Islamic Law and Society in Iran

The relationship between Islamic law and society is an important issue in Iran under the Islamic Republic. Although Islamic law was a pivotal element in the traditional Iranian society, no comprehensive research has been made until today. This is because modern reformers emphasized the lack of rule of law in nineteenth-century Iran. However, a legal system did exist, and Islamic law was a substantial part of it.

This is the first book on the relationship between Islamic law and the Iranian society during the nineteenth century. The author explores the legal aspects of urban society in Iran and provides the social context in which political process occurred and examines how authorities applied law in society, how people utilized the law, and how the law regulated society. Based on rich archival sources including court records and private deeds from Qajar Tehran, this book explores how Islamic law functioned in Iranian society. The judicial system, shari'a court, and religious endowments (*vaqf*) are fully discussed, and the role of 'ulama as legal experts is highlighted throughout the book. It challenges nationalist and modernist views on nineteenth-century Iran and provides a unique model in terms of the relationship between Islamic law and society, which is rather different from the Ottoman case.

Providing an understanding of this legal system in Iran and its role in society, this book offers a basis for assessing the motives and results of modern reforms as well as the modernist discourse. This book will be of interest to students of Middle Eastern and Iranian Studies.

Nobuaki Kondo is a Professor at Research Institute for Languages and Cultures of Asia and Africa, Tokyo University of Foreign Studies. His research interests cover early modern history of Iran and the Persianate societies. His most important publication is *Persian Documents* (Routledge, 2003).

Royal Asiatic Society Books

The Royal Asiatic Society was founded in 1823 'for the investigation of subjects connected with, and for the encouragement of science, literature and the arts in relation to, Asia'. Informed by these goals, the policy of the Society's Editorial Board is to make available in appropriate formats the results of original research in the humanities and social sciences having to do with Asia, defined in the broadest geographical and cultural sense and up to the present day.

The Man in the Panther's Skin
Shota Rustaveli
Translated from the Georgian by M. S. Wardrop
New Foreword by Donald Rayfield

Studies in Turkic and Mongolic Linguistics
Gerard Clauson
New Introduction by C. Edmund Bosworth

Women, Religion and Culture in Iran
Edited by Sarah Ansari and Vanessa Martin

The History of the Mohammedan Dynasties in Spain
Ahmed ibn Mohammed al-Makkari
Translated from the Arabic by Pascual de Gayangos
New Introduction by Michael Brett

Society, Politics and Economics in Mazandaran, Iran 1848–1914
Mohammad Ali Kazembeyki

The Courts of Pre-Colonial South India
Jennifer Howes

The Zen Arts
Rupert Cox

The Theory of Citrasutras in Indian Painting
A Critical Re-Evaluation of their Uses and Interpretations
Isabella Nardi

Persian Literature: A Bio-bibliographical Survey
Volume V: Poetry of the Pre-Mongol Period
François de Blois

Tribal Politics in Iran
Rural Conflict and the New State, 1921–1941
Stephanie Cronin

Muslims in India since 1947
Islamic Perspectives on Inter-Faith Relations
Yoginder Sikand

Muslim Women, Reform and Princely Patronage
Nawab Sultan Jahan Begam of Bhopal
Siobhan Lambert-Hurley

The Origins of Himalayan Studies
Brian Houghton Hodgson in Nepal and Darjeeling 1820–1858
Edited by David M Waterhouse

Hindi Poetry in a Musical Genre
Thumri Lyrics
Lalita Du Perron

The Cheitharol Kumpapa: The Court Chronicle of the Kings of Manipur
Original Text, Translation and Notes Vol. 1. 33–1763 CE
Saroj Nalini Arambam Parratt

The Development of Modern Medicine in Non-Western Countries
Historical Perspectives
Edited by Hormoz Ebrahimnejad

Anglo-Iranian Relations Since 1800
Edited by Vanessa Martin

State Violence and Punishment in India
Taylor C. Sherman

The British Occupation of Indonesia 1945–1946
Britain, the Netherlands and the Indonesian Revolution
Richard McMillan

The Making of Western Indology
Henry Thomas Colebrooke and the East India Company
Ludo Rocher and Rosane Rocher

The Politics of Self-Expression
The Urdu Middleclass Milieu in Mid-Twentieth Century India and Pakistan
Markus Daechsel

The Rise of the Ottoman Empire
Studies in the History of Turkey, 13th–15th Centuries
Paul Wittek, edited by Colin Heywood

Urbanisation, Citizenship and Conflict in India
Ahmedabad 1900–2000
Tommaso Bobbio

Islamic Law and Society in Iran
A Social History of Qajar Tehran
Nobuaki Kondo

Royal Asiatic Society Books: Ibrahim Pasha of Egypt Series

The Royal Asiatic Society's Ibrahim Pasha of Egypt Fund, established in 2001 by Princess Fazilé Ibrahim, encourages the growth and development of Ottoman studies internationally by publishing Ottoman documents and manuscripts of historical importance from the classical period up to 1839, with transliteration, full or part translation and scholarly commentaries

Grievance Administration (*Şikayet*) in an Ottoman Province
The Kaymakam of Rumelia's 'Record Book of Complaints' of 1781–1783
Michael Ursinus

Islamic Law and Society in Iran

A Social History of Qajar Tehran

Nobuaki Kondo

Routledge
Taylor & Francis Group
LONDON AND NEW YORK

First published 2017
by Routledge
2 Park Square, Milton Park, Abingdon, Oxon OX14 4RN

and by Routledge
711 Third Avenue, New York, NY 10017

Routledge is an imprint of the Taylor & Francis Group, an informa business

British Library Cataloguing-in-Publication Data
A catalogue record for this book is available from the British Library

Library of Congress Cataloging-in-Publication Data
Names: Kondo, Nobuaki, 1966–, author.
Title: Islamic law and society in Iran : a social history of Qajar Tehran / Nobuaki Kondo.
Description: New York, NY : Routledge, 2017. | Series: Royal Asiatic Society books | Includes bibliographical references and index.
Identifiers: LCCN 2016048063 | ISBN 9780415711371 (hardback) | ISBN 9781315201832 (ebook)
Subjects: LCSH: Islamic law—Iran—Tehran. | Waqf—Iran—Tehran. | Justice, Administration of—Iran—Tehran. | Sociological jurisprudence—Iran—Tehran.
Classification: LCC KBP63.3 .K66 2017 | DDC 340/.115095525—dc23
LC record available at https://lccn.loc.gov/2016048063

ISBN: 978-0-415-71137-1 (hbk)
ISBN: 978-1-315-20183-2 (ebk)

Typeset in Times New Roman
by Apex CoVantage, LLC

Contents

Figures

Tables

Maps

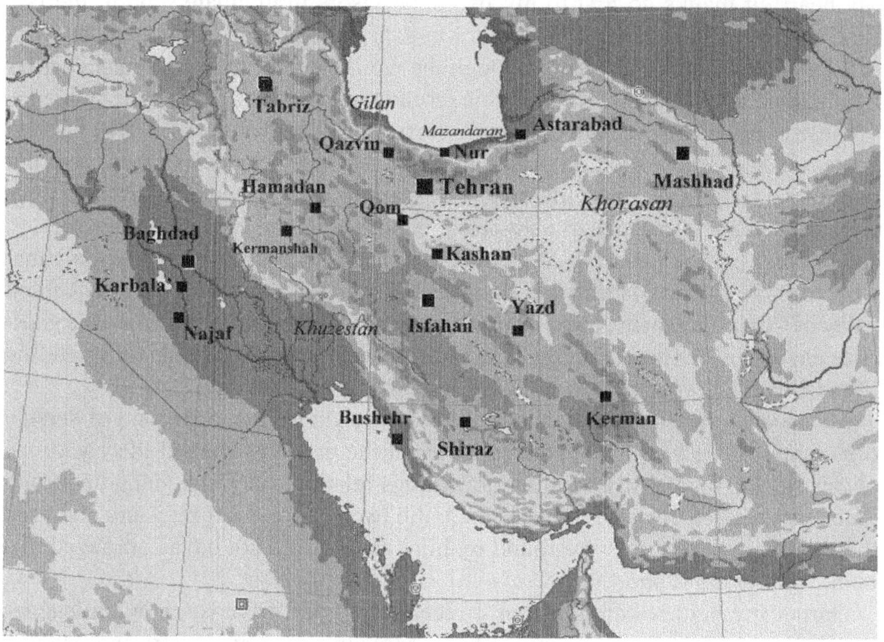

Map 0.1 Map of Iran and Iraq

Acknowledgements

My heartfelt thanks go first to my two supervisors in graduate school, the late Professor Tsugitaka Sato and Professor Masashi Haneda, who taught me the basics of Islamic and Iranian history. Although the work for this study commenced after I completed my Ph.D. dissertation, this research nonetheless reflects the influence of these two academics. I am extremely sorry that I could not present this book to Professor Sato in his lifetime. Also, although Professor Shohei Komaki was not my official supervisor, his guidance and cooperation as a specialist in Qajar history were invaluable to me, generously providing me with some important sources.

My study of the Qajar shari'a court documents started in 1997, when I met Christoph Werner, a respected colleague. His in-depth knowledge and excellent study of Qajar documents completely changed my academic life. Further, his guidance enabled me to access archives in Iran. I sincerely appreciate his longstanding friendship and cooperation.

My special gratitude goes to Omid Reza'i, who guided me in the field of Persian diplomatics. The years we spent together in the archives shaped the backbone of this book. He is always finding new things relating to Persian documents and graciously shares them with me. Indeed, the two shari'a court registers analyzed thoroughly in this book were found by him, and I could not have completed this book without his support.

During my field research in Iran, I received support from so many colleagues that I am unable to name them all here. Mohammad Reza Nasiri and Mansur Sefatgol always received me warmly and provided generous support. Ha'ede Lale introduced me to the *Vaqf* Organization, which played a critical role in my research. The staff members in archives such as the *Vaqf* Organization, University of Tehran, Golestan Museum, Iranian National Archives, and Institute for Iranian Contemporary Historical Studies were always helpful, facilitating my research. Bahman Bayani, Sirus Sa'dvandiyan, and Mohammad Hasan Tabataba'i gave me the opportunity to read unpublished documents that I otherwise could not have accessed.

I would also like to thank my Japanese colleagues, especially those at the Tokyo Metropolitan University and the Research Institute for Languages and Cultures of Asia and Africa (ILCAA), my current institution. They allowed me to take frequent and lengthy leaves in order to go to Iran and other places to engage in field research. My gratitude likewise goes to Kazuo Morimoto, who provided me with the opportunity to undertake my first long field trip in Iran in 1998. I should note that my research trips were supported by various research projects, which were funded by the Japan Society for the Promotion of Science (KAKENHI Grant Number 15710179, 23320149, 15H01895) and ILCAA. I would like to express my gratitude to Bernard Hourcade, who joined our project "Human Mobility and Multi-ethnic Coexistence in Middle Eastern Urban Societies," and shared his insightful knowledge on Tehran. He also kindly provided me with excellent maps of Tehran for this book.

I would like to thank my British colleagues who cooperated with me in completing this book. Edmund Herzig generously accepted me for a sabbatical in Oxford, where I completed a number of the chapters for this book. Zahir Bhalloo patiently read my early drafts and helped me polish the manuscript.

I also wish to express my gratitude to Vanessa Martin and the Editorial Board of the Royal Asiatic Society of Great Britain and Ireland for their help and encouragement in the publication of this book.

Naturally, all the responsibility for any errors in this book remains my own.

Note on the transliteration

The system of transliteration in this book is a modified version of that recommended by the *Iranian Studies*. The only modification is that the silent *h* is not written as *Dowle*.

Introduction

Law has been a key issue in the history of modern Iran. Many researchers have described how modern or Western law was introduced into Iran. During the nineteenth century, Iranian intellectuals such as Malkom Khan and Mostashar al-Dowle claimed that Western-type law was indispensable for the modernization of Iran. The term *qanun* represented such Western-type law.[1] These intellectuals insisted that there was no law in Iran and nothing that prevented despotic authorities from committing an injustice. It is a well-known fact that their claims introduced a modern concept of law to Iran and paved the way for the Iranian Constitutional Revolution and the establishment of the Constitution in 1906. On the other hand, it is also well known that Sheykh Fazl-allah Nuri, a leading *mojtahed* at the time of the Constitutional Revolution, wanted a shari'a-based constitution (*mashrute-e mashru'*). His claim was reflected in Article Two of the Supplementary Fundamental Law enacted in October 1907.[2]

Although these modernist and Islamist discourses have been well documented and studied, the actual structure of the legal and judicial system of the nineteenth century, which was closely related to Islamic law, has received little attention. Researchers have been interested more in the modernizing reforms than in the original judicial system as they were following the modernist discourse. However, even if the process of introducing Western concepts and institutions was rather slow, it does not necessarily mean that there was no law or no substantial judicial system at all in Qajar Iran. Moreover, from a Muslim perspective, Islamic law can never be outdated because it is God's law. Naturally, most Muslim countries today claim that their law is based on Islamic law, or shari'a, even though their actual policies vary. Even the Iranian Civil Code established in 1928–1936 under the secular Pahlavi regime used Shi'i *fiqh* books as primary sources.[3] Thus, even if one stands by the modernist position, it is difficult to understand these modernist discourses in their proper context without an adequate knowledge of the legal and judicial system.

This book examines legal practice in the urban society of nineteenth-century Iran. It investigates how Islamic law was executed and how it affected urban society. The main focus of the book is the court system and the *vaqf*, or the Islamic pious endowment. The setting is Tehran, the capital city of Qajar Iran. Instead of analyzing political discourse, this book is based on archival sources and describes nineteenth-century Iran from the perspective of social history, examining the relationship between modernity and Islam from a legal perspective. The Iranian government had already begun judicial reform in the nineteenth century, and the reform raised the same question that persists today about the relationship of modern institutions with shari'a. Adopting a view akin to that of an anthropologist who investigates societies other than those of the West, I avoid a modernist approach and treat shari'a simply as a system of law that differs from that of Western law: I do not discuss any "progress" or "failure" of modernization in Iran here.

In recent years, studies of Islamic law and its relation to society as a whole have developed considerably. A special academic journal has been published since 1994 (*Islamic Law and Society*), and there are two book series (*Studies in Islamic Law and Society* and the *Harvard Series in Islamic Law*) that comprise more than forty volumes combined. Cases from the Ottoman Empire, in particular, have been well documented, particularly those based on shari'a court records.[4] However, with regard to Iran, very few studies have been published for a variety of reasons.

First, in comparison with Sunni law, Shi'i law has long been neglected by researchers. When one reads a standard reader on Islamic law, Schacht's *An Introduction to Islamic Law,* one finds very few descriptions of Shi'i law. Nor does the book introduce the Ja'fari school, a byname of the Shi'i school of Islamic law.[5] Although Twelver Shi'ism and the Shi'i school of law prevailed in West Asia after the emergence of the Safavid Empire, the research on Shi'i law falls far behind Sunni law. Mudarresi Tabataba'i's detailed bibliography is immensely helpful, but it does not contain much in the way of detail about Shi'i law.[6] Works by such scholars as Norman Calder, Devin Stewart, and Robert Gleave are very important, but they deal with the theoretical framework of Shi'i law and do not explain its detailed provisions.[7]

Second, well-known historians of Iran, such as A.K.S. Lambton and W. Floor, have not considered the critical importance of the shari'a for Iranian society. They have emphasized the distinction between two jurisdictions, shari'a and *'orf* (*'urf,* "custom") in Iran. While the qadis administered the shari'a courts on the basis of the shari'a, political authority presided over the *'orf* courts, which were sometimes called *mazalem* courts (courts for complaints) and derived from Sasanian practice. And then, they emphasize the dominant position of the *'orf* courts over shari'a courts.[8] At least, the distinction between two judicatures, the shari'a and the *'orf* courts, was widely accepted by other scholars, although their view varied in understanding the relationship between the two courts.[9] This book will challenge this two-judicature theory, and offer a new interpretation of the Qajar judicial system. We will see the degree to which the political authorities were affected by the shari'a and the shari'a court.

The third problem relates to sources. In the past, the Iranian archives were not well organized and access was restricted, especially for non-Iranian researchers. However, that situation changed after the late 1990s when some shari'a court records were published by Iranian scholars. Reading these documents is not an easy task, but it has enhanced the possibility of new research; this study is based on fourteen years of field research in the Iranian archives.

This book contributes to our understanding of the political role of the Iranian ʻulama during the late nineteenth and early twentieth centuries, which has been a focus of discussion for scholars with respect to the Constitutional Revolution of 1906 and the 1979 Islamic Revolution. However, previous studies have primarily characterized the ʻulama as clerics or religious leaders.[10] Their role as legal experts, one of their most important roles, has rarely been discussed, probably because previous researchers did not have enough sources for such an investigation, or enough of an understanding of the legal system of the time.

While many studies on the history of Tehran have been published in Persian, only a few works have been completed in Western languages. In particular, this book deals thoroughly with the subject of Tehran's *vaqfs*. Though *vaqfs* comprise one of the most important fields in historical urban studies on Muslim cities,[11] little is known about their role in the development of Iranian cities.

One might think that the main subjects of this book, the court system and the *vaqfs*, are not related and that the study of *vaqfs* is considered to be an independent field. In my opinion, the reason for this comes from the fact that *vaqf* documents were preserved longer than other court documents because of the perpetuity of the *vaqfs*. I was unable to find any other large collection of legal deeds other than *vaqf* deeds. However, when one begins to work on shariʻa court records, one comes to understand that the *vaqf* is also a legal contract recorded in court registers. In other words, from a legal point of view, there is no difference between a *vaqf* and other shariʻa contracts. Moreover, the archives preserved many documents concerning *vaqf* litigations, which provide us with knowledge about the actual court cases during the nineteenth century: three cases will be presented in this book.

Previous works

Willem Floor published a pioneering article on the Qajar judicial system in 1983, and many researchers still follow his view, including his description of two judicatures, the shariʻa and *ʻorf* courts. According to him, the shariʻa, or religious court, presided over by the ʻulama, dealt with affairs of a civil nature, in particular with those concerning personal status, while the *ʻorf* courts, administered by government officials, were concerned with offences against the state, including rebellion, embezzlement, theft, and drunkenness.[12] The problem is that his arguments relied heavily on European sources, which were sometimes strongly biased, as did his article on the Safavid "secular" judicial system.[13] However, it should be noted that when Persian primary sources of the nineteenth century are examined, the term *ʻorf* court is rarely found. The concept of the *ʻorf* court as a secular court does not exist in Islamic jurisprudence, either, even though the term *ʻorf* originates from Islamic jurisprudence, and denotes custom or customary law or indeed any rulings other than the shariʻa. . In fact, *ʻorf* customary law, as applied in the *ʻorf* courts, tended to be emphasized in European sources in a secular sense after the seventeenth century.[14] It is true that the judicial powers were divided between the shariʻa courts for shariʻa matters (*sharʻiyat*) and the ʻAdliye courts for *ʻorf* matters (*ʻorfiyat*) in the Supplementary Fundamental Law of 1907,[15] but it was as a result of judicial reform during the second half of the nineteenth century. An analysis of Persian documents generates a better understanding of the intricate judicial systems in Qajar Iran. Schneider also published an article on the jurisdiction of Mohammad Baqer Shafti, a famous *mojtahed* in Isfahan. However, the article was based not on the documents, but on anecdotal biographies of members of the ʻulama.[16]

Christoph Werner's monograph on Tabriz, published in 2000, is an important step in this field.[17] This is a study based on numerous Persian legal documents: it concerns the urban society of Tabriz during the second half of the eighteenth and the first half of the nineteenth centuries. Werner makes three important suggestions. First, he denies the hierarchy of Qajar shariʻa courts described by John Malcolm (i.e., *sheykh al-eslam* – qadi (*qazi*) – *molla*), which was frequently cited by the previous literature. Instead, he argues that all Tabrizi ʻulama were considered to be *mojtaheds*, and, contrary to Malcolm's description, they received grants from the state.[18] Second, Werner states that the main function of the shariʻa courts was that of a notary rather than that of a judge. All prominent ʻulama would endorse the legal documents equally.[19] Third, he criticizes the basis of the distinction made between the shariʻa and *ʻorf* courts. He prefers to consider this distinction to be a differentiation between the Islamic law and the "executive powers."[20] His analysis of the transformation of the *vaqfs* is also quite inspiring. His new book deals with *vaqfs* in Iran from the fourteenth to twentieth century, and gives new insight on cultural, religious, and social aspects of Iranian *vaqf*, although it is not concerned with a specific city or specific period. This book tries to develop some of his ideas from the cases for a different place and time, using more extensive sources, including the court registers. Zahir Bhaloo's recent article describes a series of shariʻa litigation and investigates the impact of Usulism on the Qajar shariʻa court system, but does not cover whole court system.[21] Another recent article by Naofumi Abe also deals with a land dispute in nineteenth-century Azerbaijan but it rather questions the position of landlord than the judicial system.[22] Hadi Enayat's monograph on the legal reform between 1906 and 1941 is not directly concerned with the nineteenth century, but it gives a good summary of the subject.[23]

By contrast, Iranian authors refer to the Qajar judicial system in their studies of the judicial system in Iran. For example, in 1972, Mohammad Mohit-e Tabataba'i referred to the notary function of the shariʻa court in his long article on the judicial history of Iran.[24] In 1994, Ahmad Mahdavi Damghani published two short articles on the Qajar judicial system. His framework on the shariʻa and *ʻorf* courts is not very different from that of Floor's, but he does describe the role of shariʻa courts as notary offices, though without referring to any shariʻa documents to support this description.[25]

After the 1990s, shariʻa court documents including *vaqf* deeds attracted more interest among Iranian researchers. The journal, *Vaqf, Miras-e Javidan* (1993–) continues to publish various articles on *vaqfs* and related documents. Although the pioneering work on formal aspects of the Qajar shariʻa documents was carried out by Werner,[26] Omid Reza'i undertook a more comprehensive study. His book *Introduction to Shariʻa Documents from Qajar Iran* uses numerous examples to explain various types of shari'a documents, enabling the reader to understand them.[27] He has also published articles on the basis of his deep knowledge of Persian diplomatics dealing with the shari'a courts in Tehran, Shiraz, and Bushehr.[28] Some of his articles have been compiled into a two-volume publication.[29] In addition, Hoseyni Eshkevari's book categorizes shari'a documents with their facsimiles, although it does not include diplomatic explanations.[30] This book is indebted to these studies. However, these studies do not discuss the complete court system or Iranian society of the time, and none of them refers to the court registers.

In this regard, the publication of two court registers in 2006 and 2008, one by Mansure Ettehadiye and Sa'id Ruhi, the other by Omid Reza'i, has changed the situation, which will be discussed below. A few other Iranian researchers are also interested in shari'a courts. Mohammad Hoseyn Soleymani has attempted to investigate shari'a courts in Mashhad, although he has not been able to locate any court registers yet.[31] Mas'ud Habibi Mozaheri has published some examples of records from shari'a court registers compiled in the early twentieth century, but they have not been analyzed in great detail.[32]

For the history of Tehran during the nineteenth century, the volume of collected essays edited by Chahryar Adle and Bernard Hourcade is still the most important work in a Western language. It includes important papers on Qajar Tehran by John Gurney, Jennifer Scarce, and Mansure Ettehadiye.[33] However, in comparison to Safavid Isfahan, Qajar Tehran appears not to attract much attention outside Iran.

In Iran, by contrast, many books have been published on Qajar Tehran. Hoseyni Balaghi's book is a comprehensive history of Tehran that includes abundant information especially on religious buildings and *vaqfs*.[34] Ja'far Shahri's two magnificent books, *Social History of Tehran* and *Old Tehran* also deserve mention.[35] They are descriptive, encyclopedic works and contain information on every aspect of the city.

Mansure Ettehadiye's collection of papers can be considered the most important study of the social history of Tehran: she examines various topics, such as urban development, the structure of the Grand Bazaar, *vaqf* endowments, crimes and punishments, and women.[36] She has edited several new original sources and analyzed them for her research. In this regard, she is a pioneer of the document-based social history of Tehran. Indeed, some of the documents included in this study were first investigated by her. Another significant study is the historical geography of Tehran written by Mohsen Mo'tamadi.[37] On the basis of old maps and building surveys, he has collected as much geographical information on Qajar Tehran from published sources as possible. Moreover, the Iranology Foundation (Bonyad-e Iranshenasi) has recently completed a number of projects on Tehran and published three huge volumes as a result: *Emamzade Shrines and Tombs in Tehran, Rey and Shemiran* (2009), *Old Mosques in Tehran* (2009), and *History of the Grand Bazaar of Tehran* (2010).[38] Based on field research and written sources, they also feature some documents related to the buildings in Tehran, although these are not analyzed in the volumes.

In recent years, studies of Persian documents and of the history of Tehran have developed significantly in Iran. However, these studies are not well integrated, nor have the results in Iran been communicated to the international academic world; the resulting gap is what this book tries to bridge.

Sources

The most important of the Persian documents that form the basis for this book are the shari'a court registers recently found and/or published.[39] Though Ottoman studies indicate how useful such sources are for research on social history, no similar attempt has been made in the field of Iranian history. Three registers that I refer to consist of two registers of Sayyed Mohammad Sadeq Sangelaji and one register of Sheykh Fazl-allah Nuri, covering a number of years between 1867 and 1889. It is difficult to understand the entire function of the shari'a courts from individual documents because the documents are concerned with individual cases. However, the court registers used for this study contain more than six thousand transactions and reveal the overall function of the shari'a courts. They are fully analyzed in Chapters three and five.

The second category of documents to which I refer comprises individual *vaqf*-related documents, particularly unpublished documents from the archives of the *Vaqf* Organization in Tehran, which are among the richest for historical documents in Iran. The preliminary catalog of documents for Tehran was published by 'Emad al-Din Sheykh al-Hokama'i in 2000 in the journal *Vaqf, Miras-e Javidan*.[40] Eventually, in 2007, Reza'i published a two-volume catalog for the same documents, which is more comprehensive and includes information on endowed properties, conditions of expenditure, and ways in which the original, the transcribed copy, and the photo-copy differ from one another.[41] The archives were established for administrative purposes by the *Vaqf* Organization and are still used for those purposes; they contain many transcribed copies and photocopies of the documents.[42] I refer not only to the originals but also to the transcripts and the photocopies. A list of the *vaqf* deeds to which I refer in Chapter 6, including published texts and inscriptions, appears in the appendix.

The third group of sources comprises various governmental documents, mainly surveys and reports. The most important are two building surveys of Tehran from 1853 and 1899–1900. In principle, they cover all the buildings located in Tehran, along with the names of the owners. The survey of 1853 appears to be more accurate and provides us with information on the types of shops, whereas the survey of 1899–1900 appears to omit some buildings. Both surveys were published in 1990 by Sa'dvandiyan and Ettehadiye.[43] However, to ensure accuracy, I refer to the original manuscripts.[44] They are quite useful, especially for an analysis of the role of the *vaqf* in urban society.

The inventories compiled at the Qajar court also include information on the properties in Tehran. An inventory of the royal property dated 1843 and another one compiled between 1851 and 1858 are still in existence. They refer not only to the royal properties but also to the *vaqf* properties.[45] I was able to access the manuscript inventory of the deeds and documents preserved in the royal treasury and storage, which shows details of the royal and confiscated properties.[46] The inventory shows that even the Qajar Shahs retained the documents for their properties:

their right to the properties was legally secured by these documents drawn up at the shari'a courts.

The Qajar state would draw up the budget, settle the accounts, and compile fiscal booklets every solar year. The budget was called the *dastur al-'amal* while the settlement was referred to simply as *jam' va kharj* (income and expenditure) or *mofassa hesab* (account settlement): the accounts were written in *siyaq* (bookkeeping numerals).[47] I refer to two fiscal books from Tehran dated 1849 and 1870: they show the amount of pension that the *mojtaheds* received as well as the *vaqf* income under state control.[48] The fiscal book for 1886–1887 covers all the provinces, including Tehran.[49] There is much work to be done on these fiscal books and this study is a first attempt to utilize them.

Notes

1 Hamid Algar, *Mirza Malkum Khan* (Berkeley and Los Angeles, 1973), 29, 190; A. A. Seyed-Gohrab and S. McGlinn, *The Essence of Modernity* (Amsterdam and West Lafayette, 2008), xi, xiii.

2 Vanessa Martin, *Islam and Modernism* (New York, 1989), 126–127, 140–141.

3 Naser Yeganeh, s.v. "Civil Code," *Encyclopaedia Iranica* 5 (1992): 648–650.

4 Dror Ze'evi, "The Use of Ottoman Shari'a Court Records as a Source for Middle Eastern Social History: A Reappraisal," *Islamic Law and Society* 5 (1998): 35–56.

5 Joseph Schacht, *An Introduction to Islamic Law* (Oxford, 1982).

6 Hossein Modarressi Tabataba'i, *Introduction to Shi 'i Law* (London, 1984).

7 Norman Calder, "The Structure of Authority in Imami Shi'i Jurisprudence" (Ph.D Dissertation, University of London, 1980); Devin J. Stewart, *Islamic Legal Orthodoxy* (Salt Lake City, 1998); Robert Gleave, *Inevitable Doubt* (Leiden, 2000).

8 Ann K. S Lambton, s.v. "Mahkama 3. Iran," *The Encyclopaedia of Islam*, New Edition, 6 (1991): 11–22; Willem Floor, s.v. "Judicial and Legal Systems: IV. Judicial System from the Advent of Islam through the 19th Century." *Encyclopedia Iranica* 15 (2009): 199–204.

9 Hamid Algar, *Religion and State in Iran 1785–1906* (Berkeley and Los Angeles, 1969), 12–14; Said Amir Arjomand, *The Shadow of God and the Hidden Imam* (Chicago, 1984), 233; Martin, *Islam and Modernism*, 7–8; Irene Schneider, *The Petitioning System in Iran* (Wiesbaden, 2006), 21–22.

10 For example, Algar used the term "clerical." Algar, *Religion and State in Iran*.

11 See Masashi Haneda and Toru Miura, *Islamic Urban Studies* (London, 1994), 337–338; Miriam Hoexter, "Waqf Studies in the Twentieth Century," *Journal of the Economic and Social History of the Orient* 41 (1998): 482–483; Randi Deguilhem, "The Waqf in the City," in *The City in the Islamic World*, eds. Renata Holod, Attilio Petruccioli, and André Raymond (Leiden, 2008), 2:923–950.

12 Willem Floor, "Change and Development in the Judicial System of Qajar Iran (1800–1925)," in *Qajar Iran: Political, Social and Cultural Exchange*, ed. E. Bosworth and C. Hillenbrand (Edinburgh, 1983), 113.

13 Willem Floor, "The Secular Justice System in Safavid Persia," *Studia Iranica* 29 (2000): 9–60.

14 Christoph Werner, "'Orf oder Gewohnheitsrecht in Iran," in *Rechtspluralismus in Der Islamischen Welt Gewohnheitsrecht Zwischen Staat Und Gesellschaft*, eds. Michael Kemper and Maurus Reinkowski (Berlin, 2005), 155–159.

15 *Motammem-e Qanun-e Asasi*, 29 Sha'ban 1325AH, 27–2.

16 Irene Schneider, "Muhammad Baqir Šafti (1180–1260/1766–1844) und Die Isfahaner Gerichtsbarkeit," *Der Islam* 79 (2002): 240–273.

17 Christoph Werner, *An Iranian Town in Transition* (Wiesbaden, 2000).
18 Ibid., 239, 252.
19 Ibid., 232–233.
20 Ibid., 235.
21 Zahir Bhalloo, "Judging the Judge: Judicial Competence in 19th Century Iran," *Bulletin D'études Orientales* 63 (2014): 276–293.
22 Naofumi Abe, "The Ambivalent Position of the Landloard," *Islamic Law and Society* 23 (2016): 52–88.
23 Hadi Enayati, *Law, State, and Society in Modern Iran* (New York, 2013), 23–48.
24 Mohammad Mohit-e Tabataba'i, "Dadgostari dar Iran az Sadr-e Eslam ta Aghaz-e Mashrutiyat," *Kanun-e Vokala'* 119 (1351Kh.): 114. Ravandi just cited it in his book. Mortaza Ravandi, *Seyr-e Qanun va Dadgostari dar Iran* (Tehran and Babol, 1368Kh), 248.
25 Ahmad Mahdavi Damghani, "Mahakem-e Qaza'i dar Zaman-e Qajariye," *Hafez* no.3 (1383Kh.): 30–35; idem. "Tarikheche-e Mahzar va Daftar-e Asnad-e Rasmi," *Hafez* no.7 (1383Kh.): 17–18.
26 Christoph Werner, "Formal Aspects of Qajar Deeds of Sale," in *Persian Documents: Social History of Iran and Turan in the Fifteenth-Nineteenth Centuries*, ed. Nobuaki Kondo (London, 2003), 13–49.
27 Omid Reza'i, *Dar-amadi bar Asnad-e Shar'i-e Dowre-e Qajar* (Tokyo, 2008).
28 For Tehran, Omid Reza'i, "Aqa Sayyed Sadeq Mojtahed Sangelaji va Neveshtejat-e Shar'iye," *Vaqf, Miras-e Javidan* no.56 (1385Kh): 57–68; idem. "Jaygah-e Khanedan-e Behbahani dar Towlid va Sabt-e Neveshtejat-e Dowre-e Qajariye," *Vaqf, Miras-e Javidan* no.57 (1386Kh): 44–55. For Shiraz, Omid Reza'i, "Selsele-e Sheykh al-Eslamiye-e Tamami-e Shiraz Pishgam-e dar Sabt-e Neveshtejat-e Shar'iye-e Dowre-e Qajar," *Vaqf, Miras-e Javidan* no.54 (1385Kh): 77–94; idem. "Barrasi va Tahlil-e Mohrha-ye bi-Yaddasht dar Qabaleha-ye Dar al-'Elm-e Shiraz," *Vaqf, Miras-e Javidan* no.60 (1386Kh): 26–38. For Bushehr, Omid Reza'i, "Pishine va Nahve-e Sabt-e Asnad-e Shar'i dar Bandar-e Bushehr (1308HQ–1350HQ)," *Asnad-e Baharestan* no.1 (1390Kh): 79–94.
29 Omid Reza'i, *Jostarhayi dar Sanad-shenasi-e Farsi* (Tehran, 1385Kh); idem. *Qabale-haye Parsi* (Tehran, 1388Kh).
30 Sayyed Sadeq Hoseyni Eshkevari, *Asnad-e Shar'i dar Ketabkhane-e Mirza Mohammad Kazemeyni* (Qom, 1387Kh).
31 Mohammad Hoseyn Soleymani, "Dar al-Shar'-e Mashhad dar Dowre-e Qajar va Barrasi-e Chand Saj'-e Mohr," *Payam-e Baharestan* no.21 (1392Kh): 211–223; idem. "Sakhtar-e Dar al-Shar' va Sazokar-e Tahrir-e Ashnad-e Shar'i," *Ketab-e Mah, Tarikh va Joghrafiya* 192 (1393Kh): 45–48.
32 Mas'ud Habibi Mozaheri, "Bargozide-e Aznad-e Tanzimi dar Mahzar-e Sayyed Mohammad Mojtahed Tabataba'i," *Payam-e Baharestan, Vizhename-e Qanun va Hoquq* no.3 (1391Kh): 354–406; idem. "Gozide-e Asnad-e Tanzimi dar Mahazer-e Shar'," *Payam-e Baharestan, Vizhename-e Maliye va Eqtesad* no.1 (1392Kh): 381–404.
33 Chahryar Adle and Bernard Hourcade, eds. *Téhéran: Capitale bicentenaire* (Paris and Tehran, 1992).
34 Sayyed 'Abd al-Hojjat Hoseyni Balaghi, *Tarikh-e Tehran*, 2 vols. (Qom, 1350Kh).
35 Ja'far Shahri, *Tarikh-e Tehran dar Qarn-e Sizdahom* (Tehran, 1367Kh); idem. *Tehran-e Qadim* (Tehran, 1371Kh).
36 Mansure Ettehadiye, *Inja Tehran Ast* (Tehran, 1377Kh).
37 Mohsen Mo'tamadi, *Joghrafiya-ye Tarikhi-e Tehran* (Tehran, 1381Kh).
38 Hasan Habibi, ed. *Emamzadeha va Torbat-e Barkhi az Pakan va Niyakan-e Tehran, Shemiranat va Shahr-e Rey*, vol. 1 (Tehran, 1388Kh); idem. *Masajed-e Dirinesal-e Tehran* (Tehran, 1388Kh); Shahram Yusofifar and Hasan Habibi, *Sargozasht-e Bazar-e Bozorg-e Tehran* (Tehran, Bonyad-e Iranshenasi, 1389Kh).

39 Mansure Ettehadiye and Sa'id Ruhi, eds. *Dar Mahzar-e Sheykh Fazl-allah Nuri* (Tehran, 1385Kh); Omid Reza'i, ed. *Asnad-e Mahkame-e Sayyed Sadeq Tabataba'i (Sangelaji) Mojtahed-e 'Asr-e Naseri* (Tehran, 1387Kh); *Daftar-e Shar'i-e Sangelaji*. Arshiv-e Melli, Tehran. In August, 2006, Ettehadiye gave a paper on Nuri's register at the Six Biennial Conference of Iranian Studies held at SOAS, London, which fortunately I attended. Concerning the Sangelaji's registers, first I received information from Omid Reza'i in 2007. I would like to express my deep gratitude to Omid Reza'i and Mohammad Hasan Tabataba'i for allowing me access to the unpublished register of Sangelaji before it was transferred to Arshiv-e Melli-e Iran.

40 'Emad al-Din Sheykh al-Hokama'i, "Asnad-e Vaqf-e Ostan-e Tehran dar Baygani-e Markazi-e Sazman-e Owqaf va Omur-e Kheyriye," *Vaqf, Miras-e Javidan* no.28 (1378Kh): 141–167.

41 Omid Reza'i, *Fehrest-e Asnad-e Mowqufat-e Iran, vol. 4: Ostan-e Tehran va Tababe'* (Tehran, 1386Kh).

42 The archives belong to Daftar-e Asnad va Shenasayi-e Mowqufat (Office for Vaqf documents and Identification) of the Vaqf Organization. For its history, see Omid Reza'i, "Ashnayi ba Daftar-e Asnad va Shenasayi-e Mowqufat-e Sazman-e Owqaf," *Ganjine-e Asnad* no.51/52 (1382Kh): 10–13. Concerning early *vaqf* administration after the Constitutional Revolution, see Omid Reza'i, "Ravande Shekrgiri-e Edare-e Ma'aref va Owqaf-e Kerman va Qom," *Vaqf, Miras-e Javidan* no.31/32 (1379Kh): 47–57. For comparison of the original *vaqf* deeds and its transcripts in the archives, see Omid Reza'i, "Barrasi-e Runeveshtha-ye Vezarat-e Ma'aref va Owqaf as Asl-e Vaqf-nameha," *Vaqf, Miras-e Javidan* 38(1381Kh): 87–94. For the transcribing activity in the *vaqf* administration in the early twentieth century, see Omid Reza'i, "Dastur al-'Amalha-ye Edari-e Owqaf be Edarat-e Nowbonyad dar khosus-e 'Estensakh-e Vaqf-name' va 'Estekhlas-e Mowqufe'," *Vaqf, Miras-e Javidan* no.39/40 (1381Kh): 36–41.

43 Sirus Sa'dvandiyan and Mansure Ettehadiye, eds. *Amar-e Dar al-Khelafe-e Tehran* (Tehran, 1368Kh). The summary of the surveys is found in Sirus Sa'dvandiyan, *'Adad-e Abniye, Shomar-e Nofus az Dar al-Khelafe ta Tehran 1231–1311 Khorshidi* (Tehran, 1380Kh), 11–97, 161–238. For an introduction to this type of source, Sirus Sa'dvandiyan, *Dar-amadi bar Jam'iyat-shenasi-e Tarikhi-e Iran dar 'Asr-e Qajar* (Tehran, 1379Kh).

44 *Surat-e 'Adad-e Khaneha va Sayer-e Benaha-ye Dar al-Khelafe-e Bahere-e Tehran*. Or Ms. K9(9), E.G. Browne Collection, Cambridge University; Hasan Akhzar 'Ali Shah, *Ta'in va Sabt-e Mahat-e Khandaq-e Shahr-e Dar al-Khelafe-e Bahere*, MS Adabiyat 20-ba, Central Library, University of Tehran.

45 *Surat-e Khalesejat va Mowqufat va Raqabat*. I. MS 7619, Ketabkhane-e Majles-e Showra-ye Eslami, Tehran; II. MS Mar'ashi Library, microfilm 4819, Central Library, University of Tehran; *Ketabche-e Dehat-e Khalese va Mowqufat va Amlak-e Enteqali-e Divan-e A'la*, I. MS 8891, Central Library, University of Tehran; II. MS 7868, Mar'ashi Library, Qom. Unfortunately, the edition by Bayani and Ettehadiye confused the two different versions and changed the order of the chapters. Bahman Bayani and Mansure Ettehadiye, ed. *Ketabche-e Qabalejat-e Khazane-e Mobarake, Amlak-e Haji Mirza Aqasi, Khalasejat va Mowqufat-e Divan-e A'la* (Tehran, 1387Kh), 157–568.

46 *Ketabche-e Sabt-e Qavalejat va Neveshtejat-e mowjudi dar Khazane-e Mobarake-e Andaruni va Sanduqkhane-e Mobarake*, MS Mr. Bahman Bayani Private Library. I would like to express my gratitude to Mr. Bayani for letting me access the manuscript. The edition is found in Bayani and Ettehadiye, eds. *Ketabche-e Qabalejat*, 27–155.

47 These fiscal books (*ketabche*) were preserved in Iranian libraries and archives from various provinces: most of them are from the second half of the nineteenth century. Floor explains them briefly without referring to any of them. Willem Floor, *A Fiscal History of Iran in the Safavid and Qajar Periods, 1500–1925* (New York, 1998), 281–282, 284.

48 *Ketabche-e Jam' va Kharj-e hazih al-Sane-e Takhaqoy-' il-e Dar al-Khelafe-e Tehran Abvab-jam'i-e 'Alijenab Moqarrab al-Khaqan 'Isa Khan Beglarbegi*, MS Hoquq J-371, Central Library, University of Tehran; *Dastur al-'Amal-e Hazih al-Sane-e Yunat-'il-e Kheyriyat-Tahvil-e Dar al-Khelafe-e Tehran*, MS J-373, Central Library, University of Tehran.

49 *Ketabche-e Jam' va Kharj-e Koll-e hazih al-Sanat-e It-'il-e Mamlekat-e Mahruse motabeq-e Sanne-e 1304 Hejri*, MS 776, Majles Library; Bahman Bayani, ed. *Ketabche-e Jam' va Kharj-e Koll-e hazih al-Sanat-e It-'il-e Mamlekat-e Mahruse motabeq-e Sanne-e 1304 Hejri* (Tehran, 1391Kh).

1 The historical development of Tehran

Tehran before the Qajars

Tehran lies on the southern slopes of the Alborz Mountains at an altitude of 1,158 meters above sea level. The old capital city of this region, Rey, is located south of Tehran and includes several historical sites such as the shrine of Shah 'Abd al-'Aziz and Chashme-e 'Ali. Tehran's northern suburb, Shemran, connects the city to the Alborz Mountains and was used as a summer residence for the inhabitants of Tehran. Tehran has a dry climate, just like other cities on the Iranian plateau, because the Alborz blocks wet winds from the Caspian Sea. Snow on the mountains turns into water and irrigates the city via traditional irrigation canals known as *qanat*. According to Olivier, a French traveler, Tehran was hot and insanitary during the summer. It was not uncommon for people to leave the city or send their family to the villages in the vicinity in order to escape the dangerous epidemics that prevailed there during the summer season.[1]

Originally, Tehran was a village on the outskirts north of Rey. However, by the first half of the fourteenth century, Hamd-allah Mostowfi refers to it as a *qasabe*, a small city.[2] In the sixteenth century, Tehran began to be called a *shahr* (a city). According to a Safavid source, *Haft Eqlim* (dated 1593–1594),

> Tehran was adorned with a city wall and markets, and received the rank of a city (*samt-e shahr*) during the reign of Shah Tahmasp Safavi, the ruler of Iran.[3]

Another Safavid writer, Majd al-Din Mohammad Hoseyni stated,

> It (Tehran) was a small city (*qasabe*) before, but the late victorious king (Shah Tahmasp) made efforts to develop it and built a city wall, which was 6 *farsang* (=about 36 km) long. Now it prospers.[4]

One of the most well-known descriptions of Safavid Tehran is by E'temad al-Saltane. Writing in the second half of the nineteenth century, he notes:

> In 961 AH, Shah Tahmasp ordered a city wall to be constructed around Tehran, which was 6000 steps around the city. A hundred and fourteen towers

> (*borj*) were constructed on the wall equal to the auspicious number of chapters of the Qur'an. A chapter of the Holy Qur'an was concealed in each tower.[5]

However, there are two points that need to be examined in this description. First, the date, 961AH (=1553–1554) is problematic. It is not mentioned in any of the contemporary sources, though in most of the secondary literature it is accepted as a fact.[6] According to a late Safavid source, it was in the Year of the Dragon/963–964AH/1556–1557 that the construction of the city wall first began.[7] When one compares events before and after the construction with a contemporary source, one will find the exact date was the Year of the Snake/964–965AH/1557–1558.[8] We know for example that Shah Tahmasp visited Karaj, a small city located near Tehran the year before.[9] According to a nineteenth-century source, Shah Tahmasp spent a long time visiting the Emamzade Hamze, located next to Shah 'Abd al-'Azim, and hunting in the region, and then ordered the construction of the city wall.[10] The date 964–965/1557–1558 is also more probable because in 961/1553–1554 Tahmasp was engaged in war with the Ottoman ruler Suleyman I.

The second point is the story of the Qur'anic towers. What is curious is that a similar description can be found in *Golshan-e Morad*, an eighteenth-century Zand chronicle. In around 1760, the entire city wall built by Shah Tahmasp was in ruins. Karim Khan Zand is said to have ordered the city wall to be rebuilt with 114 towers, a number equal to the total number of chapters of the Qur'an, which was a good omen.[11]

The Zand chronicle, however, does not mention the Qur'anic chapters being concealed in the towers. It is likely that Karim Khan wanted to connect the city with the Holy Qur'an as he had done when he rebuilt the gate of the Qur'an in Shiraz. As none of the Safavid sources mention 114 towers, it is almost certain that E'temad al-Saltane altered the description found in *Golshan-e Morad* and connected the 114-tower story with the Safavids in his own geographical work.

E'temad al-Saltane also wrote that no palace was built in Tehran during the Safavid period and gardens occupied two-thirds of the city area.[12] This might be the reason why Chahryar Adle describes Tehran before the eighteenth century as *"le jardin habité."* Though the concept of "the inhabited garden" is very attractive, one cannot ignore the fact that Tehran was considered a city (*shahr*) in contemporary sources. For example, Mirza Mofid Mostowfi stated in the seventeenth century that Tehran was one of the famous cities in Central Iran (*shahrha-ye mashhure-e 'eraq*).[13] Though a European traveler named Della Valle emphasized the small size of the population of Tehran at that time,[14] another traveler named Thomas Herbert counted 3,000 houses. Since, according to him, more than twelve people resided in each house,[15] one can estimate the population of the city to have been around 30,000, not an insignificant number for Iranian cities at that time. The Safavids appointed Qezelbash Amirs as the provincial governors of Tehran during the reign of Shah 'Abbas.[16] They sent a jurist as *sheykh al-eslam* as in other major cities in the empire during the seventeenth century.[17] Five *madrases* were built in Tehran during the Safavid Period. Moreover, at that time, it was normal that a city contained vast gardens. Isfahan for example had many such gardens like the *chahar bagh*.

The Zand chronicle, *Golshan-e Morad*, states that Karim Khan renovated Tehran because it was located between Central Iran and Azerbaijan and was a famous city in Central Iran.[18] He built an audience hall and a residence which still exists today. Although it is not clear if Karim Khan intended to make Tehran his capital city as Perry claims, he probably expected to stay there for a while in order to confront the Qajars in the north.

In brief, Tehran was not merely an inhabited garden after the seventeenth century as not only did it have a large population but was of considerable political, cultural, and strategic significance. It is no accident that Aqa Mohammad Khan Qajar chose Tehran as his capital.

The early Qajars and Tehran

How and why the Qajars chose Tehran as their capital city is not clear from previous studies. There is also confusion about when Tehran became the Qajar capital.[19] Naturally, as Adle and Hourcade have pointed out, the concept of the capital must also be defined clearly.[20] We can reach more concrete conclusions only after examining the early Qajar chronicles such as Saravi's *Tarikh-e Mohammadi* and Chulavi's *Tarikh-e Molk-ara*, which have not been considered hitherto in studies on Tehran.

After the death of Karim Khan Zand, Aqa Mohammad Khan escaped from Shiraz to Astarabad, and began his military operations to subdue various regions in Iran. In autumn of 1785, he entered Tehran with his army.[21] According to the chronicles, he had decided to make Tehran his capital (*maqarr-e asas-e soltani, maqarr-e eyalat va markaz-e khelafat*) when he left Isfahan and for this reason he took many builders, artisans, and engineers with him. Saravi considered that he chose Tehran because it was the center of his conquered regions, while Chulavi gave the following two reasons: Tehran was located between Mazandaran and Central Iran; and no strong general ruled there.[22] In other words, Aqa Mohammad Khan chose Tehran as his capital for geographical and strategic reasons. At that time, he confronted the Zands whose stronghold was Shiraz. Tehran became his capital once he entered the city.

Immediately, Aqa Mohammad Khan brought his mother and all the people of his *haram* from Mazandaran to Tehran.[23] The title of the capital city *dar al-saltane* ("the house of the King") is found in a sale deed dated as early as September–October 1787.[24] The title can also be seen in a sale deed dated October–November 1818,[25] but is not found in later documents. After that Tehran held the more majestic title, *dar al-khelafe* ("the house of the Caliphate").[26]

What did the capital city mean for the Qajars? First, it was the city where the shahs stayed longer than any other place. The shahs, Aqa Mohammad Khan and Fath ʻAli Shah, spent more than six months in Tehran in a year.

They renovated the palace and added many buildings there. Also, Tehran provided a hub for their travel itinerary. Even in years that the shahs stayed there for shorter periods, they always came back to Tehran before going on another trip. They rarely stayed in Tehran during the summer because of climate, hygienic, or political reasons, but always sojourned in the capital for some time in other seasons.[27]

Secondly, Tehran was where the Qajar court ceremonies were held. According to Saravi, Aqa Mohammad Khan had his coronation ceremony in Tehran in spring 1796.[28] It occurred during his eighteen-day stopover in Tehran in-between the Georgian and Khorasan expeditions.[29] His successors also had their coronations in Tehran.

Another ceremony that was held in Tehran was the New Year ceremony. Aqa Mohammad Khan and Fath 'Ali Shah were almost always in Tehran for the Persian New Year (*Nowruz*), which corresponds to the vernal equinox. Even when they spent winter in places other than Tehran, they would return to Tehran before the New Year to hold the ceremony there. This custom related to the legend of Jamshid, an ancient mythical king of Iran.[30]

Tehran was indeed the capital city of Qajar Iran and there can be no doubt that the presence of the royal court contributed to its development.

Expansion and population growth

After becoming the Qajar capital, Tehran's population increased rapidly during the nineteenth century.[31] Olivier, a French traveler, estimated its population at 15,000, including the shah's servants and soldiers, in 1796. According to him, the buildings occupied only a half of the city area.[32] Twelve years later, Dupré, another French traveler, who visited Tehran in 1808, calculated the population to be roughly between 45,000 and 50,000 in winter.[33] Thus, the population more than tripled after 1796. Forty years later, in 1851, an English traveler named Binning noted that the city population was about 80,000–90,000,[34] while another Englishman, Eastwick, reported that it was around 100,000 in 1860.[35]

Iranian official sources after 1860 offer some data on the city's population. However, the data is confusing. For example, the population survey of 1868 suggests that the number of inhabitants was 155,736,[36] while the yearbooks of the Iranian government state that Tehran had a population of 250,000 in 1873 and 280,000 in 1874.[37] According to the Iranian official gazette, in 1877 the population of the city had reached 300,000,[38] while a later survey conducted in 1884 gives the figure of 361,131 people, although the sum of the numbers of the residents in all the houses and buildings recorded in the survey reached only 106,944.[39] A population of more than 360,000 is highly unlikely because even the 1932–1933 census indicated that the city population was 310,139.[40]

We can say around 200,000 is a reasonable number for the city's population in the late nineteenth century because this number is found in both European and Iranian sources: 210,000 by *Almanach de Gotha* (1891), 250,000 by 'Abd al-Ghaffar (1891), 200,000–220,000 by Curzon (1892), and 250, 000 by Stahl (1900).[41] Also one has to take into consideration the fact that the survey of 1922–23 gives us the number of 210,000.[42]

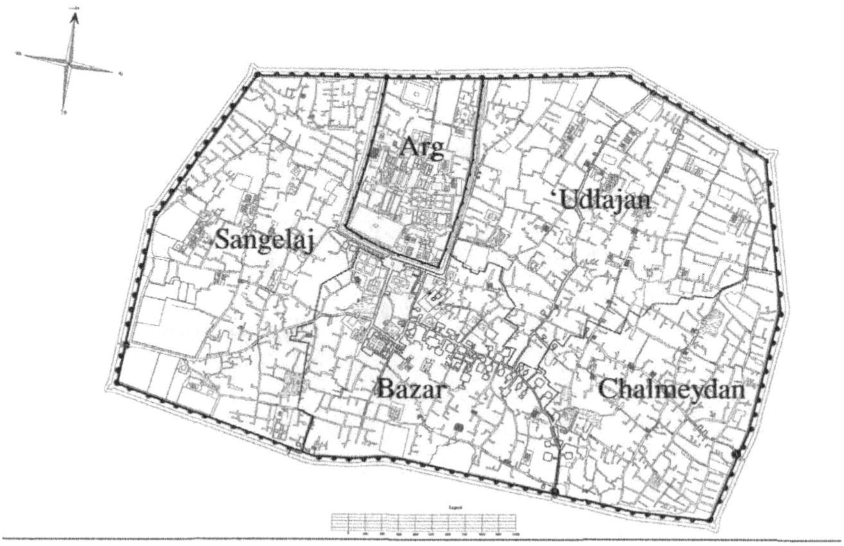

Map 1.1 Tehran in 1858 after Krziz

If these numbers are accurate, the population of Tehran grew thirteen times from what it had been in 1796 over a period of 100 years. As Gilbar remarked, the growth of Tehran was more considerable than that of any major city in Iran in the late nineteenth century.[43] Thus, it can be said that during the nineteenth century, Tehran had developed quite rapidly. The main reason for this development was the migration of people from other provinces.[44]

Furthermore, the city experienced significant changes in the latter half of the nineteenth century with its expansion.[45] Until then, Tehran had maintained the city wall that was first built during the sixteenth century. The city area stretched for 2.7 km from north to south and 1.8 km from east to west and was divided into five districts: Arg, 'Udlajan, Sangelaj, Bazar, and Chalmeydan, which are clearly shown in the map of Krziz in 1858 (Map1.1).[46] Because of the increase in population, the government began expanding the city in December 1867.[47] The new city area was 3.3 kilometers from east to west and 3.6 kilometers from north to south. In 1881, five new districts (*mahalle*), Dowlat, 'Udlajan, Sangelaj, Bazar, and Chalmeydan were established and appear in 'Abd al-Ghaffar's map of 1891 (Map 1.2).[48] Each district encompassed a new area that lay outside the old city wall. In particular, the Dowlat district, which contained foreign embassies, a hospital, and large mansions of the notables, became a Europeanized part of the city.[49] Although these new districts were units of local administration, even after 1881, shari'a court records tended to use old district and city gate names when they referred to urban properties.

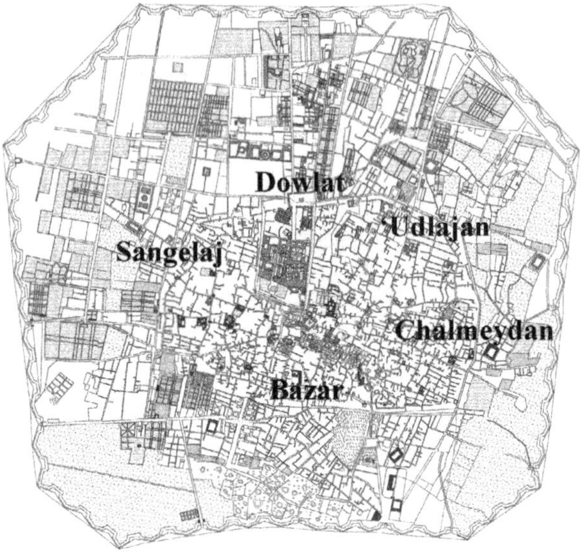

Map 1.2 Tehran in 1891 after 'Abd al-Ghaffar

Central and local administration

Since Tehran was the capital for the Qajar shahs, the royal family and bureaucrats also lived in Tehran, distinguishing it from other cities in Iran. According to Olivier, the total population of 15,000 included 3,000 bureaucrats and soldiers in 1796.[50] The building survey of 1853 categorized Muslim owners of houses into three groups: (a) *amir*s and *khan*s (royal family and high ranking officials), (b) *nowkar*s (other central and local officials) and (c) *ra'iyat*s (none-officials such as merchants and artisans). The *amir*s and *khan*s' owned 27 houses in the Arg district, while 2,122 houses (27%) belonged to the *nowkar*s and 4,695 houses (59%) were in the hands of the *ra'iyats*.[51]

The central and local administration of Tehran sometimes overlapped. The *divankhane*, to which people brought their petitions, was also located in Tehran and the *amir-e divan*, the officer who superintended it, resided in the city. During the second half of the nineteenth century, the Qajars frequently reorganized the central administration. In 1858, after dismissing Aqa Khan Nuri, Naser al-Din Shah abolished the position of *sadr-e a'zam* (Grand Vazir) and established six ministries: the Ministry of Interior, Ministry of Foreign Affairs, Ministry of War, Ministry of Finance, Ministry of Justice, and Ministry of Pensions and Endowments.[52] Among them, the Minister of Justice was a new position and was responsible for judicial affairs in place of the *amir-e divan* although the latter continued to work at least until 1868.[53] Even after that, the government implemented several judicial reforms including the most famous one by Mirza Hoseyn Khan Sepahsalar.[54] However, when one examines the actual cases brought to the minister, its basic function did not change until the end of the nineteenth century.

The Ministry of Pensions and Endowments was a little older than the Ministry of Justice, established in 1854, when the records of pensions and endowments were transferred from the *daftarkhane* (the fiscal department) to the hands of the new minister, Azod al-Molk.[55] The ministry remained unchanged at least until 1901.[56] The ministry was said not to have full control of the *vaqf*s,[57] but this will be reexamined in Chapter 6.

The Qajar shahs appointed a governor and a *vazir* for Tehran. The *vazir*s of Tehran supervised mainly financial matters but sometimes administered the local government in place of the governor. People could present their petitions to the central *divankhane* as well as to the governor or *vazir* of Tehran.

For the city administration, the offices of *kalantar* and *kadkhoda* were important. A major duty of the *kalantar*, who European sources described as mayor of the city,[58] was to maintain public order. He investigated cases of theft and was responsible for finding stolen goods. Under his command, the *kadkhoda*s, i.e., chiefs of districts (*mahalle*s), arrested the thieves and recovered stolen goods. According to the *salname*, there were four *kadkhoda*s in Tehran in 1873, who were probably chiefs of ʻUdlajan, Sangelaj, Chalmeydan, and Bazar districts.[59] In 1876, the *salname* mentioned five *kadkhoda*s, including those of Arg-e Homayun and Sangelaj.[60]

Naser al-Din Shah also implemented reforms in the city administration. In 1878, the Shah appointed the Italian Conte di Monteforte to the position of chief of the newly established police force (*polis* or *nazmiye*).[61] Consequently, in 1880, the office of *kadkhoda* had changed into the office of *ra'is-e mahalle* (chief of the district) under the command of Conte. Also, after this year the position of *kalantar* disappeared from the *salname*.[62] The duty of chiefs of the districts was clearly shown in the Polis Reports, which are analyzed in Chapter 2. However, it was also true that before the reform, the *kadkhoda* prepared reports concerning the events that happened in his district every day.[63] In this regard, the duties of *kadkhoda* and *ra'is-e mahalle* were quite similar.

What is important is that there was no office that controlled the shariʻa courts in both central and local administration. The Qajars did not have any office comparable to the Ottoman *şeyhülislam* or Safavid *sadr*. During the early Qajar period, the office of *molla-bashi* (literally "chief cleric") existed. However, the main role of the *molla-bashi* appears to have been to tutor princes.[64] Unlike the Safavids, the Qajars appointed no one to be a qadi. Although names of *mojtahed*s, most of whom held shariʻa courts, are found in government yearbooks (*salnames*), it does not mean that the *mojtahed*s were employed by the government; the yearbooks also include the names of notable and famous merchants. As we will see later, the shariʻa courts were quite independent of the government.

Notes

1 G. A. Olivier, *Voyage dans l'Empire ottoman, l'Égypte et la Perse* (Paris, 1801–1807), 5:91.
2 Hamd -allah Mostowfi, *Nozhat al-Qolub*, ed. G. Le Strange (1915; reprint, Tehran, 1362), 55.
3 Ahmad Amin Razi, *Haft Eqlim*, ed. Javad Fazeli (Tehran, n.d.), 3:7.
4 Majd al-Din Mohammad Hoseyni, *Zinat al-Majales*, ed. Ahmad Ahmadi (Tehran, 1362Kh), 768.
5 Mohammad Hasan Khan E'temad al-Saltane, *Mer'at al-Boldan*, ed. 'Abd al-Hoseyn Nava'i and Mir Hashem Mohaddes (Tehran, 1367Kh), 828; Mohammad Taqi Hakim, *Ganj-e Danesh*, ed. Mohammad 'Ali Suti and Jamshid Kiyanfar (Tehran, 1366Kh), 457.
6 V. Minorsky, s.v. "Teheran," *The Encyclopaedia of Islam*, 1st Edition, 4 (1927): 715; Chahryar Adle, "Le jardin habité, ou Téhéran de jadis des origines aux Safavides," in *Téhéran: capitale bicentenaire*, ed. Chahryar Adle and Bernard Hourcade (Paris and Tehran, 1992), 30, 33–34; Mo'tamadi, *Joghrafiya-ye Tarikhi*, 24; Mas'ud Nurbakhsh, *Tehran be-Revayat-e Tarikh* (Tehran, 1381Kh), 1:62.
7 Sayyed Hasan Hoseyni Astarabadi, *Az Sheykh Safi ta Shah Safi az Tarikh-e Soltani*, ed. Ehsan Eshraqi (Tehran, 1364Kh), 82.
8 Qazi Ahmad Qommi, *Kholasat al-Tavarikh*, ed. Ehsan Eshraqi (Tehran, 1363Kh), 387–392.
9 Ibid., 386.
10 Mohammad Baqer Va'ez Kojuri, *Ruh va Reyhan ya Jannat al-Na'im va al-'Eysh al-Salim*, ed. Sayyed Sadeq Hoseyni Eshkevari (Qom, 1382Kh), 4:193.
11 Abu al-Hasan Ghaffari, *Golshan-e Morad*, ed. Gholam Hoseyn Tabatabayi Majd (Tehran, 1369Kh), 135. Perry has not given an adequate explanation of this description. He has followed the statement of E'temad al-Saltane. Also he has mistakenly shown a picture of Qasr-e Qajar as the palace built by Karim Khan, when it was in fact built by Fath 'Ali Shah. The buildings built by Karim Khan are now part of the Golestan Palace located in Central Tehran. See John R. Perry, *Karim Khan Zand* (Chicago, 1979), 242, 284.
12 E'temad al-Saltane, *Mer'at al-Boldan*, 828–829.
13 Mohammad Mofid Mostowfi Bafqi, *Mokhtasar-e Mofid*, ed. Iraj Afshar (Tehran, 1390Kh), 111.
14 Pietro Della Valle, *I Viaggi di Pietro Della Valle*, ed. F. Gaeta and L. Lockhart (Rome, 1972), 290.
15 Thomas Herbert, *Travels in Persia, 1627–1629*, ed. William Foster (London, 1928), 194, 322.
16 Qommi, *Kholasat al-Tavarikh*, 873, 906.
17 Mohammad Taher Nasr-abadi, *Tazkere-e Nasr-abadi*, ed. Mohsen Naji Nasr-abadi (Tehran, 1378Kh), 1:261; Muhammad b. al-Hasan al-Hurr al-Amili, *Amal al-Amil*, ed. Ahmad al-Husayni (Baghdad, 1385AH), 1:30.
18 Ghaffari, *Golshan-e Morad*, 135.
19 Many scholars, such as Minorsky, Lambton, Calmard, Hambly, Mo'tamadi, and Nurbakhsh, give the year 1200/1786. Minorsky, s.v. "Teheran," 4:716; A. K. S. Lambton, s.v. "Kadjar," *The Encyclopaedia of Islam*, New Edition, 4 (1978): 391; J. Calmard, s.v. "Tihran: Urbanization, Monuments," *The Encyclopaedia of Islam*, New Edition, 10 (2000): 490; Gavin R.G. Hambly, "Agha Muhammad Khan and the Establishment of the Qajar Dynasty," in *The Cambridge History of Iran*, eds. Peter Avery, Gavin Hambly, and Charles Melville (Cambridge, 1991), 7:118; Mo'tamadi, *Joghrafiya-ye Tarikh*, 65; Nurbakhsh, *Tehran be-Revayat-e Tarikh*, 1:174. Their claim is based on *Ma'aser-e Soltaniya* and *Rowzat al-Safa*, which however were compiled later than *Tarikh-e Mohammadi*. The author of the *Ma'aser* mistakenly gives the date as 1200AH instead of 1199AH mentioned in *Tarikh-e Mohammadi*. See, 'Abd al-Razzaq Donboli,

Ma'aser-e Soltaniye: az ru-ye Noskhe-e Muze-e Boretaniya, ed. Firuz Mansuri (Tehran, 1383Kh), 27; Mohammad Fath-allah b. Mohammad Taqi Saravi, *Tarikh-e Mohammadi: Ahsan al-Tavarikh*, ed. Gholam Hoseyn Tabatabayi Majd (Tehran, 1371Kh), 152. Hedayat's description in *Rowzat al-Safa* concerns the coronation of Aqa Mohammad Khan and is not related to the choice of the capital. The description of the coronation is itself quite doubtful. Reza Qoli Khan Hedayat, *Malhaqat-e Rowzat al-Safa-ye Naseri* (Tehran, 1339Kh), 9:200–201. Finally, it should be noted that Perry gives the year as 1203/1788–9 while Ettehadiye has 1788. Both, however, give no evidence. John R. Perry, s.v. "Aga Mohammad Khan," *Encyclopaedia Iranica*, 1 (1984): 603; Mansoureh Ettehadieh, "Emergence of Tehran as the Cultural Centre of Iran," in *Téhéran: capitale bicentenaire*, ed. Chahryar Adle and Bernard Hourcade (Paris and Tehran, 1992), 127.

20 Adle and Hourcade, eds. *Téhéran: capitale bicentenaire*, 7–8.

21 Saravi, *Tarikh-e Mohammadi*, 152; Mirza 'Ali Qoli Eqbal Chulavi, *Tarikh-e Molk-ara*, MS 4161, Malek Library, Tehran, 118a. Both mentioned the date, 27 Shavval/ 2 September, but in *Mohammadi* this is the date when Aqa Mohammad Khan left Hamadan for Tehran while in *Molk-ara* Aqa Mohammad Khan entered the city on this date.

22 Saravi, *Tarikh-e Mohammadi*, 151–152; Chulavi, *Tarikh-e Molk-ara*, 118a.

23 Chulavi, *Tarikh-e Molk-ara*, 118a.

24 Sale deed of Qanat-e Haji Mohammad Reza, dated 10 Zihejje 1201 AH, Golestan no.3028.

25 Sale deed of a house by Mohammad Khan Hajilar Yuzbashi-e Gholaman dated Moharram 1234 AH, Golestan no.3584,

26 A *vaqf* deed dated August–September 1818 is the oldest example of this that I have found. Owqaf, no.36, the *vaqf* deed of Mirza Mohammad Shafi' Sadr, dated Shavval 1233AH.

27 For more detail about this, see Nobuaki Kondo, "Between Tehran and Sultaniyya: Early Qajar Rulers and Their Itineraries." in *Turko-Mongol Rulers, Cities and City Life*, ed. David Durand-Guédy (Leiden, 2013), 387–406.

28 Saravi, *Tarikh-e Mohammadi*, 280, 283–285.

29 *Tarikh-e Molk-ara* and *Rawzat al-Safa* mentions the coronation took place in 1200AH/1786, but there is no such description in *Tarikh-e Mohammadi*, the most reliable source. Some of the secondary literature makes the claim that Aqa Mohammad Khan had his coronation ceremony at the Mughan plain, but there is no evidence for this.

30 Kondo, "Between Tehran and Sultaniyya," 407–411.

31 Rough estimates of the population have been made by some authors before although information from Persian sources was not fully utilized. Frédy Bémont, *Les Villes de l'Iran: cités d'autrefois à l'urbanisme contemporain* (Paris, 1969–1973), 1:118; Ettehadieh Nezam-Mafi, Mansoureh (Ettehadiye, Mansure), "Patterns in Urban Development: The Growth of Tehran (1852–1903)," in *Qajar Iran: Political, Social and Cultural Exchange*, eds. Edmond Bosworth and Carole Hillenbrand (Edinburgh, 1983), 199.

32 Olivier, *Voyage*, 5:89–90.

33 A. Dupré, *Voyage en Perse fait dans les années 1807, 1808, et 1809* (Paris, 1819), 2:186.

34 Robert B. M.Binning, *A Journal of Two Years' Travel in Persia, Ceylon etc* (London, 1857), 2:215.

35 Edward B. Eastwick, *Journal of a Diplomat's Three Years' Residence in Persia* (London, 1864), 1:217.

36 Mirza 'Abd al-Ghaffar Najm al-Dowle, "Tashkhis-e Nofus-e Dar al-Khelafe," ed. Naser Pakdaman, *Farhang-i Iran-zamin* 20 (1353Kh): 353. For the details of this survey, see Tsutomu Sakamoto, "The Demoghraphic Census of Teheran in 1868," *Oriento* 27 (1984): 92–108.

37 *Salname-e Iran*, 1290AH, 72; 1291 AH, 41.

38 *Ruzname-e Iran*, no.318:6. 9 Rabi' II 1294 AH.

39 *Ketabche-e Te'dad-e Nofus-e Mahallat-e Dar al-Khelafe-e Tehran*, MS Melli Library, Tehran. Later statistics that appears to be based on the same survey and published by

Tehran municipality in 1923–1924 described the total population of 1884 as 106,482. See, Baladiye-e Tehran, *Sarshomari-e Nofus-e Shahr-e Tehran* (1312Kh; reprint in Ja'far Shahri, *Tarikh-e Tehran dar Qarn-e Sizdahom*), 1:12; Sa'dvandiyan, *'Adad-e Abniye*, 119.

40 Sa'dvandiyan, *'Adad-e Abniye*, 315.

41 *Almanach de Gotha: cent-vingt-huitième année* (Gotha, 1891), 977; 'Abd al-Ghaffar, *Naqshe-e Dar al-Khelafe-e Naseri* (Tehran, 1891); George N. Curzon, *Persia and the Persian Question* (1892; reprint, London, 1966), 1:333; A.F. Stahl, "Teheran und Umgegend," *Dr. A. Petermanns Mitteilungen aus Justus Perthes' geographischer Anstalt* 46 (1900): 53.

42 Baladiye-e Tehran, *Sarshomari-e Nofus*, 13; Sa'dvandiyan, *'Adad-e Abniye*, 258.

43 Gad G. Gilbar, "Demographic Developments in Late Qajar Persia, 1870–1906," *Asian and African Studies* 11 (1976): 150. We can compare this data with Hambly's estimate of city populations in the early nineteenth century. Garvin R.G. Hambly, "An Introduction to the Economic Organization of Early Qajar Iran," *Iran* 2 (1964): 72–73. See also Garvin R.G. Hambly, "The Traditional Iranian City in the Qajar Period," in *The Cambridge History of Iran*, eds. Peter Avery, Gavin Hambly, and Charles Melville (Cambridge, 1991), 7:544–548.

44 For migration to Tehran during the Qajar period, see Nobuaki Kondo, "Migration and Multi-Ethnic Coexistence in Qajar Tehran," in *Human Mobility and Mutliethinic Coexistence in Middle Eastern Urban Societies 1*, ed. Hidemitsu Kuroki (Fuchu, 2015), 6–11.

45 For these changes, see John Gurney, "The Transformation of Tehran in the Later Nineteenth Century," In *Téhéran: capitale bicentenaire*, eds. Chahryar Adle and Bernard Hourcade (Paris and Tehran, 1992), 51–71; Ettehadiye, *Inja Tehran Ast*, 25–51.

46 A. Krziz, *Naqshe-e Dar al-Khelafe-e Tehran* (1275AH; reprint, Tehran, 1370Kh).

47 *Ruzname-e Dowlat-e 'Aliye-e Iran* no.613:1–3, 29 Sha'ban 1284AH; Mohammad Hasan Khan E'temad al-Saltanae, *al-Ma'aser al-Asar*, ed. Iraj Afshar (Tehran, 1363Kh), 104; Gurney, "Transformation of Tehran," 52.

48 *Salname-e Iran* 1298AH, 18; 'Abd al-Ghaffar, *Naqshe-e Dar al-Khelafe*.

49 Gurney, "Transformation of Tehran," 57; Mo'tamadi, *Joghrafiya-ye Tarikhi*, 195–198.

50 Olivier, *Voyage*, 5:90.

51 *Surat-e 'Adad-e Khaneha*. The survey lacked information about the *nowkar/ra'iyat* status of the owners of 579 houses in the Sangelaj district and 114 houses outside the city wall.

52 *Ruzname-e Vaqaye'e al-Ettefaqiye* no.397:2–3, 30 Moharram 1275AH; Mohammad Hasan Khan E'temad al-Saltane, *Tarikh-e Montazam-e Naseri*, ed. Mohammad Esma'il Rezvani (Tehran, 1363–67Kh), 1809. See also Ann K.S. Lambton, *Qajar Persia: Eleven Studies* (Austin, 1987), 291; Abbas Amanat, *Pivot of the Universe, Nasir al-Din Shah Qajar and the Iranian Monarchy 1851–1896* (London, 1997), 355–356.

53 *Ruzname-e Dowlat-e 'Aliye-e Iran* no.620:3, 18 Rabi' I 1285AH.

54 Concerning his judicial reform see, Shaul Bakhash, *Iran: Monarcy, Burecracy & Reform under the Qajars: 1858–1896* (London, 1978), 83–91; Guity Nashat, *The Origins of Modern Reform in Iran, 1870–1880* (Urbana, 1982), 43–54.

55 *Ruzname-e Vaqaye'e al-Ettefaqiye* no.179:1–2, 8 Shavval 1270AH.

56 *Ruzname-e Iran* no.1005:2, 10 Sha'ban 1319AH.

57 A. Reza Sheikholeslami, *Structure of Central Authority in Qajar Iran 1871–1896* (Atlanta, 1997), 206.

58 On the various duties of the *kalantar*, see Willem Floor, "The Office of Kalantar in Qajar Persia," *Journal of the Economic and Social History of the Orient* 14, no.3 (1971): 253–268, although this article needs to be revised in light of newer sources.

59 *Salname-e Iran*, 1290AH, 74.

60 Ibid., 1294AH, 32.

61 Mortaza Seyfi Fami Tafreshi, *Nazm va Nazmiye dar Dowre-e Qajariye* (Tehran, 1362Kh), 55. See also E'temad al-Saltane, *al-Ma'aser va al-Asar*, 163–164; *Ruzname-e Iran* no.392:1–2, 12 Rabi' I 1296AH; Willem Floor, "Police in Qajar Persia," *ZDMG* 123 (1973): 299; Ettehadiye, *Inja Tehran Ast*, 123–124.

62 *Salname-e Iran*, 1297AH, 9–11.

63 Unfortunately, only fragments of the reports have survived. See, Iraj Afshar, ed. "Ruzname-e Mahallat-e Dar al-Khelafe 1292," in *Daftar-e Tarikh*, ed. Iraj Afshar (Tehran, 1389Kh), 4:267–277. The report is dated 16 Safar 1292AH.

64 For a list of offices under Fath 'Ali Shah, see Farhad Mirza Mo'tamad al-Dowle, *Zanbil* (Tehran, 1367Kh), 124–128. It includes *sadr al-mamalek* and *molla-bashi* in the same column. The first holder of the office was Molla 'Ali Asghar Hezarjaribi Mazandarani. Although Algar considered him as one of the 'ulama, he was described as tutor of the princes (*adib-e shahzadegan*) in Persian sources. He taught 'Abbas Mirza and other princes. See, Algar, *Religion and State in Iran*, 52; Saravi, *Tarikh-e Mohammadi*, 299; Qajar Mahmud Mirza, *Tarikh-e Sahebqerani*, ed. Nadere Jalali (Tehran, 1389Kh), 74.

2 Judicial system

'Orf courts or "executive powers"?

Shari'a court vs. 'orf court?

Much of the secondary literature has described the Qajar judicial system as a combination of two different judicatures. One is the shari'a court, which was presided over by the 'ulama and was concerned with civil matters, and the other was the "secular" or *'orf* court, which was administered by government officials and dealt with criminal matters such as riots, embezzlement, theft, and inebriation.[1] According to John Malcolm,

> in Persia, there is another branch of judicature, termed Urf, that is known or customary: The secular magistrates who administer it, are to decide all cases brought before them according to precedent, or custom. This law if it can be termed such, is never written.[2]

Certainly, *shar'* and *'orf* were used together in Persian sources, for example, "*shar'an 'orfan*" (in law and custom) in the closing phrase of private deeds. The term *'orf* has multiple meanings. As a general term, *'orf*, like *'ada*, means custom or customary law.[3] In Islamic jurisprudence, it denotes local or temporary custom and also an abstract tool to educe customary practices in substantive law.[4] In Shi'i jurisprudence, although Vahid Behbahani refuted the idea that the shari'a could have its source in *'orf* (common practice), he also stated that *'orf* is useful for understanding Muslim duties.[5] Uriel Heyd explains how the Ottoman usage of the term *'orf* was complicated. Originally, it denoted "common usage," but it could mean Ottoman *qanun*, "commands of the sovereigns," or even "torture."[6] Werner's detailed discussion also indicates that the term *'orf* had been used in various ways depending on the sources and contexts.[7]

However, this theory of two judicatures in Iranian history, i.e., the shari'a and '*orf* courts, is not directly derived from Islamic legal theory; No modern work on Islamic legal theory ever mentions the "*orf* court." Instead, the theory was largely based on European sources, which described the judicial system too simplistically. As Christoph Werner points out, the concept of *'orf* in Iran was particularly developed by European travelers who visited there from the seventeenth to the nineteenth centuries.[8] Therefore, those who described these two judicatures needed to cite first European sources such as Malcolm's *History of Persia*.[9]

The problem is there were few sources that describe in detail the *'orf* courts and their process of trial in the primary sources from Qajar Iran.[10] It is, in fact, questionable if an *orf* court, as an independent "secular" court of justice with its own "secular" law code, actually did exist. For this reason, Werner interpreted these two judicatures rather as a differentiation between law (here meaning Islamic law and its actual practices) and "executive powers." In his opinion, the latter included "police activities, implementation of bodily and pecuniary penalties, and overriding judgments made by the governors in response to petitions of every kind."[11] Although his opinion was at least worth considering, Floor and Schneider totally ignored this in their later works.[12]

How then should we interpret the so-called *'orf* court? According to Floor, the highest *'orf* court was the *divan* of the Shahs, and the next in rank was that of the provincial governors.[13] However, obviously, the function of the *divan* of the Shahs was not limited to judicial matters. Lambton understands the *'orf* court in the framework of the *mazalem* tradition, while Schneider distinguished the *'orf* court from the *mazalem* system.[14] In other words, the concept of the *'orf* court is still ambiguous in the secondary literature, and there is no consensus as to its role.

For this reason, I use a different approach. Instead of investigating the ambiguous *'orf* court, I examine two concrete issues which are characteristic of the so-called *'orf* court: criminal cases and complaints/petitions. The latter concerned both the *divankhane*s and so-called the *mazalem* system, and from this we will see how criminal cases and people's complaints/petitions were dealt with by the authorities, and what law was referred to in the process.

Criminal cases

Criminal cases are rarely mentioned in the narrative sources. However, the official gazette that was first issued in 1851 provides some information on criminal cases in Tehran. Most of them were cases of murder, theft, inebriation, and assault.

The first question is who dealt with the cases. From 1851 to 1871, the governors of Tehran dealt with forty-nine cases, five of which were handled by the *vazir*s of Tehran and three cases were managed by both together. The gazette describes the cases as follows:

> This week, the *kalantar* and the *kadkhoda*s arrested four thieves. His highness, noble Prince Ardashir Mirza, the Governor of Tehran and the surroundings, ordered them to be punished. By his order, they were punished at Meydan-e Qapuq in order to warn others away from theft and crime.[15]

In most of the cases found in the official gazette, the governor or his deputy (*vazir*) decided the case, while the *kalantar* and *kadkhoda*s arrested the criminals. Among the cases decided by the governor, forty-one cases concerned theft and four cases related to inebriation.

On the other hand, Naser al-Din Shah decided only four cases including two cases of murder.[16] Naturally, the Shah presided over more serious cases than the governor. Crimes such as theft and inebriation were managed by the governor. This situation did not change even after the foundation of a modern police force in 1878. Criminals like thieves and drunkards arrested by the police were then sent to the governor's *divankhane* for punishment.[17] Moreover, in the same year, Naser al-Din Shah ordered that only the governor's prison in Tehran was to be used instead of the state and military prisons and any officers outside this jurisdiction did not have right to restrain criminals. State and military prisons remained but their use was restricted to the confinement of special criminals.[18]

The gazette sometimes mentions punishments such as whipping, the cutting of hands and earlobes, and expulsion from the province. What is noteworthy here is that in some cases the gazette mentions Islamic law when deciding on the penalty. For example:

> Last week, the three persons that committed thefts and inappropriate acts and deserved capital punishment according to Islamic law (*qanun-e shar'-e mota'*) were executed on the scaffold in Tehran.[19]
>
> By the order of his highness (the governor) and Islamic law (*qanun-e shar'*), he was decided to be punished again. His hand was cut off due to his theft. He was enchained, marched around the markets and expelled (from the city).[20]

The gazette claimed that the punishment accorded with Islamic law. Moreover, there was a case of murder for which *qisas/qesas*, the retaliation principle in Islamic law, was applied. The murderer was killed by the successors of the victim.[21] The gazette refers to Islamic law (*shar'*) and never mentions *'orf* at all. Therefore, it is clear that the governor was expected to deal with the cases on the basis of Islamic law, not on the basis of *'orf*. The gazette also provides some evidence of discretion being taken by the governors:

> Although his hand must be cut off according to Islamic law, his two earlobes were cut off by the order of his highness (the governor). He was enchained, marched around the markets and expelled (from the city).[22]

The cutting of a hand for theft is written in the Qur'an and is a part of the fixed punishment (*hadd*) in Islamic law which cannot be changed or reduced.[23] However, here the governor did not order the cutting off of the thief's hand but rather his earlobes, which is not found in Islamic law. The punishment of cutting earlobes was not an unusual one in the gazette: one finds seven other cases from the years 1851–1871.[24] There is no reference to the punishment of the cutting off of a leg that is also one of the *hadd* punishments.[25] The governors, thus, outwardly respected Islamic law, but often implemented the penalties for criminal cases at their own discretion.

One finds the same sense of outward respect for Islamic law along with discretionary measures in the police regulations given to officers written by the Italian officer Conte di Monteforte in 1879. The regulations stipulated that murders must be judged in accordance with Islamic law, but for other crimes, it introduced imprisonments and fixed fines, never found in Islamic law.[26] Despite these innovations, the police were still ordered to "execute all the regulations of shari'a" and "observe all the regulations of Islamic law."[27] Here, again, there is no indication of *'orf*. Conte di Monteforte had introduced modern elements into the details of the regulations which were supposedly in accordance with Islamic law.

All procedures dealing with criminal cases were quickly carried out by the local government. In other words, criminal cases were handled as a part of the local administration. With regard to criminal cases, therefore, it is difficult to find what might be considered an independent *'orf* court, which opened regularly and conducted sessions. If the law was supposed to be referred to at all, it was Islamic law not *'orf* or customary law that is mentioned explicitly in the sources.

The central divankhane

Making a direct appeal to rulers or high dignitaries was a tradition in Muslim societies. The court of appeal was called the *mazalim* court. *Mazalim/mazalem* denotes various injustices and oppressions. Theoretically a just ruler must get rid of them of all. In the seventeenth century, the Safavid ruler Shah 'Abbas II fixed a day of the week to hear appeals and petitions from people.[28] We will see another example later: a man appealed to the *divankhane* of Mohammad Shah for the return of his property in 1835.[29]

In the first half of the nineteenth century, the officer who administered the affairs of the *divankhane* was given the title Amir-i Divan. In 1858, during institutional reform, the Minister of Justice (*vazir-e 'adliye*) took over the central *divankhane*.[30] The central *divankhane* (*divankhane-e mobarake*) gradually came to be referred to as the *divankhane* of justice (*divankhane-e 'adliye*), and the Minister of Justice, not the Shah, came to hear the appeals of the people.[31] The government tried to consolidate the position of the *divankhane* and confer upon it the Shah's authority. In 1854, the government decided to hang a curtain with the Shah's portrait on it at the *divankhane*. The official gazette explained, "the place with the shah's portrait is the shah's presence, and a just order is issued there."[32] The proclamation of 1862 emphasized that provincial governors, nobles, and ordinary people must pay high regard to the orders issued by the *divankhane* and consider them next to a royal edict because they were looked over by the Shah.[33]

Since the concept of an "*'orf* court" is somewhat ambiguous, Faridun Adamiyat used the term *divankhane* to denote a court system other than the shari'a court.[34] However, without an analysis of actual cases from the *divankhane*, it is difficult to determine its character: it could function as a means of presenting petitions as well as a judicial court. Below, I shall refer to two sources which shed light on the functions of the central *divankhane*, which include forty cases from the years 1860–1867 that were described in the official gazette and ninety-two cases around 1900 published by 'Abbas Zare'i.[35]

The official gazette mentions two functions of the *divankhane*. First, the *divankhane* was the court where one person accused another. In other words, it dealt with civil cases, and its function overlapped with that of the shari'a courts. According to the proclamation of 1858, "if someone has a claim or a complaint, it will be investigated at the *divankhanes* of justice and the shari'a courts of the 'ulama (*mahzar-e 'ulama-ye shar'-e diniye*)."[36] When one person complained about another at the *divankhane*, not only the plaintiffs but also the defendants had to attend the *divankhane*.[37] The other function was to remove injustice and oppression by central and local officials. The proclamation of 1863 stated that in order to complain against an official, people did not need to attend the *divankhane* in Tehran: it was enough to send a letter of complaint to the *divankhane*.[38] In short, the official gazette clearly describes the *divankhane* both as a judicial court and as a petitioning institution.

Of the forty cases from 1860–1867, thirty-three (or more than 80 percent) were civil cases. Among them, eighteen cases were concerned with land rights and real estate, eight cases related to inheritance, and seven cases pertained to the repayment of debts. For example,

> Mirza Mohammad Qoli and Mirza Javad complained about some matters at the *divankhane* of justice: some people in Yazd had usurped some of their [Mohamamd Qoli and Javad's] lands, shops, a garden, money and goods, and oppressed and abused them. A royal edict was issued from the *divankhane* of justice that Saheb-e Divan, the governor of Yazd should investigate the case thoroughly and recover their right, and then send the report.[39]

On the other hand, only five cases concerned officials and administration. Among them were three cases that related to injustice and oppression by a local governor, a tax collector and a military officer:

> Farmers in a certain Lanjrud village, which belonged to the *toyul* of 'Ali Naqi Khan, the brigadier (*sartip*), complained at the royal court about the oppression of the brigadier. After investigation, an edict was issued from the *divankhane* of justice, which ordered Nosrat al-Dowle, the Governor of (Persian) 'Eraq, to occupy the village and pay the salary of the brigadier himself.[40]

Another case pertained to financial support from the government for repairing an irrigation canal,[41] and the final case concerned compensation for a house that had been destroyed by the expansion of military exercise fields.[42]

Here, we can consider the *divankhane* as a court of justice in terms of civil cases. However, the *divankhane* also accepted complaints about local officers and in this regard it was a part of the central administration.

Also among the ninety-two cases brought to the central *divankhane* around 1900, sixty-nine cases (75 percent) concerned civil matters. Among them, thirty cases concerned disputes over land and property, twenty-eight cases related to debts, eight cases pertained to leases and sales, and five cases were about inheritance. Only four cases were concerned with administration and taxation. A difference from the 1860s is that sixteen criminal cases were included: plundering (eight cases), theft (five cases), homicide (two cases), and assault (one case). As mentioned above, usually local governors handled criminal cases, but here the plaintiffs directly referred to the *divankhane* as follows:

> Mohammad Beg Garrusi complained to the Ministry of Justice as follows. "The persons, Seyf-allah Khan, Lotf ʻAli Khan, Haji Baqer and the son of Fardin Soltan, without any reason, plundered my money and furniture. I came to Tehran to complain and to recover my rights." Therefore, the Minister of Justice ordered Mohammad Hoseyn Khan, the royal musketeer, to be sent to Garrus to investigate the case thoroughly with the consent of ʻAli Reza Khan, the Governor of Garrus. (The minister decreed that) the royal musketeer should retake, without exception, all money and furniture that is proven according to the Holy Shariʻa to have been plundered and seized from the plaintiff and to have caused him loss and damage. It should be returned to the plaintiff, a receipt should be taken from him, and sent along with a report to the *divan* of justice to inform us.[43]

It is not clear when the *divankhane* began to deal with criminal cases. We do know however that following judicial reform in 1871 Mirza Hoseyn Khan Sepahsalar divided the Ministry of Justice into four departments including a criminal department (*majles-e jenayat*).[44]

Petitioning system

Irene Schneider published an interesting book on the "petitioning system," or *mazalem,* institution in Qajar Iran. She analyzed sixteen folios of a large register of petitions, which were sent from the provinces by post to Naser al-Din Shah and handled by the Grievance Investigation Department (*majles-e tahqiq-e mazalem*) around 1883. She uses the term "petitioning system" as a synonym of "*mazalem* institutions," which she concludes was "an inherent part of the political system."[45] While there can be no doubt that the "petitioning system" had political implications, Schneider fails to provide a clear account of where the "petitioning system" is to be located within the wider Qajar judicial system. It appears that she located this "petitioning system" outside of the jurisdictional institutions such as the sharʻia and the so-called *ʻorf* courts.[46]

To begin with, it is not accurate to consider the petitioning system examined by Schneider as the sole *mazalem* institution in Qajar Iran. In fact, as mentioned above, the *divankhane* can be considered the main *mazalem* institution. The description of the *divankhane*s in official gazettes is quite similar to those of the petitioning system: "(Minister of Justice) controlled the central *divankhane*, investigated petitions (*ʻaraʼez*) and problems of ordinary people, and protected the right of the oppressed (*mazlumin*) and the depressed (*malhumin*)."[47] This is understandable because the *divakhane* was originally the council that the Shah attended in person and accepted petitions from his subjects.

Secondly, though its institutional development is rather complicated,[48] there can be little doubt that the petitioning system was closely related to the Ministry of Justice and the *divankhane*. The origin of the petitioning system can be traced back to 1860 when Naser al-Din Shah proclaimed that he would attend the Divan-e Mazalem on Sundays. At this time he decided to accept petitions that people sent by post (*chapar*) from the provinces. Since the Minister of Justice and Nayeb-e Sadr-e Divankhane had major roles in this Sunday Divan-e Mazalem, the petitions from the provinces were also handled by these officers of the *divankhane*,[49] although the Sunday Divan-e Mazalem appears to have been abandoned shortly afterwards.

According to a declaration of the government in 1863, people in the provinces could also send petitions on the injustice of local officers to the central *divankhane* by post.[50] However, the petitioning system was developed considerably by the formal establishment of the so-called Box of Justice (*sanduq-e 'adalat*) in 1864. Though the details of the initial system of the Box are not clear, petitions concerning matters in the provinces arrived in Tehran through the system, and the Minister of Justice was responsible for the execution of the Shah's orders in response to them.[51] In 1866, when the government clarified the duty of each ministry, it demanded that the Ministry of Justice deal with both the appeals at the *divankhane* and the petitions in the Box of Justice.[52] As has been described so far, the petitioning system was thus developed alongside the Ministry of Justice and the *divankhane*.

In January 1875, Naser al-Din Shah appointed 'Azod al-Molk to supervise the newly implemented Box of Justice in the provinces: the petitions put into the provincial boxes were brought to Tehran by post.[53] This is the direct origin of the petitioning system that produced the register of petitions analyzed by Schneider. 'Azod al-Molk was given the position of the Chief of the Grievance Department (*ra'is-e divan-e mazalem*) in the *Salname* of the next year (1292 AH) and it appears from then on no public *divan* was held with the Shah in attendance.[54] In the summer of 1875, 'Azod al-Molk was appointed the Minister of Justice. He was responsible for the supervision of both the *divankhane* and the Box of Justice because, according to the official gazette, the two duties were closely related.[55] The Grievance Department is also mentioned as being part of the Ministry of Justice in the *Salname*s of the years 1877 to 1881.[56] The only exceptions are the *Salname*s of the years 1882 and 1883. They do not refer to the Grievance Department. Instead, one finds a department, in the Ministry of Justice, named "Department for Investigation (*majles-e tahqiq*)." This "Department for Investigation (*majles-e tahqiq*)" had been presided over by Mohammad Rahim Khan Qajar, who had been the chief of the Grievance Department since 1878.[57] Though the 1882 and 1883 *Salnames* omit the last word "*mazalem*," no doubt this shortened name denotes the Grievance Investigation Department (*majles-e tahqiq-e mazalem*), where the register of petitions studied by Schneider was compiled. In other words the department still belonged to the Ministry of Justice.

When one examines the petitions that Schneider has published, of the sixty-seven petitions, only twenty-one are related to civil cases like land and property, debt, sale, and lease. Seven petitions concern criminal cases. There were more petitions concerning officials and administration: nineteen petitions complained about injustice from officials, and four petitions asked for tax exemptions. In addition, there were nine petitions that asked the Shah for pensions, salaries, or financial support.[58] The difference from the *divankhanes*, where 75 percent of the cases heard were of civil matters, is obvious. The percentages that Schneider provides also confirm this.[59]

What is the reason for the difference between the *divankhane* and the petitioning system? We may assume that it is because the petitioning system supplemented the role played by the *divankhane*. In fact, the newly styled Grievance Investigation Department was part of the Ministry of Justice, which also administrated the *divankhane*. In other words, it is quite unlikely that the petitioning system was an independent system from the *divankhane*.

The petitioning system developed along with the reforms of the *divankhane*. The *divankhane* was originally the central council of the rulers to which people presented petitions on both legal and administrative matters, on the basis of the *mazalem* tradition. In the second half of the nineteenth century, as the central *divankhane*, presided over by the Minister of Justice, gradually came to accept more judicial matters than people's petitions. This means that people lost the opportunity to present petitions directly to the Shah. It was because of this that the government needed other institutions like the petitioning system to supplement the *divankhane* and keep up the tradition of *mazalem*.

Local governors

The *divankhane* and the petitioning system that I have discussed above were part of the central government in Tehran. Were there any counterparts in local governments that dealt with criminal cases?

In the regulations relating to the *divankhane* issued in 1862, inhabitants of Tehran and surrounding areas had the option to complain at the *divankhane* of justice or before the governor and *vazir* of Tehran. The governor and *vazir* must not prevent people from complaining at the *divankhane*. The cases directly related to the governor or *vazir* should be heard at the *divankhane*. If the governor or *vazir* neglected to hear the case for more than five days, the case had to be brought to the *divankhane*. The governor and *vazir* also had a duty to execute the orders of the *divankhane*. Regarding other provinces, the regulations stipulated that the *divankhane* would appoint an official who would supervise whether the governor executed the orders of the *divankhane* and handled complaints brought by the inhabitants adequately.[60] People could also complain before their local governors.

In 1871, the government tried to reform the office of the *vazir* of Tehran. According to the official gazette, prior to that the engagement of the *vazir* in administration and other bureaucratic procedures prevented him from handling complaints and protecting the right of the oppressed. Therefore, the *vazir* would now establish an investigative council (*majles al-tahqiqi*) and assign officials to preside over it: a chief, the *kalantar*, four *kadkhodas*, five elders (*rishsefidan*), and two secretaries.

The officials were expected to sit and hear the cases from morning to noon every day except Monday and Friday.[61]

Unfortunately, there is no detailed information on complaints brought before the governors and *vazir*s. However, it appears that two differences existed between the local governors and the central institutions such as the central *divankhane* and the petitioning system. First, the central institutions belonged to the Shah and had much more authority than the local governors. The official gazette freely used a full range of literary expressions to describe the Shah and his institutions, and attempted to portray the Shah as a holy person. The local governors on the other hand did not demonstrate such holiness. The edicts issued by the Shah were more effective than those issued by the governors. Second, the reform of the local governments started considerably later than that of the central government. In 1858, Naser al-Din Shah attempted to establish a *divankhane* similar to the central one in the provinces: he sent out officers named *divanbegi*.[62] However, the *divanbegi*s could not establish their positions in the provinces because of resistance from the local governors.[63] It was not until 1877 that the first local *divankhane* was established by the governors.[64] Before that, apparently, the provincial governments did not have their own separate judicial departments. Therefore, it must have been difficult for local governors to deal with many legal cases without such judicial departments as was the case of Tehran.

In concluding this section, it has become clear that the so-called *'orf* court was not a single organized judicial institution. It was a complex amalgamation of administrative institutions at various levels that dealt with criminal and judicial matters as well as people's petitions. Though modern reforms did bring the *divankhane* closer to a judicial court, it nevertheless still handled administrative matters and people's petitions. Also, it is difficult to find any explicit reference to the term *'orf* in primary sources concerning the so-called "*'orf* court." This will be shown more clearly in the following section when we investigate the relationship between these institutions and the shari'a court.

Relationship with shari'a courts

As mentioned above 70 percent of cases that were brought to the central *divankhane* were civil cases, one might wonder therefore how the *divankhane* coexisted with the shari'a courts which also dealt with civil cases. Also, since local governors dealt with criminal cases in accordance with Islamic law, it is natural that they had some relationship with the shari'a courts. Here, I examine the role of the shari'a courts in criminal cases tried at the local government level and in criminal cases referred to the central *divankhane*.

Criminal cases and shari'a courts

As far as the official gazettes are concerned, there is little information about the role played by jurists in criminal cases. However, the police reports from 1886–1888 frequently mention shari'a courts in connection with criminal cases. For example, in Ziqa'de 1303/August 1886, twenty-six of the eighty-one cases of theft (about one third of all the cases) were brought to shari'a courts by the police or heads of the districts in the city of Tehran. At that time, inhabitants of Tehran also complained to the heads of districts about civil matters such as debts and marriages. The heads in turn sent thirteen cases to shari'a courts in the same month.[65] It is notable that there were twice as many theft cases as there were civil matters.

On what occasions did the police and heads of districts bring the cases to shari'a courts? There were two possibilities. First, the cases were complicated and not easy to determine. Occasionally, they had legal backgrounds similar to the following case:

> Yesterday, Mashhadi Hoseyn Qoli, a cloth seller, told the head of the district: "a brother of my wife has stolen from her articles that valued 10 *tomans*." The head sent a person to bring the brother in front of him. The head interrogated the brother, and found that there was a legal dispute behind the case. He sent the case to a shari'a court and made them continue proceedings there.[66]

Apparently, there was a dispute between the wife and her brother over articles and the brother claimed that the articles belonged to him. Cases of theft committed by neighbors, family and apprentices tended to be brought to shari'a courts. It is reasonable to assume that these sorts of theft had problems regarding property rights and the police could not handle them.

Second, the cases needed to be judged under oath (*be-qeyd-e qasam*).[67] Complicated cases might be more suitably judged at the shari'a court under oath because people were under pressure to avoid lying there. The shari'a court allowed defendants to swear an oath on the Qur'an and to be found not guilty when the plaintiff could not prove his claim, as we will see later.

Divankhane and shari'a courts

It can be said that all the civil cases examined in this study that were brought to the *divankhane* involved the shari'a court, as most of the documentary evidence brought to the *divankhane* was arranged beforehand at the shari'a court even when the case involved disputes about land, inheritance or unpaid debts. However, in five cases from 1860 to 1867, and in eleven cases from around 1900, legal edicts (*hokms*) issued by a shari'a court, which provided a *mojtahed*'s opinion, were brought to the *divankhane*. In those cases, the decision of the *divankhane* followed the legal edicts. Here is an example.

> Some time ago, Nasr-allah Khan b. 'Abd-allah Khan Amin al-Dowle sued Khan Baba Khan Chalah-shatri and claimed that the latter had usurped a part of the inherited property of the former illegally. Many sessions were held at the Divan-e 'Adalat, and documents and legal edicts issued by 'ulama of Najaf al-Ashraf and Isfahan were shown there. The process was reported to the Shah. After investigation by the Supreme Council (*majles-e showra-ye*

> *kobra*) and in recognition of his legitimate right, the *divankhane* ordered on the basis of the legal edicts that the property should be returned to Nasr-allah Khan and Khan Baba Khan must not intervene in the property.[68]

The case was brought not only to the *divankhane* but also to the Shah and the Supreme Council. In the end, the order of the *divankhane* followed the legal edicts of ʻulama in Najaf and Isfahan.

The reverse process can also be found in the sources. Eleven cases from 1860–67 and ten cases from around 1900 were first brought to the *divankhane*, and then referred to shariʻa courts. In addition to these cases, seven cases from around 1900 included a sentence in the final section as follows: "if you have a matter that needs a shariʻa lawsuit (*morafe ʻe-e sharʻi*) go to a shariʻa court, which both of you agree with, and close the case."[69] Even after closing the case at the *divankhane*, sometimes plaintiffs and defendants needed to bring the case to a shariʻa court.

Let us review the content of the cases. Among the eleven cases from 1860–1867 where the cases were sent from the *divankhane* to a shariʻa court, five cases concerned inheritance, four cases related to property and two cases pertained to debt. Here is an example of an inheritance case:

> A daughter of late Haji Esmaʻil Khan Qajar complained that after the death of her father even a *dinar* of her share of his legacy, which is 60,000 *tomans* in value comprising cash, goods and properties, was not given to her. After two sides attended (the *divankhane*), (the case) was referred to the (shariʻa) court of the Mojtahed of the Age, Haji Molla Mirza Mohammad (Andarmani) and whatever his edict is, it will be executed (by the *divankhane*).[70]

It is clear that the *divankhane* entrusted the case totally to the shariʻa court. There is no explanation given but the reason appears to be the complexity of inheritance law.

On the other hand, the cases from around 1900 included a murder. Mirza Akbar Khan complained at the *divankhane* that Nabi Khan had killed a farmer on his estate. The local governor arrested and detained Nabi Khan. However, a relative of the father of Nabi Khan sent a false telegram from Tehran, requesting Nabi Khan's release for his trial in Tehran. As a result, Nabi Khan was released. The *divankhane* ordered the governor to investigate the case with officials from the *divankhane* and, if Nabi Khan committed the murder, to re-arrest him. The procedure was determined in this way: the relatives of the victim were to refer to a shariʻa court and receive confirmation of the murder. The governor was to punish the murderer in accordance with the edict of the shariʻa court and with the consent of the central government.[71]

In this case, the role of the shariʻa court was to confirm and certify the legal fact of the murder. In other words, the *divankhane* referred to the shariʻa court in criminal cases as well as in civil cases when it needed legal certification from a shariʻa court. There is another case from around 1900, in which a shariʻa court confirmed the occurrence of a murder.[72] In addition, two theft cases were also referred to the shari'a court while two robbery cases were expected to be presented at shari'a courts if necessary.[73] It is not a surprise that the murder case of Bibi Asilu analyzed by Vanessa Martin involved a *mojtahed*.[74]

The *divankhane* sent a case to a shari'a court when procedures which fell under the jurisdiction of shari'a courts were necessary. One such procedure was an oath, as mentioned above. The case of Mast Mah Gowhar Khanom is described in a document from around 1900. She lent Fateme Khanom 400 *tomans* cash. When Fateme died, Mast Mah Gowhar claimed Fateme's husband was required to pay back the debt from her legacy, but did not do so. Mast Mah Gowhar complained at the *divankhane*, but the husband denied the debt. They referred the case to the shari'a court of a *mojtahed*, Sheykh Fazl-allah Nuri. Finally, Mast Mah Gowhar could not find a witness, who would support her claim. Fateme's husband swore an oath on the Qur'an that he did not have any debts, and the *mojtahed* arranged an oath deed. The deed was submitted to the *divankhane*, and the husband was exempt from payment of the debt.[75] In Islamic law, an oath was a measure to close a case with victory for the defendant when the plaintiff could not submit enough evidence. This procedure was possible at a shari'a court but not at the *divankhane*.

Another procedure, which was possible only at shari'a courts, was a settlement. Here is an example:

> Mirza Taqi Nuri complained at the *divankhane* of justice: half (3 *dang*) of the village of Reza-abad in Savojbolagh, in the possession of Ja'far Qoli Khan, had originally been part of the property of Shahrut Beg Eshtehardi and his heirs. Shahrut Beg Eshtehardi and his heirs transferred their right to me [Mirza Taqi] by a settlement. Both parties [Mirza Taqi and Ja'far Qoli Khan] attended, and after the investigations, it became clear that Shahrut Beg made a settlement with Ja'far Qoli Khan and renounced his claim (over the property) after Shahrut Beg had transferred his right to Mirza Taqi. Since Shahrut Beg had already died, (Mirza Taqi) made a settlement with Ja'far Qoli Khan at the court of Hajji Molla Mirza Mohammad (Andarmani); receiving 120 *tomans*, Mirza Taqi renounced his claim leaving the property in the hands of Ja'far Qoli Khan.[76]

The case was heard at the *divankhane*, but in the last stage, the case was brought to the shari'a court in order to make a settlement, since that was the only place where a settlement was possible. A settlement was a contract, which was frequently arranged at a shari'a court. A deed of settlement was also drawn up there.

Therefore, shari'a courts were necessary for the *divankhane* for two reasons. First, shari'a courts produced documents that were used as proof at trials at the *divankhane*. Private deeds and legal edicts were submitted at trials in order to confirm legal facts, and these considerably influenced final decisions. Second, the *divankhane* needed to entrust a case to a shari'a court when the case was difficult to close or had a legal problem. In these cases, the *divankhane* executed legal edicts from shari'a courts, or the shari'a courts closed the cases by oath or settlement.

In fact, as will be described in the next chapter, it was only possible to arrange legal deeds and confirm legal facts via shari'a courts, as the local governors or the *divankhane* did not have authority over these matters. What the *divankhane* did was solve problems in the execution of cases where there was no legal aspect in doubt. When there were doubts on any legal aspect, the *divankhane* was obliged to entrust the case to the shari'a court.

Schneider claims that the shari'a courts were subordinate to the state because the legal edicts from a shari'a court were not executed quickly.[77] However, this is a one-sided view. The *divankhane* and the Grievances Investigation Department used shari'a documents as proof, and when a case was legally complicated, the institutions had to rely on the shari'a courts to solve the case. The shari'a court and the state had different roles in the judicial system: the former specialized in the law while the latter was responsible for the execution of the law. Concerning problems related to the details of the law, the state was subordinate to the shari'a court.

State/local authorities and shari'a: a conclusion

In this chapter, three points must be emphasized. First, criminal cases were mainly handled by local governors as part of the local administration. The governors respected the shari'a as the only single legal standard, but they sometimes determined penalties at their own discretion. Second, the central *divankhane* was the most prestigious organization that managed complaints and petitions. It accepted various legal and administrative complaints along with the Grievance Investigation Department. However, more than 70 percent of the complaints at the *divankhane* related to civil cases. In this regard, we can say it gradually became a court of justice. Third, although the *divankhane* was concerned with civil cases, its character was different from that of the shari'a court. The governors and the *divankhane* could not deal with cases that had complicated legal backgrounds, including criminal cases that were also brought to shari'a courts. Unlike the shari'a court, they could not use oath or settlement to close cases. Therefore, they referred such cases to a shari'a court if necessary.

The government authorities were not experts in Islamic law. Therefore they endeavoured to conform to Islamic law whilst applying previous practice where there was no evident or practicable guidance available to them. It is true that the shari'a and the *'orf* are a pair of concepts in Islamic jurisprudence. Therefore, it might be natural that European travelers summarized the political authorities' commitment into the judicial sphere by simplistically describing it as an "'*orf* court." However, although the term "court" was used for both, their nature was quite different. While the shari'a court was a concrete single institution operated by *mojtahed*s as we will see below, the so-called *'orf* court was not an actual single institution. As described above, the *divankhane* and the criminal administration were totally different institutions, and it is not reasonable to discuss both as being the same as the *'orf* court.

However, what is important here is that the *divankhane* and the criminal administration were operated with executive power, which the state and local authorities possessed and the shari'a court lacked. Wael B. Hallaq, in his book, clearly distinguished *siyasat shar'iya* (the state perspective of Islamic law) from *'urf* (local custom or customary law), both of which depended on Islamic law.[78] Although the term *siyasat shar'iya* is never found in Qajar sources, his suggestion can be applied to the Qajar judicial system: State and local authorities, i.e., shahs and governors, claimed to execute not *'orf* but shari'a under the *mojtaheds*' guidance, even though this shari'a naturally included local customs.

Notes

1 Floor, "Change and Development," 113; Floor, s.v. "Judicial and Legal Systems."
2 John Malcolm, *The History of Persia from the Most Early Period to the Present Time*, New Edition (London, 1829), 2:311.
3 G. Libson and F.H. Stewart, s.v. "'Urf," *Encyclopaedia of Islam*, New edition, 10 (2000): 887–892.
4 Ayman Shabana, *Custom in Islamic Law and Legal Theory* (New York, 2010), 5.
5 Gleave, *Inevitable Doubt*, 213, 216.
6 Uriel Heyd, *Studies in Old Ottoman Criminal Law*, ed. V.L. Ménage (Oxford, 1973), 168–171.
7 Werner, "'Orf oder Gewohnheitsrecht."
8 Ibid., 155–159.
9 Floor, "Secular Justice System," 10 (cited Raphael du Mans); Schneider, *Petitioning System*, 21 (cited Curzon).
10 The only example I have found is "*mahkame-e 'orfi*" in a local history of Yazd, *Jame'-e Ja'fari*. Here, a *sayyed* was whipped. See Mohammad Ja'far Na'ini Tarab, *Jame'-i Ja'fari*, ed. Iraj Afshar (Tehran, 1353Kh), 505.
11 Werner, *An Iranian Town*, 235.
12 Floor, s.v. "Judicial and Legal Systems"; Schneider, *Petitioning System*, 21–25.
13 Floor, "Change and Development," 114.
14 Lambton, s.v. "Mahkama 3. Iran"; Schneider, *Petitioning System*, 21–25, 30–37.
15 *Ruzname-e Vaqaye' al-Ettefaqiye* no.130:2, 21 Shavval 1269AH.
16 Ibid. no.13:1, 23 Jomada II 1267AH; no.55:2, 28 Rabi' II 1268AH.
17 Anise Sheykh Reza'i and Shahla Azari, eds. *Gozareshha-ye Nazmiye az Mahallat-e Tehran* (Tehran, 1377Kh), 25, 49, 58, 59, 62, 66, 71, 98.
18 *Ruzname-e Iran* no.347:1, 6 Rabi' I 1295AH.
19 *Ruzname-e Vaqaye' al-Ettefaqiye* no.13:1.
20 Ibid. no.311:4, 18 Jomada II 1273AH.
21 Ibid. no.361:1, 14 Jomada I 1274AH.
22 Ibid. no.311:4.
23 Schacht, *An Introduction to Islamic Law*, 178–181.
24 *Ruzname-e Vaqaye' al-Ettefaqiye* no.221:3, 9 Sha'ban 1271AH; no.231:2, 9 Shavval 1271AH; no.276:2, 10 Ramazan 1272AH; no.323:4, 13 Sha'ban 1273AH.
25 Schacht, *An Introduction to Islamic Law*, 180.
26 Conte di Monteforte, *Ketabche-e Avval-e Qanun* (Tehran, 1296AH; reprint, in Seyfi Fami Tafreshi, *Nazm va Nazmiye*), 4, 7, 11–12.
27 Ibid., 4–5.
28 Mirza Mohammad Taher Vahid Qazvini, *Tarikh-e Jahan-ara-ye 'Abbasi*, ed. Sayyed Sa'id Mir Mohammad Sadeq (Tehran, 1383Kh), 557.
29 See Chapter 5.
30 *Ruzname-e Vaqaye' al-Ettefaqiye* no.397:3, 30 Muḥarram 1275AH.
31 The earliest reference to the term *divankhane-e adliye* that I have found is dated 23 Zihejje 1273AH/14 August 1857. See Hedayat, *Rowzat al-Safa*, 10:780. However, even

in 1883, the term *divankhane-e mobarake* was still used. *Ruzname-e Iran* no.523:2, 24 Ramazan 1300AH.

32 *Ruzname-e Vaqaye' al-Ettefaqiye* no.157:1, 4 Jomada I 1270AH.

33 *Ruzname-e Dowlat-e 'Aliye-e Iran* no.535:3, 17 Rajab 1279AH.

34 Faridun Adamiyat, *Amir-e Kabir va Iran* (Tehran, 1354Kh), 307–308.

35 'Abbas Zare'i Mehrvarz, "Asnad-e Divan-e 'Adalat-e 'Ozma," in *Khaterat va Asnad-e Mohammad 'Ali Ghaffari*, ed. 'Abbas Zare'i Mehrvarz (Tehran, 1380Kh), 271–319.

36 *Ruzname-e Vaqaye' al-Ettefaqiye* no.371:1, 24 Rajab 1274AH.

37 Ibid. no.157:1.

38 *Ruzname-e Dowlat-e 'Aliye-e Iran* no.551:2–3, 28 Jomada II 1280AH. Lambton interpreted the proclamation of 1863 as follows: "it was announced that disputes over land were to be referred to the local department of Justice. This was further encroachment on Shari'a jurisdiction" (Lambton, *Qajar Persia*, 292). However, the main point of the proclamation was to permit people referring to the *divankhane* in Tehran by post concerning the injustice of local officials. In addition, the text of the proclamation clearly shows that disputes over land were to be referred directly to the *divankhane* in Tehran by person, not to those in the provinces. Moreover, there is no mention of the shari'a courts at all and people continued to refer to the shari'a courts, as we will see later.

39 *Ruzname-e Vaqaye' al-Ettefaqiye* no.459:3, 18 Jomada II 1276AH.

40 *Ruzname-e Dowlat-e 'Aliye-e Iran* no.521:3–4, 18 Ziqa'da 1278AH.

41 *Ruzname-e Vaqaye' al-Ettefaqiye* no.461:3, 7 Rajab 1276AH.

42 *Ruzname-e Dowlat-e 'Aliye-e Iran* no.519:6, 17 Shavval 1278AH.

43 Zare'i Mehrvarz, "Asnad-e Divan," 306. For the translation, I have omitted all the honorific titles of the parties involved.

44 *Vaqaye'-e 'Adliye* no.1, Zihejje 1287AH; Shaul Bakhash, *Iran: Monarchy, Bureaucracy and Reform under the Qajars: 1858–1896* (London, 1978), 86–87; Nashat, *Origins of Modern Reform*, 45, 47.

45 Schneider, *Petitioning System*, IX.

46 Ibid., 59.

47 *Ruzname-e Vaqaye' al-Ettefaqiye* no.410:3, 3 Jomada I 1275AH.

48 The secondary literature is confused on this point as little attention was paid to the official yearbooks known as *salname*. For example, Damghani does not mention the establishment of the Box of Justice in 1864. Floor mentions it but cites wrong sources. Mostowfi and Curzon cited by Floor refer in fact to the re-installment of the Box in 1875. Schneider follows Floor. Mohammad Taqi Damghani, *Avvalin Qavanin-e Iran qabl az Mashrutiyat* (Tehran, 1357Kh), 94; Floor, "Change and Development," 121; Schneider, *Petitioning System*, 35.

49 *Ruzname-e Vaqaye' al-Ettefaqiye* no.471:3–4, 28 Moharram 1277AH.

50 *Ruzname-e Dowlat-e 'Aliye-e Iran* no.551:2–3, 28 Jomada II 1280AH.

51 Ibid. no.562:1, 6, 29 Safar 1281AH.

52 Ibid. no.589:5, 21 Safar 1283AH.

53 *Ruzname-e Iran* no.243:2, 5 Zihejje 1291AH, which includes the edict of Naser al-Din Shah. Mostowfi cited the edict, but he did not mention the title of 'Azod al-Molk correctly. See, 'Abd -allah Mostowfi, *Sharh-e Zendegani-e Man* (Tehran, 1365Kh), 1:135–137.

54 *Salname-e Iran* 1292AH, 54.

55 *Ruzname-e Iran* no.256:1, 11 Jomada II 1292AH.

56 *Salname-e Iran* 1294AH, 28; 1295AH, 31; 1296AH, 10; 1297AH, 13; 1298AH, 20, 1299AH, 21.

57 Ibid. 1300AH, 24; 1301AH, 45; *Ruzname-e Iran* no.349:1, 28 Rabi' I 1295AH.

58 Schneider, *Petitioning System*, 106–203, Plate I–XVI.

59 According to Schneider, the breakdown of cases is as follows: 42 percent are civil cases, 9 percent are criminal cases, 26 percent are complaints about or statements of

satisfaction with officials, and 23 percent are requests. Schneider, *Petitioning System*, 40–49. In her previous article, she provided a different set of percentages: 19 percent were civil cases, 6 percent were criminal cases, 45 percent were the result of oppression by state officials, 11 percent were injustices from officials in their fiscal duties, and a further 11 percent were requests for financial support. Irene Schneider, “Religious and State Jurisdiction during Naser al-Din Shah’s Reign,” in *Religion and Society in Qajar Iran*, ed. Robert Gleave (London, 2005), 88–89.

60 *Ruzname-e Dowlat-e ‘Aliye-e Iran* no.535:4–6, 17 Rajab 1279AH; E‘temad al-Saltane, *Mer’at al-Boldan*, 1425–1428.

61 *Ruzname-e Iran* no.7:1–2, 3 Ṣafar 1288AH.

62 *Ruzname-e Vaqaye‘ al-Ettefaqiye* no.407:2–4, 11 Rabi‘ II 1275AH.

63 The situation in Kordestan province is well documented. The *divanbegi* of Kordestan was imprisoned by the governor of the province. See, Mirza Hoseyn Khan Divanbegi, *Khaterat-e Divanbegi*, ed. Iraj Afshar and Mohammad Rasul Daryagasht (Tehran, 1383Kh), 31–33. Two documents relating to the duties of the divan-begi were published in the appendix. Ibid., 273–278.

64 The *divankhane-e ‘adliye* was founded in Fars province in the years between 1877 and 1881 by the governor, Farhad Mirza. Haj Mirza Hasan Hoseyni Fasa’i, *Farsname-e Naseri*, ed. Mansur Rastegar Fasa’i (Tehran, 1367Kh), 857. The earliest mention of a *divankhane* in Tabriz can be found in a directory of government officials in 1882. *Salname* 1300AH, 49. Damghani cited the regulations of the *divankhane* in Tabriz, but the date of its founding is not clear. Damghani, *Avvalin Qavanin*, 222–237.

65 Sheykh Reza’i and Azari, eds. *Gozareshha-ye Nazmiye*, 1–98.

66 Ibid., 10–11.

67 Ibid., 81–82, 92–93, 97.

68 *Ruzname-e Dowlat-e ‘Aliye-e Iran* no.533:4–5, 4 Jomada II 1279AH.

69 Zare‘i Mehrvarz, “Asnad-e Divan,” 311.

70 *Ruzname-e Vaqaye‘ al-Ettefaqiye* no.459:3–4, 18 Jumada II 1276AH.

71 Zare‘i Mehrvarz, “Asnad-e Divan,” 299.

72 Ibid., 303. Another murder case, which was confirmed by a shari‘a court, is found in a petition published in Schneider, *Petitioning System*, 198.

73 Zare‘i Mehrvarz, “Asnad-e Divan,” 278, 303, 307, 311.

74 Vanessa Martin, “Murder in Bushehr in 1844: The Case of Bibi Asilu,” *Iran* no.46 (2008): 287.

75 Zare‘i Mehrvarz, “Asnad-e Divan,” 276–277.

76 *Ruzname-e Dowlat-e ‘Aliye-e Iran* no.519:5–6, 17 Shavval 1278AH.

77 Schneider, “Religious and State Jurisdiction,” 91–93, 95, 98.

78 Wael B. Hallaq, *Shari‘a: Theory, Practice, Transformations* (Cambridge, 2009), 55, 199, 316, 368.

3 Shari'a court

Who presided over shari'a courts?

In his *Encyclopaedia Iranica* article published in 2009, Willem Floor repeated his theory regarding the hierarchy of the shari'a courts, which dealt with civil cases. In a large town, a *sheykh al-eslam*, assisted by one or more subordinate judges, presided over the court. Small towns only had one judge, while in large villages, local religious leaders (*molla*) pronounced judgments. Shari'a judges were also appointed by the Shah and in some cases, *mojtahed*s also agreed to adjudicate disputes, assisted by their students and witnesses.[1]

Christoph Werner provides a completely different interpretation of the shari'a courts. According to Werner, the hierarchy of *sheykh al-eslam–qazi–molla* did not exist in Qajar Tabriz. All the major members of the 'ulama, who were also referred to as *mojtahed*s, engaged in legal matters, regardless of their title. At times, they received stipends from the government but they were not appointed to an office by the Shah.[2] Werner's suggestion is quite convincing because it is based on an analysis of legal deeds and other documents.

However, one must also examine other cities because Tabriz might have been an exception. Here, I examine the case of Tehran during the nineteenth century, which was one of the largest contemporary cities in Iran.

Among the cases brought to the *divankhane*, mentioned in the previous chapter, none referred to the *sheykh al-eslam* of Tehran. Cases were referred by the *divankhane* to Haji Molla Mirza Mohammad Andarmani (five cases), Sayyed Mohammad Sadeq Sangelaji (two cases), and Haji Molla 'Ali Kani (one case) who all had the title of *mojtahed* but not the titles of *sheykh al-eslam* or *qazi*.[3] The cases from the *divankhane* must have been entrusted to the high-ranking authorities of the shari'a, but the *sheykh al-eslam* was not among them.

The *Salname* of 1290 AH comprised the list of 'ulama and shari'a judges (*hokkam-e shar'*). The list included twelve names: Mirza Zeyn al-'Abedin Emam Jom'e, Aqa Sayyed (Mohammad) Sadeq (Sangelaji) (d.1883), Aqa Sayyed Esma'il Behbahani, Haji Molla 'Ali (Kani), Aqa Sayyed Saleh 'Arab, Sadr al- 'Olama, Haji Molla Hadi Modarres, Haji Aqa Mohammad, Haji Molla Mohammad Ja'far (Chalmeydani), Haji Sayyed Hoseyn (Kashani), Haji Molla Mohammad Taqi (Kashani), and Mirza Ahmad Sheykh al-Eslam.[4] This list includes the name

Sheykh al-Eslam, and as it was written in the margin one gets the impression that Sheykh al-Eslam was not especially important among the shari'a judges. None possessed the title of *qazi*.

On the other hand, in the *Salname* of 1291 AH, the heading of the list changed to simply 'ulama.[5] The list included sixteen names, twelve of which were the same as those from 1290 AH. Mirza Ahmad Sheykh al-Eslam was inserted in the main text, but his name appears in the penultimate position on the list. It is difficult to suggest that Mirza Ahmad had a special role, such as that of the chief justice, among the 'ulama. One might be inclined to believe that these jurists were appointed to an office of the state because their names were included in the *Salname*. However, the *Salnames* also contained the names of notable people (*a'yan*) and merchants (*tojjar*), most of whom did not have a title or an office.

Moreover, a useful article by 'Omid Reza'i, which surveyed seals on shari'a documents, including those of shari'a judges in Qajar Tehran, preserved in the archives of the *Vaqf* Organization, does not mention the occurrence of seals of any *sheykh al-eslam*.[6] Very little evidence in the documents suggests that the *sheykh al-eslam* presided over the shari'a court.

On the other hand, plenty of evidence indicates that most high-ranking 'ulama engaged in legal transactions. Most of the abovementioned shari'a judges in the *Salname* of 1290 AH were also mentioned in Reza'i's article, and these 'ulama were considered *mojtaheds* at that time. The juridical situation in Tehran was thus exactly the same as that in Tabriz as described by Werner.

The term *mojtahed* denotes those who reached the stage of *ejtehad*, as an understanding of *ejtehad* was indispensable in jurisdiction in Qajar Iran. Here, *ejtehad* does not indicate the ability to make an independent or personal judgment but rather to technically deduce legal rules from legal sources.[7] Those who engaged in legal transactions and presided over shari'a courts had to have acquired this ability. A question – answer edict recorded in Sangelaji's court register clearly demonstrates this:

> [QUESTION] Aqa Mirza Mohammad Hasan Ashtiyani is not famous, but anyway you must know him. So, do you think he is a *mojtahed* and able to issue *fatvas*, and Muslims are able to bring a lawsuit to him, or not? We need to know and ask you if he is a *mojtahed* and able to issue *fatvas*, please write about his character and stamp your seal on the top of this petition.
>
> *[ANSWER] The pillar of the learned 'ulama, Aqa Mirza Mohammad Hasan Ashtiyani is the most honorable among jurists and* mojtaheds *and able to issue* fatvas *and* hokms. *May God increase persons like him.*[8]

It is clear that even Mirza Mohammad Hasan Ashtiyani, the well-known *mojtahed* as leader of the 'Tobacco Protest' in 1891, was unknown among people in his youth and needed Sangelaji's *hokm* of confirmation for judicial duties. The relevant point here is that the questioner considered three issues in tandem: being a *mojtahed*, issuing *fatvas*, and dealing with lawsuits. Sayyed Mohammad Sadeq Sangelaji's response also mentioned these three: being a *mojtahed* and issuing *fatva*s and *hokm*s. Being a *mojtahed* closely related to presiding over a shari'a court.

An episode concerning Molla Abu al-Hasan Tehrani (d.1855–1856) also tells us about a similar situation. After Tehrani began to administer the law (*hokumat va qazavat*) in Tehran, some denied the legitimacy of his *ejtehad* and came to doubt it. They sent a letter to Tehrani's professor, Haji Mohammad Ebrahim Kalbasi (d.1845), in Isfahan enquiring about Tehrani's *ejtehad*. Kalbasi replied confirming Tehrani's *ejtehad* and after that his credibility was established as people believed in his *ejtehad* and brought many lawsuits to his court.[9]

The combination of three elements (*qaza, fatva,* and *ejtehad*) is also seen in a famous *fiqh* work translated in the nineteenth century. The Persian translation of Muhaqqiq al-Hilli's *Shara'i' al-Islam* says a *qazi* must have the ability to issue *fatva*s independently and must be a *mojtahed*.[10] In this regard, theory corresponded well with practice.

The question, however remains regarding appointing someone to be a shari'a judge. The examples of Ashtiyani and Abu al-Hasan Tehrani indicate that they did not have a special position or title except that of *mojtahed*. If they were *mojtahed*s, they could manage legal matters and did not need to be appointed by the state. Consequently, one needed social recognition to be a *mojtahed* and acquire clients. During the nineteenth century, there were many examples in which people asked other *mojtahed*s if a scholar was a *mojtahed* or not, as in the cases of Ashtiyani and Tehrani.[11] This was a serious problem for the people because the jurist's decisions and his arrangement of contracts were invalid if he was not a *mojtahed*.[12] In this way, a type of peer review system was in place.

This is a system unique to Qajar Iran in Islamic history. As far as we know, a *qadi* was appointed by the state under all other historical dynasties. Why did such a unique system appear in nineteenth-century Iran?

One possible reason is the theoretical background in Shi'ite Iran. Twelver Shi'ism considers the twelve Imams and Imam 'Ali and his descendants, to be legitimate rulers. Theoretically, only Imams can appoint a qadi.[13] Moreover, the Usuli theory, which recognizes *mojtahed*s as deputies of the hidden Imam, prevailed in Iran after the eighteenth century. The state that was not the deputy of the hidden Imam did not have the right to appoint a qadi. The Qajar system concurred with these theories.

However, it is difficult to hold that only theoretical developments produced this system.[14] Another possible reason is the social and historical context. After the fall of the Safavid dynasty in the eighteenth century, the center of Shi'i religious learning shifted to the 'Atabat in Iraq and shrine cities such as Najaf and Karbala'. In other words, religious learning developed in the 'Atabat without the protection of political authority during the eighteenth century, and the 'Atabat continued to attract many students of Shi'i religious and legal sciences during the nineteenth century. We see a recurrent career pattern among the *mojtahed*s in Tehran in which they spent many years learning in the 'Atabat, including the following examples:

- Haji Abu al-Qasem Kalantari from Tehran (d.1875)

  At the age of twenty, he moved to the 'Atabat. He returned to Tehran around the age of forty.[15]

- Haji Molla 'Ali Kani from Tehran (d.1888)

  After the age of twenty, he moved to the 'Atabat. He returned to Tehran around the age of forty-two.[16]

- Sayyed Mohammad Sadeq Sangelaji from Isfahan (d.1883)

  At the age of four, he moved to Karbala'. He started his studies at the age of fourteen and completed them at the age of twenty-one. He moved to Hamadan, then to Mashhad. At the age of thirty-three, he moved to Tehran.[17]

- Haji Mohammad Hasan Ashtiyani from Ashtiyan (d.1901)

  At the age of thirteen, he moved to Borujerd. He then moved to Najaf at the age of eighteen and to Tehran around the age of thirty-four.[18]

- Sheykh Hadi Najm-abadi from Tehran (d.1902)

  At the age of twelve, he moved to Najaf. He finished the elementary stage of his education and returned to Tehran at the age of twenty. He moved again to Najaf and returned to Tehran after he turned thirty.[19]

These men stayed in the 'Atabat from seven to twenty years learning religious sciences, and they then returned or moved to Tehran in their thirties or the first half of their forties. In addition, Sheykh Fazl-allah Nuri (d.1909), who moved to the 'Atabat after he finished the elementary stage of his education, settled in Tehran at the age of forty-two and engaged in legal matters forty days after his arrival.[20]

These examples indicate that these men obtained the most important part of their education (i.e., becoming a *mojtahed*) in the Ottoman territory of the 'Atabat, where the Qajar government could not intervene. Unlike the Ottomans who controlled the education of the 'ulama, the Qajars could not control it at all.

The only means the Qajars could use to control the 'ulama was through the stipends that were given to them. Werner stated that all the important 'ulama in Tabriz received regular and considerable grants from the state.[21] When one examines two fiscal books of the Tehran Province, one from 1849 and the other from 1870, several names of the leading members of the 'ulama are listed: Mirza Abu al-Hasan Tehrani and Molla Mirza Mohammad (Andarmani) in 1849, and Aqa Sayyed (Mohammad) Sadeq Mojtahed (Sangelaji), Haji Sheykh Mohammad (leader of prayers at the Old Friday Mosque), and Haji Molla Mohammad Ja'far (Chalmeydani) in 1870.[22] The fiscal book of all the provinces, dated 1887–1888, mentioned stipends for Zeyn al-'Abedin Emam Jom'e and a famous leader of the Constitutional Revolution, Aqa Sayyed Mohammad Tabataba'i, b. Aqa Sayyed Sadeq.[23] However, it is questionable whether all the leading 'ulama received the stipends because the fiscal books do not contain all the members of the 'ulama. In addition, the stipend amounts differed greatly among them. Haji Sheykh Mohammad received only ten *kharvar* grains, Chalmeydani obtained just ten *tomans* in cash in a year, and Sangelaji acquired 300 *tomans* in cash and sixteen *kharvar* in grain.[24] Zeyn al-'Abedin Emam Jom'e received 635.5 *tomans* per year, but the stipends for Tabataba'i amounted to just 101.6 *tomans* in cash and eight *kharvar* in grain in a year.[25] The books also show that various types of people, such as princes, bureaucrats, militaries, *sayyeds*, and notables, received stipends, and that heirs of famous persons sometimes received stipends. Their positions and stipends were not directly connected, and it is natural that a notable family had greater opportunities to acquire stipends. The Tabrizi ʻulama, described by Werner, belonged to notable families, while there were no such notable families in Tehran at the time.

For this reason, it is improbable that the Qajars intended to control the ʻulama through stipends. However, they granted stipends whenever they wished, and the manner in which they did so was not systematic or strategic. In other words, the ʻulama in Tehran enjoyed their independence even if they received stipends.

A judge or a notary public?

Another point to be discussed is the function of the shariʻa courts. As mentioned above, Willem Floor dealt with the shariʻa courts as part of the judicial system. According to him, shariʻa courts were places in which a judge (*sheykh al-eslam*s, *qazi*s, or *molla*s) sat in judgment on lawsuits. However, citing a royal edict from 1770, Christoph Werner emphasized that the *qazi* was perceived as a notary, whose professional daily routine involved the promulgation and authorization of legal deeds.[26] While Floor's description seems to be based on his own framework of modern or Western jurisdiction which tends to ignore contemporary views on the role of the shariʻa court, Werner's argument was based on the contemporary understanding of the shariʻa court, found in Persian archival sources. Moreover, Mortaza Ravandi divides the main functions of the shariʻa courts (*mahzar-e shar'*) into two parts: investigating conflicts and drawing up deeds for sales, marriages, and divorces.[27]

It is well known that in the pre-modern Islamic world, a qadi would generally not only judge lawsuits but also attest deeds of contracts arranged in accordance with Islamic law. Ottoman shariʻa court records included many such deeds, and an individual deed included the seal of a qadi at the top. The *qazi* of Isfahan under the Safavids also had the same duties:

> In his house, every day except Friday, he judged lawsuits of the people, stamped his seal on documents and deeds (*asnad va qavalejat*), and wrote down his legal decisions (*hokm-e shar'i*) on them, which the *'orf* authorities (*hokkam-e 'orf*) would execute.[28]

The *'orf* authorities also executed the legal decisions of a *qazi*. In addition, the bulk of legal documents from the Qajar period, which are preserved in Iranian archives, were the kinds of deeds attested by the *mojtahed*s.

However, it is difficult to conclude that notarizing was the main daily function of the shariʻa courts without referring to Iranian shariʻa court records, which cover most of the transactions at the court. As no studies of Iranian court records have been undertaken, the examination of court records from nineteenth-century Tehran in the next section provides an important starting point.

Shari'a court records

It is unclear whether every Qajar shari'a court compiled court records, although Omid Reza'i found marginal notes in original deeds from various regions proving that the deeds were registered at court.[29] A collection of shari'a documents' specimens state that the author, who was obliged to draw up the documents, had to collect the specimens one by one; he could not compile the book systematically because he did not have access to a pre-existing collection of documents.[30] This might suggest that he did not have a good court register to which he could refer.

Recently, three shari'a court registers from Qajar Iran were discovered, two of which have been published. These registers have changed research on Iranian shari'a courts during the nineteenth century. The registers I refer to here are as follows:

(a) *Sangelaji I*

This register belonged to Sayyed Mohammad Sadeq Tabataba'i Sangelaji; it covers the period from December 1867 to December 1868. The register contains 992 items, which are mostly in chronological order. Omid Reza'i published a facsimile edition in 2008–2009.[31]

Sangelaji arrived in Tehran in around 1845. He lived in Golbandak Street in the Sangelaj district and taught at the Chalhesar Madrase, also located in the same district.

(b) *Sangelaji II*

This register also concerns Sangelaji; it covers the period from December 1875 to November 1879. The register includes 4,312 items but their order is quite confusing. It has not been published yet.[32] The original is now preserved in the National Library and Archives of Iran.

(c) *Nuri*

This register belonged to the famous *mojtahed* Sheykh Fazl-allah Nuri; it covers the period from January 1886 to July 1889. It was edited and published by Mansure Ettehadiye and Sa'id Ruhi in 2007.[33] According to the introduction, the original consists of two volumes, but there is no indication of which part belongs to which volume. Moreover, there is no mention of original folios or pages in the edition, and it is difficult to understand its original composition. Another problem is how to categorize the items. The editors appear to have had little knowledge of shari'a contracts, and the divisions, headings, and titles of the items are not always correct. According to the edition, the register contains 1,452 items, but by my account it includes 1,524 items.

Sheykh Fazl-allah Nuri arrived in Tehran in 1885. He lived in the Sangelaj district and was associated with the Yunos Khan Madrase. The register begins forty days after his arrival in Tehran.

These three registers concerned the Sangelaj district of Tehran. However, this does not mean the registers relate only to this district. Moreover, besides the courts of

Sangelaji and Nuri, the registers mention the courts of Aqa Mohammad Najm-abadi (d.1885/6) and Aqa Sheykh Hadi Najm-abadi (d.1902), who were also active in the Sangelaj district.

The most significant difference from the Ottoman shari'a records, however, is that the records belonged to individual *mojtaheds* and not to a city district or an administrative region. Naturally, this difference is also reflected in the court system. It is also the reason court records from Qajar Iran are rarely included in state archives.

Contents and composition of the court records

The registers contain a summary of each legal transaction. For example, a transaction of a house described in Sangelaji's record reads as follows:

> (In Arabic) The proposer of settlement mentioned below stated the content below on the settlement, the reception of the price and the waiver of the options in my presence on 12 holy Ziqa'de 1284 AH.
>
> (In Persian) the proposer of settlement: Shir Mohammad Beg Gholam, son of the late Karim Khan. The accepter of settlement: Mohammad Taqi Beg Gholam, son of the late Rahim Beg. One quarter share of one house (*khayat*), a half of which was owned by the settler and located in Qurkhane-e Kohne Street, the Sangelaj district, one of the districts of Tehran, which had four boundaries is as follows: the house of Molla Sha'ban 'Ali, the house of Feyz-allah Khan, the stable of Feyz-allah Khan and public street, along with other belongings of the share of the house, was transferred from the settler to the settled through the settlement contract for the price of 12 *toman*s of panah-abad silver coins with a weight of 13 *nokhod*. In addition to the contract, all the options with the contract were waived by the both sides. The contract was agreed on 9 holy Ziqa'de 1284 AH.[34]

It is clear that the record summarized the sale deed by the *mosalehe* contract.[35] The record retains some original information from the deed: it cites the text of his endorsement (*sejell*) literally, and it includes the boundaries of the house and the kind and weight of the coins which paid for it. On the other hand, Nuri's record mentions that "the deed had a seal and an endorsement" and does not cite the text of the endorsement, nor does it mention the boundaries or the kind of coins. According to Reza'i, Sangelaji introduced a special technique for preparing legal deeds,[36] thus it is understandable that his registers were more precise and more informative than Nuri's. Although the styles of Sangelaji and Nuri were quite different, both registers contained a summary of documents they endorsed or issued. The difference also indicates that they compiled their registers independently.

Table 3.1 shows the composition of the records in each register. There are some differences among the registers, but the general trend is clear; most records are deeds. The deeds of economic transactions (i.e., the deeds of sale, "conditional sale," loan, lease, and donation) form a large percentage: 55.6 percent, 55.2 percent, and

Table 3.1 Composition of records in the court registers

	Sangelaji I		*Sangelaji II*		*Nuri*	
Sale	194	19.5%	1,174	27.2%	247	16.2%
Conditional sale	174	17.5%	519	12.0%	271	17.8%
Loan and credit	128	12.9%	359	8.3%	303	19.9%
Q & A *hokm*	79	8.0%	379	8.8%	2	0.1%
Settlement	69	7.0%	204	4.7%	189	12.4%
Procuration	66	6.7%	266	6.2%	47	3.1%
Confirmation	60	6.0%	419	9.7%	7	0.5%
Lease	47	4.7%	198	4.6%	130	8.5%
Transcription	35	3.5%	182	4.2%	22	1.4%
Hokm	32	3.2%	122	2.8%	5	0.3%
Postscript	19	1.9%	83	1.9%	5	0.3%
Divorce	13	1.3%	19	0.4%	42	2.8%
Receipt	10	1.0%	49	1.1%	47	3.1%
Donation	9	0.9%	134	3.1%	30	2.4%
Marriage	9	0.9%	36	0.8%	42	2.8%
Statement	9	0.9%	41	0.9%	16	1.0%
Guardianship	7	0.7%	17	0.4%	4	0.2%
Duty	6	0.6%	19	0.4%	13	0.9%
Employment	6	0.6%	15	0.3%	12	0.8%
Vaqf	5	0.5%	11	0.3%	26	1.7%
Will and testament	5	0.5%	16	0.4%	21	1.4%
Examination of old records	3	0.3%	5	0.1%	1	0.1%
Oath	2	0.2%	1	0.0%	3	0.2%
Fatva	1	0.1%	17	0.4%	0	0%
Testimony	1	0.1%	2	0.0%	2	0.1%
Partnership	0	0%	3	0.1%	3	0.2%
Partition of a heritage	0	0%	2	0.0%	7	0.5%
Bailment	0	0%	2	0.0%	4	0.3%
Release of security	0	0%	0	0%	2	0.1%
Others	4	0.4%	25	0.6%	22	1.4%
Total	993	100.0%	4319	100.0%	1524	100.0%
Cancellation/imperfect	2		39			

64.8 percent, respectively, in each register. Deeds that relate to family law (such as marriage, divorce, guardianship, and partition of an inheritance) formed a very small proportion: only 2.7 percent, 1.6 percent, and 6.3 percent, respectively, in each register. Similarly, items related to lawsuits or disputes did not form a large proportion. Two types of *hokm*s formed 11.3 percent, 11.6 percent, and 0.4 percent, respectively, of the total while the deeds of settlement comprised 7.0 percent, 4.7 percent, and 12.4 percent, respectively, of the total.

Consequently, the numbers of items in the three registers indicates that the shari'a courts mainly engaged in endorsing deeds (especially, economic deeds). This coincides with the fact that most of Esfahani's specimens of shari'a documents were not *hokm*s but deeds.[37] This supports Werner's theory, which points to the importance of the notarial function of Qajar shari'a courts.

Documents for solving disputes

The deeds and the *mojtahed's* endorsements on them have been relatively well studied.[38] However, little is known about the mechanisms of how Qajar shari'a courts solved disputes. Here, I introduce some types of documents related to disputes.

An important question involves whether the documents issued by *mojtahed*s had binding power. In the Sunni world, the qadis/*qazi*s issued a *hukm/hokm*, which had binding power and was executed by the state, while the muftis/*mofti*s issued a fatwa/*fatva*, which was a legal opinion that did not have decisive binding power. A *qadi* could be a mufti at the same time; however, under the Ottomans, *qadis* and muftis were appointed by the state separately. In a legal process, qadis sometimes asked muftis for their opinions as fatwas.

On the other hand, in the famous Shi'i *'usul* textbook, *Ma'alim al-Din*, written around the sixteenth century, the term "*mujtahid*" was used interchangeably with the term "mufti."[39] This is also true in a *fiqh* work from the nineteenth century, as we saw above. Because the *mojtahed*s played the role of *qazi*s during the nineteenth century, it logically follows that the *mojtahed*s were *qazi*s and *mofti*s at that time. This made things complicated. Being only one person, a *mojtahed* always played both roles, and it is difficult to distinguish documents issued by the *mojtahed*s as being *hokm*s by *qazi*s or *fatva*s by *mofti*s. At the same time, it is difficult to evaluate the binding power of the documents issued by the *mojtahed*s.

A royal edict of Naser al-Din Shah for the *amir-e divan* indicates that the documents issued by 'ulama could be referred to as *fatva*s even in the nineteenth century:

> All the orders (*hokm*) issued from the *divankhane* along with the written accusation of the plaintiffs and details of *fatva*s from religious 'ulama (*fatva-ye 'olama-ye din*) belonged to the cases must be shown to the Shah (*mowjez-e haqq-shenas*).[40]

Here, the edict used the term *fatva* for the documents issued by 'ulama for cases at the *divankhane*, while it used the term *hokm* for orders of the *divankhane*. The edict appears to claim that the document issued by 'ulama was just an opinion and that only the orders of the *divankhane* had binding power.

However, as we saw in the previous chapter, the term *hokm* was applied in the official gazettes for documents issued by the 'ulama. Moreover, all documents issued by the *mojtahed*s tended to be called *hokm*s in shari'a court documents. Using the term *hokm* implies that people must have followed the document. We can assume that the usage concerns the position of *mojtaheds* in Shi'i Usuli theory; a non *mojtahed* must choose a *mojtahed* and follow his instruction. In that case, it was natural for the non-*mojtaheds* to follow all documents issued by the *mojtahed*, whether it was a *fatva* or a *hokm*. Therefore, the differences between a *fatva* and a *hokm* became obscure, and any given documents tended to be described as a *hokm*. In other words, the strong position of the *mojtaheds* in theory reflects usage.

Deed-type hokm

A *hokm* therefore denotes not only a *qazi*'s judgment issued by a *mojtahed* but also every document issued by a *mojtahed*, excluding the documents attested to by him such as deeds.

The question is how we understand the character of the *hokms* and how we can categorize them. For example, Werner translated each *hokm* as a "shari'a court verdict," "shari'a court statement," "shari'a court protocol," and "shari'a court protocol and verdict" when he introduced the relevant documents.[41] It is unclear how Werner categorized these *hokms*. Reza'i does not see any categories among *hokms*. According to Reza'i, in many cases, *hokms* were written down on the upper part of the petitions (*'arize*), and when needed, they were written on independent papers.[42] Reza'i's book on petitions and *hokms* also includes fourteen *hokms* without petitions.[43] However, there is no evidence that *hokms* written in independent papers were always responses to petitions.

On the other hand, it is easy to separate a question–answer type or *hokms* with petitions from others in terms of the form of the documents. A non-question-and-answer type document had an Arabic endorsement and a seal of a *mojtahed* on the upper part of the document as did other deeds. Reza'i published an original *hokm* issued by Sangelaji in 1870.[44] The records in Sangelaji's registers also keep original Arabic endorsements. Because these *hokms* without petitions kept the original form of deeds, one might suspect that they were more authentic or that they served a different function from the question-and-answer type, although both were referred to as *hokms*. For convenience, I call them deed-type *hokms*, based on their forms.

Some deed-type *hokms* relate to lawsuits, as seen in the following:

> (Arabic) The order (*al-amr*) was just as recorded and transcribed below. It was written on 13th of the month of Rabi' I 1285AH.
>
> (Persian) It must not be concealed that on Tuesday, 13th, Haji Qasem 'Arab sued (*modda'i shod*) the wife of late Aqa Musa, a coffee seller (*qahvechi*), whose name was Khasse, for the cash of 6 *tomans* and 6,000 [*dinars*] that he had delivered to her. At last, she confessed that the cash was delivered to her. On the basis of her confession, the above-mentioned cash of 6 *tomans* and 6,000 [*dinars*] is her debt. She must pay back the above-mentioned Haji. This occurred on the day mentioned in the month of Rabi'I 1285AH.[45]

Because the form of the record is the same as other deed-type *hokms*, there is no need to separate it from the others.[46] It is clear that the record concerned the lawsuit and that Sangelaji provided a decision. Both the plaintiff and the defendant attended the court session. This evidence proved that people sued at the shari'a courts and that the *mojtaheds* adjudicated the case. This kind of lawsuit was not restricted to civil cases. The second register of Sangelaji included a criminal case. Akhond Molla Mohammad 'Ali 'Eraqi sued Mashhadi 'Abd al-Razzaq Ordubadi for theft of 86.5 *tomans*: both attended the court session, and the defendant denied the theft. He made an oath of "not guilty" and the case was closed.[47]

However, it is problematic that only a small number of the *hokms* were records of a lawsuit: five records in the first register and seven records in the second register of Sangelaji. These records made up 19 percent (six records) and 6 percent (seven records), respectively, of the total deed-type *hokms* in each register, consisting of 1.5 percent and 0.1 percent, respectively, of the total records for each register. In addition, there is no such record in Nuri's register.

What, then, were the majority of the *hokms*? Here is an example:

> (Arabic) The order (*al-amr*) was just as recorded. It was written in the night of the 5th of the month of Ramazan 1284 AH.
>
> (Persian) The following fact must not be concealed. On the basis of testimonies of many reliable and trustworthy witnesses, what is not only fixed and ascertained but also clear in the highest extent to this smallest servant of holy shari'a is that Aqa 'Ali Akbar, a cloth dealer (*bazzaz*), became needy and poor, and legally destitute and is bankrupt. In accordance with (the verse of Qur'an) "and if someone is in hardship,"[48] It is necessary and has been decided that his creditors should grant him grace and not claim the payment from him right now until God of the world gives him money and he can afford to pay for his debts. (Arabic) I have already judged (*hakamtu*) this in the night of the 5th of month of Ramazan 1284AH.[49]

Here, Sangelaji merely confirmed that the cloth dealer was bankrupt.[50] In the background, it is likely that there was a dispute between the creditors and the cloth dealer. However, Sangelaji acknowledged the legal fact of the cloth dealer's bankruptcy based on witness testimonies.

In fact, most of the *hokms* belong to this group. Sangelaji acknowledged various kinds of facts: the owner of a private property; the administrator of a *vaqf*; the heir of a deceased person; and an amount of a debt. The main purpose for this group of *hokms* was to prove a legal fact. These *hokms* functioned as certificates to prove the legitimate legal rights of people.

Another type of *hokm* was issued for the appointment of a duty:

> (Arabic) The order (*al-amr*) was just as recorded and described in the main text and the margin. It was written on 9th of honored Rajab 1295 AH.
>
> Because Sayyed Razi Orji(?) passed away and an infant named Belqis Begom inherited some of the estates of the deceased, by the legal general authority (*velayat-e 'am-e shar'iye*), I authorize and permit (*morakhkhas va ma'zun namud*) Sayyede Khatun, mother of the infant, to control and keep

the infant's inheritance from the late *sayyed*'s property. Consulting with the infant's maternal uncle, Jan Mohammad and the elder of the village, Aqa Sayyed Hoseyn and considering profits and tutelage, she has to take possession of the estates. If, by the law of shari'a, the deceased's debt was fixed, after the claimer is proved and gives oath, the debt will be repaid from the deceased's inheritance with her consent. Also, after confirming this legally, she will receive her dowry (*sedaq*). On the 9th of honored Rajab 1295AH.[51]

The point is the expression of the "legal general authority." It is a qadi's authority and duty to protect the property of infants.[52] In this case, there might also be a dispute among the deceased's relatives, but the *hokm* was merely told that the mother had been entrusted by the *mojtahed* to control the infant's inheritance.

Thus far, although several *hokms* related directly to lawsuits, most *hokms* simply certified legal facts or entrusted duties by legal authority of the *mojtahed*. In other words, most *hokms* were not sentences handed down during lawsuits, as we are led to believe from the initial meaning of the term.

Question–answer hokm

As shown in Table 3.1, this type of *hokm* was more common than the deed-type *hokm*. Omid Reza'i has introduced 29 examples of this type of *hokm*,[53] while the shari'a court registers contain over 450 examples. Contrary to the deed-type *hokms*, the question–answer *hokms* did not contain Arabic endorsements. The questions were written in the lower parts while the *mojtaheds* wrote their answers in the upper parts.

The topic of the questions varied widely. As we can see above, a group of questions concerned the status of *mojtaheds* and witnesses. Here is another example:

[QUESTION] Hojjat al-Eslam, please write down two words and put your seal on what is clear to you concerning Akhond Molla Gholam Hoseyn from Jabolagh near Borujerd, if he has enough ability to deal with legal matters (*omur-e shar'i*), to lead the Friday prayer and to do other things such as testify.

[ANSWER] Pious people must know that Akhond Molla Gholam Hoseyn is proved to be trustworthy and honest, and it is possible to ask him to recite the Qur'an, to explain legal questions in place of mojtaheds *– May God increase them –, and to lead Friday prayers. This is the end. The humble servant wrote this on 19th day of the revered month Shavval 1295AH.*[54]

In this case, Sangelaji confirmed that Akhond Molla Gholam Hoseyn could perform some religious and legal duties in place of the *mojtaheds*.

Other records relate to a lawsuit:

[QUESTION] Hojjat al-Eslam, two people agreed to go to the court of Aqa Sayyed Esma'il to settle a lawsuit. He issued a *hokm*. After a while the loser wanted to bring the same case to a court of one of the other judges. Is it lawful after Aqa Sayyed Esma'il heard the case and issued a *hokm*? Or is it illegal? Write a reply. May God make you eternal!

[ANSWER] *If the axis of jurists and* mojtaheds, *Aqa Sayyed Esma'il Behbahani may God make him eternal, issued the* hokm, *he is one of the shari'a judges who can hear the case. A new trial is unlawful and illegal. It is finished with information and favor. The most humble servant wrote this on 28th day of the month of Ziqa'dah 1284AH.*[55]

However, it is difficult to consider this record to be a record of a trial because it is unclear whether both parties attended the court session. It is possible to speculate that the loser went to another court and sued the winner. However, from the text of the record, we only know that Sangelaji denied retrial.

We can find large numbers of question–answer type *hokm*s in the course of long-lasting legal disputes, as I will show using examples in the next chapter. However, it is difficult to consider them court orders. Instead, questioners asked for the *mojtahed*s' opinions on legal matters, including legal disputes, and the *mojtahed*s confirmed the legal facts.

There are a few examples related to criminal cases:

[QUESTION] Hojjat al-Eslam, what do you say about the *hokm* issued by the powerful among the ulama', the leader among the jurists, Akhond Molla 'Ali Zanjani, May God protect him, regarding the murder that occurred? He issued the *hokm* that the murderer must be punished through *qesas*, and you actually looked at the *hokm*. If you recognize him as a completely qualified *mojtahed* whose *hokm* is effective, write down two words on the top of this petition and put your seal so that the person who has a right can exercise his right. May God give you peace and mercy.

[ANSWER] *A leader among the jurists and the* mojtaheds, *Akhond Molla 'Ali Zanjani is righteous and acceptable. This was written on 29th of the sacred month of Ziqa'de, 1284AH.*[56]

Here Sangelaji confirmed the *hokm* issued by Zanjani concerning a murder case. In most question–answer *hokm*s, the questioners asked Sangelaji to prove a legal fact on both criminal and civil matters. The following *hokm* concerns a deed of a transaction:

[QUESTION] Hojjat al-Eslam, what do you say about the bond for 30 *tomans* that Mohammad Kazem and Aqa 'Ali received and testified about before you as you wrote? If their debt is lawfully accepted, please write it and put your seal.

[ANSWER] *Mohammad Kazem and Aqa 'Ali testified before this servant of the Holy shari'a about the debt of this sum that they owe you, Haji Mirza Hedayat. According to this testimony, they owe you lawfully and must pay you. This is the end. The most humble servant wrote it on 28th day of the month of Rabi' II 1295AH.*[57]

Here Sangelaji confirmed that Mohammad Kazem and Aqa 'Ali had a debt of thirty *tomans* to Haji Mirza Hedayat.

Although the forms of the two types of *hokms* (the deed-type and the question–answer type) differed, we can say that their functions were almost the same: both were issued to prove a legal fact.

Fatva

As discussed above, a *mojtahed* played the roles of both qadi and mufti under the Qajar legal system. This system was distinguished from the Ottoman system, in which the qadis and the muftis held different official positions. Therefore, the Qajar shari'a court records contained a number of *fatvas* issued by the *mojtaheds*, while the Ottoman qadis rarely issued fatwas and the court records contained only muftis *fatvas*, which related to the lawsuits.[58]

When we refer to Iranian archives, we rarely come across this type of document.[59] I have already introduced one *fatva*, which was transcribed in the margin of a *vaqf* deed.[60] As Table 3.1 shows, only Sangelaji's registers contained *fatvas*: the first register included one *fatva*, and the second contained seventeen *fatvas*.

In terms of the form, a *fatva* was a set of questions and answers. Just like the question–answer *hokms*, the *mojtaheds*' answer were written in the upper part of the questions. One might wonder if there were differences between *fatvas* and the question–answer *hokms*. However, unlike the question–answer *hokms*, the *fatva* did not concern a specific case. The *mojtaheds* advanced an opinion on general matters through their *fatvas*. Here is an example:

> [QUESTION] Emami scholars, what do you say about this? A certain Zeyd grabbed an 'Amr's collar, saying, "You killed my relative," and brought him before one of religious scholars for a trial. When the scholar asked 'Amr, he answered "The murder happened. Zeyd here grabbed my collar and blamed me for the murder. I have no idea who killed the victim." By this statement, can the murder of 'Amr be proved or not? Please write down (the reply) in the upper part. On 12th day of the month of holy Moharram 1285AH.
>
> *[ANSWER] If 'Amr correctly said these words, his murder is not legally proved, in the case that there are no other words that prove his murder. On 14th day of the month of holy Moharram 1285AH.*[61]

This *fatva* used the fictitious names Zeyd and 'Amr. The content was hypothetical. It might concern a real murder case, but Sangelaji did not prove any legal facts. In this regard, this *fatva* can be clearly distinguished from question–answer *hokms* and can be compared with the Ottoman fatwas that also used fictitious names.[62] In addition, as *fatvas* are considered a weak form of evidence they were not used by people to prove their rights, and, for this reason, individual *fatvas* were not kept by people.

Settlement

Floor states that religious judges could only arbitrate between two parties who consented to lay their case before him.[63] Although we know the shari'a courts could not only arbitrate but also provide a decision, we can assume that arbitration and settlement must have been important at shari'a courts. In Ottoman Adana and Uskudar courts, *solh* consisted of 7 percent and 3 percent of all the cases.[64]

Another problem is that contracts of "settlement" (*solh* or *mosalehe*) were used for multiple transactions under the Qajars, as we explain later. Reza'i introduced three types of *solh/mosalehe* deeds: a (normal) *solh-name*, a *mosalehe-name* for lease, and a *mosaleh-name* for sale.[65] I will analyze the first in this section.

The record of settlements comprises 4.7 to 12.4 percent of total transactions in each register. Like deed-type *hokm*s, the records did not provide much information about the detailed processes at the court. Nevertheless, one can find a few terms concerning disputes in the records: *modda'i* (claimant), *da'va* (accusation), and *da'avi* (accusations):

> (Arabic) After understanding it, he stated the content below on the settlement, the reception of the price and the waiver in my presence on 4th day of the month of Rabi 'I 1296AH.
>
> (Persian) Proposer of settlement: Mohammad Beg, a stonemason (*sang-bori*), son of late Qorban. Accepter of settlement: Mashhadi 'Ali Mohammad, a baker (*khabbaz*), son of late Hajji Mohammad Taqi, a baker. All claims (*da'avi*) and rights (*hoquq*) to the heir of the late Mohammad Javad, a baker, which the proposer had concerning the wage for bringing a load of flour to him, and all other claims and rights to his children has been withdrawn completely, on the condition that the accepter gives 6 *toman*s in 26 *nokhod*s in silver *riyal* coins and 1 *sir* of yellow sugar candy from Tehran to the proposer for the settlement. Both parties have withdrawn all of their claims and the contract of settlement has been validated on 2nd day of the month of Rabi' I 1296AH.[66]

It is clear that there was a dispute between the stonemason and the baker over the wage and that they agreed to resolve the dispute with the settlement. The person who accepted the settlement paid six *toman*s to the proposer, while the proposer dropped all claims. A deed of settlement was arranged and endorsed by Sangelaji, who recorded the deed in his register to prevent further disputes in the future.

In all, thirty-eight records of settlement from Sangelaji's first register, 104 from Sangelaji's second register, and 135 from Nuri's register contain terms on governing disputes. When one compares these records with records of lawsuits in the form of deed-type *hokms* (*Sangelaji I* 6, *Sangelaji II* 7, *Nuri* 0), one can say that most disputes brought to the shari'a court were resolved by settlements and the attendance of both parties.

However, settlements of disputes were not the only things recorded in the legal frame work of the registers; renunciations of rights were also recorded in the same legal framework in the registers:

> On the 13th day of the month of Ramazan, Gol Badan, a daughter of Mohsen, from Kandi village, made a settlement to renounce all the rights that she had

for her husband, Nayeb Karim, including, her dowry (*mehriye*), necessary expenses for living (*nafaqe*) and clothes (*kesvat*) with the price of 1 *sir* of sugar candy. Beside the contract, the above-mentioned Mohsen was obliged to take responsibility if corruption was found in this settlement during the next fifty years.

The deed of settlement was sealed and has an endorsement.[67]

The wife described had legitimate rights to receive her dowry, necessary expenses for living, and clothes, and Gol Badan renounced those rights. From the court records, we know her husband divorced his wife and gave three *tomans* to her as necessary expenses for living during the period prohibiting remarriage.[68] It is unclear whether there was a dispute between the husband and the wife. At the least, this is a record of settlement or agreement between the husband and the wife during the process of their divorce. We can find other records of settlement for dowries in the registers: nine records in *Sangelaji I*, twenty-two in *Sangelaji II*, and ten in *Nuri*.

Another issue that caused people to propose settlements was inheritance. Among the records of settlement, seventeen records in *Sangelaji I*, fifty-eight in *Sangelaji II*, and eleven in *Nuri* concern inheritances.

These settlements were formally arranged at the shari'a court. A deed of settlement was drawn up, and endorsed by a *mojtahed.* The form of the deeds does not tell us much about the process of settlements. As we saw in the previous chapter, the *divankhane* could refer the case to a shari'a court to make a settlement. In such a case, it is unclear whether both parties negotiated at the court or not. It is possible that they negotiated at the *divankhane* or somewhere else and that the shari'a court simply issued the deed of settlement based on the negotiated terms. C. J. Wills described how disputing merchants compromised outside court, arranged documents, and then went to legal or religious authorities to ask them to fix their seals on it.[69] In this case, the shari'a court simply endorsed the private deed because the negotiation for the settlement was made outside of court.

If these cases were a majority, it would be difficult to say that people brought a case to the shari'a court and that the court solved the case using a settlement. Instead, we can suppose that two parties negotiated somewhere else, reached a settlement, and then came to the shari'a court to allow the deed of settlement to be endorsed by a *mojtahed.* If so, the shari'a court did not intervene in negotiations at all: it simply arranged the settlement deeds and endorsed them after negotiations.

Shari'a court: a reappraisal

After investigating the court records, we understand how the shari'a court functioned in Qajar Tehran. The court was presided over not by state-appointed *sheykh al-eslams* or *qazis* but by *mojtaheds*, who studied in the shrine cities in Iraq for many years. The Qajar government never controlled the shari'a courts through an appointment to posts or offer of pensions. Based on an analysis of the court records, it is difficult to consider the shari'a court as a genuine court of justice.

Most records in the register concerned deeds of transactions, such as sales, "conditional sales," loans, leases, and donations. In this regard, it can be said that notarizing deeds was the daily business at the shari'a court. More details of such transactions will be examined in Chapter 5.

Even so, the shari'a courts played a role in solving disputes. The *mojtaheds* issued *hokms*, some of which concerned disputes. The registers contained thirteen records, which can be considered as records of judicial trials. One can understand from deed-type *hokms* that both plaintiffs and defendants attended the court session and that the *mojtahed* made decisions. However, these types of records of trials comprised less than 1.5 percent of the total records in the registers. Other *hokms*, both deed-type and question–answer type, might have been related to disputes, but they were not records of judicial trials. In particular, the question–answer *hokms* appear to indicate only the *mojhahed*'s opinions on specific legal problems; it is difficult to consider them decisions made at judicial trials because it is unclear whether the other side of the dispute also attended the court sessions. As we will see in the next chapter, these *hokms* could affect the course of disputes, but they were not likely to be final judgments in judicial trials.

On the other hand, the shari'a courts arranged settlements between two parties to solve disputes. Approximately 5 to 12 percent of all the transactions concern these settlements, which are more abundant than deed-type *hokms* concerning trials. However, in most cases, the records do not tell us how the negotiations for the settlements proceeded (it is unclear whether they were negotiated at the court or somewhere else). It is clear that the parties attended the court to prepare the settlement deeds.

Therefore, if one considers the function of the shari'a court, the most straightforward answer here might be that the court was a place for endorsing or issuing legally valid documents including *deeds* and *hokms*. The *mojtaheds* could adjudicate cases or arbitrate between two disputing parties. However, their most important role involved preparing legal documents, which proved legal facts, regardless of whether they were the result of arbitration at the court. Though I use the term "shari'a court," it differs from a modern court of justice in many ways.

Notes

1 Floor, s.v. "Judicial and Legal Systems."
2 Werner, *An Iranian Town*, 229–254.
3 *Ruzname-e Vaqaye' al-Ettefaqiye* no.459:3–4, 18 Jomada II 1276AH; no.461:3, 7 Rajab 1276AH; no.464:3, 27 Ramazan 1276AH; *Ruzname-e Dowlat-e 'Aliye-e Iran* no.509:5–6, 16 Jomada II 1278AH; no.511:4–5, 15 Rajab 1278AH; no.515:5, 27 Sha'ban 1278AH; no.519:5–6, 17 Shavval 1278AH.
4 *Salname-e Iran* 1290AH, 73–74.
5 Ibid. 1291AH, 43.
6 Omid Reza'i, "Khatt va Mohr-e Omana-ye Shar'-e Tehran dar Dowre-e Qajar," *Vaqf, Miras-e Javidan* no.43/44 (1382Kh.): 62–87.
7 Nobuaki Kondo, "Shi'i Ulama and *Ijaza* during the Nineteenth Century," *Orient* 44 (2009): 71–73.

8 Reza'i, ed. *Asnad-e Mahkame*, 119, 12 Safar 1285AH.
9 *Name-e Daneshvaran-e Naseri: dar Sharh-e Hal-e Sheshsad Tan az Daneshmandan-e Nami* (Qom, 1338Kh), 1:424–425.
10 Muhaqqiq al-Hilli, *Tarjome-e Farsi-e Sharayi' al-Eslam*, trans. Abu al-Qasem b. Ahmad Yazdi Abu al-Qasem b. Ahmad Yazdi, ed. Mohammad Taqi Daneshpazhuh, 4 vols. (Tehran, 1373Kh), 1624. The latter half does not exist in the original and was inserted by the Persian translator in the nineteenth century; it might reflect actual practice during the nineteenth century. Cf. Muhaqqiq al-Hilli, *Shara'i' al-Islam fi masa'il al-Halal wa al-Haram*, ed. 'Abd al-Husayn Muhammad 'Ali Baqqal (Qom, 1377Kh), 4:59.
11 One can find five other examples in Sangelaji's first register, and three in Sangelaji's second register; an episode in *Qesas al-'Olama* confirms that fact. When Aqa Sayyed Mohammad b. Aqa Sayyed 'Ali Tabataba'i visited Qazvin, people asked him about Molla Mohammad Saleh Baragani and Molla Mohammad Taqi Baraghani if they were *mojtaheds* or not. Tabataba'i recognized Mohammad Saleh as a *mojtahed* immediately, but hesitated to do so for Mohammad Taqi. At last, he recognized Mohammad Taqi and went to the mosque and addressed the masses on the *menbar* to let people know. Mohammad b. Soleyman Tonekaboni, *Qesas al-'Olama*, eds. Mohammad Reza Barzgar Khaleqi and 'Effat Karbasi (Tehran, 1383Kh), 28.
12 In fact, the first *vaqf* deed of Ostad 'Abbas was claimed to be invalid, being said that the deed was not arranged by a *mojtahed*. See, Nobuaki Kondo, "The Waqf of Ustad 'Abbas: Rewrites of Deeds in Qajar Tehran," in *Persian Documents*, ed. Nobuaki Kondo (London, 2003), 116.
13 al-Hilli, *Tarjome-e Farsi-e Sharaye'*, 1637.
14 On this point, I do not agree with the approach of Zahir Bhaloo, who thinks that the "de-centralization" of Iranian judicial system was caused by the triumph of Usulism. Bhalloo, "Judging the Judge."
15 *Name-e Daneshvaran*, 2:364–365.
16 Mirza Mohammad 'Ali Mo'allem Habib-abadi, *Makarem al-Asar dar Akhval-e Do Qarn-e 13 va 14 Hejri* (Isfahan, 1337–1381Kh), 696–697.
17 *Ruzname-e Iran* no.511:3, 5 Jomada I 1300AH.
18 Agha Buzurg al-Tihrani, *Nuqaba' al-Bashar al-Qarn al-Rabi' 'Ashar* (Mashhad, 1404AH), 380; Sayyid Musin al-Amin, *A'yan al-Shi'a*, ed. Sayyid Hasan al-Amin (Beirut, 1998), 8:54.
19 Kamal Haj Sayyed Javadi and 'Abd al-Hoseyn Nava'i, eds. *Asar-e Afarinan: Zendeginame-e Nam-avaran-e Farhangi-e Irani* (Tehran, 1377–80Kh), 6:25; Mo'allem Habib-abadi, *Makarem al-Asar*, 1377.
20 Ettehadiye and Ruhi, eds. *Dar Mahzar*, 49.
21 Werner, *An Iranian Town*, 252.
22 *Ketabche-e Jam' va Kharj-e Takhaqoy-'il*, 15b, 18a; *Dastur al-'Amal-e Yunat-'il*, 9b–10a.
23 *Ketabche-e Jam' va Kharj-e Koll*, MS, 1025–1026; Bayani, ed. *Ketabche-e Jam' va Kharj-e Koll*, 831–832.
24 *Dastur al-'Amal-e Yunat-'il*, 9b–10a.
25 *Ketabche-e Jam' va Kharj-e Koll*, MS, 1025–1026; Bayani, ed. *Ketabche-e Jam' va Kharj-e Koll*, 831–832.
26 Werner, *An Iranian Town*, 232.
27 Morteza Ravandi, *Tarikh-e Ejtema'i-e Iran* (Tehran, 1341Kh), 4:1227; idem, *Seyr-e Qanun va Dadgostari*, 148.
28 Mirza Rafi'a Ansari, "Dastur al-Moluk," in *Daftar-e Tarikh*, ed. Iraj Afshar (Tehran, 1380Kh), 1:497. It should be noted that Sadrs and Sheykh al-Eslam also stamped their seals on the documents and deeds. Ibid., 493, 497.
29 For, Shiraz see Reza'i, "Selsele-e Sheykh al-Eslami-e Tamami"; idem. "Mohrha-ye bi-Yaddasht." For Bushehr, see Reza'i, "Sabt-e Asnad-e Shar'i dar Bandar-e Bushehr." For Tehran, Reza'i, "Aqa Sayyed Sadeq Mojtahed Sangelaji"; idem. "Jaygah-e Khanedan-e Behbahani."

30 Mohammad b. Sabz 'Ali Esfahani, *Vajizat al-Tahrir: dar Chegunegi-e Tanzim-e Asnad Shar'i, Melli va Hoquqi dar Dowre-'e Safavi va Qajar*, ed. Rasul Ja'fariyan (Qom, 1393Kh), 37, 73.
31 Reza'i, ed. *Asnad-e Mahkame*.
32 *Daftar-e Shar 'i-e Sangelaji*. I express my deep gratitude to Omid Reza'i who made the register accessible to me.
33 Ettehadiye and Ruhi, eds. *Dar Mahzar*.
34 Reza'i, ed. *Asnad-e Mahkame*, 57.
35 For *mosalehe* contract, see Chapter 5.
36 Reza'i, "Aqa Sayyed Sadeq Mojtahed Sangelaji."
37 Esfahani, *Vajizat al-Tahrir*.
38 See, Werner, "Formal Aspects."; idem. "Pious Merchants: Religious Sentiments in Wills and Testaments," in *Religion and Society in Qajar Iran*, ed. Robert Gleave (London, 2005), 211–226; Reza'i, *Dar-amadi*, 60–182; Hoseyni Eshkevari, *Asnad-e Shar'i*.
39 Shaykh Hasan b. Zayn al-Din al-'Amili, *Ma'alim al-Din wa Maladh al-Mujtahidin* (Qom, 1417AH), 242–246. Another example is found in *Tarikh-e 'Abbasi* for a title of Sheykh Baha al-Din 'Ameli (Sheykh Baha'i) as "*mofti al-zamani*." Molla Jalal al-Din Monajjem, *Tarikh-e 'Abbasi ya Ruzname-e Molla Jalal*, ed. Seyf-allah Vahid-niya (Tehran, 1366Kh), 347.
40 Jahangir Qa'em-maqami, ed. "Asnad-e Khanedan -e Amir Divan-e Nuri," *Barrasiha-ye Tarikhi* 8, no.1 (1352Kh): 294. The edict was dated Zihejje 1273AH.
41 Werner, *An Iranian Town*, 388–389.
42 Reza'i, *Dar-amadi*, 189. Rezai terms this type of documents a "*hokm* document." (*varaqe-e hokmiye*).
43 Omid Reza'i, ed. *Panjah va Yek 'Arize va Hokm-e Shar'i az 'Olama-ye Dowre-e Qajar dar bare-e Omur-e Jari-e Mowqufat* (Tehran, 1383Kh), 17–39, 58–73, 88–93,126–128, 145–147,195–197, 203–205.
44 Reza'i, *Dar-amadi*, 190.
45 Reza'i, ed. *Asnad-e Mahkame*, 138.
46 Reza'i deals with *hokm*s related to lawsuits separately, which he terms "a written declaration and a qadi's decision (*ezhar-name va hokm-e qazi*)." However, the document introduced by him is dated 1904 and is thus relatively late and had a quite different form from those in Sangelaji's registers. Reza'i, *Dar-amadi*, 185–187.
47 *Daftar-e Shar'i-e Sangelaji*, 194b.
48 Qur'an 2–280.
49 Reza'i, ed. *Asnad-e Mahkame*, 34.
50 Floor's article did not touch the legal procedure for bankruptcy, but it is clear from the records that the shari'a court decided it. Willem Floor, "Bankruptcy in Qajar Iran," *ZDMG* 127 (1977): 61–76.
51 *Daftar-e Shar'i-e Sangelaji*, 370a.
52 Schacht, *An Introduction to Islamic Law*, 188.
53 Reza'i, ed. *'Arize va Hokm-e Shar'i*, 40–57, 73–87, 94–125, 129–144, 148–155, 183–194, 198–202.
54 *Daftar-e Shar'i-e Sangelaji*, 317a.
55 Reza'i, ed. *Asnad-e Mahkame*, 74.
56 Ibid., 75.
57 *Daftar-e Shar'i-e Sangelaji*, 302b.
58 Ronald C. Jennings, "Kadi, Court and Legal Procedure in 17th C. Ottoman Kayseri," *Studia Islamica* 48 (1978): 134.
59 As rare published examples, Masih Zabihi and Manuchehr Sotude, eds. *Az Astara ta Estarbad* (Tehran, 1349–1380Kh), 6:253; 10:15–18; Reza'i, ed. *'Arize va Hokm-e Shar'i*, 156–182.
60 Kondo, "Waqf of Ustad 'Abbas," 117.
61 Reza'i, ed. *Asnad-e Mahkame*, 97.

62 Uriel Heyd, "Some Aspects of the Ottoman Fetva," *Bulletin of the School of Oriental and African Studies* 32 (1969): 41.
63 Floor, "Judicial System," 114.
64 Işık Tamdoğan, "*Sulh* and the 18th Century Ottoman Courts of Üsküdar and Adana," *Islamic Law and Society* 15 (2008): 61.
65 Reza'i, *Dar-amadi*, 151–163. Hoseyni Eshkevari cites Mohammad Naseri's explanation on *solh* and introduces nine types of *solh* contracts. However, the explanation does not correspond well to actual documents. Hoseyni Eshkevari, *Asnad-e Shar'i*, 106–107.
66 *Daftar-e Shar'i-e Sangelaji*, 164b.
67 Ettehadiye and Ruhi, eds. *Dar Mahzar*, 205.
68 Ibid., 206–207.
69 C.J. Wills, *Persia as It Is: Being Sketches of Modern Persian Life and Character* (London, 1886), 45.

4 An actual dispute

The case of double *vaqf*

After investigating the legal system and shari'a courts, we will now examine an actual case of a dispute involving both the shari'a courts and executive power. How did the Qajar shari'a courts function as courts of justice for legal disputes? What was the relationship between the state and the shari'a courts in the process of lawsuits? Though we have a few case studies of lawsuits under the Qajars, they do not focus on legal procedures.[1] In order to answer these questions, we will investigate an actual case of what can be termed the "the case of the double *vaqf*."[2] In this particular case, two individuals, each of whom claimed to own a village, established endowments within the same village for different purposes. The situation naturally produced disputes between the two parties involved, and many members of the 'ulama participated in the process of resolving these disputes. Although this case is extremely complicated, after describing and analyzing the process of dispute resolution, we will see that it provides us with clues that can help answer our questions.

The first *vaqf* (document 1, 1835)

The first *vaqf* was established in January 1835 by a female member of the Qajar royal family, Hajiye Badr Nesa' Khanom.[3] The list of her endowments included the following:

1 Village of Bord-abad in Shariyar County in the western suburb of Tehran.[4] It included two *qanat*s and other attachments.
2 Two public baths located near Madrase-e Aqa Mohammad Khaje in the Sangelaj district of the city of Tehran.
3 Three shops (a confectionary, bakery, and shoemaker's shop) in Bazar-e Now (new bazaar) located in the Grand Bazaar of Tehran

Hajiye Badr Nesa' Khanom endowed the village of Bord-abad located in the eastern suburb of Tehran as well as the public baths and shops in the city of Tehran on behalf of Imam Husayn. The *vaqf* income was to be used as follows:

1 Salary of the *vaqf*-administrator: 20%
2 Candles to be lit at the shrines of Husayn and 'Abbas in Karbala': 20%

3 Mourning ceremonies on behalf of Husayn and 'Abbas and foods for the participants of the ceremonies: 20%
4 Purchasing or transcribing books of religious sciences and endowing the books as *vaqf*: 20%.
5 Aid to pilgrims visiting the shrines of Imam Husayn (in Karbala') and Imam Rida (Emam Reza in Mashhad) or for sending deputies for pilgrimages: 10%
6 Aid to the poor (*sayyed*s and non-*sayyeds*): 10%

The first *vaqf* administrator was Badr Nesa' herself; later, she was followed by Akhond Molla Mohammad Hasan Yazdi and his descendants. There is no mention of the supervisor (*nazer*) in the main text of the *vaqf* deed, but in the margin of the deed it states that Molla Mohammad Taqi was appointed as the supervisor, who received a 5 percent salary, which was included in the 20 percent salary of the *vaqf* administrator.[5]

The *vaqf* concerned Shi'i shrines and mourning ceremonies for Imams, and this can be considered as a normal Shi'i *vaqf* for this period.[6] It was originally established by a female member of the Qajar royal family. Because her child passed away at an early age, she appointed a jurist to be the *vaqf* administrator after her. In addition, she included the Shrines in Karbala' as the object of the *vaqf* because she intended to be buried in the 'Atabat after her death.

The *vaqf* deed does not suggest any connection between Badr Nesa' and Molla Mohammad Hasan, who is described as the "*mojtahed* of the age" in the deed. According to Tonekaboni, he was a famous scholar in Iran who was extremely pious and devoted to God. In addition, he always mourned for Imam Husayn and other Imams. During the reign of Fath 'Ali Shah he relocated from Yazd to Tehran. The Shah wanted Mohammad Hasan's son to marry a princess but Mohammad Hasan did not agree to the marriage. He eventually migrated to Karbala' and died there.[7] He might have had a good connection with Qajar courtiers because Hoseyn 'Ali Khan Mo'ayyer-bashi also appointed him as the *vaqf* administrator in another *vaqf* deed dated 1831.[8]

However, the date of the deed was a little problematic because of the interim period between the death of Fath 'Ali Shah and the accession of Mohammad Shah. Furthermore, although the form of the deed was not problematic, its terms eventually caused a long-lasting dispute.

The first lawsuit (documents 2 and 3, February and March 1835)

One month after the *vaqf* was established, three sons of Yahya Khan Nasaqchi-bashi filed a lawsuit against the second *vaqf*-administrator, Molla Mohammad Hasan for possession of the village of Bord-abad. An additional memorandum written by Mirza Nabi Khan Amir-e Divan[9] suggests that the plaintiffs first petitioned the royal *divankhane* (*divankhane-e mobarake*); then the Amir-e Divan sent the petition to Mir Mohammad Mahdi Emam Jom'e of Tehran for investigation. The Emam Jom'e eventually issued a document on February 4, 1835.[10]

The document is a deed-type *hokm*.[11] According to the document, after the death of Yahya Khan, his son, Yahya Khan II sold the village of Bord-abad to Badr Nesa' Khanom without the consent of his brothers (the plaintiffs), in spite of the fact that the village was to be inherited by, and divided among, them. Therefore, the sale of the portions of Bord-abad that should have been inherited by the plaintiffs was invalid. After hearing the testimony, Emam Jom'e approved the entire claim of the plaintiffs. In other words, Emam Jom'e found that the contract of sale before the establishment of the *vaqf* included a major problem.

Next, the plaintiffs presented Emam Jom'e's *hokm* along with a new petition (*'arze-dasht*) to the Shah.[12] The petition suggested that the sale between Yahya Khan II and Badr Nesa' Khanom was not a normal one but a "conditional sale."[13] In fact, Yahya Khan II borrowed money from Badr Nesa', using the village as a security. However, he could not pay her back in the due time and the village was eventually foreclosed by her. After that, she established the *vaqf* with the village.

After receiving the petition and the *hokm*, Mohamamd Shah issued a royal edict (Document 3–2) in which he ordered Bahman Mirza, the governor of Tehran, to deliver portions of the village to the plaintiffs.[14]

In this case, we see two institutions. The first is the royal *divankhane* supervised by the Amir-e Divan. It received the petition and issued the royal degree. Document 3 is a typical petition-royal edict pattern document. The copy referred to is a later transcript, but it shows that the Shah himself wrote "I examined carefully" in the document and that many other officials affixed their seals behind the document.

Floor claims that the royal *divankhane* was the supreme *'orf* court. However, if its main function was receiving a petition and issuing a royal edict for a response, it is difficult to say that it was a genuine judicial institution because it also must have received numerous non-judicial petitions and issued royal degrees regarding non-judicial matters. In other words, it appears to have been an administrative institution that focused on various administrative matters, although it also occasionally dealt with judicial cases.

The second institution is that of Mir Mohammad Mahdi Khatun-abadi Emam Jom'e. He was invited from Isfahan by Fath 'Ali Shah to lead the Friday prayers at the Shah Mosque (Masjed-e Shah) in 1820–1.[15] We already know that like other *mojtaheds* he endorsed a deed of sale for property in Tehran and arranged a settlement related to the control of Zahiriye *vaqf* in Tabriz.[16] However, this was the first case in which he was referred to by the royal *divankhane*, heard testimony, issued a *hokm* with his seal and handed it over to the plaintiff. As mentioned in Chapter 2, there are many examples during the second half of the nineteenth century where the *Divankhane-e 'Adliye* entrusted complicated and difficult cases to *mojtaheds*. This case shows that the same procedure also existed during the first half of the century.

The document issued by Emam Jom'e has a problem of terminology. Here I use the term *hokm* for the document because it is referred to as a *hokm* in a later document.[17] However, it was called a *fatva* in both the petition and the royal edict of Document 3. This is another example of the distinction between a *hokm* and a *fatva* becoming obscure during the nineteenth century.[18]

Contrary to the widely held view of an inefficient Qajar bureaucracy, the case was settled quickly and logically, and there appears to have been no contested points concerning the judgment and royal edict. According to a later document, after the first lawsuit the plaintiffs recovered their share of the village. One of the plaintiffs, ʻAli Khan, sold half of the village in 1839 to a Georgian courtier, Sohrab Khan, for the sum of 800 *tomans*. Emam Jomʻe arranged this sale contract as well as another settlement deed in 1842, which resulted in Sohrab Khan acquiring thirteen-fifteenths of the village in total.[19] However, the case still continued.

The second hokm (document 4, 1844)

In 1844, a jurist named Haji Molla ʻAli Asghar issued another deed-type *hokm*. After hearing several testimonies of reliable witnesses in his shariʻa court (*mahzar-e sharʻ*), he supported the first *vaqf* and proved that the entire village of Bord-abad was *vaqf* property on behalf of Imam Husayn. In addition, he ordered that it must be controlled by the legitimate *vaqf* administrator, Aqa ʻAbd al-Hoseyn, b. Molla Mohammad Hasan. This is a deed-type *hokm*, which was issued to "be a proof when it is needed."[20]

Contrary to the *hokm* of Emam Jomʻe, this *hokm* was issued without any request by the Shah. It appears that Aqa ʻAbd al-Hoseyn had asked the jurist to issue the *hokm*. In this case, there is no information on the issuer of the *hokm*, Haji Molla ʻAli Asghar. At least, his name was not included among the seventeen well-known members of the ʻulama of Mohammad Shah's reign in the chronicle, *Eksir al-Tavarikh*, while Emam Jomʻe, who had denied the *vaqf*, was included among them.[21] However, ʻAli Asghar's *hokm* clearly reversed the *hokm* of Emam Jomʻe and the content of the royal edict nine years earlier. Here we can see that neither the *hokm* of Emam Jomʻe, who still held office at the time of the reversal, nor the royal edict of the Shah, who was still on the throne, were decisive among jurists.

What is striking is that the *hokm* significantly affected the course of the dispute although it was issued by an unknown jurist. The reason was an Arabic endorsement written in the top center of the main text.

> Molla ʻAli Asghar, may God give him peace and protect him, is a bona fide *mojtahed* who is fully qualified to issue *hokms*. To refuse his *hokm* is to refuse *hokms* of God and his Prophet and the holy Imams.[22]

The jurist who made the endorsement was Sheykh Mohammad Hasan Najafi (d.1850) of Najaf. He was the author of one of the most important works in Shiʻi *fiqh*, *Jawahir al-Kalam*, and is sometimes considered to be the first *marjaʻ-e taqlid* – the supreme authority in the Shiʻi world of learning.[23] Najafi confirmed the position of the issuer for the *hokm* as a *mojtahed* and verified the *hokm*.

Najafi's endorsement was so important that the other five endorsements did not confirm the main *hokm*, but rather verified Najafi's endorsement on the basis of his seal and handwriting:

> This happy handwriting and noble seal belonged to late Sahib al-Jawahir (Najafi) – May God elevate his position – and (his endorsement) is to be followed and obeyed.[24]

This endorsement was made by Mirza Abu al-Qasem Emam Jom'e (1800/1801–1855),[25] who was the nephew and successor of Mir Mohammad Mahdi Emam Jom'e mentioned above. Two famous *mojtaheds* during the constitutional period, Sheykh Fazl-allah Nuri and Sayyed 'Abd-allah Behbahani (1840–1910), also confirmed Najafi's endorsement.[26] Behbahani's confirmation was dated 1907, which suggests that the *hokm* was referred to more than 60 years later.

While the *hokm* of Molla 'Ali Asghar was never mentioned in later documents, Najafi's endorsement was frequently referred to as the most important proof, which was called a "*hokm*," for legitimizing the first *vaqf*.[27] In fact, what changed the course of the dispute was not the *hokm* itself but Najafi's endorsement.

Now the case was brought out from the realm of Iran to Karbala' in Iraq in Ottoman territory. In addition, Najafi was not the sole 'Atabat jurist who participated in the case, as we will see below.

The second *vaqf* (document 5, 1848)

Sohrab Khan Gorji, the Georgian courtier, who purchased one half of the village of Bord-abad in 1839, established a *vaqf* on it in 1848. Sohrab Khan was a military man, who fought in the Russo-Iranian war, and was also appointed as *Gholam-e Pishkhedmat-bashi* (chief of the attendant pages) and *tahvildar* (cash keeper). He married the thirty-ninth princess of Fath 'Ali Shah,[28] and was known by the nickname 'Naqdi (the pecuniary) as he managed the pocket money of Naser al-Din Shah. Later, he became a chief customs officer.[29]

In this case, the *vaqf* property was one half of the village. The description of the boundaries showed that another village named Kordzar was also owned by Sohrab Khan.[30] The *vaqf* deed stipulated that the income should be spent for the mourning ceremony of Emam Hoseyn and his descendants held at Takye-e Chehel Tan in the Grand Bazaar. Sohrab Khan appointed a prominent *mojtahed*, Haji Molla 'Ali Kani (1805/06–1888) as the *vaqf* administrator and he was to be succeeded by the most learned jurist in Tehran. In addition, the deed appointed Aqa Bozorg (Sheykh Mohammad, d.1877), the prayer leader of Old Friday Mosque, as the *vaqf* supervisor (*nazer*).[31] An annotation in the margin of the deed stipulated that the *vaqf* administrator should consult with Mohammad 'Ali Khan, the second son of Sohrab Khan, and a certain Mashhadi Baqer Kolahduz (hatter) Tehrani and spend the *vaqf* income for the mourning ceremony every year.[32]

The *vaqf* deed was endorsed by six jurists including well-known *mojtaheds* such as Sheykh 'Abd al-Hoseyn Tehrani and Aqa Mahmud Kermanshahi.[33] One of the endorsements, dated 1891, shows that the deed was referred to more than forty years later.

Now we understand how two *vaqf*s were established over the same village. If we assume that the deed is not a forgery, then we can conclude that it was written in contradiction to the *hokm* issued four years earlier. Sohrab Khan occupied at least one half of the village of Bord-abad and established the *vaqf* on it. In other words, the *hokm* of 1844 was not executed and the jurists who arranged the *vaqf* deed did not doubt Sohrab Khan's ownership of his half of the village. The *vaqf* deed was drawn up as if the *hokm* of 1844 simply did not exist.

However, it is unclear whether the *vaqf* deed was related to the *hokm* of 1844 or not, because Mirza Abu al-Qasem Emam Jom'e wrote in his deed-type *hokm* (no date, before 1855) that the dispute over Bord-abad still continued and it should be resolved first. Sohrab Khan might have established this *vaqf* in opposition to the first *vaqf*. However, even the reason for jurists permitting him to establish a *vaqf* over disputed land is unknown.

It is certain that Sohrab Khan had some relation to Takye-e Chehel Tan. Naser al-Din Shah wrote in his diary.

> The *pishkhedmat*s (attendants) Vali Khan and Hoseyn Khan (sons of Suhrab Khan) were also there. They also prepared their own Takye-e Chehel Tan (for the mourning ceremony). Mirza Abu Taleb, who was *mobasher* (overseer) of the Takye-e Chehel Tan in the time of Sohrab Khan, is still its *mobasher* and engaged in his work also in this year.[34]

In this case, Sohrab Khan and his sons owned or supported the Takye. On the other hand, there was no mention of either Haji Molla 'Ali Kani, the *vaqf* administrator or Sheykh Mohammad, the *vaqf* supervisor.

Moreover, two other points were strange. First, Hajji Molla 'Ali Kani, the *vaqf* administrator and Sheykh 'Abd al-Hoseyn Tehrani, an endorser of the (second) *vaqf*, ignored the *vaqf* deed and issued *hokm*s for supporting the first *vaqf* of 1835. Second, the contents of the *vaqf* deed were referred to in the documents only after forty years; Document 15 dated 1888 first confirmed the content of the *vaqf* deed as we will see below. These points suggest the possibility that the *vaqf* deed might be concealed, lost, or forged.

Four hokms (document 6–9, 1848–1856)

After the second *vaqf* deed was drawn up, four *hokm*s were issued by three jurists in Tehran. All of them supported the first *vaqf* and completely ignored the second one.

- ***Document 6 and 7, 1848 and no date***

Abu al-Qasem Emam Jom'e issued two deed-type *hokm*s. The first one was dated November 1848, five months after the second *vaqf* deed was drawn up. On the basis of *hokm*s issued by jurists in the 'Atabat, he stated that Bord-abad was the *vaqf* property of the first *vaqf*, and Aqa 'Abd al-Hoseyn, son of the first administrator, was the legitimate *vaqf* administrator. In addition, he informed the Shah's favorite (i.e., Sohrab Khan) that he had to make a statement in ten days if he had any objection.[35]

The second one was not dated but it appears to be issued after Document 6. He confirmed that the village belonged to the first *vaqf*. In addition, he stated that the case was stagnated for a while and needed to be solved because it concerned Imam Husayn.[36]

- ***Document 8, 1849–1850***

Sheykh 'Abd al-Hoseyn Tehrani issued a question-answer type *hokm* in 1849–1850. As mentioned above, he endorsed the second *vaqf* deed. However, this *hokm* completely ignored the second *vaqf* deed as follows:

> [QUESTION] I am saying to the noble and holy person. Concerning the case that Sohrab Khan and Aqa Esma'il illegally occupied the village of Bord-abad, late Najafi and late Aqa Sayyed Ebrahim Qazvini – may God raise their positions – issued *hokm*s. In order to confirm these *hokm*s and to close the case, I would like to ask a question. The defendants were sued at *Divankhane-e 'Adliye*, and you replied to it. Please write down what we should do and stamp your seal so that we know what to do. In 1266 AH.
>
> *[ANSWER] I reply. As I have said and written several times, no one was permitted to oppose the* hokms *issued by the jurists who were pillars of religion and sacred law and orders of religion and creed. If the defendants had a deed, they should submit it immediately. In any case, you must follow the* hokms.[37]

- ***Document 9, 1856***

Haji Mirza Abu al-Qasem Kalantari (1821–1875) issued a deed-type *hokm* in July 1856. He confirmed that the first *vaqf* was legitimate and Sohrab Khan illegally occupied the *vaqf* village. However, Kalantari appears not to have known much about the case. For example, he wrote that he himself might have attended the meeting for arranging the first *vaqf* deed.[38] In fact, the first *vaqf* deed did not have his endorsement. It is improbable because he was just fourteen years old when the *vaqf* deed was drawn up.

Each of these three *hokm*s confirmed the authority of the first *vaqf* and considered Sohrab Khan as a usurper. Their grounds were the *hokm*s issued by jurists in the 'Atabat. Sheykh 'Abd al-Hoseyn mentioned the names of Najafi and Sayyed Ebrahim Qazvini (d.1846) in which the former's "*hokm*" denoted the endorsement mentioned above and the latter's *hokm* was not found in the archives. Qazvini was a top level *mojtahed* and a rival of Najafi.[39] Here we can see how greatly 'Atabat's foremost 'ulama influenced the Tehrani 'ulama in their *hokm*s. This is because most of the jurists in Tehran had studied under these foremost 'ulama in the 'Atabat. For instance, Sheykh 'Abd al-Hoseyn studied under both Najafi and Qazvini while Kalantari learned from Qazvini.[40] In other words, Tehrani ʻulama followed their professors' *hokm*.

Abu al-Qasem Emam Jomʻe and Sheykh ʻAbd al-Hoseyn gave Sohrab Khan opportunities to object to the *hokm*. In particular, Sheykh ʻAbd al-Hoseyn stated that Sohrab could bring deeds if possible. However, there was no sign that Sohrab would do so. It is natural to think that he did not bring the second *vaqf* deed because it did not prove his status as the *vaqf* administrator. However, it is strange that Sheykh ʻAbd al-Hoseyn, who endorsed the deed, did not mention it at all. Instead, he recognized Sohrab Khan as a usurper.

On the other hand, it is clear that the village of Bord-abad was still in the hands of Sohrab Khan twelve years after the second *hokm* of 1844 and after the three *hokm*s of the Tehrani *mojtahed*s were issued. In addition, Aqa ʻAbd al-Hoseyn, the administrator of the first *vaqf*, not only referred to the three *mojtahed*s in Tehran but also appears to have appealed at Divankhane-e ʻAdliye. Nevertheless, Sohrab Khan still occupied the village even though his position was weak in relation to the *hokm*s that issued against him.

Joint trial in 1866 (document 10–14)

Several members of the ʻulama held a joint trial of this case at the house of Mirza Sayyed Mortaza Sadr al-ʻOlama',[41] by the order of the government. Two issues were at stake here: the possession of the village of Bord-abad and the 2,100 *tomans* debt of Sohrab Khan, who had already died. The debt suggests that there were certain negotiations between Sohrab Khan and Aqa ʻAbd al-Hoseyn, the administrator of the first *vaqf*, but the details are unknown. Aqa ʻAbd al-Hoseyn first petitioned the Grand Vazir,[42] who then ordered the members of the ʻulama to have a joint trial in order to investigate the proof. The defendants included Vali Khan (Irikli Khan), son of Suhrab Khan and Haji Abu Taleb, a merchant from Tehran. Vali Khan was a royal attendant of Naser al-Din Shah along with his younger brother, Hoseyn Khan,[43] whereas Haji Abu Taleb was the manager (*mobasher*) of Takye-e Chehel Tan and sponsor of the Shiʻi passion play (*taz'iye-khani*) presented there.[44]

Upon completion of the trial, four *hokms* were issued by different jurists. Documents 10 and 11 were issued on the day of the trial, while Document 12 was drawn up four days later.[45] Document 13 was not dated.[46] Although it was a joint trial, the results were issued separately as four question-answer type *hokm*s. In addition, another document was prepared six months later for confirmation because the three *hokm*s and related documents that the Grand Vazir presented to Naser al-Din Shah were too complicated for him to handle.[47] The following is a list of *mojtahed*s that stamped their seal on each *hokm*. The first jurist in each document denotes the main issuer and the rest endorsed the document in the margins:

Document 10 (a) Haji Sayyed Mohammad Baqir[48]

Document 11 (b) Haji Sayyed Baqer [same as (a)?](c) Sheykh ʻAbd al-Nabi (Mazandarani)[49](d) Haji Mirza Abu al-Qasem Kalantari (e) Haji Molla ʻAli Kani

Document 12 (f) Haji Mirza Abu al-Qasem Tehrani (Kalantari)
Document 13 (g) Sayyed Hoseyn Kashani (d.1879)[50]
Document 14 (h) Haji Mirza Mohammad Andarmani (i) Haji Mirza Abu al-Qasem Tehrani (Kalantari) (j) Haji Fakhr al-Din Yazdi (k) Sayyed (Mohammad) Sadiq Tabataba'i (Sangelaji)

Most of the jurists are so well-known that their names are found in biographical dictionaries. In this case, all of them supported the petitioner, Aqa 'Abd al-Hoseyn, the administrator of the first *vaqf*. The jurists ordered the heirs of the late Sohrab Khan to repay his 2100 *tomans* debt from his inheritance. In addition, they confirmed that the village of Bord-abad was the *vaqf* property of the first *vaqf* and that Aqa 'Abd al-Hoseyn was its administrator. The defendants were then ordered to deliver the village to the *vaqf* administrator.

The grounds of these *hokm*s were again the *hokm*s of the jurists in the 'Atabat, in particular, those of Qazvini and Najafi mentioned earlier. According to Document 12, Qazvini's *hokm* annulled the 1835 *hokm* of Emam Jom'e, which stated that the village had been sold without the heirs' consent. Thus, Qazvini confirmed this.

What is notable here is the claim of the defendants. The first time, they insisted that half Bord-abad was the *vaqf* property established by Sohrab Khan and that they were its administrators.[51] They also stated that there were two administrators other than Valii Khan and Haji Abu Taleb.[52] However, when the jurists requested the related documents to the *vaqf*, they replied that they had the documents but could not produce them at that moment.[53] Since the second *vaqf* deed was not submitted in the trial as proof, it determined the outcome.

Accordingly, this raises the question as to why the defendants did not submit the second *vaqf* deed in the trial, even if it was authentic. As shown earlier, the deed did not mention Vali Khan or Haji Abu Taleb, but it showed Haji Molla 'Ali Kani as the *vaqf* administrator. In other words, the deed did not support Vali Khan's claim to *vaqf* control.

However, it was embarrassing that Haji Molla 'Ali Kani supported the first *vaqf* and did not refer to the second *vaqf* deed in his endorsement,[54] although the second *vaqf* deed appointed him as the *vaqf* administrator. It is incredible that a *vaqf* administrator denied the validity of the *vaqf* that he controlled.

Therefore, it is probable that the second *vaqf* was not managed in accordance with the deed. It is certain that Vali Khan and Haji Abu Taleb controlled both Takye-e Chehel Tan and half of Bord-abad, and maybe even spent income from the village for the mourning ceremonies held at the *takye*. Even then, this management did not relate to the stipulations of the second *vaqf* deed, and therefore, the deed was not suitable to submit in the trial. Additionally, it is possible that the second *vaqf* deed was a forgery.

This consequence shows one feature of the shari'a court. In principle, the *mojtaheds* only investigated the documents submitted in the trial by both parties. Therefore, each party could ignore or conceal the documents that did not support their initial claim. The state officials as well as the *mojtahed*s could not access the other documents because there were no central archives for *vaqf* and other private deeds.

Even if the deed was a forgery, when its format was well prepared, there were no differences from authentic deeds except for the date and jurists' endorsements. This was one of the main reasons why the second *vaqf* deed was eventually recognized as authentic.

After the joint trial

Although the joint trial of 1865 confirmed that the village of Bord-abad belonged to the first *vaqf*, the portion of the village was not delivered to the administrator of the first *vaqf*. There is no record to explain the reason, but probably it was because of the fact that Vali Khan was very close to Naser al-Din Shah. Nevertheless, the dispute still continued after the trial and even after the *mojtahed*s issued numerous *hokm*s.

It is striking that two *hokm*s were issued in favor of the second *vaqf* as follows:

- ***Document 15, 1888***

Sayyed 'Abd-allah Behbahani issued a deed-type *hokm* dated 9 October, 1888. Contrary to many other *hokm*s, this particular *hokm* confirmed the validity of the second *vaqf*. According to it, Haji Abu Taleb, the merchant, acquired Haji Molla 'Ali Kani's permission to control half of Bord-abad as *vaqf* property and to spend the *vaqf* income for the mourning ceremonies held at Takye-e Chehel Tan. Since Kani passed away, Behbahani ordered him to continue to spend the *vaqf* income in the same way.[55]

- ***Document 23, 1891***

Gholam Hoseyn Tehrani[56] replied to the petition of Haji Abu Taleb in July – August 1891, which supported the second *vaqf*. According to the document, the second *vaqf* was managed properly for more than fifty years. However, the original *vaqf* deed had been preserved by the late Kani and it was impossible to access. Therefore, Gholam Hoseyn proved the contents of the *vaqf* deed at the request of the petitioner.[57]

It is obvious that these two *hokm*s contradicted the results of the joint trial in 1866. As shown earlier, Kani had denied the existence of the second *vaqf* before 1888. It was improbable that Kani would have entrusted the control of the second *vaqf* to Haji Abu Taleb. Now that these new *hokm*s confirmed for the first time the validity of the second *vaqf* deed, the real competition between the two *vaqf*s had started.

The *hokm*s that supported the second *vaqf* appeared at this time probably because Haji Molla 'Ali Kani passed away on October 7, 1888.[58] Behbahani issued his *hokm* (Document 15) only a few days after Kani's death. Because the second *vaqf* deed appointed Kani as the *vaqf* administrator, Vali Khan and Haji Abu Taleb did not ignore Kani's opinion. If Kani denied it, then they did not have any measures to oppose it at the trial. However, after his death, they could claim that Kani had entrusted them with control of the *vaqf*.

However, Behbahani's position was completely inconsistent. As shown earlier, he confirmed the endorsement of Najafi, in which he indirectly supported the first *vaqf*. In addition, he confirmed the first *vaqf* in the margin of Document 45, dated January 1907.[59] It appears that he made spontaneous decisions and did not care about the consistency of such decisions. This might also be true for Sheykh 'Abd al-Hoseyn and Kani, whose names were found in the second *vaqf* deed but issued the *hokm*s in favor of the first *vaqf*.

Many more *hokms* were issued in support of the first *vaqf*, among them, two *hokm*s were particularly important:

- ***Document 18, 1890***

A well-known *mojtahed* and leader of the Tobacco Protest, Mirza Mohammad Hasan Ashtiyani issued a question and answer *hokm* in April–May 1890 after Sheykh Mahmud, the son of Aqa 'Abd al-Hoseyn and the fourth administrator of the first *vaqf*, petitioned him. Ashtiyani confirmed that all Bord-abad was property of the first *vaqf* and it should be controlled by Sheykh Mahmud. In addition, Mirza Hasan Shirazi, prominent Marja'-e Taqlid at the time of the Tobacco protest, endorsed the *hokm*.[60]

- ***Document 35, 1901***

Akhond Molla Mohammad Kazem Khorasani, also known as Akhond-e Khorasani (1839–1911),[61] issued a question-answer type *hokm* that supported Sheykh Mahmud's control over Bord-abad in 1901. Akhond-e Khorasani resided in Najaf and was later considered as a Marja'-e Taqlid. He was also known for his support of the Constitutional Revolution in Iran.[62]

Here the leading jurists in the 'Atabat still issued the *hokm*s in favor of the first *vaqf*, even after two *hokm*s supported the second one.

On the other hand, the second *vaqf* was gradually recognized by the authorities. A *hokm* of a jurist described the possessors and their shares of Bord-abad in August 1896 as follows:

> Sheykh Mahmud b. Aqa 'Abd al-Hoseyn: five twenty-fourths (the first *vaqf*)
> Vali Khan b. Sohrab Khan: seven twenty-fourths (private property)
> Haji Abu Taleb: one half (the second *vaqf*)[63]

The *hokm* recognized that Haji Abu Taleb possessed one half of the village as a *vaqf* administrator. It also excluded Vali Khan from among the *vaqf* administrators although he claimed to be an administrator at the joint trial of 1866. In other words, the *hokm* was issued in accordance with the second *vaqf* deed. In addition, as a settlement, the *hokm* proposed that the Minister of the Interior should take control of the *vaqf*. In this case, the *hokm* considered the continuity of the second *vaqf* as more important than the *vaqf* administrator. In sum, the second *vaqf* was recognized as authentic, and it was to be controlled in accordance with the second *vaqf* deed.

Finally in 1914, the Ministry of *Vaqf* recognized the second *vaqf* just as the above-mentioned *hokm* did.[64] Accordingly, the state refused to accept all *hokms* issued by the most learned jurists in the ‘Atabat in favor of the first *vaqf*. This may suggest that the state became more independent from the ‘Atabat jurists and more close to a nation-state.

Disputes in reality

In this actual case, we have seen that both parties frequently referred to the state and religious authority. They petitioned the *divankhanes* as well as the shari‘a courts about the case, and it appears that there was no preference or distinction in their choice. In other words, both parties used every measure possible to obtain favor. The Amir-e Divan and the Grand Vazir asked for the *mojtahed*'s opinion, while the *hokms* from the shari‘a court were brought to the *divankhane* as a proof. For solving such a complicated case, the state and shari‘a court were involved in an intricate way. This case also suggests that the two institutions were connected, and it was not likely to be a dual system as emphasized in some previous studies.

The primary function of the shari‘a courts seen here can be summarized as issuing *hokms*. However, because no *hokm* was decisive, it could not terminate the dispute, although the term *hokm* implies that it had binding power. Instead, as described in Document 4, it was drawn up to "be a proof when it is needed" and had the same function as legal deeds and endorsements on such deeds. Furthermore, the shari‘a court provided the legal grounds to the customer and in turn, the customer brought the *hokms* along with the related deeds to the state and claimed his right at the *divankhane*.

There was no sign that the state intervened in the shari‘a court. In fact, a jurist could issue a *hokm* against the royal edict of the reigning Shah. The only authority that affected the shari‘a court in a significant way was the supreme members of the ‘ulama in the ‘Atabat. It is interesting that Sayyed Ebrahim Qazvini, Sheykh Mohammad Hasan Najafi, Mirza Hasan Shirazi, and Akhond-e Khorasani, who were the most learned Shi‘i jurists of their age and lived in Iraq, confirmed the validity of the first *vaqf* over a village near Tehran. In this case, the first *vaqf* party went to Iraq in order to obtain confirmation and gain an advantage in the dispute. One of the reasons for the ‘Atabat ‘ulama's support of the first *vaqf* in the disputes is that the *vaqf* also benefitted the ‘Atabat shrines. In addition, the second administrator of the first *vaqf* resided in the ‘Atabat in his later years, and he might have had good relations with the ‘Atabat jurists. However, irrespective of the backgrounds of the *hokms*, the ‘Atabat *hokms* had a substantial impact on the overall course of the disputes.

We know how well Shirazi's *hokm* on the Tobacco Prohibition was observed by the Iranian people, but the *hokms* of the ‘Atabat jurists also decisively affected ordinary civil disputes in Iran. Most of the ‘ulama in Tehran had learned in ‘Atabat under these jurists. In the formative period of the Shi‘i learning hierarchy, disputes were also handled under this hierarchy.

Bord-abad, Private Property of Yahya Khan Nasaqchi-bashi
↓inherited
Yahya Khan II b. Yahya Khan
↓conditional sale (*bey'-e shart*)
1250/1835 Hajiye Badr Nesa Khanum Qajar Qavanlu
Established a *vaqf* and became the first *vaqf*-administrator [Doc. 1]
↓
1250/1835 Molla Mohammad Hasan Yazdi, the second administrator
The first lawsuit, royal edict of Mohammad Shah
[Doc.2 & 3] — Lost some shares of the village
↓ — ↓purchased
1254/1839 (Half) Sohrab Khan Gorji
↓ — ↓
Aqa Mirza 'Abd al-Hoseyn the third *vaqf*-administrator
1260/1844 The second *hokm* endorsed by Najafi [Doc. 4] — ↓
↓
1264/1848 — ↓
(Half) Aqa Mirza 'Abd al-Hoseyn — (Half) Sohrab Khan established a *vaqf* [Doc. 5]
↓ — Molla 'Ali Kani, the first *vaqf*-administrator?
1264/1848 *hokm* of Abu al-Qasem Emam Jom'e [Doc. 6]
No date *hokm* of Abu al-Qasem Emam Jom'e [Doc. 7]
1266/1849-50 *hokm* of Sheykh 'Abd al-Hoseyn [Doc.8] — ↓
1272/1856 *hokm* of Kalantari[Doc. 9]
↓ — ↓
1282/1866
(Half) Aqa Mirza 'Abd al-Hoseyn — (Half) Vali Khan b. Sohrab Khan as administrator?
Joint trial [Doc. 10–Doc.14]
1306/1888 *hokm* of Behbahani [Doc. 15]

1306/1890 Sheykh Mahmud b. 'Abd al-Hoseyn, fourth administrator
Hokm of Ashtiyani endorsed by Shirazi [Doc.18]
1308/1891 *hokm* of Gholam Hoseyn [Doc.23]

1314/1896 *hokm* of a jurist [Doc.33]
Sheykh Mahmud, *vaqf* administrator (Five twenty-fourth) — Haji Abu Taleb, *vaqf* administrator (Half) — Vali Khan (Seven twenty-fourth)

1318/1901 *hokm* of Akhond-e Khorasani [Doc.35]

Figure 4.1 Possessors of Bord-abad, their shares, and related documents

Another feature observed in the dispute was how to deal with proof and pertinent documents. The *mojtaheds* issued *hokms* on the basis of testimony and legal documents. However, there was no central archive where the documents were preserved and could be consulted for future reference. Each *mojtahed* made a decision for each particular occasion after hearing the testimony and referring to the documents that were presented to them. As Vali Khan showed, one side could conceal the existence of a given document. Therefore, a jurist's decision could contradict his previous one, as seen in the case of 'Abd-allah Behbahani.

This "double *vaqf* case" represented the complicated structure of the Qajar judicial system. The shari'a court was independent of the state, and it was affected only by the leading jurists in the 'Atabat. The *mojtahed*s made decisions and issued *hokm*s as legal experts, but the *hokm*s were not executed immediately by the state. In theory, the *hokm*s ought to have been followed and executed, but in reality, their executions depended upon particular situations. Furthermore, the *hokm*s were treated as proof for other trials in the state or the shari'a court.

The relationship between the state and the shari'a court is too complicated here to be described as "the dual judicial system." On the one hand, the state depended upon the shari'a court for judging intricate legal problems. On the other hand, the shari'a court required state cooperation for executing their proposed *hokm*s. In this case, the judicial system consisted of two different types of authority that depended upon each other under one law, the shari'a.

The mutual reliance between the state and the shari'a court did not always work well. It is certain that, in 1835, the *divankhane* and Emam Jom'e cooperated sufficiently in the first lawsuit and the royal edict was quickly issued on the basis of Emam Jom'e's *hokm*. However, on other occasions, the state did not execute the numerous *hokm*s that were issued in favor of the first *vaqf* and the administrator could not regain control of the *vaqf* property despite the terms. Furthermore, the 'ulama could issue *hokm*s without intervention from the state but they also required the cooperation of the state in order to execute the *hokm*s. This did not always succeed. By examining these situations, we can better understand the claim of some 'ulama who wanted constitutionalism based on the shari'a in the Constitutional Revolution.

Notes

1 For previous studies of Qajar lawsuits see, Ann K.S. Lambton, "The Case of Hajji Nur Al-Din, 1823–47: A Study in Land Tenure," *Bulletin of the School of Oriental and African Studies* 30 (1967): 54–72; Werner, *An Iranian Town*, 99–122; Bhalloo, "Judging the Judge." Lambton focuses on land tenure, where as Werner deals with a change of a Safavid *vaqf* in Qajar times. Martin's article describes an interesting murder case but does not focus on the procedure. Martin, "A Murder in Bushehr." See also Kondo, "Waqf of Ustad 'Abbas."

2 Related documents are preserved by the *Vaqf* Organization in Tehran in two files: Owqaf no.530 and 550.

3 She was the daughter of Mostafa Khan Qajar Qavanlu and the paternal cousin and one of the four wives of Fath 'Ali Shah, but was divorced. For her biography, Soltah Ahmad Mirza 'Azod al-Dowle, *Tarikh-e 'Azodi*, ed. 'Abd al-Hoseyn Nava'i (Tehran, 2535Sh), 12–13, 302.

4 The village, located in a flat rural area, included a population of 216. *Farhang-e Joghrafiya'i-e Iran* (Tehran, 2535Sh), 1:34.

5 Document 1, *Vaqf* deed of Badr Nesa' Khanom dated 1 Ramazan 1250AH.

6 See Chapter 6.

7 Tonekaboni, *Qeas al-'Olama'*, 121–123.

8 *Vaqf* deed of Hoseyn 'Ali Khan Mo'ayyer-bashi dated Ramazan 1246AH, Owqaf no.642. For the biography of Hoseyn 'Ali Khan, see Mahdi Bamdad, *Sharh-e Hal-e Rejal-e Iran dar Qarn-e 12 va 13 va 14 Hejri* (Tehran, 1363Kh), 6:93.

9 For his biography, see Bamdad, *Sharh-e Hal*, 6:277–279.
10 Document 2, *hokm* of Mirza Mahdi Emam Jom'e dated 5 Shavval 1250AH.
11 See Chapter 3.
12 Document 3–1, *'arze-dasht* of Mohammad Vali, Mohammad Hoseyn and 'Ali, no date.
13 See Chapter 5.
14 Document 3–2, royal edict of Mohammad Shah, dated Ziqa'de 1250AH.
15 Mo'allem-e Habib-abadi, *Makarem al-Asar*, 1703; E'temad al-Saltane, *al-Ma'aser al-Asar*, 192–193.
16 Nobuaki Kondo, "Private Property and Vaqf of Manuchehr Khan Mo'tamad al-Dowle," *Toyoshi-kenkyu* 60–61 (2001): 5–7; Werner, *An Iranian Town*, 104. For his seal, see Reza'i, "Khatt va Mohr," 83.
17 Document 12, Q &A *hokm* of Hajji Mirza Abu al-Qasem Tehrani, dated 4 Moharram 1282AH.
18 See Chapter 3.
19 Document 52, Raport-e Dayer-e Tahqiq, Edare-e Koll-e Owqaf, dated 28 Rajab 1332AH.
20 Document 4, *hokm* of Haji Molla 'Ali Asghar, dated 21 Rajab 1260AH.
21 'Ali Qoli Mirza E'tezad al-Saltane, *Eksir al-Tavarikh*, ed. Jamshid Kiyanfar (Tehran, 1370Kh), 602–603.
22 Document 4.
23 He was called "Saheb-e Javaher." Concerning Najafi and his leadership, see Ahmad Kazemi Musavi, *Religious Authority in Shi'ite Islam* (Kuala Lumpur, 1996), 200–202; Meir Litvak, *Shi'i Scholars of Nineteenth-Century Iraq* (Cambridge, 1998), 64–70.
24 Document 4.
25 For his biography, see Mo'allem-e Habib-abadi, *Makarem al-Asar*, 547–549.
26 The other two jurists who confirmed Najafi's endorsement were named Mirza Sayyed Hoseyn Qommi and Mirza Sayyed 'Ali Yazdi. However, we do not possess their biographies. The latter might be a jurist living in Karbala' at that time. E'temad al-Saltane, *al-Ma'aser va al-Asar*, 247.
27 Document 8, Q&A *hokm* of Sheykh 'Abd al-Hoseyn dated 1266AH and Document 13 Q &A *hokm* of Sayyed Hoseyn Kashani, no date.
28 Mirza Fazl-allah Shirazi Khavari, *Tarikh-e Zu al-Qarneyn*, ed. Naser Afshar-far (Tehran, 1380Kh), 737, 1030, 1149; Mohammad Ja'far Khormuji, *Haqayeq al-Akhbar-e Naseri*, ed. Hoseyn Khadivjam (Tehran, 1363Kh), 290.
29 Sayyed 'Ali Al-e Davud, ed. *Asnad va Nameha-ye Amir-e Kabir* (Tehran, 1379Kh), 214; E'temad al-Saltane, *al-Ma'aser al-Asar*, 44.
30 The village had been *khalese* (royal) land but it was transformed into private land for Sohrab Khan by a royal edict of Fath 'Ali Shah. *Surat-e Khalesejat va Mowqufat* I, 163.
31 For more information about him, see Chapter 7.
32 Document 5, *vaqf* deed of Sohrab Khan, dated Rabi' II 1264AH.
33 He was a grandson of Vahid Behbahani. For his biography, see Mo'allem-e Habib-abadi, *Makarem al-Asar*, 2002–2003.
34 Naser al-Din Shah, *Yaddashtha-ye Ruzane-e Naser al-Din Shah: 1300–1303AH*, ed. Parviz Badi'i (Tehran, 1378Kh), 500.
35 Document 6, *hokm* of Abu al-Qasem Emam Jom'e, dated 21 Zihejje 1264AH.
36 Document 7, *hokm* of Abu al-Qasem Emam Jom'e, no date.
37 Document 8.
38 Document 9, *hokm* of Haji Mirza Abu al-Qasem Kalantari, dated 26 Ziqa'de 1272AH.
39 Litvak, *Shi'i Scholars*, 61; Kazemi Musavi, *Religious Authority*, 188–189.
40 Muhammad Husayn Harz al-Din, *Ma'arif al-Rijal fi Tarajum al-'Ulama' wa al-'Udaba'* (Qom, 1405AH), 1:20, 2:35; Mo'allem-e Habib-abadi, *Makarem al-Asar*, 1018.
41 He was a brother of Mirza Abu al-Qasem Emam Jom'e. See Mohammad Sharif Razi, *Akhtaran-e Foruzan-e Rey va Tehran ya Tazkerat al-Maqaber fi Ahval al-Mafaher* (Qom, n.d.), 427–428.

42 The name of the Grand Vazir was not mentioned here, but from the date it should be Mirza Mohammad Khan Qajar Sepahsalar. See Bamdad, *Sharh-e Hal*, 3:228–232.
43 Bamdad, *Sharh-e Hal*, 5:323–324.
44 Sheykh Reza'i and Azari, eds. *Gozareshha-ye Nazmiye*, 201.
45 Document 10, *hokm* of Haji Sayyed Mohammad Baqir, dated 29 Zihejje 1282AH; Document 11, *hokm* of Hajji Sayyed Baqer and others, dated 29 Zihejje 1282AH; Document 12, *hokm* of Mirza Abu al-Qasem Tehrani, dated 4 Moharram 1282AH.
46 Document 13, *hokm* of Sayyed Hoseyn Kashani, no date.
47 Document 14, *hokm* of Haji Molla Mirza Mohammad Andarmani and others, 15 Rajab 1283AH.
48 He might be Haji Sayyed Mohammad Baqer Eraqi. See, E'temad al-Saltane, *al-Ma'aser va al-Asar*, 217.
49 Ibid., 235.
50 Ibid., 215.
51 Document 13.
52 Document 12.
53 Document 13.
54 Document 11.
55 Document 15, *hokm* of 'Abd-allah Behbahani, dated 4 Safar 1306AH.
56 He was son of Molla Abu al-Hasan Tehrani. E'temad al-Saltane, *al-Ma'aser va al-Asar*, 245.
57 Document 23, Q & A *hokm* of Gholam Hoseyn Tehrani, dated Zihejje 1308AH.
58 1 Safar 1306AH. E'temad al-Saltane, *al-Ma'aser va al-Asar*, 186–187.
59 Document 45, Q & A *hokm* of Aqa Mirza Sayyed Hoseyn Qommi, dated 8 Zihejje 1324AH.
60 Document 18, Q & A *hokm* of Mirza Mohammad Hasan Ashtiyani, dated Ramazan 1307AH.
61 For his life, see A. Hairi, s.v. "Akund Korasani: i. Life and Political Role," *Encyclopaedia Iranica*, 1(1984): 732–734.
62 Document 35, Q & A *hokm* of Akhond-e Khorasani, dated 8 Zihejje 1318AH.
63 Document 33, *hokm* of a jurist, dated 8 Rabi' I 1314AH. The seal of the jurist was illegible.
64 Document 52.

5 Attestations and transactions in shari‘a courts

As we saw in Chapter 3, shari‘a court records contain more deeds for transactions than *hokms*. Approximately 70 percent of the records concern transactions such as sales, leases, and donations. Among them, three type of transactions, namely, sales, conditional sales, and loans, comprised almost half all records in each of the three registers. As mentioned above, Sangelaji and Nuri engaged mainly in endorsing the transaction deeds in terms of the numbers of records. These will be examined in detail.

When one attempts to categorize the transactions, a common problem encountered involves contradictions between types of legal contracts and actual transactions. Influenced by the Shafi‘ school of law, the Ja‘fari school of law considers a *solh* (settlement) contract as a subdivision of five types of legal contracts: (1) *bey‘* (sale), (2) *habe* (donation), (3) *eqrar* (acknowledgement), (4) *ejare* (lease), and (5) *‘ariye* (loan of non-fungible things).[1] Therefore, under the Qajars, the *mosalehe* contract was used not only for settlement but also for sales, donations, and leases; a practice that makes categorization exceedingly difficult.[2] My classification of the transactions contained in the registers is therefore based on the nature of the transactions themselves and not on the type of legal contract used.

Major transactions

Sales

Sales were the most basic, popular transactions recorded in the court registers. Sales comprised 19.5 percent (*Sangelaji I*), 27.2 percent (*Sangelaji II*), and 16.2 percent (*Nuri*) of the transactions in each register. From a legal view point, two types of contracts were used for sales: *mobaye‘e* (sale) and *mosalehe* (settlement). The custom in the nineteenth century was to use *mosalehe* contracts for sales. The number and percentage of records of each contract type are shown in Table 5.1.

Mosalehe contracts outnumbered *mobaye‘e* contracts. We will see that this trend persists for transactions other than sales.

Table 5.1 Records sorted by the types of contract for sales

	Sangelaji I		*Sangelaji II*		*Nuri*	
mobaye'e	70	29%	442	38%	31	13%
mosalehe	124	71%	732	62%	216	87%
	194	100%	1,174	100%	247	100%

Table 5.2 Sale records sorted by sale items in the registers

	Sangelaji I		*Sangelaji II*		*Nuri*	
Houses, mansions	75	39%	346	29%	121	49%
Shops	7	3%	53	5%	14	6%
Caravanserais	3	2%	7	1%	8	3%
Baths	2	1%	3	0%	2	1%
Icehouses	2	1%	0	0%	1	0%
Gardens *(bagh)*	8	4%	59	5%	16	6%
Lands	29	15%	519	44%	35	14%
Villages, hamlets	55	28%	164	14%	33	13%
Qanats	8	4%	19	2%	6	0%
Female slaves	2	1%	5	0%	0	0%
Total records	194	100%	1,174	100%	247	100%

* The records include multiple items counted separately: therefore, total numbers do not match the total records.

What was sold at the shari'a courts? Table 5.2 provides data on the sale records. The registers suggest that the most common type of sale recorded at the shari'a court concerned real estate, such as houses, villages, and land. When a property was sold at the court, the buyer received the deed of sale, which proved ownership of the property. Therefore, it was natural that people came to the court to conduct real estate sales.

The only exception was the sale of female slaves (*kaniz*, *jariye*), for which only seven records are found.[3] Their prices ranged from twenty-eight to fifty-five *tomans*. Their ages ranged from twenty-five to forty years old; two records involve slaves sold with their children. Because slaves were expensive commodities in Qajar Tehran, transactions involving them were conducted at the shari'a court for safety.

How large were the transactions conducted at the shari'a court? Table 5.3 shows the amounts paid for the articles in each record. In over 70 percent of the records, the articles being bought cost less than 1,000 *tomans*. Of these articles, the one costing less than 200 *tomans* were more common. However, the range of prices varied. For example, four records indicate that the articles sold cost over

Table 5.3 Sale records sorted by article price

	Sangilaji I		*Sangilaji II*		*Nuri*	
3000t~	12	6%	35	3%	11	4%
2000t~3000t below	11	6%	13	1%	4	2%
1000t~2000t below	30	15%	52	4%	16	6%
Below 1000t	139	72%	1,070	91%	216	87%
800t~1000t below	8	4%	17	1%	11	0%
600t~800t below	13	7%	36	3%	18	6%
400t~600t below	15	15%	65	6%	25	14%
200t~400t below	36	19%	172	15%	31	13%
Below 200t	69	36%	780	67%	131	53%
Total records	194	100%	1,170	100%	247	100%
Average	810.6t		435.4t		721.6t	

20,000 *tomans*, a sum equivalent to one year of tax income for a small province such as Natanz:[4]

- On 4 Rajab, 1295 AH, Jan Mohammad Khan Khalaj Seyf al-Saltane sold a village, hamlets, and lands in Save to Vajh-allah Mirza Khazane-dar-e Nezam b. Soltan Ahmad Mirza 'Azod al-Dowle for 23,000 *tomans*.[5]
- On 22 Zihejje, 1296 AH, Haji Mohammad Kazem Malek al-Tojjar-e Iran sold a half of Karvansara-ye Dowlat in the Grand Bazaar to Mirza Mohammad Khan Amin-e Khalvat for 50,000 *tomans*.[6]
- On 4 Safar, 1306 AH, Princess Forugh al-Dowle sold a two-thirds share of two villages and the same share of a hamlet in the Ghar county to Haji Mohammad Hasan Amin-e Dar al-Zarb for 26,000 *tomans* with the permission of her husband Zahir al-Dowle.[7]
- On 25 Rabi' I, 1306 AH, four sons and a daughter of late Aqa Mohammad Hoseyn Arbab sold shares of four villages and a hamlet in the Varamin county that they inherited from their father to Aqa Mirza Ahmad Khan 'Ala' al-Dowle for 30,000 *tomans*. In addition, they sold crops and seeds there to 'Ala' al-Dowle for 1,000 *tomans*.[8]

In these cases, sellers and buyers were well-known people, such as a prince, a princess, and high officials, who had their titles bestowed by the Shah. These elites also attended the shari'a court or sent representatives to record their transactions.

The registers contained also contain 125 sale records for complete houses in the Sangelaj district.[9] The price of the house ranged from 32 to 18,000 *tomans*, with an average of 351.8 *tomans*. Shared parts of houses were also sold at the courts, and in most cases, their prices were less than two hundred *tomans*.

Donation

Under Islamic law, a donation contract is usually known as *hiba* in Arabic. A *habe-name* dated August–September 1824 from Tehran is preserved at the Golestan Museum.[10] No record using the term *habe* could be found in the registers. However, this does not mean the register contains no donation record. *Mosalehe* contracts were subordinate to contracts of donation, which meant that, like sale, transfer via donation were also carried out through them.

The problem is that if parties used a *mosalehe* contract for a donation, no difference in the record form is found between a sale and a donation. This was, because in most cases, the party making a donation received a small amount of money or valueless goods in exchange for the donation to avoid the donation being returned. In other words, one can find the difference between a sale and a donation within a *mosalehe* contract only by examining the prices or the substitutes. Accordingly, I include *mosalehe* transactions for less than 0.1 *tomans*, one *man* (=2.97 kilograms) of wheat, or five *sir* (=371.24 grams) of sugar candy (*nabat*) under the category of donation.

Donation records comprise 0.9 percent, 3.1 percent, and 2.4 percent of the total records for each register. Around half of the donation transactions were conducted between relatives after inheritance to avoid fragmentation of the family property. Table 5.4 shows the number of transfer records via donations carried out between family members.

Among the 173 records, 134 records (77 percent) concern the donation of real estate, whereas in twenty-seven records (16 percent), all the property and belongings the giver owned were delivered to others. In particular, donation served as an important strategy for families to control and protect their property.

Leases

In *fiqh*, the term *ijara/ejare* denotes a lease contract. However, as in the case of sales and donations, a *mosalehe* contract was used for leases in Qajar Iran. In this case, the lessor sold proceeds (*manfa'*) accruing from a property within a certain time limit to the lessee for a price, which actually comprised rent.

Another point to note concerning leases is that in some cases, two types of deeds were drawn up for one lease. If two parties used an *ejare* contract for a lease, they prepared an *ejare* deed and a *qabul-e ejare* deed. The *ejare* deed, which proved that the lessor leased a property to a lessee and received rent, was kept by the

Table 5.4 Records of donations conducted between family members

	Sangelaji I	*Sangelaji II*	*Nuri*	*Total*	
Between family members	4	62	24	90	52%
Between others	5	72	6	83	48%
Total	9	134	30	173	100%

Table 5.5 Records of lease sorted by the type of contract

	Sangelaji I	*Sangelaji II*	*Nuri*	*Total*	
Ejare contract	24	43	40	107	29%
Qabul-e ejare contract	4	16	23	43	11%
Mosalehe contract	16	107	42	165	44%
Qabul-e mosalehe contract	3	29	28	60	16%
Total	47	195	133	375	100%

Table 5.6 Records of lease sorted by items

	Sangelaji I	*Sangelaji II*	*Nuri*	*Total*	
Houses, mansions	10	43	42	95	25%
Shops, small bazaar	9	26	25	60	16%
Caravanserais	5	2	5	12	3%
Baths	3	12	5	20	5%
Coffeehouse	0	7	0	7	2%
Gardens *(bagh)*	5	11	3	19	5%
Lands	2	16	10	28	7%
Villages, hamlets	17	62	28	107	29%
Qanats	3	11	2	16	4%
Total records	47	195	133	375	100%

lessee, while the *qabul-e ejare* deed showed that the lessee rented the property from the lessor for a certain period, and the deed was remained in the hands of the lessor. When two parties concluded a *mosalehe* contract for a lease, they arranged a *mosalehe* deed and a *qabul-e mosalehe* deed.

Table 5.5 shows the range of contracts concluded for a lease. Although Nuri registered one lease transaction even though both *ejare* and *qabul-e ejare* deeds were drawn up, I have counted them separately, as Sangelaji does. At least 60 percent of lease transactions were conducted through the *mosalehe* contract. On the other hand, *qabul*-type deeds comprised just one-third of *ejare* and *mosalehe* deeds. This suggests that sometimes, only deeds for the lessor or the lessee were drawn up.

As Table 5.6 shows, the rented items related to real estate such as houses, shops, gardens, and villages.

Table 5.7 shows the rent amounts in each lease transaction. Half of all lease transactions asked for rents below one hundred *tomans*. However, some rents were very expensive. For example, a merchant (*tajer*) named Aqa Asad-allah Borujerdi b. Aqa Musa leased a plot of land containing twenty-one shops and a *saray* in Tehran, which was *vaqf* property on behalf of Takye-e Agha Bahram Khaje, from Sayyed Mohammad Sadeq Sangelaji, at 18,000 *tomans* for 120 years in 1868.[11] This is an extraordinary case in terms of the rent and the period, but these kinds of transactions were also possible.

Table 5.7 Rent amounts in each lease transaction

	Sangelaji I	*Sangelaji II*	*Nuri*	*Total*	
1000t~	9	13	12	34	9%
100t~1000t below	8	75	37	120	32%
Below 100t	24	89	74	187	50%
Articles	5	17	11	33	9%
	46	194	134	374	100%

Table 5.8 Lease contract periods

	Sangelaji I	*Sangelaji II*	*Nuri*	*Total*	
below 1 year	8	21	15	44	12%
1 year~	16	42	35	93	25%
2 years~	4	30	25	59	16%
3 years~	8	31	31	70	19%
4 years~	1	6	11	18	5%
5 years~	2	30	7	39	11%
6 years~10 years		9		9	2%
10 years~	7	26	6	39	11%
sum	46	195	130	371	100%

Table 5.8 presents data on lease periods. Of the lease transactions, 72 percent were carried out for a period of less than four years. However, in 11 percent of all lease transactions, properties were leased for longer than ten years. The longest lease contract concerned a house and land in Rasht, which Aqa Mirza Mahmud, his wife, and daughters leased to Aqa Mohammad Saleh at five thousand *dinar* for 150 years in 1876.[12]

Conditional sale

Although usury is prohibited in Islam, historically, a number of ways emerged to lend money at interest under the rule of Islamic law, as Maxime Rodinson wrote in his famous book, *Islam et capitalisme*.[13] This was also the case in Qajar Iran. The *bey'-e shart*, which literally means "a conditional sale," was one such means in Shi'i law. This is quite similar to the system of *bey'-e ja'ez* in Central Asia and *bey' bi'l-vefa* in the Ottoman Empire.[14]

The *bey'-e shart* system was rather complicated. As its name indicates, it is categorized as a type of sale (*bey'*) in Islamic law. More precisely, it is related to *khiyar al-shart*, or "stipulated option," in Shi'i law. If a sale contract includes *khiyar al-shart*, the seller has the option to recover the commodity following a refund of the purchase price during the option period (*moddat-e khiyar*). This

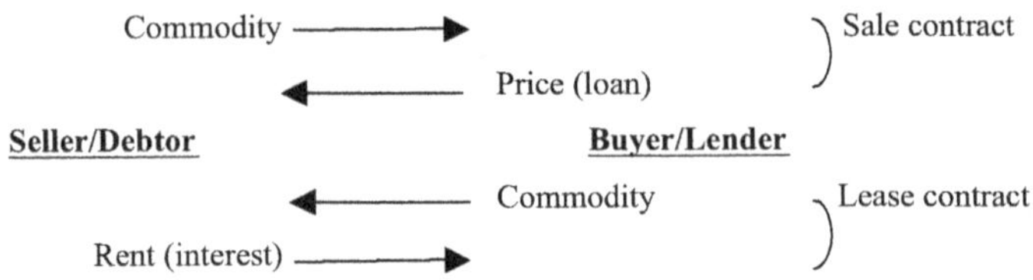

Figure 5.1 Structure of conditional sales

provision is tantamount to a "cooling-off period" and has no relation to loans or usury. However, if the seller were to lease back the commodity from the buyer in the same period in exchange for rent, the seller can keep the commodity and obtain a loan with interest. First, the seller/borrower gets money from the buyer/lender by means of the sale contract as the price of the commodity, but continues to control the commodity by means of the lease contract. Then, if the seller/borrower pays back the borrowed money and the rent for the commodity to the buyer/lender in the stipulated period, the sale contract will be cancelled, and the seller/borrower will recover ownership of the commodity. The buyer/lender will receive not only the original money but also the rent, which is actually the interest. If he does not pay the borrowed money and the rent, the lease contract will be terminated, and the buyer/lender will obtain full possession of the commodity. These transactions constitute a secured loan with interest. Here is an example:

> Abu al-Qasem, a cloth dealer (*bazzaz*), made a conditional sale to Ostad Asad-allah, a tailor (*khayyat*), who lived in Tehran. The article was a one-third share of a house, half of which belonged to the seller, located outside the Mohammadiye gate, and its border was noted below along with its belongings. The price for the sale was 20 *tomans* of silver coins of 26 grains. The contract was concluded. In addition, a condition was stipulated; the seller had right to cancel the contract if he refunded the sale price in ten days after one year from the date below. [Then,] the seller leased the sold article from the buyer at 6 *tomans* for the period, by paying 5000 *dinars* at the end of each month. On 18 Rabi' II 1295AH.[15]

In short, the cloth dealer borrowed twenty *tomans* from the tailor for a year with the security of one-third share of the house and the interest of six *tomans* for the year, which translates to an interest rate of 24 percent per year. This is a typical transaction in a conditional sale, which was a secured loan with interest.

This is a particularly Shi'i way of dealing with these transactions. Sunni law also admits *khiyar al-shart*, but only for a period no longer than three days. Moreover, Hanafi law does not accept any contracts with conditions (*shart*). Therefore, in Central Asia, a promise (*va'ade*), by which a seller could cancel the sale contract, was added to the sale contract, for the same purpose as *bey'-e shart*.[16]

Some variations existed among conditional sales in Qajar Tehran. Usually, sale contracts and lease contracts were bound in a single deed, but sometimes, the buyer/lender and the seller/borrower arranged two separate deeds for a sale and a lease. In addition, as in a regular sale, conditional sales used both *mobaye'e* contracts and *mosalehe* contracts with the terms *mobaye'e-e shartiye* and *mosalehe-e shartiye* being employed. Moreover, when a transaction did not include a lease contract, the commodity/security would remain in the hands of the buyer/lender, meaning that the seller/borrower could not use the article during the stipulated period. In this case, the transaction should be interpreted as pawning.

The *mobaye'e/mosalehe* ratio in Table 5.9 indicates that Nuri mainly used the *mosalehe* contract for conditional sales, while Sangelaji preferred the *mobaye'e* contract over the *mosalehe*. Between the two Sangelaji's registers, the latter includes *mosalehe* contracts more frequently than former. Considering that Sangelaji employed the *mosalehe* contract more than *mobaye'e* for normal sales as shown in Table 5.1, one may assume that the shift from *mobaye'e* to *mosalehe* occurred first in normal sales and then was extended to conditional sales. Moreover, the table shows that just 10 percent to approximately 20 percent of the conditional sales were used for pawning. In other words, a conditional sale usually represented a secured loan with interest.

Table 5.10 indicates loan amounts. It is clear that 90 percent of the secured loans were less than 1,000 *tomans*, with over half of them were under 200 *tomans*;

Table 5.9 Contract types for conditional sales and leases

	Sangelaji I		*Sangelaji II*		*Nuri*	
With lease	157	90%	428	82%	247	91%
mobaye'e	139	80%	281	54%	68	25%
mosalehe	18	10%	147	28%	179	66%
Without lease	17	10%	91	18%	24	19%
mobaye'e	8	5%	47	9%	7	3%
mosalehe	9	5%	44	9%	17	16%
Sum	174	100%	519	100%	271	100%

Table 5.10 Loan amounts in conditional sales

	Sangelaji I		*Sangelaji II*		*Nuri*	
3000t~	5	3%	8	2%	1	0%
2000t~3000t below	3	2%	8	2%	1	0%
1000t~2000t below	13	8%	20	5%	7	3%
Below 1000t	136	89%	394	92%	240	97%
800t~1000t below	4	3%	2	0%	5	2%
600t~800t below	4	3%	6	1%	7	3%
400t~600t below	10	6%	24	6%	5	2%
200t~400t below	31	20%	71	17%	26	10%
Below 200t	87	55%	291	68%	202	81%
Total records	157	100%	430	100%	249	100%

Table 5.11 Interest rates of conditional sales

	Sangelaji I		*Sangelaji II*		*Nuri*	
50% and over	8	5%	4	1%	9	4%
40~50%	1	1%	6	1%	2	1%
30~40%	7	4%	58	14%	17	7%
20~30%	82	52%	203	48%	142	57%
10~20%	42	27%	87	20%	55	22%
1~10%	0	0%	8	2%	4	2%
less than 1% including *nabat*	15	10%	61	14%	13	5%
in kind	2	1%	1	0%	0	0%
unknown	0	0%	0	0%	5	2%
Total	157	100%	428	100%	247	100%

one could use a house as security to borrow 200 *tomans* at that time. A few, however, were huge loans. For example, on February 14, 1889, 'Abd-allah Khan Mirpanj obtained a loan of 16,210 *tomans* from Mohammad Hoseyn Kojuri Esfahani Tajer on the security of a mansion and a stable in the city center and a village in Shemiran.[17] A Qajar princess, Qamar al-Saltane, lent 10,000 *tomans* to a courtier, Mo'ayyer al-Mamalek on the security of three villages and one *qanat* in Pashapuye, with the interest of nine hundred *tomans* for five months and twenty-three days (about 19 percent per year) on May 25, 1878.[18]

These de-facto interest rates are interesting because Islamic law forbids (high) interest (*riba*). As Lady Sheil wrote in the mid-nineteenth century, "legal interest is limited to 12 per cent; but it seldom amounts to less than 25, and often reaches 50, 60, or 100 per cent."[19] The next Table 5.11 presents the distribution of interest rates per year. Almost half of all secured loans were arranged with an interest rate between 20 percent and 30 percent per year. Contrary to Sheil's statement, of these, the most prevalent interest rate was 24 percent per year, comprising fifty-five transactions in Sangelaji's first register, 142 in his second registers, and ninety-three transactions in Nuri's register. The interest rate was also affected by the period of the loan. Higher rates were preferred when the loan period was short. For example, eight of nine secured transactions with an annual interest rate higher than 50 percent in Nuri's register had a period of less than one year: three transactions lasted one month, another three lasted for two months, one lasted for six months, and the other lasted for eight months.

Table 5.12 shows the loan period duration. Over 90 percent of all secured loans required repayment within two years. The one-year secured loan is the most common term; 68 transactions from *Sangelaji I*, 216 transactions from *Sangelaji II*, and 132 loans from Nuri's register were one-year secured loans. It is clear that the loan period was usually quite short. When people needed to borrow money for longer periods, they usually renewed a short-term contract repeatedly.

Table 5.12 Loan periods for conditional sales

	Sangelaji I		*Sangelaji II*		*Nuri*		*Total*	
below 1 year	81	51%	174	40%	101	41%	356	42%
1year~	75	47%	231	54%	139	56%	445	53%
2 years~	1	1%	18	4%	6	2%	25	3%
3 years~	3	2%	5	1%	3	1%	11	1%
4 years~			1	0%			1	0%
5 years~								
6 years~10years			1	0%			1	0%
10years~			1	0%			1	0%
Total	160	100%	431	100%	249	100%	840	100%

Table 5.13 Types of collateral for conditional sales

	Sangelaji I		*Sangelaji II*		*Nuri*	
Houses, mansions	85	54%	264	61%	121	49%
Shops	3	2%	22	5%	12	5%
Caravanserais			1	0%	3	1%
Baths	1	1%	3	1%	1	0%
Icehouses			3	1%	2	1%
Gardens *(bagh)*	5	3%	29	7%	8	3%
Lands	3	2%	15	3%	48	19%
Villages, hamlets	53	34%	89	21%	35	14%
Qanats	1	1%	10	2%	1	0%
Total records	157	100%	430	100%	249	100%

Table 5.13 shows the types of collateral offered for conditional sales. Principally, immovable property could serve as collateral. Houses and mansions were the most common collateral, followed by villages and hamlets, while the percentages of commercial properties, such as *sarays* and shops, were low.

The absence of professional lenders involved in these conditional sales is striking. The *sarrafs*, who were a sort of banker, are rarely found as lenders in the secured loan records. Only one was found in Sangelaji's second register, and two were found in Nuri's register.[20] The merchants (*tajers*) were more involved in the conditional sale transactions than were the *sarrafs*. We can find six cases in Sangelaji's first register, twenty-nine cases in the second, and eleven in Nuri's register. However, these forty-six cases comprise only 6 percent of total secured loans. In other words, secured loans were overwhelmingly transactions among individuals who were not always bankers or merchants. Merchants of the time appear to have used *barat* (draft) transactions more frequently than they used conditional sales for lending money. A famous Iranian merchant, Amin al-Zarb explained a conditional sale transaction to his agent in Mashhad as follows:

> Concerning the conditional sale with the most prominent pilgrim, Haji Mahdi, I gave him 465 *tomans* and received a deed of the conditional sale from him. The deed is enclosed. However, you must receive 470 *tomans* from him because, if he issued a promissory note (*barat*), in place of a conditional sale deed, with forty or fifty days for repayment, you would receive a profit in addition to the original amount.[21]

This collection of Amin al-Zarb's commercial documents refers to *bey'-e shart* transactions only once while it mentions *barat* transactions frequently, although he also accumulated properties through conditional sales.[22]

Another important question is what happened after the expiry of the conditional sale's option period. In principle, as mentioned above, the debtor would lose his or her property used as security if he or she could not repay the lender. What percentage of debtors did not repay and lost their properties? Unfortunately, this is difficult to know. In all, fourteen records in *Sangelaji I* and sixty-one records in *Sangelaji II* concern foreclosures for conditional sales in the form of "postscripts" below; in this case, the debtors could not repay the debts and lost their collateral property. If we compare these with the total number of conditional sale records in each register, they comprise 8 percent and 12 percent, respectively. On the contrary, Nuri's register contains thirty-seven records (15 percent) of repayments. In addition, among them, eleven records concerns the renewal of conditional sale contracts. It is not clear which cases were dominant at that time.

However, the conditional sale prevailed in late nineteenth-century Iran, although jurists had some doubt on its legality, as noted by E'temad al-Saltane.[23] In particular, foreclosures caused conflicts between lenders and debtors, as shown in relation to we saw in the double *vaqf* case discussed in the previous chapter. The official gazette also reported that disputes caused by conditional sales were brought to the *divankhane*. In 1861, a paymaster (*lashkar-nevis*) made 300 hundred *tomans* from him on the security of a house in Tehran. Even one year after the repayment time limit, the broker did not transfer the house or repay the debt and its interest to the military secretary. The *divankhane* found that the military secretary's statement was true. Because the broker could not afford to transfer the house or repay the debt, the *divankhane* made an arrangement for clearing the debt: two builders estimated the value of the house, and the debt was counted again based on a 1.5 percent interest rate. The security, i.e., the house, was delivered to the military secretary, but the broker received the balance.[24]

The Qajar government attempted to deal with disputes caused by conditional sales. Of thirty-one articles of the *divanbegis*' regulation issued in 1858, three concern conditional sales. The *divanbegi* had a duty to deliver the collateral property to the lender if foreclosure was determined by legal edict (*hokm-e shar'i*: article 22). If the collateral's value was lower than the debt, the *divanbegi* required the debtor to repay the entire debt to the lender (article 23). The *divanbegi* also had to prevent debtors from circumventing property seizure, on the pretext that the collateral belonged to the debtor's children or relatives when the debtor was listed as owning the collateral at the time of contract (article 25).[25] As mentioned in Chapter 2, the appointment of *divanbegis* to provinces failed due to resistance from provincial governors, but the state noticed problems surrounding the practice of conditional sales.

Moreover, at one point, the government tried to ban the seizure of collateral because of the number of disputes that arose from conditional sales. The Shah decided that debtors could hold their collateral with the payment of normal interest even after the due date. Furthermore, even after the property was delivered to the lender, the debtor could retake it after paying the entire debt and interest. This caused debtors to fail to settle their debts, and people avoided lending money to anyone, which had a negative effect on commerce. Therefore, in 1864 and 1867, the government instituted a one-year moratorium. If the debtor repaid within a year after the due date, he could regain rights to the property. If he failed to repay, the creditor received the collateral property one year after the due date.[26]

E'temad al-Saltane praised Naser al-Din Shah when he prohibited foreclosures arising from conditional sales.[27] However, even around 1900, the Ministry of Justice allowed the buyer/lender to seize collateral property.[28] It appears that the custom of conditional sales was so deeply rooted in Qajar society that the state could not control it.

Loans and credit

Unlike supporters of present-day Islamic banking, Qajar jurists permitted conditional sales (i.e., secured loans with interest) and even endorsed such deeds. This type of transaction was a combination of sale and lease contracts, and one could avoid obvious interest payments. Mirza Abu al-Qasem Qommi stated clearly:

> [QUESTION] Zeyd lent 4 tomans to 'Amr with 20 percent interest (per year), "cash to cash," without any conditional sale or lease. The contract continued for several years until Zeyd received 20 percent interest and the principal of 4 tomans still remained unpaid. After receiving 8 tomans, Zeyd arranged a conditional sale for the original 4 tomans debt with lease. Now the due date has come. Is this conditional sale and lease valid or not? And does 'Amr owe Zeyd or not?
>
> *[ANSWER] Since the original transaction has obvious interest, it is invalid. Zeyd has a credit of 4* tomans *to 'Amr while 'Amr has a claim of 8* tomans *to Zeyd. Therefore 'Amr must receive 4* tomans *from Zeyd.*[29]

It is clear that Qommi did not allow the "cash-to-cash" original transaction with interest, whereas he recognized the conditional sale with interest. However, when one examines the shari'a court records, one finds the "cash-to-cash" loan with interest.

Table 5.14 Contract types for loans and credit

	Sangelaji I		*Sangelaji II*		*Nuri*	
deyn/estedane	125	98%	355	99%	43	14%
Zemme	3	2%	2	0.5%	240	79%
qarz/estedane	0		0		14	5%
Others	0		2	0.5%	6	2%
Total	128	100%	359	100%	303	100%

As indicated in Table 5.14, records of loans and credit comprise 8 percent to 20 percent of the total. In Nuri's register, they were more prevalent than any other type transaction, and they were in second and fourth place in Sangelaji's registers. Consequently, we can say that endorsing deeds of loan and credit was one of the major activities of shari'a courts.

A few legal terms were used for loan and credit: *deyn/estedane, zemme*, and *qarz/esteqraz*. While Reza'i introduces two *zemme-name*s in his book, Eshkevari explains *qarz* and *deyn* separately.[30] An example of *deyn* from the court registers is as follows:

> [Arabic *sejell*] He acknowledged the debt (*deyn*) mentioned below on 9 Safar 1293AH.
>
> [Persian] Debt: 20 *tomans* by riyal silver coins with 26 grain weight. Creditor (*da'en*): Mirza Mohammad Taqi, a royal secretary (*monshi-e shah*). Debtor (*madyun*): Mirza Hashem Khan, a royal musketeer (*tofangchi-e homayun*). The debtor must repay after three months. On 9 Safar 1293AH.[31]

In contrast, the *zemme* record was slightly different:

> On 7 Rabi' II, Mr. Haji Sayyed Yusof Damavandi acknowledged his debt (*zemme*) of 175 *tomans* by riyal silver coins to Mr. 'Abd al-Karim, secretary for royal letters (*monshi-e rasa'el-e khasse*), which he will repay one year later than the day. The deed (*tamassok*) has a seal and an endorsement.[32]

As indicated in Table 5.14, Sangelaji mainly used the term *deyn/estedane*, while Nuri mainly used the term *zemme* for debt transactions. In terminology form and usage, both Sangelaji and Nuri used their own methods for debt transactions.

Some of the records mentioned security (*rahn*) and/or interest. The following example includes both security and interest:

> CREDITOR: Haji Hoseyn, potter (*fakhkhar*), from Khoy living in Tehran. Debtor: Baba Gharib, son of late Mashhadi Hoseyn from Hamadan living in Tehran. Debt: 56 *tomans* of *panah-abad* silver coins with 13 grain weight, among which the 50 *tomans* are the principal and the 6 *tomans* are the settlement

> fee (*mal al-mosalehe*) for six months. The debtor must repay the debt to the creditor or his legal deputy 6 lunar months later. Moreover, the debtor offered four-sixth share of his own house with a courtyard located near the Mohammadiye gate in Tehran in security for the debt, including the same share of all the belonging of the house. The house should be dealt with as security (*rahn*) after the period has terminated. In addition, the debtor nominated the creditor as his deputy and testamentary executor after his death. When the period of the debt has terminated, the creditor will sell the secured house at the market price of the time, collect the debt, and then transfer the surplus to the debtor if he is living or to his heirs if he is dead. Furthermore, Khan Jan Beg, captain of the royal camel-swivels, attended at the court and guaranteed all the debt so that he will pay all to the creditor if the period of the debt has terminated. The contract was closed in the way above mentioned on 4 Jomada II 1285AH.[33]

This transaction was prepared well for collecting debt; it had not only a security but also a guarantor. More interesting is that the transaction included a "settlement fee" for six months, which translate to an interest rate of 24 percent per year. This transaction clearly contradicted Qommi's opinion cited above because it is a "cash-to- cash" contract without using sale and lease contracts. As shown in Table 5.15, 16 to 18 percent of the loan and credit records are with interest. This is not the majority, but is difficult to ignore. The percentages of records with security vary in each register from 9 to 19 percent of the total loan and credit records. In addition, only thirty-six contracts recorded in the register have both interest and security, a number far less than that of conditional sales. In other words, in the case of loans with interest and security, people preferred conditional sales to the *deyn* or the *zemme*.

Checking the interest rate per year of loan and credit records with interest (135 records) in the three registers yields similar results to those for conditional sales. Of the transactions, 42 percent bore 20 to 30 percent interest per year, and 29 percent of the transactions carried an annual interest rate of 10 to 20 percent. The most popular annual interest rate was 24 percent, which was found in forty-two records, similar to that found in conditional sales. Moreover, like conditional sales, transactions were carried out not by professional lenders but various individuals: one can find only

Table 5.15 Interest and security in loan and credit records

	Sangelaji I		*Sangelaji II*		*Nuri*	
With interest	22	17%	57	16%	56	18%
With security	11	9%	67	19%	28	9%
With both	2	2%	20	6%	14	5%
Without both	107	83%	255	71%	233	77%
Total	128	100%	359	100%	303	100%

one *sarraf* and five *tajers* as lenders, which comprise just 4 percent of the total loan and credit transactions having interest.[34] Although their legal devices were different from those for conditional sales, some similarity did exist with the conditional sales.

Other business at the shari'a court

Confirmation

The legal deeds and *hokms* did not require more than a seal and an endorsement from a *mojtahed*. However, one comes across documents bearing multiple seals and endorsements from several *mojtaheds* sometimes. A good example is document 4 from the previous chapter, in which Najafi confirmed Molla 'Ali Asghar's *hokm* and other *mojtaheds* confirmed Najafi's endorsement.

Interestingly, the three court registers contained records of such confirmation: in particular, 6 to 9 percent of the records in Sangelaji's registers concerned confirmation records, i.e., Sangelaji confirmed a document that was drawn up before. An example is his confirmation of Haji Aqa Mohammad Najm-abadi's handwriting and seal, which confirmed a conditional sale deed dated Ramazan, 1254 AH.

> The attestation (*tashih*) made by the honor of scholars and *mojtaheds*, Haji Aqa Mohammad (Najm-abadi), – May God protect him –, is authentic. The most humble wrote this in the month of Rabi' II, 1294AH.
>
> The handwriting and seal of Haji Aqa Mohammad – May God protect him: Two scholars in charge, Aqa Akhond Molla 'Abd al-Karim and Aqa 'Ali – May god make their knowledge eternal – are correct in my opinion, and Akhond Molla Lotf 'Ali, who is a son of the seller, confirmed the transaction. I wrote this in Safar 1294AH.[35]

Following these two statements, the original sale deed was cited. Here we understand that the most important part of court records was the jurist's endorsements and confirmations. When Sangelaji endorsed a legal deed or confirmed another jurist's handwriting, he kept its record in his registers.

Table 5.16 shows the types of documents confirmed at the shari'a court. Because these confirmations occurred as part of disputes, as in the case of double *vaqf*, the percentages of two types of *hokms* were higher than the deeds. In most cases, jurists confirmed other jurist's endorsements even when they wrote their confirmations on the deeds:

Table 5.16 Types of confirmed documents

	Sangelaji I	*Sangelaji II*	*Nuri*
Hokms	32	124	1
Q &A *hokms*	12	163	0
Deeds	15	118	10
Hokms of *divankhane*	0	11	0
Total	59	416	11

Moreover, the registers include eleven records of confirmations on orders from the *divankhane*. For example:

> What was written here must be obeyed according to the *hokm* of the respectable shari'a, which was issued by this most humble servant of holy shari'a. I wrote this on 23 Moharram 1293AH.[36]

The order concerned a usurpation of heritage. The daughter of Aqa Sayyed Abu al-Hasan complained at the *divankhane* that Haji Ebrahim Kashani usurped her father's heritage worth 40,000 *tomans*. First, she brought the case to the Sangelaji's court and succeeded in getting a *hokm* for herself. Then, she went to the *divankhane* and acquired a *divankhane*'s order, which Sangelaji confirmed twelve days later.[37] As described in Chapter 2, Sangelaji sometimes cooperated with the *divankhane*. The record indicated that in some cases, the order of the *divankhane* needed to comply with the shari'a and be legitimized by the jurist.

Postscripts

I have used the term "postscripts" to refer to the notes added by jurists that were more than simple confirmations. Most postscripts concern the conditional sales mentioned above; fourteen out of eighteen postscripts in *Sangelaji I* and sixty-one out of eighty postscripts in *Sangelaji* II fall under this category.[38] These postscripts proved that a conditional sale was finalized, which means that the debtor had to deliver their security to the lender following a failure to repay his or her debt in due time. For example:

> Since repayment of equivalents for the price is not proved and the period of the option (*khiyar*) has passed, on the basis of shari'a (the conditional sale) has been finalized. The most humble wrote this on 22 Rabi' II, 1285AH.[39]

Following this postscript, the original conditional sale's transaction was explained. The debtor was Khosrow Khan Khamse'i, who borrowed 130 *tomans* for four months from 'Abbas Beg Vakil-e Tupkhane on the security of a one-twelfth share of a village in the Zanjan region. The interest (*mal al-mosalehe*) was forty *tomans* and the original deed dated 28 Sha'ban 1284 AH was recorded in the register.[40] In other words, the postscript was written in the original deed approximately eight months later.

We have come to understand that the court register recorded confirmations and postscripts, which the jurist wrote in the margins of the original deeds. Iranian court registers conformed well to the system of Iranian legal documents, to which the jurists added their own notes even months or years later.

Transcription and examination of old records

Transcripts (*savads*) were made when the courts transcribed existing documents and proved that they were authentic copies of the original documents. These can be distinguished from the confirmations and postscripts because the jurists added no comment to the document's content.[41] The record of transcription, for example, began with an Arabic endorsement:

> The transcript was based on the original including seven seals and seven endorsements. The most humble wrote this on 20 Rabi' II 1295AH.[42]

Following this endorsement, the text of the *vaqf* deed dated 18 Rabi' II 1295 AH was cited in the record. For cases in which the deed's text had already been recorded in the register, a short summary of the document was written following the endorsement. Most transcribed documents were deeds and *hokm*s arranged at shari'a courts, but an order from the Ministry of Foreign Affairs and a telegraph order of the government were also included in Sangelaji's registers.[43] In other words, non-shari'a documents could also be transcribed at the shari'a courts.

Another type of records concerns the examination of old records in the registers. Only three records in *Sangelaji I* and ten records in *Sangelaji II* belong to this category. However, they are significant because they indicate the main reason for compiling the court registers. For example,

> (Arabic) On the basis of the valid record (*sabt*) [in the register], it is legal. He wrote it on 4 Ziqa'de 1293AH.
>
> (Persian) This is the record of the land that E'tezad al-Saltane sold to 'Aziz-allah. The land covers 75 square *zar'* (=approximately 75 square meters) and the price was 500 *toman*s. The original transaction was totally recorded in my register on 28 Jomada II, 1291AH.[44]

It appears that Sangelaji confirmed the sale deed based on an older record of the registered sale deed because someone doubted its authenticity. In other words, the registers were sometimes utilized to check the validity of deeds or transactions. Moreover, three records from this category concern reissue of legal deeds based on the registers after the original deeds were lost.

Comparison of the registers

Returning to Table 3.1, significant differences in compositions can be observed between Sangelaji's and Nuri's registers. Nuri's register contains fewer *hokm*s, confirmations, and postscripts than Sangelaji's registers. On the other hand, it includes more records of loans, marriages, divorces, and settlements than Sangelaji's. How should we interpret this?

One interpretation is that this reflects their positions at the time when the registers were compiled. Sangelaji was more than fifty-five years old, and he had a career as a jurist spanning over twenty years at the time of the first register. He was ranked between the second to the fourth most prestigious *mojtahed* in Tehran in a governmental yearbook (*salname*) and was clearly considered as one of the most respectable.

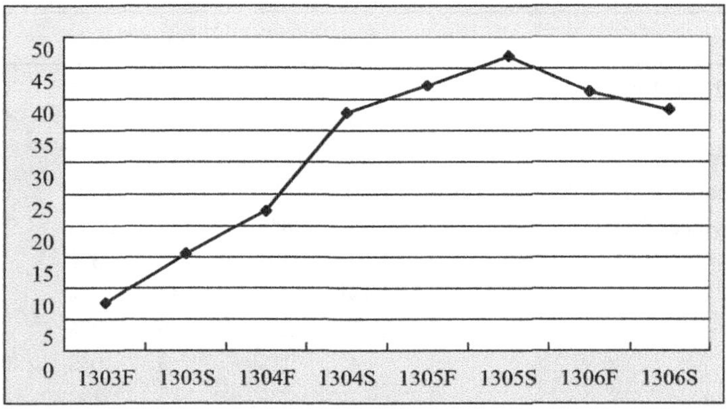

Figure 5.2 Average number of Nuri's records per month
F: the first half of the *hejri* year S: the second half of the *hejri* year

Nuri, on the other hand, was approximately forty-two years old, and as mentioned above, started keeping records forty days after he arrived in Tehran from the 'Atabat. He was thus a young newcomer at the time. He had just begun his work as a jurist. Figure 5.2 indicates the numbers of transactions per month that Nuri dealt with in six month periods.

In the first half of 1303 AH, he handled only eight transactions per month. However, that number gradually increased, and after the second half of 1304 AH, he dealt with around forty cases per month. This increase coincides with the fact that the *salname* included his name in the list of distinguished 'ulama in 1305 AH. In comparison, Sangelaji did not show an increasing trend. Sangelaji consistently handled over seventy transactions per month, and sometimes his numbers were over one hundred. In the first stage of Nuri's career as a jurist, he did not have the supreme authority among the 'ulama and did not have many clients because he was a newcomer. He initially dealt with transactions such as loans, credit, marriages, and divorces, which did not require much authority, as he tried to gain more clients.

Table 5.17 indicates the numbers of records when sorted by location of associated properties. It is natural that many of the properties were located in the city, particularly in the Sangelaj district, where the two courts were located. However, it is notable that 20 to 30 percent of the records concerned properties in other provinces. Moreover, the registers included twenty-six transactions of properties located outside Iran: all of which were related to properties in shrine cities in Ottoman Iraq. This indicates that the shari'a courts did not have an exact physical jurisdiction; if both sides agreed, a court could sell even a foreign-located property in a Tehran court.

Table 5.17 Records sorted by the location of the properties

	Sangelaji I		*Sangelaji II*		*Nuri*	
City of Tehran, Total	206	47%	753	34%	327	46%
Sangelaj	147	33%	485	22%	238	33%
Around the City	53	12%	711	32%	61	9%
Other Counties in the Tehran Province	62	14%	254	12%	110	15%
Other Provinces, Total	124	28%	484	22%	228	32%
Hamadan	24	5%	59	3%	1	0%
Qazvin	19	4%	42	2%	22	3%
Malayer	7	2%	40	2%	21	3%
Nur	4	1%	3	0%	101	14%
Outside Iran	7	2%	17	1%	2	0%
Total	440		2191		712	

Table 5.18 Records sorted by clients' *nesbe*

	Sangelaji I		*Sangelaji II*		*Nuri*	
Hamadani	29	3%	89	2%	7	0%
Qaraguzlu	17	2%	32	1%	0	0%
Nuri	34	3%	48	1%	311	20%
Tabrizi	28	3%	119	3%	39	3%
Esfahani	53	5%	139	3%	46	3%
Shirazi	34	3%	86	2%	39	3%
Qazvini	33	3%	98	2%	27	2%
Total	992	100%	4319	100%	1524	100%

The registers also reflect personal connections. Nuri's register included 101 transactions related to properties in Nur, his birthplace. Sangelaji's connection is not so obvious, but transactions concerning properties in Hamadan, Sangelaji's former living place are more numerous in Sangelaji's registers than in Nuri's register. Furthermore, Table 5.18 indicates the analysis of origin names (*nesbe*) in the registers. Transactions involving people from Nur comprise 20 percent of the total. In addition, Sangelaji's registers contain Hamadani and Qaraguzlu, a tribal group from the Hamadan province, as clients, whereas Nuri's register contains very few people from those groups. Sheykh Fazl-allah Nuri, who opened the court in Tehran for the first time, likely needed to acquire his clients among those from the same province. According to the building survey of 1853, those who came from Nur possessed more houses in the Sangelaj district than in others. This might be the reason why Nuri chose to settle in this district.

Table 5.17 reveals some other interesting trends. Sangelaji's second register concerns properties around the city (i.e., outside the old city wall) much more than other registers. Looking into the details, this is because Mirza 'Isa, the former *vazir* of Tehran,[45] sold or donated 378 pieces of vacant land between the old and new city walls. These lands were newly incorporated into the city area after the government built a new city wall and expanded the city area. This urban development project also needed to cooperate with the shari'a court because the project concerned ownership of land. In other words, the shari'a courts found clients not only among private persons but also among public figures, who ran urban development projects.

Features of Qajar shari'a courts

Based on our discussion, it is clear that shari'a courts played an important role in the economic and social life of people living in Tehran. The court registers contain details on many transactions, such as loans and credit, for which deeds are rarely preserved in Iranian archives. These transactions, along with "conditional sales," indicate that people made investments through the shari'a courts. Moreover, a shari'a court took part in the project to expand the city of Tehran; the lands of the new city area were sold or distributed through Sangelaji's court.

It is also notable that the method used to compile the three shari'a court registers fits the Qajar court system well. Because a shari'a court belonged to a *mojtahed,* a court register was compiled for a *mojtahed.* Sangelaji's registers and Nuri's register have much different forms because the two *mojtahed*s dealt with legal matters independently. While clients frequently asked Sangelaji to issue a *hokm,* Nuri rarely issued one because he was a young, inexperienced *mojtahed* at the time. The transactions the *mojtaheds* handled also somewhat reflected their personal background; one can find more clients from their birthplace than from other regions and discover more properties located there. Other business matters, such as confirmations and postscripts, were also recorded in the registers. These are unique when compared with Ottoman registers.

The flexibility of Qajar shari'a courts can also be seen. The court not only arranged contracts of conditional sales, which meant a secured loan with interest, but also offered a simple loan contract with interest, which might contradict the prohibition of *riba* in Islamic law. The *mojtahed*s undoubtedly did so because these transactions responded to social needs at that time. The convenient *mosalehe* contract prevailed for transactions such as sales, leases, and donations; of course, the *mojtaheds* respected the principles of Islamic law, but they also cared about social needs because the shari'a courts were indispensable to the city's economic and social life.

Notes

1 al-Hilli, *Tarjome-e Farsi-e Sharaye'*, 247.
2 For example, the published text of Nuri's register classifies each item, but its classifications are quite confusing and lack consistency.
3 Reza'i, ed. *Asnad-e Mahkame*, 48, 67; *Daftar-e Shar'i-e Sangelaji*, 25a, 100a, 107b, 328a, 333b.

4 The cash tax income from Natanz was around 21,158 *tomans* at that time (E'temad al-Saltane, *al-Ma'aser va al-Asar*, 323).

5 *Daftar-e Shar'i-e Sangelaji*, 311a. Seyf al-Saltane had the rank of *amir-e toman* and commander of the second Save Khalaj regiment (E'temad al-Saltane, *al-Ma'aser*, 314, 367). For bibliographical information on Vajih-allah Mirza, see Bamdad, *Sharh-e Hal*, 4:396–405.

6 *Daftar-e Shar'i-e Sangelaji*, 406b. For a biography of Haji Kazem Malek al-Tojjar, see Bamadad, *Sharh-e Hal*, 3:141–145. For Amin-e Khalvat, see ibid., 3:214–215.

7 Ettehadiye and Ruhi, eds. *Dar Mahzar*, 521. Forugh al-Dowle was a daughter of Naser al-Din Shah who married 'Ali Khan Zahir al-Dowle. See Iraj Afshar, ed. *Khaterat va Asnad-e Zahir al-Dowle* (Tehran, 1367Kh), xxxvi–xxxvii. For an excellent biography of Amin al-Zarb, see Shireen Mahdavi, *For God, Mammon and Country: A Nineteenth-Century Persian Merchant* (Boulder, 1999).

8 Ettehadiye and Ruhi, eds. *Dar Mahzar*, 555.

9 Twenty-six records in *Sangelaji I*, sixty-three in *Sangelaji II*, and thirty-six records in *Nuri*, respectively.

10 *Hebe* deed of two *qanat*s in Shemiran between Hasan 'Ali Mirza and Manuchehr Khan Mo'tamad al-Dowle, dated 1 Moharram 1240 AH, Golestan, no.4349.

11 Reza'i, ed. *Asnad-e Mahkame*, 110. Aqa Musa, father of Aqa Asad -allah, was Agha Bahram's testamentary executor and established the *vaqf* for the *takye* in 1861. *Vaqf* deed of Aqa Musa Tajer, dated 21 Shavval 1277 AH, Owqaf no.320.

12 *Daftar-e Shar'i-e Sangelaji*, 440a.

13 Maxime Rodinson, *Islam and Capitalism*, trans. Brian Pearce (London, 1974), 35–37.

14 Ken'ichi Isogai, "Research on Formal Aspects of Central Asian Documents: Deeds of Bay'-i Ja'iz," in *Historical Research on Common Identity and Islam in Central Asia*, ed. Yashushi Shinmen (Hachioji, 2002), 51–66; Abdülaziz Bayındır, s.v. "Bey' bi'l-Vefa," *Türkiye Diyanet Vakfı İslâm Ansiklopedisi* 6 (1992): 20–22.

15 *Daftar-e Shar'i-e Sangelaji*, 358a

16 Schacht, *An Introduction to Islamic Law*, 153; Isogai, "Research on Formal Aspects," 61.

17 Ettehadiye and Ruhi, eds. *Dar Mahzar*, 620–621. The interest was only one *man* of *nabat* from Yazd, the price of which was almost nothing. The debtor had a duty to repay by ten-time installments in three years and seven months.

18 *Daftar-e Shar'i-e Sangelaji*, 305a. Qamar al-Saltane was a daughter of Fath 'Ali Shah and the wife of Mirza Hoseyn Khan Sepahsalar. Dust Mohammad Khan Mo'ayyer al-Mamalek succeeded his father's title position in 1869. Bamdad, *Sharh-e Hal*, 1:425–426, 502–503; E'temad al-Saltane, *Mer'at al-Boldan*, 1588.

19 Mary Sheil, *Glimpses of Life and Manners Glimpses of Life and Manners in Persia* (London, 1856), 143.

20 *Daftar-e Shar'i-e Sangelaji*, 288a; Ettehadiye and Ruhi, eds. *Dar Mahzar*, 86, 626. Floor also did not pay much attention to secured loans in his article on *sarraf*s. Willem Floor, "Bankers (*Sarrafs*) in Qajar Iran," *ZDMG* 129 (1979), 271.

21 Asghar Mahdavi and Iraj Afshar, ed. *Asnad-e Tejarat-e Iran dar Sal-e 1287 Qamari* (Tehran, 1380Kh), 44.

22 Asghar Mahdavi, "The Significance of Private Archives for the Study of the Economic and Social History of Iran in the Late Qajar Period," *Iranian Studies* 16 (1983): 261, 276.

23 E'temad al-Saltane, *al-Ma'aser va al-Asar*, 176–177.

24 *Ruzname-e Dowlat-e 'Aliye* no.509:5, 9 Jomada II, 1278AH.

25 *Ruzname-e Vaqaye' al-Ettefaqiye* no.407:3–4, 11 Rabi ' II 1275AH.

26 *Ruzname-e Dowlat-e 'Aliye* no.562:5–6, 30 Safar 1281; Ibid. no.611:3, 10 Rajab 1284AH.

27 E'temad al-Saltane, *al-Ma'aser va al-Asar*, 176–177.

28 Zare'i Mehrvarz, "Asnad-e Divan-e 'Adalat," 295–296.

29 Mirza Abu al-Qasem Qommi, *Jame' al-Shatat*, ed. Mortaza Razavi (Tehran, 1371–1375Kh), 2:229–230.

30 Reza'i, *Dar-amadi*, 82–85, 106–107; Eshkevari, *Asnad-e Shar'i*, 48, 86–88. Reza'i called the first one *marahane-name* because it also contains stipulations about security. Eshkevari's documents do not correspond to his explanation well; he introduced two deeds of *zemme* for *qarz* and three deeds of *zemme* for *deyn*. Only one deed of *deyn* was included in his explanation of *deyn*.

31 *Daftar-e Shar'i-e Sangelaji*, 7a.

32 Ettehadiye and Ruhi, eds. *Dar Mahzar*, 564.

33 Reza'i, ed. *Asnad-e Mahkame*, 192.

34 Ibid., 42; *Daftar-e Shar'i-e Sangelaji*, 117a, 264b, 285a, 361a; Ettehadiye and Ruhi, eds. *Dar Mahzar*, 247.

35 *Daftar-e Shar'i-e Sangelaji*, 92b.

36 Ibid., 4a.

37 Ibid. Sangelaji's *hokm* that was brought to the *divankhane* was not recorded in the register. Another record concerning the dispute is found in the register: a question-answer *hokm* dated Sha'ban 1293AH. *Daftar-e Shar'i-e Sangelaji*, 226b.

38 Nuri's register contained only five records of postscripts. Among them, one record relates to a conditional sale.

39 Reza'i, ed. *Asnad-e Mahkame*, 172.

40 Ibid. The record of the original deed is found in: Reza'i, ed. *Asnad-e Mahkame*, 30.

41 For more on how the deeds (*qabales*) were annotated, transcribed, and registered in early modern Iran, see Nobuaki Kondo, "The Lives of *Qabalahs*: Annotation, Transcription and Registration of Documents in Early Modern Iran," in *Lecteurs et copistes dans les traditions manuscrites iraniennes, indiennes et centrasiatiques*, eds. Nalini Balbir and Maria Szuppe, *Eurasian Studies* 12 (2014): 561–575.

42 *Daftar-e Shar'i-e Sangelaji*, 301b.

43 Reza'i, ed. *Asnad-e Mahkame*, 134; *Daftar-e Shar'i-e Sangelaji*, 11a.

44 *Daftar-e Shar'i-e Sangelaji*, 235b. Concerning E'tezad al-Saltane, see Abbas Amanat, s.v. "E'tezad al-Saltana, 'Aliqoli Mirza," *Encyclopaedia Iranica* 8 (1998): 669–672.

45 He was the *vazir* of Tehran from 1867 to 1874 and from 1891 to 1892. His father, Mirza Musa was also the *vazir* of Tehran from 1853 to 1859 and from 1860 to 1865.

6 *Vaqf*s in Tehran

The *vaqf*, an Islamic endowment, is also an Islamic legal transaction: *vaqf* deeds were prepared at the shari'a courts and endorsed by the *mojtahed*s. In this regard, there is no difference between *vaqf*s and other transactions analyzed in the previous chapter. From Table 3.1, one realizes that records of *vaqf*s were not dominant in the court registers: they comprised only 0.3 to 1.7 percent of the total records.

The most important feature of the *vaqf*s is that in theory, once a *vaqf* is established, it is valid in perpetuity. The *vaqf* property is not to be sold or divided: it is entrusted to a *vaqf* administrator under the conditions set by the founder. For this reason, although the *vaqf* was not a dominant transaction at the shari'a court, it had a long term effect on the society. In other words, the *vaqf* is a good example through which to assess the influence of Islamic law on society.

Since a *vaqf* is perpetual, *vaqf* deeds have a longer life than other shari'a court documents. As a result, one of the largest collections of shari'a court documents in Iran is that of the Vaqf Organization in Tehran, in which *vaqf* related documents are preserved. Although *vaqf* studies on Iran have developed in recent years, most of them dealt with a few *vaqf*s as case studies. Therefore, in this chapter, I investigate 260 *vaqf*s in Tehran from the thirteenth century AH (1786–1883) and explore their impact on urban society.

Two articles have tried to investigate all of the *vaqf*s in Qajar Tehran. Ettehadiye analyzed *vaqf*s in two building surveys, while Shah Hoseyni acquired statistical information from the collection of the Vaqf Organization.[1] I will point out the technical problems in these articles. Hoseyni Balaghi's book is not a systematic work on the *vaqf*s in Tehran, but is useful because he produced a catalogue of *vaqf* properties in Tehran.[2]

State control of the *vaqf*s

Since the *vaqf* deeds were prepared at shari'a courts, the Qajar state never controlled the establishment of *vaqf*s. The *vaqf* administrators were appointed by *mojtahed*s. The shari'a court records included eight deed-type *hokm*s, by which Sangelaji and Nuri appointed persons to be *vaqf* administrators.[3] Although we know that Naser al-Din Shah issued royal edicts for appointing *vaqf* administrators, those cases are rare. For example, Naser al-Din Shah appointed Aqa Sayyed Mohammad Baqer as a *vaqf* administrator of Mirza Saleh Madrase, as indicated by a royal edict dated 1860. However, the administrator was first appointed by a member of the 'ulama in Tehran and then confirmed by Sheykh Mortaza Ansari, the leading jurist in Najaf; the royal edict was issued following these jurists' decision.[4] In other words, the state did not intervene in *vaqfs* directly.

However, this does not mean that the Qajar state did not have an interest in *vaqfs*. 'Abbas Mirza, who was Governor General of Azerbaijan from 1799 to1833, ordered a survey of *vaqf* lands along with crown lands (*khalese-e divani*) in order to use their income for the purpose of the *vaqf*: This was part of his reform program(*nezam-e jadid*).[5] In 1841, a *vaqf* inventory of Yazd province was compiled, although the inventory did not cover all the *vaqfs* in the province.[6] In 1844–1845, Mirza Mohamamad Hasan Ashtiyani Mostowfi compiled a *vaqf* inventory of all the provinces in Iran based on documents from the provinces: unfortunately, only a preface of the inventory has survived to today.[7]

Another work related to *vaqfs* is "the inventory of the royal property (*Surat-e Amlak-e Khasse*)," dated 1843.[8] This covers all the provinces in Iran, including Tehran. According to the preface, Haji Mirza Aqasi, Grand Vazir at the time, ordered a compilation of the inventory because documents concerning the royal property and *vaqf* property of sacred places had been confused for a long time. The staff of the fiscal department (*daftarkhane*) compared old inventories with current taxation, compiled a perfect inventory, and kept the documents in the royal treasury. This was in order to protect royal and *vaqf* property from injustice and usurpation.[9]

Table 6.1 indicates *vaqf* property in the city of Tehran listed in the inventory.[10] Only eight *vaqf* properties are mentioned. The most obvious one is the *vaqf* on behalf of Shah Mosque (Majed-e Shah). The mosque was built by the order of Fath 'Ali Shah in 1830. According to the summary of the *vaqf* deed, the Shah endowed the mosque with thirty-six shops and a public bath,[11] so the inventory

Table 6.1 Vaqf property in the inventory of the royal property dated 1843

Vaqf *property*	*Number, quantity*	Vaqf *purpose*
Small bazaar in Arg	all	Masjed-e Daftar
Shops in the Grand Bazaar	36	Masjed-e Shah
Saray of Haji Mostafa Khan	1	Emamzade Zeyd
Saray of 'Abd-allah Khan	1	'Atabat
Public bath in the Grand Bazaar	1	Masjed-e Shah
Qanat of Mehrjerd	7 *mahche*	
Qanat of Sangelaj	4 *mahche*	
Qanat of Zu al-Qarneyn	12 *mahche*	
Land of Chahardah Ma'sum		Chahardah Ma'sum

is correct. The Daftar mosque was located near the *daftarkhane* in the south west of the Arg.[12] The *saray* of 'Abd-allah Khan was once in the possession of Aqa Mohammad Shah and Fath 'Ali Shah. It is likely that the *saray* later became a *vaqf* on behalf of the 'Atabat, i.e., Shi'i shrines in Iraq. The *vaqf* for the Chahardah Ma'sum (the fourteen infallibles in Shi'i Islam) was a special *vaqf*, first established by the Safavids in the sixteenth century, which we will discuss in detail in the last chapter. The inventory covered the *vaqfs* that had a connection with the state or the royal family. On the other hand, the *vaqf* on behalf of the Old Friday Mosque and that of Marvi Madrase, both of which had considerable properties, were not mentioned at all. This might suggest that the state control of the *vaqfs* was still quite limited at that time.

It is not clear how much the creation of the Ministry of Pension and Endowment (*Vezarat-e Vaza'ef va Mowqufat*) in 1854 changed the situation. According to the official gazette, the first minister, Mirza Mohammad Hoseyn 'Azod al-Molk, received the registers of pensions and endowments from the royal *daftarkhane*. The gazette proclaimed that all of the *vaqf* administrators and those related to the *vaqf* property must not intervene in the affairs of the *vaqf* without consulting the minister or his agent.[13] Officially, the Minister of Pension and Endowment had a duty to make sure the *vaqf* income was used for the purpose stipulated by the *vaqf*-deed.[14]

However, the revised inventory of the royal property, which was compiled under the Grand Vazir, Mirza Aqa Khan Nuri, 1851–1858, did not contain any new *vaqf* property in Tehran.[15] The building survey of 1853 included valuable information on *vaqf* property in the city, as we will see below, but the structure of the survey was difficult to use for controlling the *vaqfs*. On the other hand, we know that 'Azod al-Molk conducted a survey of *vaqf* property for Emam Reza Shrine in Mashhad in 1857; this was the first full scale survey after the Afsharid period.[16]

The fiscal book of the Tehran province in 1870 and that of Iran in 1886–1887 contained information on some *vaqf* properties in the province. Table 6.2 indicates the details from the book of 1870.[17] The *vaqfs* on behalf of five shrines,[18] four *madrases*, and three graves of political figures were mentioned. The book indicates that for these *vaqf* properties, the local government had the means to know their income.

However, since there were twenty-five *madrases* in Tehran at that time, less than one-sixth of the *madrases*' *vaqfs* were controlled by the local government. None of the nine shrines in the city (including the most famous, Emamzade Zeyd) that were listed in the building survey of 1853 was included in the fiscal book. It is likely that the local government controlled only a small part of the *vaqfs* in Tehran. The situation did not change much in the fiscal book of 1886–1887. Three more shrines[19] were included in the book, while Manuchehriye and the Saray of Armenians were excluded from the book.[20] In sum, even towards the end of the nineteenth century, the *vaqf* property controlled by the state is quite limited.

Table 6.2 Vaqf property in the fiscal book of the Tehran province in 1870

Vaqf *purpose*	Vaqf *property*	*Income in cash*	*Income in kind*
Emam Reza Shrine	Evin Village	3.4983 t	17.34 kh
	Pigeon Tower	2.6866 t	Fodder 10.86 kh
	Khordin Village	100 t	Straw 10.86 kh
	Rashid-abad Village in Ghar	0.16 t	100 kh
Public bath of Shah 'Abd al-'Azim	*karvansara* and shops at the shrine	145 t	
Emamzade Gazorsang	Meshgin-abad Village in Savojbolagh	38.92 t	0.80 kh
Candle for the Shrine of Lot	Peygambar Qoli Hamlet	2.08 t	Wheat 1 kh Barely 1 kh
Emamzade Voshgin	Voshgin Hamlet	2.5 t	3 kh
Madrase-e Fakhriye (Marvi Madrase)	Sarchashme Garden in Tajrish	12 t	
	Do baradaran Village	10 t	
Madrase and Mosque of Sepahsalar	Karim-abad Village	8 t	6 kh
Madrase-e Molla Aqa Reza (Nezam al-'Olama)	Firuz-abad Village	100 t	Fodder 100 kh Straw 100 kh
Madrase-e Haji Mirza Reza Qoli	Riye Village		Fodder 30 kh Straw 30 kh
Grave of Zell al-Soltan (For candles)	Saray of Armenians* (Sabze Meydan)	100 t 30 t	
Grave of Haji Mirza Aqasi	Hammam-e Chal Hammam at the Mosque's gate	145 t 160 t	
Candles for the grave of Manuchehr Khan	Manuchehriye Village*	100 t	
Mourning ceremonies at *takyes*		100 t	Grains 5 kh
The poor (Nezam al-'Olama)	Firuz-abad Village		Fodder 30 kh Straw 30 kh
Descendants of Molla 'Abd-allah	*Khalese* shops	102 t	
Haji Mohammad Taqi, locksmith	Shops	7.2 t	
Minors of Esma'il Dorqor-abadi	A hamlet	5 t	Fodder 20 kh Straw 20 kh
	Qeysariye (in the Grand Bazaar?)	60 t	
	Hesar-e Amir Village	125 t	
	Amin-abad Village	10 t	10kh

* Property does not appear in the fiscal book of 1886–1887 t: *toman* kh: *kharvar*

Table 6.3 New *vaqf* entries in the fiscal book of 1886–1887

	Place	*Income in Cash*	*Income in Goods*
Candles for Emamzade Saleh	Tajrish	11.98 t	
Candles for Emamzade Hasan	Mahal-e Ji	14.4 t	
Staff for Emamzade Andarman	Andarman	0.16 t	8 kh
Old *sayyed* land-owners	Zeyn-abad	10 t	10 kh

t: *toman* kh: *kharvar*

The reason is obvious. When one wanted to establish a *vaqf*, one would go to a shari'a court and prepare the *vaqf* deed there. In this process, the state had no chance to register the *vaqf*. Some *vaqfs*, especially *vaqfs* for the shrines, were under state control, but the majority was out of the control of the state.

General survey of *vaqfs* in Tehran

Since the state did not have full control over the *vaqfs*, there was no complete inventory of them. As we saw above, we have only a partial list of the *vaqfs* that appear to be controlled by the state. Instead of a *vaqf* inventory, two types of sources are available for general survey of the *vaqfs* in Tehran. One is the building surveys of 1853 and 1899–1900, which cover all the building in Tehran and indicate the ownership of the buildings, including the *vaqfs*, at that time. Ettehadiye published an article giving an analysis of the surveys, but here we will see a more accurate analysis based on the database.

The other is the *vaqf* deeds from Qajar Tehran. I have collected 260 *vaqf* deeds, both published and unpublished, dated to the thirteenth century AH (between 1201/1786 and 1300/1882), from archives and other sources. These concern the *vaqfs* with properties or endowed institutions located in the city. Among them, 229 deeds are preserved in the Vaqf Organization in Tehran, seventeen deeds are found in the shari'a court registers, three deeds are from other libraries, one deed is from the wall inscription, and ten deeds have been published in various journals and books. As mentioned in Chapter 1, since Tehran became a Qajar capital in the fall of 1785 (1200AH), the date range of the *vaqf* deeds is almost identical to the first 100 years under the Qajar rule over the city. As mentioned above, Shah Hoseyni published a short article based on the documents preserved by the Vaqf Organization in Tehran. However, her analysis is too rough to understand the general trend of the *vaqfs*.[21] Also, it is unknown which documents she referred to. I include a list of the deeds in the appendix.

Before the analysis, let us take a look at the distribution of the dates of the *vaqf* deeds (Table 6.4). The deeds dated after 1260/1846–1847 reach 191 and comprise 73 percent of the total. This is partly because later deeds had a better chance to survive, but also because the city of Tehran developed rapidly during the nineteenth century. The more people lived in Tehran, the more *vaqfs* were established there.

Table 6.4 Dates of the *vaqf* deeds analyzed in Chapter 6

Years (Hijra/C.E)	*Number of* vaqf *deeds*
1201/1786–7~1210/1795–6	1
1211/1796–7~1220/1805–6	7
1221/1806–7~1230/1814–5	8
1231/1815–6~1240/1824–5	6
1241/1825–6~1250/1834–5	19
1251/1835–6~1260/1844–5	28
1261/1845–6~1270/1853–4	39
1271/1854–5~1280/1863–4	38
1281/1864–5~1290/1873–4	51
1291/1874–5~1300/1882–3	63
Total	260

Founder (vaqef)

Who established *vaqfs* in Qajar Tehran? Among the 260 *vaqf* deeds, 51 deeds (10 percent) include a female founder.[22] Therefore, 209 *vaqfs* were established by exclusively male founders. That percentage almost coincides with the case of Yazd: nine female founders were found among forty-two *vaqfs*, of which the founders were identified in the *vaqf* survey of 1841.[23]

One can investigate the social status of the founders as far as one has suitable information. Eighteen *vaqfs* (7 percent) were established by founders from the Qajar royal family and seventy-two *vaqfs* (28 percent) were donated by bureaucrats and military officers. Twenty-six ‘ulama’s *vaqfs* (10 percent) are found in the *vaqf* deeds, while the merchants and the artisans established sixty-eight *vaqfs* (26 percent). We can say that bureaucrats, military officers, merchants, and artisans had major roles in the establishment of *vaqfs* in Qajar Tehran. On the other hand, the *sayyeds* (descendants of Prophet Mohammad) contributed to nineteen *vaqfs* as founders. However, it is difficult to consider this as one social group because they included various people: two were ‘ulama, three were merchants and artisans, and one was a bureaucrat.[24]

It is possible to identify the social status of the fifty-one female founders from their fathers or husbands: thirteen founders were from the royal family, eleven from the merchants and artisans, ten from the bureaucrats and military officers, and two from the ‘ulama. The female founders from the royal family are remarkable because they surpass the male founders from the royal family (five *vaqfs*).

Among 260 founders, thirty-four founders (14 percent) are founders not in reality but in form. They established the *vaqfs* as testamentary executors (*vasi*) appointed by deceased persons in accordance with the latter’s will. Among them, thirteen executors were relatives of the deceased, while another thirteen executors were from the ‘ulama class. In other words, half of the *vaqf* founders from the ‘ulama class founded them as testamentary executors. Six merchants and artisans and one bureaucrat appointed the ‘ulama as executor for the *vaqf*.

More details are following:

(a) Royal family

Only three *vaqf*s were established by the Shahs: Fath ‘Ali Shah’s *vaqf* on behalf of Shah Mosque a *vaqf* for a new mosque, and a *vaqf* of a new *qanat* by Naser al-Din Shah. The Shah’s wives, including Naser al-Din Shah’s mother, Mahd-e ‘Olya, and his influential wives in the *haram*, Amin-e Aqdas and Anis al-Dowle, founded six *vaqf*s.

(b) Bureaucrats and military officers

Seven Grand Vazirs’ *vaqf*s were included in this category. Mirza Mohammad Shafi‘ (two *vaqf*s), Mohammad Khan Qajar Sepahsalar, and Mirza Hoseyn Khan Sepahsalar established *vaqf*s on behalf of *madrase*s that they had founded. Aqa Khan Nuri endowed his new mosque with the *vaqf*. He also established the other two *vaqf*s of *qanat*s.

Among financial officers, accountants (*mostowfi*s) founded six *vaqf*s: one of them, the *vaqf* of Mirza Yusof Ashrafi, was huge, including two villages in Ghar county, public bathes, shops in Mazandaran province, and shops and baths in the Sangelaj district of Tehran.[25] In addition, treasurers (*sanduqdar*, *khazane-dar*) established four *vaqf*s. Besides the financial officers, royal attendants such as *gholam-e pishkhedmat* and *pishkhedmat-e khasse* founded five *vaqf*s.

Local officers also established *vaqf*s. ‘Isa Khan Qajar, the governor of Tehran province, endowed the mourning ceremonies for Shi‘i Imams with his five *vaqf*s. Another governor, Qanbar ‘Ali Khan, founded a *vaqf* on behalf of his *madrase*. Mahmud Khan Kalantar, who took over the city administration, established two *vaqf*s. Another *vaqf* was founded by his heirs. All of them concerned the mourning ceremonies for the Imams.

Genuine military officers are not so considerable among the founders. A brigadier-general (*sartip*) and two majors (*yavar*s) established a total of three *vaqf*s. A large *vaqf* of a *qanat* for the Chalmeydan district was established by Hoseyn Khan Shehab al-Molk. He was from a Turkic tribal group, the Shahsavan, had a long career as a military officer, and received the rank of commander of ten thousand soldiers (*amir-e toman*). In addition, a paymaster (*lashkar-nevis*) and another military administrator (*vakil-e lashkar*) established two *vaqf*s.

Thirteen *vaqf*s were established by non-royal Qajars, including those of the Grand Vazir and the governor of Tehran. Among them, the Shambayati subgroup founded four *vaqf*s. It was common for those from the tribal groups to establish *vaqf*s.

(c) ‘Ulama

As mentioned above, the ‘ulama established thirteen *vaqf*s as testamentary executors. Prominent jurists, such as Molla ‘Ali Kani, Hadi Najm-abadi, and Fazl-allah Nuri, were included among these executor-founders. In addition, though he was not an executor, Sheykh ‘Abd al-Hoseyn Sheykh al-‘Eraqeyn founded a *vaqf* in place of the mother of Mirza Taqi Khan Amir Kabir, the famous reformer. This was a complicated transaction: first she transferred the property to Sheykh 'Abd al-Hoseyn, then the jurist established a *vaqf*, part of which benefited her.

Among the other twelve founders of the *vaqf*s, the most famous jurist was Esma'il Behbahani, father of 'Abd-allah Behbahani. He endowed those of his descendants who became jurists with the *vaqf*. In total, the 'ulama's endowments were limited in number.

(d) Merchants and artisans

Among the sixty-eight founders who were merchants and artisans, the wholesale merchants (*tajer*s) are the most remarkable: thirty *tajer*s established *vaqf*s. However, among them, eleven were executor-founders; four of them were executors for their families, while in three cases they executed the wills of a eunuch, a bureaucrat, and a business partner.

Two of the merchant *vaqf*s were of a large scale: one was the *vaqf* on behalf of Fathiye Madrase established by Haji Abu al-Fath Tehrani, and the other was the *vaqf* for Jazayeri Mosque founded by Haji Mohammad Ebrahim Esfahani. In addition, Haji Aqa Tajer Tehrani built a mosque and a water reservoir (*ab-e anbar*) on the outside of the Dulab gate, made them a *vaqf*, and endowed them with a *vaqf* shop.

Various kinds of merchants and artisans established *vaqf*s: Four cloth dealers (*bazzaz*), four architects (*me'mar*), three dealers of spices and perfumes (*'attar*), two gold-lace makers (*'alaqeband*), two butchers (*qassab*), two tobacco sellers (*tanbakuforush*), two bath keepers (*hammami*), a banker (*sarraf*), a goldsmith (*zargar*), a cook (*ashpaz*), a baker (*khabbaz*), a grocer (*baqqal*), a dyer (*sabbagh*), a tanner (*dabbagh*), a stonemason (*hajjar*), and a potter (*kuzegar*). The founders were not always influential persons but often ordinary people.

Vaqf *property*

Table 6.5 indicates the *vaqf* properties described in the 260 *vaqf* deeds. More than half of the *vaqf*s contained shops, while twenty-three percent of them included houses. Urban properties surpassed rural properties in number: villages and hamlets were contained by only nine percent of the *vaqf*s. Naturally, villages and hamlets had more economic value and the *vaqf*s that contained them were of a larger scale. However, a greater number of *vaqf*s held shops as their property.

This coincides with the columns in the table denoting locations of the *vaqf* properties. Most *vaqf*s contained urban property. Among the districts of the city, the properties located in the Grand Bazaar and 'Udlajan are notable. On the other hand, properties in the counties and other provinces are not so many. Of course, the table did not count all the *vaqf* property located in the counties and other provinces: more properties in those places were included in the *vaqf*s that did not relate to Tehran. However, it can be said that the *vaqf*s did not contribute to the transferal of rural wealth to the city, although some researchers emphasize the transferal as a function of the *vaqf* institution. This is probably because the city had exceptionally developed and attracted endowments to such an extent that the *vaqf* properties in rural areas became fairly small in number in comparison with the urban properties.

Table 6.5 Number of *vaqfs* and their locations sorted by types of property

Included vaqf *property*	Vaqfs *total*	*Inside the city*							*Outside the city*	*Counties*	*Other provinces*
		Sum	*A*	*U*	*S*	*C*	*B*	*GB*			
Shops	148 (57%)	136	2	33	19	14	15	39	14	2	1
Houses	62 (23%)	51		20	10	12	7		6		2
Sarays	41 (16%)	35		12		5		18	5	2	1
Public Baths	29 (11%)	26		5	6	4	6	4	3		1
Villages or hamlets	23 (9%)									18	9
Pieces of land	21 (8%)	12		3	3	6			5	4	1
Bagh	11 (4%)	3		2	1	2			3	6	1
Ice house	9 (3%)	2		1	1				7		
Qanat	8 (3%)	3	1		1	1	3		3	1	2
Small bazaar	6 (2%)	6			4			1			
Water mill	4 (2%)								1	3	
Total	260 (100%)	250 (96%)	4	64	36	32	31	58	32 (12%)	24 (9%)	11 (4%)

A: Arg, U:'Udlajan, S: Sangelaj, C: Chalmeydan, D: Bazar district, GB: Grand Bazaar

Here we give the details of *vaqf* properties:

(a) Shops, houses, sarays, and public baths

Among the *vaqfs* endowed with shops listed in Table 6.6, seventy-eight *vaqfs* did not have any other property than shops. Out of these seventy-eight *vaqfs*, sixty-four had only five shops or less. On the other hand, out of thirty-four *vaqfs* endowed only with houses, thirty-three included only a house: the other one consisted of two houses. If one considers *vaqfs* with five shops or less and with two houses or less as small *vaqfs*, 107 *vaqfs* (41 percent of the total) belonged to this category. Out of these 107 small *vaqfs*, twenty-one were established by bureaucrats and military officers, thirty-three were founded by merchants and artisans, and twenty-six were created by women. In fact, half of women's *vaqfs* in general can be considered small.

The building surveys provide detailed information on the *vaqf* properties in the city. Table 6.6 indicates the number of *vaqfs* and total shops in each district in Tehran. As far as the building surveys show, only ten percent of the total shops belonged to the *vaqfs*. One can doubt the reliability of this information. In particular, the survey of 1899–1900 does not indicate the type of shops, and ignores the *vaqf* property of Shah Mosque and Old Friday Mosque, which could lower the *vaqf* rate. However, the survey of 1853 refers to the owner and type of each shop, and appears to be more reliable.

Concerning districts in 1853, one can see a higher *vaqf* rate of shops in the Arg, the Bazar districts, and the Grand Bazaar, while the Chalmeydan district and area outside of the city wall did not have many *vaqfs*. Chalmeydan was a very dirty district and even a rubbish heap was found there: no *madrase* was built there until 1859–1860.[26] On the other hand, in 1899–1900, the Bazar and 'Udlajan districts

Table 6.6 Vaqf and total shops in the building surveys

1853			*1899–1900*		
Districts	*Total*	Vaqf *shops*	*Districts*	*Total*	Vaqf *shops*
Arg	123	26 (21.1%)	Dowlat	2114	127 (6.0%)
'Udlajan	1127	125 (11.1%)	'Udlajan	1246	140 (11.2%)
Sangelaj	525	60 (11.4%)	Sangelaj	1000	86 (8.6%)
Chalmeydan	485	29 (6.0%)	Chalmeydan	1428	120 (8.4%)
Bazar district	653	120 (18.4%)	Bazar district	1006	138 (13.7%)
Grand Bazaar	1204	176 (14.6%)	Grand Bazaar	1218	115 (9.4%)
Outside City Wall	203	1 (0.5%)			
Sum	4320	537 (12.4%)		8012	726 (9.1%)

had higher *vaqf* rates of shops while the rate of the Dowlat district was lower. The Dowlat district was an area newly developed after 1881, and it included mainly the former Arg district and northern lands outside of the old city wall: foreign embassies and mansions of political figures were located there. It can be said that the newly developed area did not have many *vaqf* shops because the *vaqf* shop rate was higher in the oldest commercial districts of Bazar and 'Udlajan.

On *vaqf* houses, the building survey does not have any information. In the survey of 1853, there were only twenty-nine *vaqf* houses, which comprised 0.4 percent of the total houses. The survey of 1899–1900 did not provide different results: it contained 116 houses, which made up 0.8 percent of the total houses.[27] These percentages appear to be too low and the surveys might not have counted *vaqf* houses accurately. Even so, it is not possible to suppose that the *vaqfs* of houses prevailed in Qajar Tehran. Unlike Ottoman Istanbul, where the *vaqfs* of houses were very common,[28] Qajar Tehran did not see many of such *vaqfs*.

Also concerning *sarays* the building surveys are unreliable. The survey of 1853 referred to only one *vaqf timche* in districts other than the Grand Bazaar,[29] while it lists twenty-one *sarays* there. The *vaqf* deeds indicate that at least one *saray* in 'Udlajan and two *sarays* in Chalmeydan became *vaqf* property before 1853.[30] The survey of 1899–1900 lists twelve *vaqf sarays* (seven percent) among 168 *sarays* in districts other than the Grand Bazaar, which appears too few. At least sixteen *sarays* are mentioned as *vaqf* property in the *vaqf* deeds from the years 1786–1883. The details of the *sarays* in the Grand Bazaar will be discussed in the next chapter.

The public baths (*hammam*) were also important *vaqf* property. The building survey of 1853 lists fourteen *vaqf* public baths, which comprise 10 percent of 146 total public baths in the city. The survey of 1899–1900 is not reliable for information on *vaqf* public baths, and refers to only 7 out of 185 baths in the city. At least from the *vaqf* deeds, one can find thirty-eight *hammams*, a part or the whole of which became *vaqf* properties. For example, five-sixths of a share of Hammam-e Qeble with two buildings, which is not referred to as a *vaqf* in the building survey, became part of the *vaqf* established by Haji Aqa Mohammad Qazvini in 1859.[31]

Though the building surveys omitted some *vaqf* properties, there is no evidence that most of the *sarays* and public baths belonged to the *vaqfs*. Since *vaqf* founders purchased existing *sarays* and public baths more than they built new ones for establishing a *vaqf*, these properties had been private properties until then. The case of the Grand Bazaar will be analyzed in the next chapter.

(b) Villages, lands, and qanats

Mainly, the bureaucrats and the military officers founded the *vaqfs* that included villages. They established twelve *vaqfs* of villages while, other than them, only a surgeon and a woman established such *vaqfs*. Also, the *vaqfs* that contained the properties outside of the city of Tehran (i.e., in the counties of the province or in the other provinces) were established mainly by the bureaucrats and the military officers (twelve *vaqfs*). The merchants and the artisans founded three such *vaqfs* and women established three. It is natural that the large scale *vaqfs* that contained villages or properties in other provinces were mainly established by the bureaucrats and the military officers.

Nineteen *vaqfs* included properties in the counties of Tehran Province: seven in Varamin, six in Ghar, and five in Shahriyar. Among the other provinces, five *vaqfs* contained villages in Mazandaran, and two *vaqfs* included villages in Qazvin.

Three large-scale *vaqfs* are found in the collection of *vaqf* deeds. The first one is the *vaqf* of Mirza Karim Mostowfi Tehrani, established in 1797 mainly for his descendants, which included ten villages in Tehran Province.[32] The second was established by Aqa Sayyed ‘Aliya Mostowfi in 1802, mainly on behalf of his descendants, which contained shares of thirty-five villages in Qazvin, Shahriyar, Savojbolagh, and Tarom.[33] The last was the *vaqf* of Mirza Hoseyn Khan Sepahsalar, a famous modern reformer, on behalf of Madrase-e Naseri (Madrase-e Sepahsalar or Mottahari) established in 1880, which included ten villages in Zanjan, Qazvin, Ghar, Varamin, and Taleqan.[34]

The *vaqf* founders endowed pieces of land for various purposes: they built a *takye*, shops, or houses in those lands in the city. Two *vaqf* pieces of land outside the city wall were used for a graveyard and a mortuary (*ghassalkhane*), while another was an agricultural land.[35] In the counties and other provinces, four pieces of agricultural land became *vaqf* property. In more common cases, the founders endowed lands along with buildings or preferred villages as *vaqf* property.

Though only seven *vaqfs* were included in our collection, the *vaqfs* of *qanats* were also important to the city of Tehran because the water supply through *qanats* was indispensable for the inhabitants. Already in the Safavid period, shares of Sangelaj and Mehrjerd Qanats were contained in the large *vaqf* of Madrase-e Hakim Hashem dated 1691.[36] As shown in Table 6.7, the inventory of royal properties included shares of Sangelaj, Mehrjerd, and Zu al-Qarneyn Qanats as *vaqfs*. Shares of these three *qanats* were endowed by Mirza Karim Mostowfi in 1797. ‘Abedin Beg Sandqdar purchased a one-twentieth share of Mehrjerd Qanat at the price of eighteen *tomans*, and made it a *vaqf* mainly for the Arg and the Grand Bazaar in 1799.[37] These *qanats* might be all that the city of Tehran had until the early nineteenth century.[38]

Table 6.7 Main purposes of the *vaqfs* in Tehran

	Number of vaqfs *and Percentage*	*Details*	
Madrase	20 (8%)		
Mosque	26 (10%)		
Takye	16 (6%)		
Shrine	7 (3%)	Candles for the shrines	5
		Pilgrimages to the shrines	2
Mourning ceremony	114 (44%)		
Descendants, relatives	22 (8%)		
Poor	19 (7%)		
Water supply	7 (3%)	*Qanat*	5
		Drinking fountain	1
		Water reservoir	1
Grave, funeral	5 (2%)	Personal graves	2
		Ghassal-khane	2
		Graveyards	1
Liquidation after death	2 (1%)		
Plural purposes	12 (5%)		
General welfare	15 (6%)		
Total	260 (100%)		

As the city population grew, the city needed a larger water supply and *qanats*. E'temad al-Saltane listed ten *qanats* built in the first part of the forty-year reign of Naser al-Din Shah.[39] Naser al-Din Shah built the large Naseri Qanat and made it a *vaqf* in 1856, which will be analyzed below. Aqa Khan Nuri, the Grand Vazir, built two *qanats*, Sadr-abad and Kazem-abad, and endowed four-sevenths of their share as *vaqfs* in 1857. The *qanats* supplied water to the 'Udlajan and Bazar districts after they watered some gardens and mansions in the north of Tehran.[40] Haji Mohammad Hoseyn Khan Shehab al-Molk Amir-e Toman constructed a new *qanat* and endowed all of it to the inhabitants of the Chalmeydan district and in Kuche-e Ghariban in 1867.[41] Those *vaqfs* were established by high ranking officers.

In many cases, villages and *qanats* were included among the large *vaqfs* established by the bureaucrats and military officers. However, the *vaqfs* consisting of shops and houses surpassed these large *vaqfs* in number.

Objects and purposes of the vaqfs

Table 6.7 indicates the objects and purposes of 260 *vaqfs* in Tehran. Many of them had plural objects or purposes. In these cases, the objects that received the most expenditure were selected. If there were two main objects for which the same amounts would be spent, then both purposes were chosen. In the case that more than two main objects had received equal amounts, they were categorized into "plural purposes."

The mosques and *madrases* are common objects of the *vaqf* in Sunni regions. The *vaqfs* for the shrines are also popular in Sunni regions, although Shi'ism particularly respected the shrines of the Imams and their descendants. On the other hand, the *takyes* are Shi'i institutions, where the mourning ceremonies for Shi'i Imams, in particular for Imam Husayn, were performed. The police report from 1886–1888 described the mourning ceremony at thirty-two *takyes* in Tehran: most of them were passion plays (*ta'ziye-khani*) of Imam Husayn and others.

However, it is clear that the *vaqfs* on behalf of these religious institutions were only sixty-nine in number and comprise 27 percent of the totals. We generally suppose that most *vaqfs* were established on behalf of religious institutions, but this was not the case in Qajar Tehran.

The most popular purpose of the *vaqf* was the mourning ceremonies of the Imams: 114 *vaqfs* are concerned with the ceremonies, which comprise 44 percent of the totals. All the necessary expenditures for the ceremonies are mentioned in the *vaqf* deeds: buying carpets, dishes, and copper wares, payments for recitation of the ceremonies (*rowze-khani*) every year, and serving meals every week. It was unusual to stipulate spending for passion plays (*ta'ziye-khani* or *shabih-khani*): the *vaqf* deeds mention the more general term of mourning ceremonies (*ta'ziye-dari*). The ceremonies were held mainly in the months of Moharram and Safar.

When one researches the founders of the 114 *vaqfs* for the mourning ceremonies, it is discovered that 30 *vaqfs* were established by bureaucrats and military officers and 32 *vaqfs* were founded by merchants and artisans: it is unlikely that a special social group contributed to these *vaqfs*. However, it is true that twenty-seven *vaqfs* for the ceremonies were established by women, which is more than half of the total fifty-one women's *vaqfs*. This is probably related to the sizes of the *vaqfs*: of fifty-nine *vaqfs*, more than half were small, containing less than six shops or three houses as *vaqf* property.

In a broader sense, the *vaqfs* on behalf of *takyes* denote the *vaqf* for the mourning ceremony, which must be held at particular *takyes*. To sum up, of 130 *vaqfs*, half of the total *vaqfs* concerned the mourning ceremony. Moreover, all the twelve *vaqfs* of "plural purposes" also spent money on the ceremonies, and twelve of the fifteen *vaqfs* for "general welfare" mentioned expenditure for the ceremonies as examples. In addition, thirty-four *vaqfs* paid for the mourning ceremonies as minor expenditures. In other words, 180 of the total 260 *vaqfs* (72 percent) were expected to, more or less, support the mourning ceremonies. No doubt a mourning ceremony for the Imams was the most popular purpose of the *vaqfs*. This indicates the Shi'i aspect of the *vaqfs* in Tehran.

Nineteen *vaqf*s mainly concerned aid for the poor. Among them, eight *vaqfs* offered the same amount of money to the *sayyed* poor and non-*sayyed* poor. One can say that these *vaqfs* still favored the *sayyeds*, but these were not like the Safavid large *vaqfs* for the *sayyeds*, which one will see later. The Shi'i aspect is also found here, because four *vaqfs* stipulated that aid for the poor would be given at the time of the Ghadir festival.[42] Other than the nineteen *vaqfs* of this category, seven *vaqfs* of "plural purposes" paid for the poor, while seven other *vaqfs* stipulated spending part of their income for aid to the poor.

On the other hand, only twenty-three *vaqfs* mainly benefited descendants and relatives, which comprised nine percent of the total. Also, one can find only three *vaqfs* that supported the family among the category of "plural purposes," and only one other *vaqf* in other categories that partially helped descendants and relatives. In other words, in Qajar Tehran, so-called family *vaqfs* were very rare, and people seldom used *vaqfs* as tools to avoid Islamic inheritance law, which stipulated dividing legacies among the heirs. Although in most cases the *vaqf* administers were descendants of the founders and received a salary from the *vaqf* income, the descendants were rarely the main objects of the *vaqfs*.

The minor purposes of the *vaqfs* are not shown in the table. One can find thirteen *vaqfs* aiding pilgrims (other than the category of "shrine"), eight *vaqfs* serving dinner in the month of Ramazan, seven *vaqfs* purchasing or transcribing books, and two *vaqfs* helping orphans.

The building surveys offer another way to analyze the *vaqfs*. The surveys recorded an object or a purpose not of each *vaqf* but of each *vaqf* property. Table 6.8 indicates numbers of religious institutions and their *vaqf* properties. Though *vaqf* properties with purposes unknown are considerable (the purposes of 19 percent of *vaqf* shops in 1853 and 33 percent of those in 1899–1900 are unknown), still one can understand the general trends. First, *madrases* and mosques had considerable *vaqf* properties. We already know that the *vaqfs* for these institutions were not dominant among all *vaqfs*: this means that these *vaqfs* were larger than other *vaqfs*. In 1899–1900, the *vaqf* properties for the mosques were much fewer than those for *madrases*, but this data did not include the properties for two large mosques, the Shah mosque and the Old Friday Mosque, as will be mentioned later.

Table 6.8 Religious institutions and *vaqf* properties in Tehran

	1853					*1899–1900*				
	Institution	Vaqf *Property*				*Institution*	Vaqf *Property*			
		Shop	*House*	*Saray*	*Bath*		*Shop*	*House*	*Saray*	*Bath*
Madrase	18	123	3	3	5	25	211	10	5	3
Mosque	112	103	1	1	1	57	81	4		
Takye	55	102	2		1	46	119	9	1	1
Leader of the martyrs		77		3	1		63	2		
Shrine	9	23	3	1		1	14	0	1	
Others		5					1	4		
Unknown		104	20	8	6		237	87	10	3
Total		537	29	16	14		726	116	17	7

The *takye*s (places of the mourning ceremonies for Shi'i Imams) also had considerable *vaqf* properties. On the contrary, another important institution in Shi'ism, the shrine, did not have much *vaqf* property in the city of Tehran. Among the celebrated shrines in other provinces, the Emam Reza Shrine in Mashhad had only a *vaqf* shop in 1853, while the Imam 'Ali shrine in Najaf held seven shops and a *saray*.[43] Both the 'Abd al-'Azim shrine in Rey and the Ma'sume shrine in Qom had only a one-sixth share of a public bath located in the Grand Bazaar. In spite of the fact that a large number of pilgrims visited those shrines during the nineteenth century, the *vaqf*s in Tehran did not contribute much to them.

The four institutions, the mosques, the *madrase*s, the *takye*s, and the shrines, held 65 percent of *vaqf* shops in 1853 and 59 percent of *vaqf* shops in 1899–1900. The building surveys did not list many of the *vaqf* houses, *saray*s, and public baths of these institutions. However, since most of such *vaqf* properties are unknown, more *vaqf* properties might belong to these four institutions.

The category "Leader of the Martyrs (Sayyed al-Shohada)," which denotes Imam Husayn, is a little complicated. It is reasonable to assume that this category of property belonged to *vaqf*s established for supporting the mourning ceremonies, which were frequently mentioned in *vaqf* deeds. However, a part of these

Table 6.9 Major endowed institutions in Tehran

	1853				*1899–1900*				*1970–1*			
	Sh	*H*	*S*	*B*	*Sh*	*H*	*S*	*B*	*Sh*	*H*	*S*	*B*
Masjed-e Shah	43		1						53			2
Masjed-e Jame'	33	1	1		1				40			2
Takye-e Reza Qoli Khan	22					3			25			
Takye-e Dar-e Khanegah	15				2							
Madrase-e Marvi	13	3		3	75	4	2	1	81	3	4	1
Madrase-e Sadr	11				9		1		11		1	1
Chehel Tan	10	1	1									
Madrase-e Mohammadiye	9		2		9	2			25	26	2	
Emamzade Zeyd	8											
Takye-e Chalhesar	5				16							
Madrase-e Naseri					31		2	1	53			2
takye ('Udlajan district)					22							
Madrase-e Sepahsalar					18			1	18			1
Masjed-e Haji 'Abd al-Hoseyn					14							
Madrase-e Sheykh 'Abd al-Hoseyn					13				36	1		
Takye-e Emamzade Zeyd					11							
Takye-e Dabbaghkhane					8							
madrase (Sangelaj district)					8							
takye ('Udlajan district)					8							

Sh: shop, H: house, S: *saray*, B: bath

properties could concern the Shrine of Imam Husayn in Karbala'. Nevertheless, along with the categories of the *takye*s and the shrines, this category of *vaqf* property represents the Shi'i aspect of the *vaqf*s.

The next table shows major endowed institutions that had more *vaqf* properties. In 1853 two mosques, the Shah Mosque and the Old Friday Mosque, had more *vaqf* shops than other institutions, but the survey of 1899–1900 contains little data about them. When one sees Balaghi's data from the 1970s, it is unlikely that these two mosques had only one *vaqf* shop. Though they were mentioned as a private property in the survey, forty-seven shops of Emam Jom'e and sixteen shops of Soltan al-'Olama's should correspond to the *vaqf* property of the two mosques. Even so, Marvi Madrase had the most *vaqf* properties in 1899–1900. Another major endowed institution was Naseri Madrase (Mottahari Mosque and Madrase today).

Other than these four major institutions, the *takye*s are notable. Since the *takye*s were mainly used for passion plays of Imams and did not need to employ servants permanently like *madrase*s, the numbers of their *vaqf* properties did not match those of larger *madrase*s or mosques. Among the shrines, Emamzade Zeyd and Chehel Tan,[44] which are located in the Grand Bazaar, had *vaqf* properties in the city. Their *vaqf* properties were not as many as those of *madrase*s, either.

Administrators, supervisors, and their salaries

In the *vaqf* system, once a *vaqf* was established, it was controlled by the *vaqf* administrator. The *vaqf* administrator was elected in accordance with the stipulation in the *vaqf* deed. Out of 260 *vaqf* deeds analyzed, 175 deeds (67 percent) nominated the founder as the first *vaqf* administrator. Among them, 141 deeds (54 percent of the total) stipulated that the second administrator would be a descendant of the founder. Other second *vaqf* administrators were the relatives of the founder (sixteen cases), 'ulama (six cases), and so on.

In eighty-five cases (33 percent of the total), the first *vaqf* administrator was not the founder. Among them, in twenty-two cases the founder's children were nominated as the first administrators. Also, in six cases the founder's relatives became the first administrators. Five *vaqf*s, which were established in accordance with the last wills and testaments, appointed the testator's children in four cases and the testator's relative in one case to be the first administrator. On the other hand, 'ulama were appointed as first administrators only in twenty-eight cases (11 percent of the total). Among them, the second administrator also had to be a part of the 'ulama in eight cases, while in eighteen cases, the descendants of the first 'ulama administrator succeeded him.

In sum, more than 70 percent of the deeds appointed the founders or founder's relatives as the *vaqf* administrators. When 'ulama were nominated as administrators, in most cases the 'ulama's successors were their descendants and not necessarily jurists. In Shi'i law, if there is not a legitimate administrator, a jurist should take over the *vaqf*. Even so, the founders always tried to keep the *vaqf* property in the hands of their descendants and relatives as much as possible.

Table 6.10 The first and second administrators of *vaqfs* in Tehran

First administrator	*Second administrator*
Founder 175 (67%)	Founder's descendant 141(54%)
	Founder's relative 16
	'Ulama 6
	Testator's descendant 2
	Unspecified 10
Founder's children 22 (8%)	First administrator's descendant 14
	Unspecified 8
Founder's relative 6	First administrator's descendant 4
	Unspecified 2
Testator's children 4	First administrator's descendant 4
Testator's relative 1	First administrator's descendant 1
'Ulama 28(11%)	'Ulama 8
	First administrator's descendant 18
	Founder's descendant 1
	Unspecified 1
Shah 2	Shah 2
Others 17	First administrator's descendant 9
	Founder 1
	Testator's descendant 1
	'Ulama 1
	Other 1
	Unspecified 4
Unspecified 5	Unspecified 5

Out of fifty-five *vaqfs* that involved women among the founders, only twenty-seven *vaqfs* had a woman as the first *vaqf* administrator. In addition, male founders appointed women as the first administrators in only three cases. Moreover, one can find just three cases in which the wives of the founders were appointed as second administrators. The founders tended to prefer male administrators rather than female ones. 143 deeds mentioned the preference for male descendants of the founders or the first administrator, etc. Only fifty-five deeds did not care about the gender of the descendants. The *vaqf* system did not exclude women totally. However, men could inherit the *vaqf* more easily than women could.

Some *vaqfs* appointed persons as *vaqf* supervisors (*nazer*). Though the term *nazer* denotes a *vaqf* administrator (*motavalli*) in *fiqh* works, the *vaqf* deeds nominated persons other than *motavallis* for supervising the *vaqf*.[45] According to my investigation, there is no mention about the position of the *vaqf* supervisors in Islamic legal works. However, some *vaqf* deeds stipulate even the salary for the supervisor, which was usually equal to or less than the salary of the administrator.

Out of a total of 260 *vaqf* deeds, 61 deeds (23 percent) made stipulations about *vaqf* supervisors. Twelve of them nominated the founder as the supervisor, and nine of them appointed the founder as the *vaqf* administrator, too. In those cases, different persons were appointed as the second *vaqf* administrator and the second supervisor: for example, in six deeds, the administrator would be the male descendant of the founder while the supervisor would be the founder's nephew and his descendants. Moreover, in seventeen cases, the founder chose one of his or her relatives or descendants as *vaqf* supervisor.

However, twenty-two *vaqf* deeds appointed ʻulama as the first *vaqf* supervisor, which comprised more than one-third of the *vaqfs* with a supervisor. Only eight *vaqf* deeds appointed a third party to the supervisory role. Though most of the *vaqf* founders preferred their descendants and relatives to be *vaqf* administrators, they sometimes needed other persons, including the ʻulama, for the protection of their *vaqfs*.

The salaries of the *vaqf* administrators (*haqq al-towliye*) were stipulated in the *vaqf* deeds. 133 *vaqf* deeds, almost half of the total, mentioned the exact amount of the administrators' salaries. The most preferred amount was one-tenth of the total *vaqf* income, and this was stipulated in eighty *vaqf* deeds. In other cases, the amounts of two-fifteenths (eight cases), three-twentieths (four cases), one-sixth (two cases), and one-fifth (twenty-three cases) are found in the *vaqf* deeds. In sum, 116 *vaqf* administrators would have received from 10 percent to 20 percent of the total *vaqf* incomes.

In other cases, there is no stipulation on the salaries of the *vaqf* administrators. Among them, in six cases, the administrators were totally entrusted with spending the *vaqf* income. It is possible that the administrators received all the money they wanted in these cases. However, in other cases the *vaqf* deeds stipulated every expense precisely; it might have been difficult for the administrators to receive their salaries. In general, the administrators received only a limited portion of the *vaqf* income.

The *vaqf* supervisors also received their salaries (*haqq al-nezarat*). Out of sixty-one *vaqf* deeds that nominated the supervisors, forty-seven deeds stipulated their salaries: one-twentieth (twenty cases), one-tenth (fifteen cases), three-fortieths (one case), and so on. In sum, their salaries were mostly from 5 percent to 10 percent of the total *vaqf* incomes. The salaries of the supervisors were not as much as those of the administrators.

Vaqf *holders*

A *vaqf* deed is drawn up when the *vaqf* has been established. It stipulates the conditions of the *vaqf* administrator and supervisor. However, it does not indicate who actually controls the *vaqf* after it has been established. Fortunately, the building surveys contained the names of actual *vaqf* holders, who controlled forty percent of *vaqf* property in the city of Tehran. The next table shows major *vaqf* holders according to the surveys.

In the survey of 1853, Mirza Abu al-Qasem Emam Jomʻe (d. 1854) held considerable *vaqf* properties: he was the leader of prayer at the Shah Mosque and *vaqf* administrator of the mosque's *vaqf*. Mirza Abu al-Hasan was son of Mirza Masih Astarabadi (d. 1847–1848), a famous *mojtahed* in Tehran. Mirza Beg served Grand Vazir Mirza Aqa Khan Nuri as chief of the servants (*farrash-bashi*). Mirza Aqasi and Haji Esma'il were probably merchants or artisans. Mirza Aqasi's *vaqf* deed is preserved in the archives of the Vaqf Organization.[46] One spice dealer named Haji Esma'il is found in Sangelaji district in the survey;[47] he might be the same person as the *vaqf* holder.

Also in the survey of 1899–1900, a few 'ulama are found among the *vaqf* holders. Sayyed 'Ali Akbar Tafreshi was a prominent *mojtahed*,[48] while Sheykh Ja'far Soltan al-'Olama was the leader of prayer at the Old Friday Mosque (d. 1917–1918). Haji Sheykh 'Ali is supposed to be a jurist from his title. Though the *vaqf* for Takye of Emamzade Zeyd appears to have been the same as Mirza Aqasi's *vaqf*, it was not the founder's descendants but the jurist who controlled it, probably because no descendants remained in 1899–1900. Akhavi Sayyeds controlled the *vaqf* properties for their *takye*; At least three of their *vaqf* deeds are found in the archive of the *Vaqf* Organization.[49] Yusof Khan appears to have been a military officer, while Karbala'i Mahdi was a merchant or an artisan.[50] Haji Abu Taleb was a merchant (*tajer*) who founded at least two *vaqf*s.[51]

Table 6.11 Major *vaqf* holders in the building surveys

1853

Vaqf *holders*	Vaqf *property*	*Location*	*Object of the* vaqf
Emam Jom'e	40 shops, 1 small shop, 1 bath	Grand Bazaar	Shah Mosque
Mirza Aqasi	12 shops	Grand Bazaar	Sayyed al-Shohada'
Haji Esma'il	8 shops, 1 warehouse	Sangelaj	Sayyed al-Shohada'
Mirza Beg, *farrash-bashi* of Grand Vazir	6 shops, 2 warehouses	'Udlajan	
Mirza Abu al-Hasan b. Mirza Masih	3 shops, 3 small shops	Grand Bazaar	Old Friday Mosque
	1 bath, 2 small shops		Sayyed al-Shohada'
	3 shops, 2 small shops		

1899–1900

Vaqf *holders*	Vaqf *property*	*Location*	*Object of the* vaqf
Aqa Sayyed 'Ali Akbar	11 shops	Grand Bazaar	Takye of Emamzade Zeyd
	11 shops, 1 house	Chalmeydan	
	5 shops, 1 house	'Udlajan	
(Akhavi) "Sayyeds"	22 shops	'Udlajan	Takye of Akhavi Sayyeds
Soltan al-'Olama'	19 shops, 1 *saray*	'Udlajan	
Haji Sheykh 'Ali	15 shops	Dowlat	
Haji Abu Taleb's grandson	14 shops	Grand Bazaar	
Yusof Khan	12 shops, 1 *saray*	Chalmeydan	
Karbala'i Mahdi	11 shops	Grand Bazaar	

Large *vaqfs*, which usually endowed a *madrase* or a mosque, tended to be controlled by the ‘ulama. Also, the ‘ulama acquired *vaqf* properties after the descendants of the *vaqf* administrator had vanished. In this regard, the ‘ulama had an advantage for controlling *vaqfs*. However, one can see a military officer, a bureaucrat, and merchants or artisans among the major *vaqf* holders. In other words, the ‘ulama could not monopolize the *vaqf* properties because of the conditions set by the founder.

Major *vaqfs*

Marvi Madrase

Marvi Madrase had been the most important among *madrases* in Tehran until Naseri Madrase was established.[52] The founder was Haji Mohammad Hoseyn Khan Qajar ‘Ezz al-Dinlu from Marv, whose father, Beyram ‘Ali Khan was the governor. After Beyram ‘Ali was defeated by a Bukharan ruler, Shah Morad, and lost his life in 1799–1800, his son Mohammad Hoseyn escaped from Bukhara and sought asylum at Fath ‘Ali Shah's court. Mohammad Hoseyn became a speaker at the assembly (*mokhateb-e bar*) and the leader (*sarkheyl*) of prominent *amirs*. After serving twenty years, he passed away in 1819.[53]

His *vaqf* deed was dated Ziqa‘de 1231/November-December 1816.[54] The deed consists of five different *vaqfs*, as follows:

(i) *Vaqf* of the main *madrase*, including two mosques, a toilet, a warehouse, a kitchen, two rooms, books, carpets, and dishes, on behalf of students of religious sciences.
(ii) *Vaqf* on behalf of people in the *madrase*. The *vaqf* property was (a) Sadeqabad village in Varamin, (b) a garden located next to the founder's house along with a water supply from Mehrjerd Qanat, (c) an ice house located next to the *madrase*, (d) a public bath located next the *madrase*, and (e) an ice house located next to the founder's house.[55]
(iii) *Vaqf* for maintenance of a water well next to the *madrase*, lamps at the two mosques, the salary of the announcer of prayer time (*mo'azzen*), and carpets. The *vaqf* properties were three shops: a fodder shop in the Grand Bazaar, a bakery in the Chalmeydan district, and a *kabab* shop in the ‘Udlajan district.[56]
(iv) *Vaqf* on behalf of the founder's son, Mirza Esma‘il Khan, and his descendants. The *vaqf* property was a private room in the corner of the *madrase* where Esma‘il would read books, including two bookshelves, a storage room, and a coffee room. After his death, his descendants succeeded him generation by generation.
(v) *Vaqf* of a small *madrase*[57] on behalf of religious students. The founder built a small *madrase* by the side of the main *madrase*.

The income of the *vaqf* (ii) was to be spent as follows: first, the salary of the *vaqf* administrator (10 percent), that of the *vaqf* supervisor (5 percent), and that of the professor (5 percent) must be paid. Secondly, if there is damage on the *madrase* and other facilities, they must be repaired. Third, the salaries of one chief servant and two servants, light for the toilet, seeds and other expenses for land, and salary of the gardener should be paid. Then, the rest must be paid to the students living in the *madrase* month by month.[58]

The first administrator was a famous *mojtahed*, Mirza Masih Astarabadi (d.1847–1848), and he would be succeeded by a fully conditioned *mojtahed* in Tehran. The first *vaqf* supervisor (*nazer*) was a certain Molla Mohammad 'Ali Tehrani, and he was followed by his descendants generation by generation.

The structure of the *vaqf* deed was rather complicated. However, the distinguishing feature of this deed was to appoint a *mojtahed* to the position of *vaqf* administrator. As mentioned above, most founders tried to keep the position in the hands of their families, and if not possible, in the family of the first administrator. The *vaqfs* for *madrases* were no exception: out of nineteen *vaqf* deeds on behalf of *madrases*, sixteen appointed founders' or the first administrators' families to the position of administrator.[59] In other words, the Marvi Madrase was one of the exceptional institutions fully controlled by the *mojtaheds*. In fact, the prominent *mojtaheds* such as Molla Mirza Mohammad Andarmani (d.1866), Haji Molla 'Ali Kani (d.1888), and Mirza Zeyn al-'Abedin Emam Jom'e (d.1903–1904) took over the *vaqf* of the *madrase*.[60]

Though the size of the initial *vaqf* property was not huge, the *madrase* continued to attract endowments. In 1855, Hajiye Nane, wife of Haji Mir Taqi Larijani endowed the cistern of the *madrase* with one shop and a half in the Grand Bazaar. Hesareyn Village in Damavand was donated to the *madrase* by Haji Molla Reza Qoli in 1882.[61] Moreover, as indicated in Table 6.9, the Marvi Madrase came to control the most number of *vaqf* shops in Tehran before the end of the nineteenth century.

The Qajar Shahs and the Grand Vazir also supported the *madrase*. Fath 'Ali Shah issued the royal edict for exempting all the taxes on the *vaqf* property of the *madrase*. Naser al-Din Shah also decided to exempt taxes from the newly endowed Hesareyn Village.[62] Moreover, Fath 'Ali Shah invited Molla 'Abd-allah Zanuzi (d. 1841) from Isfahan to teach philosophy at the *madrase*: this was the beginning of the School of Tehran in Islamic philosophy.[63] In 1841–1842, Haji Mirza Aqasi, the Grand Vazir, brought Molla Mohammad Taqi Ardakani (d.1851–1852) from Yazd to Tehran: he became the professor at the *madrase*.[64] This support contributed to the development of the *madrase*. The Marvi Madrase held fifty-six students in 1884, second after Emamzade Zeyd Madrase among the *madrases* in Tehran.[65]

Qanat-e Naseriye

Naser al-Din Shah constructed this *qanat*; it ran from the west side of the city. After the *qanat* supplied water to the royal buildings, it irrigated the buildings in the city and became a *vaqf*. The *vaqf* deed, dated October–November 1856, states that the increase of the population and the buildings in Tehran caused a shortage of water, although older *qanat*s had provided much water to the city.[66] Though the *vaqf* deed stipulated the distribution of water, a note on the matter was drawn up and signed by the 'ulama in October 1859. According to the note, the water must be distributed as follows:

> Friday night and Saturday: the royal buildings and inhabitants of the Arg district.
> Wednesday night and Tuesday: the royal garden, armory, and arsenal.
> Saturday night and Sunday: Mosque and Madrase of Sheykh 'Abd al-Hoseyn, new public bath of Mirza Kazem Khan Nezam al-Molk, and Malek-abad Avenue.
> Monday night and Thursday: 'Abbas-abad Quarter.
> Tuesday night and Wednesday: Sheykh Reza, Amin al-Dowle, and Kuche-e Ghariban.
> Sunday night and Monday: the house of Haji Molla Kani and Haft Tan Avenue.
> Thursday night and Friday: The house of Sayyed Mohammad Sadeq Sangelaji and Haji 'Ali Khan Hajeb al-Dowle, and the Sagnelaj district.[67]

The *qanat* supplied water to the Arg, Bazar and Sangelaj districts. The total *vaqf* administrator was the ruler of the time. However, it is notable that the *vaqf* deed appointed the *mojtahed*s as administrators for each share of the water, except water for the royal buildings:

MALEK-ABAD AND 'ABBAS-ABAD: Sheykh 'Abd al-Hoseyn. After him, the most distinguished scholar who lived in this area would succeed him, generation by generation.

KUCHE-E GHARIBAN: Sheykh Reza. After him, the son of his brother, Sheykh Mohammad. After Mohammad, the scholar who was the leader of prayers at the Old Friday Mosque would succeed him.[68]

HAFT TAN: Haji Molla 'Ali Kani. After him, the most distinguished scholar who lived in this area would succeed him, generation by generation.

SANGELAJ: Aqa Sayyed (Mohammad) Sadeq Tabataba'i (Sangelaji). After him, the most distinguished scholar who lived in this district would succeed him, generation by generation.

All of them were prominent *mojtahed*s: each was living in the area where water of the *qanat* was supplied.

Water supply was essential for inhabitants of the city. One can consider the construction of the Qanat-e Naseriye as part of the public policy of Naser al-Din Shah. The *vaqf*, which involved prominent *mojtahed*s in the city, contributed to the maintenance of the *qanat* and the distribution of water. The *vaqf* deed was still useful for the distribution of water in 1928, and this was the reason why Reza Shah published the *vaqf* deed in that year.[69]

Merchant and women's vaqfs

As mentioned above, merchants and artisans also established a considerable number of *vaqfs*. Haji Mohammad Ebrahim Esfahani, a merchant of tobacco (*tajer-e tanbaku* or *tanbakuforush*) was one such merchant. His file in the Vaqf Organization contained three documents: a sale deed dated 1839, a *vaqf* deed dated 1839, and another *vaqf* deed dated 1850.[70]

First, by the sale deed of 1839, Khanom Jan Khanom, Mohammad Ebrahim's wife, sold half of three shops and of a stand to her husband at the price of fifty *tomans*. Apparently, the wife had owned all of the shops and the stand that were located in 'Abbas-abad Quarter in Tehran.

Then, Mohammad Ebrahim and Khanom Jan founded a *vaqf* on behalf of mourning ceremonies for Imam Husayn with the shops and the stand. A half share of the property owned by the husband and one-sixth share of the property belonging to the wife were entrusted to Akhond Molla Mohammad Mahdi, a leader of prayers. After Mohammad Mahdi's death, his male descendants would succeed him generation by generation. The one-third share of the shops and the stand, which was owned by the wife, was managed by Mohammad Ebrahim, the husband. He was decided to be an administrator (*motavalli*) of the *vaqf*. After his death, his male descendants should take over the one-third share generation by generation.

Molla Mohammad Mahdi received three-fourths of the total income: after he deducted necessary expenses, he should spend the rest for the recital of stories of martyrs (*rowze-khani*) in the first ten days of the month of Moharram. The rest, one third of the income, was controlled by Mohammad Ebrahim. After deducting necessary expenses, the income should be spent for the recital of the martyrs, mourning ceremony, and meals for the participants of the ceremony, which should be held in the last ten days of the month of Safar.

This is a typical small simple *vaqf* on behalf of the Shi'i mourning ceremonies. However, in this case, the descendants of the founders controlled only one-fourth of the *vaqf* property, and the rest was entrusted to an 'ulama family. This might be a reason for the next *vaqf* in 1850.

This second *vaqf* was established for the maintenance of the 'Abbas-abad Mosque,[71] which Mohammad Ebrahim had built. He also built shops attached to the mosque and made them a *vaqf*. He endowed the mosque with eight shops and a stand: five shops and a stand on behalf of maintenance of the mosque and three shops for the imam of the mosque. The first *vaqf* administrator was Mohammad Ebrahim himself, to be succeeded by his male descendants: the administrators should receive one tenth of the total revenue as their salary. Nine *vaqf* shops were recorded in the building surveys of 1853, 1899–1900, and the Vaqf Organization.[72] The police reports tell that Aqa Mir Mohammad 'Ali Shushtari (d.1889) preached and led prayers at the mosque in 1888.[73]

These two *vaqfs* contributed to the religious life of the local people: They made it possible for people in the neighborhood to use the neighboring mosque and join the mourning ceremonies in the neighborhood. Also, the founders cared about their descendants' lives: more than eight shops were expected to be controlled by their descendants. Though the *vaqfs* were comparatively small and quite local, they supported the religious life of the inhabitants as well as the lives of their descendants.

Features of the *vaqfs*

So far, we have seen some features of the *vaqfs* in Qajar Tehran. First, the Qajar state controlled only a limited part of the *vaqfs*. The inventories of the royal property and fiscal books referred to some *vaqf* properties, but did not cover the majority of them. Sometimes the Shah issued royal edicts on the *vaqfs*, but usually these were based on the edicts of the *mojtaheds*. People could go to the shari'a court to establish a *vaqf* without referring to the state. Since the shari'a courts were independent from the state, the *vaqfs* were not totally controlled by the state.

One might say that the *vaqfs* concerned society more than the state. Two groups were major *vaqf* founders: bureaucrats/military officers and merchants/artisans. More than half of the *vaqfs* were established by these two groups. On the other hand, 'ulama's *vaqfs* were limited in number. In fact, since most *vaqf* deeds nominated the founders and their descendants as administrators, the 'ulama were not to be administrators soon after the *vaqfs* were established. However, for a long term, if the line of descendants ended, the *vaqfs* were entrusted to the 'ulama.

Among the purpose of the *vaqfs*, the mourning ceremony (*ta'ziye-dari*) of the Imams was the most popular in Qajar Tehran: those *vaqfs* comprised half of the total *vaqfs* and were more than the *vaqfs* for the *madrases*, mosques, and shrines. These *vaqfs* were simple and comparatively small in size. Women's *vaqfs* were notable in number among these *vaqfs*. These *vaqfs* oblige us to get rid of our preconceived ideas that *vaqfs* contributed to institutions such as *madrases* and mosques. However, unlike the case of Tabriz,[74] a few large scale *vaqfs* were also established in Qajar Tehran. In this regard, Lambton's statement that the Qajar period was not notable for the construction of *vaqfs*[75] is not acceptable. The various sizes of *vaqfs* were established by various people, and the *vaqfs* supported various aspects of the society, at least in Tehran.

Notes

1 Ettehadiye, *Inja Tehran Ast*, 177–193; Mansure Ettehadiye, "Mowqufat-e Tehran va Tahavvol-e Shahr, 1269–1320 H.Q.," *Vaqf, Miras-e Javidan* no.28 (1378): 7–16; Parvane Shah Hoseyni, "*Vaqf* shenasi-e Joghrafiyayi-e Shahr-e Tehran: Dowre-e Qajar va Pahlavi," *Tahqiqat-e Joghrafiya'i* 42 (1375Kh): 117–133. The data in two versions of Ettehadiye's article are slightly different.
2 Hoseyni Balaghi, *Tarikh-e Tehran*.
3 Reza'i, ed. *Asnad-e Mahkame*, 105; *Daftar-e Shar'i-e Sangelaji*, 63b, 101b, 187b, 352b, 366a, 369a; Ettehadiye and Ruhi, eds. *Dar Mahzar*, 49.
4 Owqaf no.1527.
5 'Abd al-Razzaq Donboli, *Ma'aser-e Soltaniye*, ed. Gholam Hoseyn Zargarinezhad (Tehran, 1383Kh), 214.
6 See 'Abd al-Vahhab Taraz, "Ketabche-e Mowqufat-e Yazd," ed. Iraj Afshar, *Farhang-e Iran-zamin* 10 (1341Kh): 5–123. As an analysis of this inventory, Michael Bonine, "Islam and Commerce: Waqf and the Bazaar of Yazd, Iran," *Erdkunde* 41 (1987):

182–196. A recently published collection of the deeds contained more than sixty *vaqf* deeds, which were not mentioned in Taraz's work. Mohamamd Reza Tasdiqi, ed. *Yadgar-e Mandegar: Majmu'e-e Mowqufat-e Yazd*, vol. 1 (Tehran, 1380Kh).

7 Mirza Mohammad Monshi Forugh, *Safinat al-Faramin: Safinat al-Ensha'*, ed. Mohammad Golbon (Khorram-abad, 1377Kh), 87–90.

8 Here I referred to the Majles manuscript and the microfilm of the Mar'ashi manuscript that is preserved in the Central Library of the University of Tehran. Unfortunately, the recent edition has technical problems and is not reliable, although the preface that the manuscripts lack is included in it. Bayani and Ettehadiye, ed. *Ketabche-e Qabalejat-e Khazane-e Mobarake*, 343–568. Concerning this inventory, see Hushang Sa'edlu, "Ketabche-e Raqabat-e Mohammad Shahi va Naser al-Din Shahi," in *Haftad Maqale*, ed. Yahya Mahdavi and Iraj Afshar (Tehran, 1369Kh), 1:189–197. What he saw appears to have been the original, and he cited some additional notes that are not found in other versions. See also Mohammad Dabir-e Siyaqi, "Ketabche-e Amlak va Khalse va Arbabi-e Iran," *Vaqf, Miras-e Javidan* no.56 (1385Kh): 25–32. Modarresi Tabataba'i introduced the Mar'ashi manuscript but he mistakenly considered it from the Naser al-Din Shah period dated Ramazan, 1299AH. The content of the manuscript is identical with the Majles manuscript, but it contains an addition, which other versions lack. The date is not clear in the manuscript but it should be read as 1259AH. Hoseyn Modarresi Tabataba'i, "Ketabche-e Sabt-e Mowqufat va Khalesejat-e Keshvar dar Dowre-e Naseri," *Rahnama-ye Ketab* 18, no.4–6 (1354Kh): 435–442." Floor mentioned the inventory but he did not refer to it. Floor, *A Fiscal History of Iran*, 337.

9 Bayani and Ettehadiye, ed. *Ketabche-e Qabalejat-e Khazane-e Mobarake*, 344.

10 *Surat-e Amlak-e Khasse*, Majles, 150–151; Mar'ashi, 165–166.

11 *Vaqf* deed of Masjed-e Shah, Owqaf no.816. The same text is also inscribed at the north gate of the mosque (Masjed-e Emam) today.

12 Mo'tamadi, *Joghrafiya-ye Tarikhi-e Tehran*, 456.

13 *Ruzname-e Vaqaye'-e Ettefaqiye* no.179:1–2, 8 Shavval 1270AH.

14 *Ruzname-e Dowlat* no.579:4, 18 Rajab 1282AH.

15 *Ketabche-e Dehat-e Khalese*, University, 104–105; Mar'ashi, 147–148.

16 The survey was published in Haji Mirza Esma'il Khan Mostowfi Hamadani, *Asar al-Razaviye* (Tehran, 1317AH), 69–131.

17 *Dastur al-'Amal-e Yunat-'il*, 26b–27b.

18 Except for Emam Reza Shrine in Mashhad and Shah 'Abd al-'Azim in Rey, they are located in the villages of Tehran province. Gazorsang (Emamzade Hasan/Abu al-Hasan) and Voshgin (Emamzede Yusof) are located in Savojbolagh, while Lot's shrine is laid in Robat-e Karim. See Naomi Shimizu and Koji Kamioka, *Sacred Places in Tehran Province* (Fuchu, 2009), 55, 150, 154; Mohammad Ja'far Sarvqadi, *Beqa'-e Motabarakke-e Ostan-e Tehran* (Tehran, 1383Kh), 56, 76; Hasan Habib, ed. *Shomari az Boq'eha, Marqadha va Mazarha-ye Ostanha-ye Tehran va Alborz* (Tehran, 1389Kh), 1:233–234, 310–312, 2:45–48.

19 Emamzade Saleh is located at Tajrish square today. Emamzade Hasan is laid in the Ji, district located in the west of Tehran. The *emamzade* in Andarman probably denotes Emamzade Abu al-Hasan located near Rey. See Shimizu and Kamioka, *Sacred Places in Tehran Province*, 19, 29, 40; Sarvqadi, *Beqa'-e Motabarakke*, 23, 26, 99; Habibi, ed. *Emamzadeha va Torbat-e Barkhi az Pakan va Niyakan*, 50–54, 111–117, 233–242.

20 *Ketabche-e Jam' va Kharj-e Koll*, MS, 1033–34; Bayani, ed. *Ketabche-e Jam' va Kharj-e Koll*, 840–842.

21 For example, she categorizes the *vaqf* property from Qajar Tehran into five purposes: religion (1189 properties), education (86), medicine (17), welfare (120), and the others, but the standard of her categorization is not clear. See, Shah Hoseyni, "*Vaqf* shenasi-e Joghrafiyayi," 123.

22 Three *vaqfs* by women from Qajar Tehran were analyzed by Werner. Christoph Werner, "Zanan-e Vaqef dar Tehran-e 'Ahd-e Qajar," trans. Nasim Majidi Qahrudi, *Vaqf, Miras-e Javidan* no.28 (1378Kh): 115–122; idem. "Stiftungen von Frauen im Teheran der Qagarenzeit," in *Akten des 27. Deutschen Orientalistentages (Bonn-28, September bis 2. Oktober 1998)*, ed. Stefan Wild and Hartmut Schild (Würzburg, 2001), 797–807.
23 Taraz, "Ketabche-e Mowqufat-e Yazd," 8–59.
24 Sayyed Yahya Akhavi was a famous scholar. Mirza Sayyed Kazem was a financial officer (*mostowfi-e divan*). Besides them, a *sayyed* merchant, a *sayyed* cloth dealer, and a *sayyed* bath-keeper (*hammami*) are found among the endowers.
25 Manuchehr Sotude, ed. "Vaqf-name-e Mirza Mohammad Yusof Ashrafi," *Vaqf, Miras-e Javidan* no.18 (1376Kh): 39–45.
26 E'temad al-Saltane, *Mer'at al-Boldan*, 1972; Kojuri, *Ruh va Reyhan*, 4:336.
27 The population survey of 1881 refers to thirteen *vaqf* houses, which comprise 0.1 percent of the total 10,822 houses. See, *Ketabche-e Te'dad-e Nofus*.
28 Hayashi estimates that 15.5 percent of the houses in sixteenth-century Istanbul belonged to *vaqfs*. Kayoko Hayashi, "The Vakıf Institution in 16th-Century Istanbul," *The Memoires of the Research Department of the Toyo Bunko* 50 (1992): 103.
29 *Surat-e 'Adad-e Khaneha*, 84a. The *timche*, located in the Bazar district, was a *vaqf* on behalf of Chehel Tan Shrine.
30 *Vaqf* deed of Mirza Mohammad Shafi', date 1 Rabi' I 1227AH, Owqaf no.36; *Vaqf* deed of Mahmud Khan Kalantar, dated 1250AH, Owqaf no.52; *Vaqf* deed of 'Isa Khan Beglarbegi, dated Safar 1259AH, Owqaf no.135; *Vaqf* deed of Haji Qasem Dabbagh, dated 25 Sha'ban 1264AH, Owqaf no.1308.
31 Akhzar 'Ali Shah, *Ta'in va Sabt-e Mahat-e Khandaq*, Bazar 42; *Vaqf* deed of Haji Aqa Mohammad Qazvini, dated 16 Sha'ban 1275AH, Owqaf no.522.
32 *Vaqf* deed of Mohammad Karim Mostowfi, dated 1 Safar 1212AH, Owqaf no.856; Sa'id Haji 'Abbasi and Omid Reza'i, eds. *Asnad-e Mowqufat-e Boluk-e Ghar va Fashapuye* (Tehran, 1387Kh), 29–44.
33 *Vaqf* deed of Aqa Sayyed 'Aliya, dated Ziqa'de 1216AH, Owqaf no.798.
34 *Vaqf-name-e Madrase-e Naseri*, MS 463, Madrase-e 'Ali-e Mottahari Library, Tehran; Abu al-Qasem Sahab, *Tarikh-e Madrase-e 'Ali-e Sepahsalar* (Tehran, 1329Kh), 51–102; 'Emad al-Din Sheykh al-Hokama'i, *Asnad-e Me'mari-e Iran* (Tehran, 1388Kh), 1:93–138. Lambton's explanation of the *madrase* is totally wrong. See Ann K.S. Lambton, s.v. "Wakf III in Persia," *The Encyclopaedia of Islam*, New Edition, 11 (2002): 81–87.
35 *Vaqf* deed of 'Isa Khan Beglarbegi, dated 5 Safar 1259AH, Owqaf no.135; *Vaqf* deed of Haji Gorgin Beg Gorji, dated 2 Rabi' 1261AH, Owqaf no.1831; *Vaqf* deed of Mashhadi Rahim Tehrani, dated 25 Ziqa'de 1299AH, Owqaf no.1837.
36 *Vaqf* deed of Mohammad Hashem Tabib, dated 26 Ramazan 1102AH, Owqaf no.162; Omid Reza'i, "Tabibi Mosannaf ba Masjed, Madrase va Ketabkhane-e Vaqfi-ash dar Tehran-e Dowre-e Shah Soleyman Safavi," *Owraq-e 'Atiq* 2 (1389Kh): 288.
37 *Vaqf* deed of 'Abedin Beg, dated 8 Safar 1214AH, Owqaf no.484.
38 For the Mehrjerd and Sangelaj Qanats, see Mo'tamadi, *Joghrafiya-ye Tarikhi-e Tehran*, 544, 554–556. He does not mention the Zu al-Qarneyn Qanat.
39 E'temad al-Saltane, *al-Ma'aser va al-Asar*, 124.
40 Owqaf no.666. Dabir-e Siyaqi's edition lacks a word for describing the water share: *tamami az chahar sahm az koll-e shesh dang*, instead of *tamami as chahar sahm az haft sahm az koll shesh dang*. Sayyed Mohammad Dabir-e Siyaqi, ed. "Vaqf-name-e Do Qanat-e Sadr-abad va Kazem-abad va Dokkanha-ye Piramun-e Bagh-e Nezamiye-e Tehran," *Vaqf, Miras-e Javidan* no.28 (1378Kh): 32. See also E'temad al-Saltane, *al-Ma'aser va al-Asar*, 123.
41 *Vaqf* deed of Haji Mohammad Hasan Khan Shehab al-Molk, dated 19 Zihejje 1283AH, Owqaf no.742; Marziye Mortazavi, ed. "Vaqf-name-e Qanat-e Hoseyniye-e Tehran," *Vaqf, Miras-e Javidan* no.84 (1392Kh): 128–136. For this Qanat, see Mo'tamedi,

Joghrafiya-ye Tarikhi-e Tehran, 554. For the bibliography of Shehab al-Molk, Bamdad, *Sharh-e Hal*, 1:393–394.

42 18 Zihejje is the 'Eyd-e Ghadir for Shi'i Muslims, who believe that Prophet Muhammad appointed Imam 'Ali as his successor at the place named Ghadir Khumm on that day, and who celebrate that anniversary.

43 Akhzar 'Ali Shah, *Ta'in va Sabt-e Mahat-e Khandaq*, Bazar 5, 82.

44 For these shrines, see Hoseyni Balaghi, *Tarikh-e Tehran: Tarikh-e Markazi-e Tehran*, 9–13; Shimizu and Kamioka, *Sacred Places*, 24–25; Habibi, ed. *Emamzadeha va Torbat-e Barkhi az Pakan va Niyakan*, 109–110, 141–151.

45 Nozhat Ahmadi, *Dar bab-e Owqaf-e Safavi* (Tehran, 1390Kh), 23. Ahmadi shows that a *vaqf* deed dated 1647 appointed a *vaqf* supervisor other than the *vaqf* administrator. Ibid., 106–107.

46 *Vaqf* deed of Mirza Aqasi Tehrani, dated 26 Jomada II 1281, Owqaf no.681. The deed is probably a revised version of the original deed.

47 *Surat-e 'Adad-e Khaneha*, 126b.

48 H. Picot, "Bibliographical Notices of Members of the Royal Family, Notable, Merchants, and Clergy." United Kingdom, National Archives, FO881/7028, December 1897, 69.

49 *Vaqf* deed of Aqa Sayyed Sadeq Akhavi, dated 2 Sha'ban 1273AH, Owqaf no.874; *Vaqf* deed of Aqa Sayyed Yahya Akhavi, dated 20 Ziqa'de 1284AH, Owqaf no.234; *Vaqf* deed of Haji Sayyed Yahya Akhavi, dated 9 Rajab 1299AH, Owqaf no.234. For this family, see Sharif Razi, *Akhtaran-e Foruzan*, 398–400.

50 Yusof Khan, a brigadier-general (*sartip*), and Yusof Khan, a colonel (*sarhang*) possessed houses in the Chalmeydan district. Two persons named Karbala'i Mahdi are found in the Bazar district of the survey. One is a patcher (*pareduz*) and the other is a tobacco seller (*tanbakuforush*). Akhzar 'Ali Shah, *Ta'in va Sabt-e Mahat-e Khandaq*, Bazar, 20–21.

51 Two *vaqf* deeds of Haji Abu Taleb Tajer, dated 16 Ramazan 1258AH, Owqaf no.511.

52 Concerning this madrase, see Kambiz Haji Qasemi, ed. *Ganj-name, Farhang-e Asar-e Me'mari-e Eslami-e Iran vol. 3: Benaha-ye Mazhabi-e Tehran* (Tehran, 1377Kh), 134–139; Markus Ritter, *Moscheen und Madrasabauten in Iran* (Leiden, 2006), 860–865. Habibi, ed. *Masajed-e Dirinesal-e Tehran*, 226–239.

53 Khavari, *Tarikh-e Zu al-Qarneyn*, 214; Mahmud Mirza, *Tarikh-e Sahebqerani*, 217–219; Bamdad, *Sharh-e Hal*, 3:395–397.

54 *Savad-e Vaqf-name-e Madrase-e Khan-e Marvi*, MS 2850, Madrase-e 'Ali-e Mottahari Library, Tehran; Reza Ostadi, ed. "Vaqf-name-e Madrase-e Marvi," *Vaqf, Miras-e Javidan* no.13 (1375Kh): 56–71. Ostadi's edition should be read carefully because Ostadi changed the original order of the contents.

55 *Savad-e Vaqf-name-e Madrase-e Khan-e Marvi*, 13; Ostadi, ed. "Vaqf-name-e Madrase-e Marvi," 68–69.

56 *Savad-e Vaqf-name-e Madrase-e Khan-e Marvi*, 15; Ostadi, ed. "Vaqf-name-e Madrase-e Marvi," 69.

57 Haji Qasemi provides the current plans of the Marvi Madrase, but one cannot find the small *madrase* in his plans. See, Haji Qasemi, ed. *Ganj-name: Benaha-ye Mazhabi-e Tehran*, 135–138.

58 *Savad-e Vaqf-name-e Madrase-e Khan-e Marvi*, 12–14. Ostadi, ed. "Vaqf-name-e Madrase-e Marvi," 60.

59 The exceptions were the deeds of Aqa Mahmud Madrase, San'iye Madrase, and Naseri Madrase. The second and the later administrator of Aqa Mahmud Madrase was to be the prayer leader of the mosque while Sani'ye Madrase should be administered by the administrator of Marvi Madrase after the second administrator passed away. The administrator of Naseri Madrase was ruler at that time. See *vaqf* deed of Jan Jahan Khanom dated late 1291AH, Owqaf no.13; Sheykh al-Hokama'i, ed. "Masjed-Madrase-e

Me'mar-bashi-e Tehran," *Vaqf, Miras-e Javidan* no.37 (1381Kh): 32; *Vaqf-name-e Madrase-e Naseri*, 17.

60 E'temad al-Saltane, *al-Ma'aser va al-Asar*, 192, 206; idem. *Ruzname-e Khaterat* (Tehran, 2536Sh), 133.

61 Sayyed Sa'id Mir Mohammad Sadeq, "Masjed va Madrase-e Marvi," *Masjed* 29 (1375Kh): 74.

62 Both copies of the royal edicts have no date. Asnad-e Melli 246/276–50–4.

63 Seyyed Hossein Nasr, *Islamic Philosophy from Its Origin to the Present* (Albany, 2006), 237–238; Bamdad, *Sharh-e Hal*, 6:147–148.

64 E'temad al-Saltane, *al-Ma'aser va al-Asar*, 195–196.

65 *Ketabche-e Te'dad-e Nofus*, 110. Emamzade Zeyd Madrase was newly built by Naser al-Din Shah but appears not to have continued long.

66 *Savad-e Vaqf-name va Taqsim-name-e Ab-e Shah* (Tehran, 1306Kh), 2; 'Ali Karimiyan, "Vaqf-name-e Qanat-e Naseriye-e Dowlatkhane (Bagh-e Shah)," *Ganjine-e Asnad* no.45/46 (1381Kh): 102.

67 *Savad-e Vaqf-name va Taqsim-name-e Ab-e Shah*, 9–10; Karimiyan, "Vaqf-name-e Qanat-e Naseriye," 104.

68 Concerning this family, see Chapter 8.

69 *Savad-e Vaqf-name va Taqsim-name-e Ab-e Shah*, 14.

70 Sale deed of shops between Khanom Jan Khanom and Haji Mohammad Ebrahim Tajer, dated Rabi' I 1255AH; *Vaqf* deed of Haji Mohammad Ebrahim and Khanom Jan Khanom, dated 16 Rajab 1255AH; Vaqf deed of Haji Mohammad Ebrahim, dated 17 Ziqa'de 1266AH, Owqaf no.69. The third document was published: Sayyed Sa'id Mir Mohammad Sadeq, ed. "Vaqf-name-e Haj Mohammad Ebrahim Tajer Esfahani (Masjed-e Jazayeri)," *Vaqf, Miras-e Javidan* no.28 (1378Kh): 105–108.

71 The name of the mosque is found in *Surat-e 'Adad-e Khaneha*, 77a; Akhzar 'Ali Shah, *Ta'in va Sabt-e Mahat-e Khandaq*, Bazar, 16; Hoseyni Balaghi, *Tarikh-e Tehran, vol. 2: Ketab-e Masajed-e Tehran*, 49. The mosque is now called Masjed-e Jazayeri. See Habib, ed. *Masajed-e Dirinesal-e Tehran*, 151.

72 *Surat-e 'Adad-e Khaneha*, 81b; Akhzar 'Ali Shah, *Ta'in va Sabt-e Mahat-e Khandaq*, Bazar, 15–16; Hoseyni Balaghi, *Tarikh-e Tehran, vol. 2: Ketab-e Masajed-e Tehran*, 49.

73 Sheykh Reza'i and Azari, eds. *Gozareshha-ye Nazmiye*, 720.

74 cf. Werner, *An Iranian Town*, 144–145.

75 Lambton, s.v. "Wakf III in Persia."

7 *Vaqf* and private property

One way to examine the impact of the *vaqf* system on society is to investigate the relationship between *vaqf* property and private property. Two questions arise concerning this relationship. First, how much would one founder endow for a *vaqf* out of the entirety of his or her properties? And second, how many properties belonged to *vaqf*s in commercial areas such as the Grand Bazaar? To answer the first question, one needs complete lists of the founders' properties. Such lists, however, are usually difficult to obtain. Therefore, in order to piece together information concerning the extent of founders' properties, I refer to the documents related to four individuals: Mirza Mohammad Shafi' Mazadarani, the Grand Vazir, Manuchehr Khan Mo'tamad al-Dowle, the influential eunuch, Mahmud Khan Kalantar, a local officer, and Haji Mohammad Hasan Kolahduz, a merchant. All of them founded a *vaqf* and left documents concerning their *vaqf* and private property. The Qajar Shahs confiscated the properties of the first two individuals and recorded them in the inventory of the royal property – specifically the inventory of the deeds preserved in the royal court. Additionally, a deed on division of inheritance (*taqsim-name*) remained for Mahmud Khan, while Haji Mohammad Hasan prepared a last will and testament. These documents will show how these persons managed their property through legal devices including *vaqf*.[1]

Property management of individuals

Mirza Mohammad Shafi'

Mirza Mohammad Shafi' Mazandarani was the second Grand Vazir of Fath 'Ali Shah from 1801 to 1819. His ancestors were from a noble family in Isfahan, but his father moved to Bandpey, Mazandaran after the Nader Shah period. Mohammad Shafi' began to serve Aqa Mohammad Khan Qajar, when the Qajar prince gathered an army to conquer Iran. He succeeded Haji Mirza Ebrahim Shirazi, the first Grand Vazir of the Qajars.[2]

The Vaqf Organization preserved three *vaqf* deeds of Mirza Mohammad Shafi': a *vaqf* deed dated 1811 on behalf of Asefiye Madrase in Barforush, Mazandaran, a second deed dated 1812, and a third deed dated 1818 for Sadr Madrase.[3] Another document mentions his *vaqf* of Qanat-e Mahdi-abad in Ghar on behalf of Shah

Table 7.1 *Vaqf* properties endowed by Mirza Mohammad Shafi'

Location	*District*	Vaqf *Property*	*Subject*
Barforush		32 shops 1 shop (one-fifth share) 4 pieces of land 1 public bath (one-half share) 1 saray (one-tenth share) 1 house Naqib Dasht hamlet	Madrase-e Asafiyye (Barforush)
Tehran	'Udlajan 'Udlajan 'Udlajan Sangelaj Grand Bazaar Grand Bazaar	1 *saray* (five-twelfths share) 2 public baths (one-fourth share) 6 shops (one-half share) 1 public bath 1 public bath (one-half share) 1 fodder shop 2 shops	Madrase-e Sadr (Tehran)
Lavasan		Jayej village (one-half share)	Madrase-e Sadr (Tehran)
Ghar		Qanat-e Mahdi-abad	Shah 'Abd al-'Azim

'Abd al-'Azim Shrine.[4] Table 7.1 provides the details of the *vaqf* properties. A substantial number of the properties are listed. In particular, those for Asefiye Madrase are impressive, nearly matching those of top *vaqf* institutions in Tehran.

However, the inventory of deeds and documents preserved in the royal treasury and storage reveals that Mirza Mohammad Shafi' owned vast amounts of private property. The inventory contains eighty-two deeds related to his property, among which five deeds are listed twice. Each record includes the seller (to Mirza Mohammad Shafi'), an identification of the property, the price, and the date of the transaction. These deeds confirmed his property rights and were confiscated by the government after his death. Seven deeds concern his properties in Isfahan, including a house, more than eight shops, an ice house, two gardens, shares of three villages, and shares of more than five hamlets, with a total value of 3,110 *tomans*.[5] In Farahan and Central Iran, he owned six villages, a one-sixth share of four villages, a garden, lands, and a share of a *qanat*, which were collectively worth 1,892 *tomans*.[6]

Further, twenty-two deeds in the inventory concern the property of Mirza Mohammad Shafi' in Mazandaran. Among them, with regard to his property in the city of Barforush, the inventory referred to only one house, which cost sixty *tomans*. However, he owned more than twenty properties in seven villages and nine other places in rural areas.[7] Since only one hamlet was endowed as a *vaqf*, it is clear that he kept most of his private properties in the rural areas of Mazandaran.

Moreover, in Tehran, Mirza Mohammad Shafi' purchased a house and four gardens (*bagh*, *baghche*) at the total price of 589 *tomans*. The house and two of the gardens were located in the Sangelaj district, and his purchase included water shares of the Sangelaj Qanat that irrigated three additional gardens.[8] However, more notable is that thirty-three deeds concern the rural districts of the Tehran Province. According to the inventory, Mirza Mohammad Shafi‘ owned whole or part of twenty-six villages, and their total price was 3,610 *tomans*.[9] In addition, according to the inventory of the royal lands of Mohammad Shah, fifteen *khalese* villages once belonged to Mirza Mohammad Shafi‘.[10] Since he endowed the Sadr Madrase with one-half of a village, it is obvious that he established the *vaqf* with a small portion of his significant property.

Mirza Mohammad Shafi‘ had only one daughter, Mah Sharaf Begom, who married Homayun Mirza, the sixteenth son of Fath ‘Ali Shah.[11] She and her husband, however, had no connection with the *vaqfs*. The first *vaqf* administrator of the Asefiye Madrase was Mirza Mohammad Shafi‘'s paternal cousin, Mirza Nasr-allah, and the *vaqf* deed stipulated that he should be succeeded in his position by his male descendants. The position of *vaqf* supervisor of the *madrase* was entrusted to a local *sayyed* family. Moreover, a local *sayyed* in Tehran, Mirza Esma‘il Tehrani was nominated as the first *vaqf* administrator of the Sadr Madrase, and his son became the first *vaqf* supervisor. Both positions remained in the hands of this family from generation to generation. In addition, the *vaqf* of the Mohammadiye Madrase, which was founded by Mohammad Shafi‘'s wife, Nabat Khanom, was also entrusted to Mirza Esma‘il and his descendants. Therefore, these *vaqfs* did not benefit the founders' descendants.

Manuchehr Khan Mo‘tamad al-Dowle

Manuchehr Khan Mo‘tamed al-Dowle was one of the most influential political figures in Iran during the reign of Mohammad Shah. He was an Armenian from Georgia and was captured by the Iranian Army during the first Russo Iranian War. After his capture, he became a eunuch at the court of Fath ‘Ali Shah and converted to Islam. He then was appointed governor-general of Kermanshah and Khuzestan in 1836 and then governor of Isfahan in 1839. He held the governorship there until his death in 1847.[12]

We already know the details of his *vaqf*, established in 1844 mostly on behalf of his *takye* and his relatives. The *vaqf* was expected to benefit his relatives, both paternal and maternal, who accepted Shi‘i Islam: 40 percent of the revenue went to paternal relatives including his brother Mirza Gorgin Khan, while 20 percent of the revenue remained in the hands of maternal relatives.[13] The *vaqf* properties were located around Tehran as follows:

- Khanloq Village in Pashapuye County and three hamlets attached to it;
- Koleyn Village in Pashapuye County with water share of Karaj River and Ab-e Siyah;
- Eleven-thirteenths share of Maqsud-abad Village and eleven-fourteenths water share of Ab-e Bonegah and Qanat-e Kuchik in Ghar County; and
- Firuz-abad Village in Ghar County and a hamlet attached to it.

Contrary to the *vaqfs* of Mirza Mohammad Shafi‘, Manuchehr Khan endowed rural properties. This, however, does not mean that Manuchehr Khan did not own urban properties. In fact, according to the building survey of 1853, he once possessed a mansion in the Arg district and thirty-eight shops in the Bazar district along with a print house, a stable, and a *takye* in the city of Tehran.[14] He intended not to include urban properties except the *takye* in his *vaqf*.

He also had considerable private properties in the rural area of the Tehran Province. Fifteen deeds showing ownership of property in the province were recorded in the inventory of the deeds and documents preserved in the royal treasury and storage. He purchased parts of or whole villages: one in Khar, four in Pashapuye, and two in Varamin. The total value of these properties was 2,791.01 *tomans*.[15] Moreover, he possessed significant property in the provinces of Isfahan, Fars, Qazvin, and Gilan. In Isfahan, he purchased whole or part of seven villages, lands, *qanats*, and watermills, which combined were worth 4,488.4217 *tomans*.[16] His properties in Fars included three villages, fourteen hamlets, and thirty-eight pieces of land; their value was as much as 10,021 *tomans*.[17] His property in Qazvin was modest, including five villages worth 1,200.0031 *tomans*.[18] However, the property of Gilan was much larger, containing thirty-seven villages and valued at 28,997.4448 *tomans*.[19] It is clear that Manuchehr Khan's *vaqf* consisted of a very small part of his substantial property, much like that of Mirza Mohammad Shafi‘.

The Shah confiscated the *vaqf* villages mentioned in the deed along with other properties. Here, the state violated *vaqf* law, but the *takye* appears to have acquired new *vaqf* property consisting of former shops of Manuchehr Khan. In sum, the *vaqf* survived as a device for management of the *takye*, while the other properties were centers of disputes between the Christian heirs and the state.

Both Manuchehr Khan and Mirza Mohammad Shafi‘ could have established substantial *vaqfs* with their property, but they did not do so. Instead, both established modestly-sized *vaqfs* with a small part of their property. In the end, it was as if they had never used a *vaqf* as a tool for maintaining their property at all.

Mahmud Khan Kalantar

The *kalantar* was a local officer sometimes described as a "mayor" of the city in European sources. Mahmud Khan was referred to as a *kalantar* in the *vaqf* deed dated 1834–1835.[20] He remained in his office until 1861, when Naser al-Din Shah put him to death, blaming him for the scarcity of the food supply in the city.[21] Though he was executed, his property was not confiscated by the Shah.

Concerning his property, two *vaqf* deeds were preserved by the Vaqf Organization, while a deed on division of inheritance (*taqsim-name*) was recently published by Bahman Bayani.[22] Deeds on division of inheritance are rare documents, and only nine examples were included in the court registers examined in the previous chapters.[23]

The first *vaqf* of 1834–1835 was founded on behalf of the mourning ceremony of the Imams. The *vaqf* property was a one-sixth share of a *saray* and eight shops located at the end of the Grand Bazaar near Meydan-e Kahforushan (the square of straw sellers). The *vaqf* was revised in 1861 by way of precaution; Mahmud's heirs also added two pieces of land to the *vaqf* property. The second *vaqf*, dated 1854, was established also for the mourning ceremony. The *vaqf* property was a one-third share of twenty-five shops located near the moat of the Arg and the arsenal (*qurkhane*). The location was probably just south of the Arg and west of Sabze Meydan. Both *vaqf* deeds appointed the founder as the first administrator and his male descendants as his successors.

On the other hand, the *taqsim-name*, dated 1867, was drawn up for dividing his legacy among two sons and two daughters. The deed consists of seven sections. The first section concerns twenty-eight and one-half shops located in the west of Meydan-e Bolurforushan, which apparently denotes Sabze Meydan.[24] This section contains ten *vaqf* shops, which originated from the one-third share of twenty-five shops endowed in 1854. Here the ten *vaqf* shops were valued at 1,400 *tomans* while another eighteen shops, inherited by the heirs, were worth 2,890 *tomans*. Therefore, approximately one-third of his total property became *vaqf*.

The second section relates to the *saray* and shops located in Meydan-e Kahforushan. It contains thirteen shops, two shares of shops, and a one-third share of the *saray* and shops. Among them, ten shops, the two shares of shops, and a one-sixth share of the *saray* and shops were private property and inherited by the heirs, with this inheritance valued at 2,215 *tomans*. The rest of the property – the three remaining shops and a one-sixth share of the *saray* and shops – was the property of the second *vaqf*. Though the value of the *vaqf* property was not specified in the deed, one can estimate the value as seven hundred to eight hundred *tomans*. The *vaqf* property was worth less than one-third of the total property in the Meydan-e Kahforushan.

In contrast, the other five sections of the *taqsim-name* did not include any *vaqf* property. The third section concerns a one-third share of forty-three shops and one stand at the Mohammadiye Gate in addition to a house located in the 'Udalajan district; the properties were worth 2,543 *tomans* and 3,333 *dinars*. The fourth section related to a *karvansara* and other property outside of the Dulab gate, which was valued at 500 *tomans*, while the property in the fifth section, which was not divided by the heirs, including two *sarays*, a house, and a shop, and was worth 1,400 *tomans*.

Even if one ignores the last two sections concerning the undivided property and household effects, Mahmud Khan's legacy was worth approximately 9,600 *tomans*, while his *vaqf* property was valued 2,100~2,200 *tomans*. In other words, Mahmud Khan endowed less than 20 percent of his whole property as a *vaqf*.

Unlike Mirza Mohamad Shafi' and Manuchehr Khan, Mahmud Khan did not have any property outside of Tehran because his activities as a local officer were restricted to the city. Even so, he founded two *vaqfs* with only a small part of his whole property.

Haji Mohammad Hasan Kolahduz

In some cases, the property of the individuals is known through other documents such as last wills and testaments. Haji Mohammad Hasan, the hatter (*kolahduz*), is one such case. We do not know much about his life: he was a merchant (*tajer*) who passed away between 1847 and 1853. His father, Karbala'i Zeyn al-Abedin, having the *nesbe*, Khorasani, appears to have been from Khorasan. A *vaqf* deed and a last will and testament (*vasiyat-name*), both dated 1847, are preserved at the Vaqf Organization.[25] Though Werner's excellent article also addressed last wills and testaments, which included the *vaqf* provisions,[26] this will be the first case in which a *vaqf* deed and an individual's will were drawn up separately. Last wills and testaments were also recorded in the shari'a court registers, and their numbers are almost the same as those of *vaqfs*. They comprise 0.5 ~1.4 percent of the total records.

First, we must investigate Mohammad Hasan's property. With the two documents, his property can be categorized as follows.

A *Vaqf* property, which was controlled by the *vaqf* administrator on the basis of the *vaqf* deed.

Two-thirds of the *saray* that was built, including two shops, six stands, a storage, a stable, a cistern, etc., located in the Grand Bazaar.

B "One-third," which was used in accordance with his last will and testament and controlled by the executor.

One-third of his share of the two villages in Ghar: two-thirds of Esma'il-abad and all of Najm-abad, including a garden and a one-sixth share of a hamlet.
Two shops not included in Category C.

C The rest, which was to be inherited by the heirs.

Two-thirds of his share of the two villages in Ghar County.
Five and one-half shops in the Grand Bazaar.

According to Islamic law, one can devise at most one-third of his property by a last will and testament. From his last will and testament, it is clear that his cash was also divided into Category B and C, but the total amount was not specified in his will.

The *saray* of Haji Mohammad Hasan Kolahduz was the second largest *saray* in the Grand Bazaar in 1853: it contained 212 rooms with three corridors, a *timche*, a stable, a courtyard, and two stands.[27] It was built before 1839.[28] It is difficult to know the value of the *saray*, but because Saray-e Amir, which included 366 rooms, was sold at 50,000 *tomans* in 1879,[29] we know that his *saray* would have been worth approximately 20,000 to 30,000 *tomans* at that time. On the other hand, the whole of Esma'il-abad cost 6,000 *tomans* because Kayumars Mirza borrowed 3,000 *tomans* on the security of one-half of the Esma'il-abad in 1876.[30] Therefore, if we do not take cash into consideration, it appears that the *vaqf* property was more valuable than other property, although the building survey of 1853 indicates that his four *vaqf* shops and five *vaqf* stands existed in the Grand Bazaar while nine shops were owned by the heirs of Haji Mohammad Hasan.[31]

First, let us check the conditions of the *vaqf*. After deducting the necessary expenses, the *vaqf* revenue was to have been divided into fifteen portions. A two-fifteenths share was to go to the *vaqf* administrator, a one-fifteenth share was to be taken by the *vaqf* supervisor, and another one-fifteenth share was to be given to the manager (*mobasher*), who would actually take the rent from the tenants of *vaqf* property. Another thirteen portions were to be spent for different purposes, such as the mourning ceremonies, aid for poor pilgrims to the 'Atabat and Mashhad, candles of the shrines of the Shi'i Imams, aid for poor minors, aid for poor relatives and neighbors, funerals for the poor, meals at the Fetr and Ghadir festivals, etc. One may summarize the conditions as general good deeds from the Shi'i perspective.

On the other hand, the last will and testament stipulated conditions that related to the testator, Haji Mohammad Hasan. First, the executors were to have deducted his debts, the *khoms*, and the *zakat* from the whole legacy. Each of them was counted as 100 *tomans*. In theory, *khoms* should have been one-fifth of the income from the transactions, but here it was fixed perfunctorily. In the last will and testament, one-half of the *khoms* was called the Imam's share (*sahm-e emam*) and another one-half should have been spent for the *sayyeds*, which coincides with Shi'i theory. The *zakat* is the poor rate for the Muslims, but it was not specified in the last wills and testaments from Qajar Tabriz. After the deduction, one-third of the legacy, which the executor would control, should have been fixed. Then, the expenditures for the cash one-third are described: funerals, sending the body to Najaf, fifty-year fasting and prayer for the deceased, ten-year fasting and prayer on behalf of his parents, reciting Qur'an and visits to the shrines in Najaf and Karbala', deputy pilgrimage to Mecca, and atonement for the deceased's sin. All of these expenditures related to the testator in person and to his funeral, grave, and afterlife.

It is notable, however, that the real estate of the one-third was stipulated to be handled on the conditions of the *vaqf*. In other words, though properties in Category B were not *vaqf* properties, their income should be spent for the good purposes stipulated by the *vaqf* deed.

The executors nominated were his two sons, who also would be the second *vaqf* administrators after the death of Haji Mohammad Hasan. Therefore, it was possible that it would not be difficult for the executors to control both *vaqf* property and the private property. Contrary to the three previous examples, the *vaqf* property had a higher value than the private property and the conditions of *vaqf* also were applied for the private property controlled by the executors. The difference between Haji Mohammad Hasan and the three others might have arisen from his social status as a merchant.

Grand bazaar

The Grand Bazaar of Tehran flourished as a commercial center of the city in the Qajar period. In 1853, 1,204 shops (28 percent) were located in the Grand Bazaar while 4,320 shops existed in the whole city. The *sarays*, which were used for various commercial activities, were also concentrated in the Grand Bazaar. Here, the ownership of the shops and *sarays* is examined.

Shops

The building survey of 1853 indicates the kinds of shops. According to this survey, the Grand Bazaar included more than one hundred kinds of shops. Five sorts of shops were numerous and were particularly concentrated into the Grand Bazaar: cloth dealers' (*bazzazi*), gold-lace makers' (*'alaqebandi*), second-hand goods dealers' (*semsari*), hatters' (*kolahduzi*), and Russian shoes makers' (*orsiduzi*) shops. Each profession had more than forty shops in the Grand Bazaar, and they comprised more than 60 percent of the each sort of shop in the whole city. Other sorts of shops that were mainly located in the Grand Bazaar were tent materials makers' (*lavvafi*), crystal sellers' (*bolur-forushi*), quiver makers' (*tarkashduzi*), bankers' (*sarrafi*), Georgian shoes makers' (*gorjiduzi*), and pack saddle makers' (*palanduzi*) shops. Generally speaking, textile and leather products as well as precious goods were sold mainly in the Grand Bazaar.

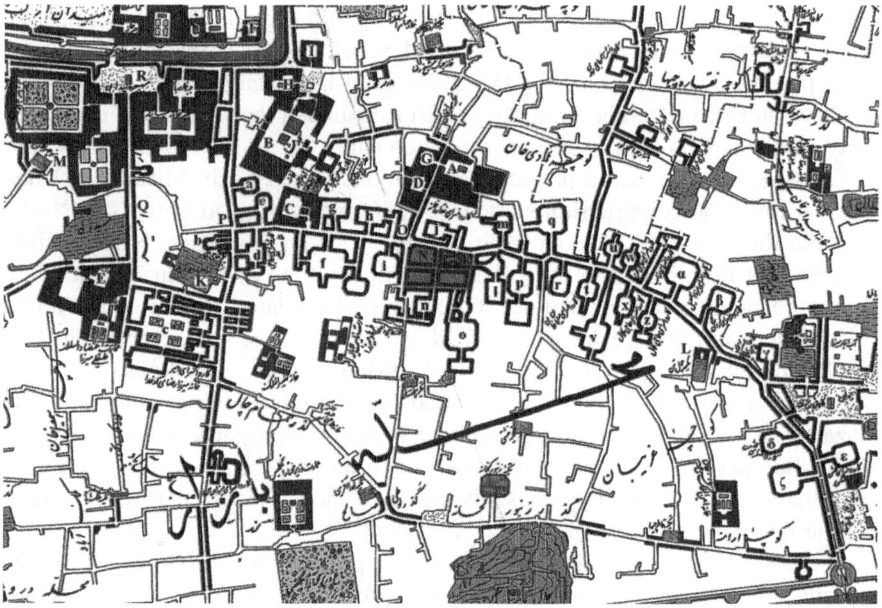

Map 7.1 The Grand Bazaar of Tehran after Krziz 1858

A: Old Friday Mosque, B: Shah Mosque, C: Sayyed 'Aziz allah Mosque,
D: Mirza Musa Mosque, E: Sheykh 'Abd al-Hoseyn Mosque, F: Madar-e Shah Madrase,
G: Mohammadiye Madrase, H: Sadr Madrase, I: Dar al-Shefa' Madrase,
K: Emamzade Zeyd, L: Haft Tan, M: Takye of Manuchehr Khan,
N: Chahar Bazar, O: Large Chahar Suq, P: Small Chahar Suq, Q: Bazaar of Amir.
R: Sabze Meydan

The names of *sarays* (a~z, α~δ) are shown in the text.

As mentioned previously, 176 shops out of a total of 1,204 shops in the Grand Bazaar belonged to the *vaqfs* in 1853. However, more precisely, 133 shops belonged to the *vaqfs* completely, while 43 shops were privately-owned buildings that were built on the *vaqf* lands. These forty-three shops were built on *vaqf* land belonging to Madrase-e Madar-e Shah (Madrase-e Hakim Hashem).[32] In short, genuine *vaqf* shops comprised only 11 percent of the total shops in the Grand Bazaar. Among them, forty-three shops were the *vaqf* for Shah Mosque and thirty shops were endowed on behalf of Imam Husayn (Sayyed al-Shohada').

If only 11 percent of the total shops were *vaqf*-owned, who owned the other shops in the Grand Bazaar? Out of the 1,204 shops recorded in the building survey, the Shah owned 91; however, the building survey did not indicate the owner of four large commercial facilities, namely, Bazar-e Amir (250 shops), Sabze Meydan (102 shops), Chahar Bazar (58 shops), and Bazarche-e Zell al-Soltani (39 shops). The Chahar Bazar had been a square named the Square of Horseshoe Makers (Meydan-e Na'albandan) before the Qajar period, but was renovated as a cruciform bazaar by the order of Aqa Mohammad Shah. Fath 'Ali Shah purchased this bazaar, which included forty-eight shops, four stands, a mint, and a *timche*, as recorded in the *khalese* inventories.[33] The Sabze Meydan was a dirty square where criminals were executed until the middle of the nineteenth century. Haji Mirza Aqasi bought 316 shops around the Sabze Meydan, which later became part of the royal property.[34] In addition, in 1852–3, Naser al-Din Shah ordered the building of a two-story commercial property, which surrounded the square and contained forty-two rooms on the first floor for the merchants.[35]

The Bazar-e Amir was a project of the famous Grand Vazir, Mirza Taqi Khan Amir Kabir. The construction started in 1850 and continued until 1855.[36] The fact that the survey of 1853 called it "Bazar-e Dowlat (Bazaar of State)" might suggest that it belonged to the government at the time of the survey, although it later became private property. In fact, a *vaqf* deed dated 1861 confirmed that thirteen shops in this bazaar were owned by the mother of Amir Kabir, while an English diplomat, Eastwick, reported in the same year, that the shops had to pay 282 *tomans* and 3,500 *dinars* for rent and 183 *tomans* as tax per month.[37] The Bazarche-e Zell al-Soltani also could have been royal property, since 'Ali Mirza Zell al-Soltan lived in exile after he had failed to succeed the throne following Fath 'Ali Shah's death. If my hypothesis is true, 540 shops (45 percent) of the Grand Bazaar belonged to the Shah or the government.

The rest, 488 shops (41 percent) were private property belonging to individuals. Among them, 105 shops belonged to merchants and artisans, sixty-eight shops belonged to the 'ulama, forty-five shops owned by bureaucrats and military personnel, and the royal family except the shah had only one shop. Among the large shop owners, Sheykh Reza, leader of prayers at the Old Friday Mosque, owned thirty-eight shops while Aqa Mahdi Navvab, a rich merchant, possessed thirty-five shops, among which fourteen and one-half shops were built on the *vaqf* site of Madrase-e Madar-e Shah.[38] Other major owners of the shops were the heirs of Haji Sayyed Hasan Tehrani (thirty-three shops), Haji 'Abd al-'Azim Harati (nineteen shops), and a merchant, Haji Mohammad Baqer Tehrani (eighteen shops and one-half). Neither bureaucrats nor the military officers are found among the major owners. In addition, only six shops had the same professions as the owner. In other words, the tenants, not the owners, operated the shops.

The situation was completely different in 1899–1900. First, there was no shop belonging to the Shah or the government. This is probably a part of Naser al-Din Shah's policy: he sold *khalese* property to rich subjects for more proper management.[39] It appears that bureaucrats and military officers had bought the property, because they owned 326 shops. The Shah's policy also benefited the members of the royal family: their shops had drastically increased to 176. The 'ulama possessed 198 shops, while the merchants and the artisans had 126.5 shops.

In fact, the royal family and high ranking bureaucrats had a considerable number of shops in the former Bazar-e Amir. The second princess of Naser al-Din Shah, 'Esmat al-Dowle, owned 102 shops of Bazar-e Orsiduzha, which was located in the back of Sabze Meydan.[40] Soltan Mas'ud Mirza Zell al-Soltan, the fourth son of Naser al-Din Shah possessed forty-five shops in the former Bazar-e Amir.[41] Mirza 'Ali Asghar Khan Amin al-Soltan, the Grand Vazir of the time, had sixty-five shops in the north of the small Chahar Suq.[42]

On the other hand, merchants represented a smaller percentage of owners. Haji Aqa Ghani owned seventeen shops; however, he was also the shareowner of sixty-two shops with four other people.[43] Haji Mohammad Hoseyn, a jeweler, owned eighteen shops in the east side of the Grand Bazaar.[44]

The shops of 'ulama in the survey of 1899–1900 were problematic. Sheykh Ja'far Soltan al-'Olama, the leader of prayers at Old Friday Mosque, owned fifty shops while Mirza Zeyn al-'Abedin Emam Jom'e possessed forty-seven shops in the Grand Bazaar, according to the survey. However, as mentioned above, most of these shops appear to belong to the *vaqf* property of each mosque that they controlled. For instance, Emam Jom'e's forty-six shops might have been all *vaqf* property for the Shah Mosque, while twenty-eight shops of Soltan al-'Olama' could have been *vaqf* property for the Old Friday Mosque. If so, the private shops owned by the 'ulama can be estimated to have totaled 123, a number that was close to the total number of shops of merchants and artisans.

The 115 *vaqf* shops in 1899–1900 could be increased to 190 if one considered these shops as *vaqf* properties for the two mosques. Even so, the *vaqf* shops comprised only 16 percent of the total 1,218 shops in the Grand Bazaar. Maybe the building surveys did not count *vaqf* properties accurately, but there are no grounds for considering most shops in the Grand Bazaar as *vaqf* property.

Sarays

The Persian word *sara* or *saray* denotes a commercial building, which wholesale traders used as an office or a storage, located in a commercial district of the city. In Qajar Tehran, the term *karvansara* was used as a synonym of *sara*. In order to avoid confusion, I use the term *saray* for these commercial buildings because the English word "caravansary" refers to an inn for caravans along the highways, which was usually called a *rebat* in Qajar usage.[45]

Naturally, *saray*s were concentrated in the Grand Bazaar. In 1853, thirty-one *saray*s, including three independent *timche*s and two independent *dalan*s, were located in the Grand Bazaar out of fifty-six *saray*s in the city.[46] Their locations are indicated in the Map 4 as a~z, α, β, δ, ε, and ζ.[47] The survey of 1853 shows the number of rooms (*hojre*s) of the each *saray*: there were two mega *saray*s (more than two hundred rooms, c and f), six large *saray*s (from 60 to 100 rooms, b, d, e, o, q, v, and y), seventeen middle-size *saray*s (from thirty to fifty-nine rooms, g, h, i, j, m, n, p, r, t, u, x, z, α, β, δ, ε, and ζ), and six small *saray*s (less than thirty rooms, a, k, l. s, w, and δ). The largest was c. Sara-ye Amir; it was a two-story building, containing 367 rooms, four corridors (*dalan*s), and four *timche*s.[48] The survey does not refer much to the usage of the rooms, but at least twenty-six rooms at the first *timche* were used as the office of the merchants (*tajer-neshin*). We know that Haji Amin-e Dar al-Zarb, the famous merchant, also had an office in this *saray*.[49] A French traveler, Orsolle mentioned that the caravans of the Ziegler Company, which almost monopolized the trade between Iran and Europe, arrived and departed every day.[50]

The survey provides more precise information about the usage of the rooms at b. Sara-ye Aqa Ahmad. It was a two-story building with two corridors, a courtyard, and seventy rooms. On the first floor around the courtyard, there were thirty-six rooms: twelve dwellings, three haberdashers (*kharraziforush*s), three cloth dealers, and eighteen stables. There were twenty rooms on the second floor: four *landare* makers (*landreduzi*), three hatters, two mosaic workers (*khatemsazi*), a haberdasher, a painter, a peddler, a tailor (*khayyat*), a rubber (*dallaki*), a fur maker (*khazduz*), a restaurant (*ashpazkhane*), a vacant room, and three dwellings, housing a merchant, a servant of Ajudanbashi, and a secretary of the *divankhane* in Tabriz. The first corridor was one story and included nine rooms: eight cloth dealers and one hatter. The second corridor was two stories with twelve rooms. On the first floor there were eight offices of merchants, while on the second floor there were three offices of merchants and one dwelling of a haberdasher.[51] Here we can say that the *saray* of a commercial complex contained offices, dwellings, stables, and various sorts of shops. It was definitely not an inn for travelers.

The building surveys provide some information about the owner of the shops. In 1853, out of thirty-two *saray*s in the Grand Bazaar, parts of fifteen of them were a *vaqf*. On the other hand, the survey of 1899–1900 listed thirty-one *saray*s. Twenty-five *saray*s overlap those of 1853, but six *saray*s are new entries, while the seven the *saray*s of 1853 have been omitted. Moreover, only five *saray*s contained shares of a *vaqf* in the survey of 1899–1900. In fact, the ownership of the *saray*s was very complicated and difficult to describe in the survey. One has to examine each *saray* one by one by analyzing the documents.

Concerning the largest *saray*, c. Sara-ye Amir, there is no evidence to indicate that any part of it was a *vaqf*. According to Eastwick, the tenants of the *saray* paid a rent of 2,400 *toman*s per year to the widow and daughter of Amir Kabir and Malek al-Tojjar.[52] Also, there was a dispute over the ownership of the *saray*, but sources do not refer to its *vaqf* share.[53] The *saray* remained wholly owned as private property. On the other hand, as mentioned above, a two-thirds share of f. Sara-ye Haji Hasan, the second largest *saray*, became a *vaqf* in 1847, and the building surveys considered the whole of it as a *vaqf*.

Seven other *sarays* that did not contain any *vaqf* portion: a. Sara-ye Zargarha, b. Sara-ye Aqa Ahmad, i. Sara-ye Haji Zaman, l. Qeysariye, s. Timche-e Sheykh Reza, u. Sara-ye Dust ‘Ali Khan, and y. Sara-ye Navvab. After analyzing documents, twenty-two other *sarays* include a *vaqf* portion. The details are as follows:[54]

d Saray of Haji Molla ‘Ali, (built after 1852, seventy-nine rooms)

The whole of the *saray* became a *vaqf* in 1888. The *vaqf* was established by the will of Mohammad Rahim Khan ‘Ala’ al-Dowle. The income was used for the salary of the administrator (ten percent), maintenance of the *saray* and *timche*, the mourning ceremony and recital of the tragedy of Karbala’ held in this *saray* (two hundred *tomans*), and the shrine of Imam Husayn in Karbala’ (one hundred *tomans*), and the rest was to be expended in clothing the poor as *radd-e mazalem* of late ‘Ala al-Dowle.[55] Though the survey of 1899–1900 describes this *saray* as the private property of ‘Ala’ al-Dowle (Ahmad Khan, son of Mohammad Rahim Khan), he appears to have controlled the *saray* as a *vaqf* administrator.

e Saray of Haji Sayyed Mohsen (built after 1830, sixty-six rooms)

This *saray* was endowed little by little as a *vaqf*. First, Haji Sayyed Mohsen, probably the founder of the *saray*, established a *vaqf* with its one-fourth share in 1830. In 1836–1837, Mirza Ebrahim founded a *vaqf* with its one-sixth share by the will of Sayyed Mohsen. Another one-twelfth share became the *vaqf* property for Madrase-e Molla Aqa Reza, probably before 1853. The building survey of 1853 noted that the larger corridor of the *saray*, including thirty-three rooms, was *vaqf* property controlled by Haji Sayyed Nasr-allah.[56] He founded another *vaqf* with one-sixth share of the *saray* by the will of Mirza Ebrahim. As a result, in 1868, two-thirds share of the *saray* was *vaqf* property controlled by Haji Molla ‘Ali Kani.[57] Though the building survey of 1899–1900 noted that the *saray* belonged to the heir of Qasem Khan and Haji Abu al-Hasan Me‘mar, it appears that at least a part of the *saray* was *vaqf*.

g Sara-ye Aramane/Gebrha (built after 1799, forty-nine rooms)

In 1799, Fath ‘Ali Shah leased the *saray* from Mirza Baba Tehrani for ninety years. In fact, this transaction means that the *saray* was owned by the Shah because it was listed as a *khalese* in the inventory of royal property.[58] The *saray* was in the hands of the family of ‘Ali Mirza Zell al-Soltan after 1843–1844, but later it became the *vaqf* for Zell al-Soltan’s tomb.[59] The building survey of 1899–1900 referred to the *saray* as owned by Moshir-e Khalvat. It is not clear how he obtained control of the *saray*.

h Sara-ye Khoda’i (built after 1826, forty rooms)

In 1835, Hajiye Shah Soltan Khanom, the eighteenth daughter of Fath ‘Ali Shah, purchased a one-fourth share of the old corridor and the courtyard and a one-twelfth share of the new corridor of the *saray* for 700 *tomans*: she made these shares a *vaqf*. After paying for maintenance and the salary of the administrator (one-tenth), one-half of the rest was to be spent for the recital of the story of martyrs while the other one-half was to be used as aid for poor *sayyeds* and non-*sayyeds*. The *vaqf* administrator was chosen from among the descendants of the founder.[60]

Moreover, in 1848, Haji Mohammad 'Ali Nuri established a *vaqf* with a one-twelfth share of the *saray* and two shops. After paying for maintenance and the salary of the administrator (one-tenth), the rest of the income was to be divided into four portions: one portion was spent for the mourning ceremony of Imam Husayn, another portion for the aid to poor students in Najaf, another for the aid to the poor, and a final portion for the purchase of religious books. The future *vaqf* administrators were the founder's son and his descendants.[61] Therefore, a one-third share of the old corridor and courtyard and a one-sixth share of the new corridor became a *vaqf*, although the building survey of 1853 did not refer to the *vaqf*.

The *saray* was owned by several co-owners and this caused decay in the *saray*. For this reason, in 1875, a deed of division (*taqsim-name*) of the *saray* was drawn up to improve the situation. The deed of division addressed the upkeep of the *saray* by establishing the owner or holder of each room. Table 7.2 indicates the intricate ownership arrangement of the *saray* set forth in the deed. Here, beside the two *vaqfs* mentioned above, two other *vaqfs* established with the shares of the *saray* and the shares of the *vaqfs* reached 4.5 dang (three-fourths) of the courtyard and a large corridor and 3.5 dang (seven-twelfths) of the small corridor. Moreover, Sheykh Mohsen and Mirza 'Abd al-Hoseyn, the heirs of late Aqa Mirza Abu al-Qasem, held the shares in three different ways: a one-twelfth share was their private property, another one-twelfth was *vaqf* property, and the use of income of the other share was directed by the last will and testament.[62]

Table 7.2 Ownership arrangement of Sara-ye Khoda'i in 1875

Owner/holder	*Portion of the saray*	*Private*	*Will*	Vaqf	*Sum*	Vaqf *founder*
Haji Sayyed	Courtyard, large corridor	0.5		1	1.5	?
Mohammad Baqer	Small corridor	1.5		1	2.5	?
Sayyed Mahmud	Whole			1.5	1.5	?
Sayyed Mortaza	Courtyard, large corridor			1.5	1.5	Shah Soltan Khanom
	Small corridor			0.5	0.5	
Sheykh Mohsen Mirza 'Abd al-Hoseyn	Whole	0.5	0.5	0.5	1.5	Haji Mohammad 'Ali
Sum	Courtyard, large corridor	1	0.5	4.5	6	
	Small corridor	2	0.5	3.5	6	

According to Reza'i, Haji Mirza Abu Fazl Mojtahed Tehrani established a *vaqf* with a one-eighth share of the *saray* in 1894. Moreover, in 1907, Sayyed Mahmud Javaheri Tehrani founded a *vaqf* with a five-twelfths share of the *saray* on behalf of Aqa Mahmud Madrase. The other *taqsim-name*, dated 1911, indicated that approximately eleven-twelfths of the *saray* became a *vaqf*.[63] The *saray* was becoming a *vaqf* portion by portion over the course of more than seventy years.

j Sara-ye Naqqarkhane (built before 1829, forty rooms)

According to the building survey, the whole *saray* was *vaqf* property for Mohammadiye Madrase in 1853. It could have been the Safavid *vaqf* because the *madrase* was built during the Safavid Period. The *saray* was in the hands of Aqa Sayyed 'Ali Akbar Tafreshi in 1899–1900.[64]

k Dalan-e Zarrabkhane/Timche-e Amin-e Aqdas (built before 1853, twenty-six rooms)

This was an independent *dalan* (corridor) without a courtyard. The building survey of 1853 noted that all of the *dalan* was a *vaqf* for Madrase-e Mohammadiye. However, in 1899–1900, it was owned by Haji Reza Khan Khazane.[65]

m Sara-ye Sheykh Ja'far (built around 1815, fifty-one rooms)

Haji Sayyed Mohsen Tajer built the *saray* and made the whole of it a *vaqf* for the Old Friday Mosque. The details of the *vaqf* of the Old Friday Mosque will be discussed in the next chapter.

n Sara-ye Haji Abu Taleb (built before 1788, thirty-eight rooms)

Haji Abu Taleb Tajer Tehrani, who is supposed to be the founder of the *saray*, established a *vaqf* with a one-third share of the *saray* along with the same share of two shops.[66] The deed was revised in 1799: the *vaqf* income should be spent on behalf of the Fourteen Infallibles (Chahardah Ma'sum) and Molla Mohammad, leader of prayers at the Old Friday Mosque, and Molla Mohammad's descendants were nominated as the *vaqf* administrators.[67] The building survey of 1853 noted that a one-third share of the *saray* was controlled by Sheykh Reza, son of Molla Mohammad.[68]

Moreover, Mirza Jani Nuri established two *vaqf*s with this *saray*. First, in 1854, he endowed a one-fourth share of the *saray* as the executor of his brother's will. Secondly, in 1855, he established a *vaqf* with a one-sixth share of the *saray*. These two *vaqf*s had the same conditions: 60 percent of income was spent for the mourning ceremonies of Imams, 20 percent for Madrase-e Mirza Zaki located in the Sangelaj district, and 20 percent for the salaries of the *vaqf* administrator and the *vaqf* supervisor. At last, in 1882, Mirza Mohammad Reza, son of Mirza Jani, founded a *vaqf* with the remaining one-fourth share of the *saray*. It was directed that 20 percent of the *vaqf* income should be spent for the salaries of the administrator and the supervisor while 80 percent should be used for the mourning ceremonies of the Imams. Here, more than ninety years after the construction, the whole *saray* became a *vaqf*.

A lease deed dated 1888 indicates how the *saray* was managed: Mirza Mohammad Reza and his brother leased their *vaqf* share (i.e., two-thirds of the *saray*) to Haji Hasan Karvasaradar Esfahani for two years at 792 *tomans*. Haji Hasan also rented the one-third share of the *saray* from Sheykh Ja'far Soltan al-'Olama', *vaqf* administrator of this share, with a separate deed.[69] In other words, though the *saray* consisted of several *vaqfs*, the management of the whole *saray* was entrusted to one *karvasaradar*. Later, Sheykh Fazl-allah acquired the control of the *vaqf* share of Mirza Mohammad Reza and his brother before 1899–1900.[70]

o Sara-ye Shah (built before 1793, ninety rooms)

An inscription of the *vaqf* deed is located at the wall of the *saray*. 'Ali Mirza Zell al-Soltan created the *vaqf* with the whole *saray*. Twenty percent of the income was allocated to the salary of the administrator, and 10 percent was for the salary of the supervisor. The rest was to be spent for the candles of the shrines of the Shi'i Imams in the 'Atabat: 'Ali's shrine in Najaf (30 percent), Husayn's shrine in Karbala' (30 percent), and the shrine of 'Abbas (brother of Husayn) in Karbala' (10 percent).[71] According to the building survey of 1899–1900, Mirza Mohammad Hasan Ashtiyani controlled the *saray* as a *vaqf*.[72]

q Sara-ye Now (built before 1852, seventy-seven rooms)

In 1855, Haji Mohammad 'Ali Tehrani founded a *vaqf* with a one-twelfth share of the *saray*. After deducting expenditures for maintenance and the salary of the administrator (10 percent), one-half of the income was to be spent for the mourning ceremonies and the other one-half was to be spent as aid for the poor at the time of the Ghadir festival. The founder appointed his son and descendants as the *vaqf* administrators.[73] The situation of the *saray* appears not to have changed until 1899–1900; the building survey noted that the *saray* was partly private property and partly *vaqf* property.[74]

p Sara-ye Haji 'Abd al-Vahhab (built before 1793, fifty-one rooms)

According to the building survey of 1853, half of the *saray* was *vaqf* property controlled by Sheykh Reza although the survey of 1899–1900 did not refer to any *vaqf* share of the *saray*.[75]

r Sara-ye Haji Nad 'Ali (built before 1826, thirty-nine rooms)

In 1887, Haji Aqa Kojuri purchased a one-eightieth share of the *saray* from Haji Mortaza Damavandi at ninety *tomans*. At the same time, Kojuri bought a one-thirtieth share of the *saray* from Aqa Mohammad Hoseyn Damavandi at 240 *tomans*.[76] It appears that Kojuri purchased small shares of the *saray* one by one. At last, in 1888, Haji Aqa Kojuri established a *vaqf* with one-half of the *saray*. After deducting the salaries of the administrator (10 percent) and the supervisor (5 percent), one-half of the *vaqf* income was to be spent for the mourning ceremony while the other one-half was to be used for aid to the poor. The *vaqf* administrators were the founders and their male descendants, while the first *vaqf* supervisor was Sheykh Fazl-allah Nuri.[77] Though the building survey of 1899–1900 noted that the *saray* was owned by Sheykh Fazl-allah,[78] at least one-half of the *saray* was the *vaqf* property controlled by him.

t Timche-e Soleyman Khan (built before 1826, thirty-nine rooms)

Though this was called *timche* or small *saray*, its structure and size was the same as a *saray* or *karvansara*: it had a courtyard and two corridors. The first *vaqf* was established in 1826 by Sayyed Mohammad Tehrani. He endowed his children with one-half of the *timche* along with shares of Sara-ye Dalan-e Deraz and nine shops. At the same time, he established a *vaqf* with a one-fourth share of the *timche* and other shares of the *saray* and shops for the mourning ceremony and aid to the poor sayyeds.[79]

In 1831, Hoseyn ‘Ali Khan, Mo‘ayyer-bashi or the Chief of Mint, founded a *vaqf* with the one-sixth share of the *timche* on behalf of the mourning ceremony of the Imams. The founder appointed Molla Mohammad Hasan Yazdi and his descendants, who were involved in the double *vaqf* case discussed in Chapter 4, as the *vaqf* administrators.[80] Now the eleven-twelfths share of the *timche* became *vaqf* property, although neither building survey refer to it as a *vaqf*.

v Sara-ye Dalan-e Deraz (built before 1800–1, eighty-one rooms)

As mentioned above, Sayyed Mohammad Tehrani founded *vaqf*s with the *saray* along with the shares of Timche-e Soleyman Khan and of nine shops in 1826. A one-third share of the *saray* became a *vaqf* on behalf of his descendants while a one-sixth share was *vaqf* property for the mourning ceremonies and the poor *sayyeds*.[81] The building surveys did not accurately described the *vaqf*; the survey of 1853 mentioned only one-third *vaqf* share, while the survey of 1899–1900 does not refer to this *saray* as a *vaqf*.

w Sara-ye Yazdiha/Gebrha (built before 1841, twenty-six rooms)

In 1841, a one-sixth share of the *saray* become *vaqf* property for Masjed-e Hakim, located in the ‘Udlajan district. The *vaqf* income was to be spent for candles, mats, a servant, a *mo’azzen,* or maintenance of the mosque.[82] According to the building survey of 1853, the share of the *vaqf* for Masjed-e Hakim had increased to one-third, while another one-third share of the *saray* became a *vaqf* on behalf of Madrase-e Haji Mohsen located in the Bazar district.[83]

Moreover, in 1892, Jan Jahan Khanom, the wife of Haji Molla ‘Ali Kani, established a *vaqf* and changed the remaining one-third share of the *saray* into *vaqf* property of Masjed-e Hakim. The income was to be spent for the students, servants, candles, and maintenance of the mosque.[84] The whole *saray* became a *vaqf* at the time, although the building survey of 1899–1900 did not note that fact.

x Sara-ye Haji Kamal Kohne (built before 1826, thirty-one rooms)

According to the building survey of 1853, a one-fourth share of the *saray* was *vaqf* property controlled by Sheykh ‘Abd al-Hoseyn.[85] In 1861, ‘Abbas Tajer Tehrani, *farshforush* (carpet seller), founded a *vaqf* with a one-fourth share of this *saray* along with shares of the other Sara-ye Haji Kamal and shares of ten shops.[86] This is also the *vaqf* on behalf of the mourning ceremony held in the house of the founder. In total, one-half of the *saray* became *vaqf* property at that time.

z Sara-ye Haji Kamal (built before 1852, thirty-two rooms)

The building survey of 1853 noted that half of the *saray* was *vaqf* property controlled by Sheykh ‘Abd al-Hoseyn. As mentioned above, in 1861, ‘Abbas Tajer established a *vaqf* also with a one-twelfth share of the *saray* on behalf of the mourning ceremony held in his house.[87] Therefore, a seven-twelfths share of the *saray* became a *vaqf* at that time.

α Sara-ye Mirza Esma‘il (built before 1852, forty-four rooms)

According to the building survey of 1853, a two-thirds share of the *saray* was *vaqf* property controlled by Haji Sayyed ‘Abd-allah.[88] However, the survey of 1899–1900 indicate that the *saray* was owed by Mirza Yusof Khan.[89]

β Sara-ye Gardan Kaj (built before 1848, 44 rooms)

The building survey of 1853 wrote that a one-fourth share of this *saray* was *vaqf* property although the *saray* was in private possession in the building survey of 1899–1900.[90]

γ Sara-ye Haji Hadi (built before 1858?)

Neither building survey refers to this *saray*, but it is found on a map in 1858. In 1848, two-thirds of the *saray* became *vaqf* property by the will of Haji ‘Ali Asghar Tehrani. After deducting the salaries of the administrator and the supervisor, and expenditure for maintenance, the *vaqf* income was to be divided into four portions: one portion to be used for the aid to the poor sayyeds, one portion for the poor non-sayyeds, one for the mourning ceremonies, and the other was to be used for a good purpose.[91]

δ Sara-ye Golshan (built before 1853, thirty-three rooms)

According to the building survey of 1853, one-half of the *saray* was *vaqf* property controlled by Sheykh Reza, the leader of prayers at the Old Friday Mosque.[92]

ε Sara-ye Goshan-Shekan (built before 1826, thirty-seven rooms)

Though the building survey of 1853 described the *saray* as private property, a related *vaqf* deed dated 1846 was preserved in the archives of the Vaqf Organization: one-third of the *saray* was endowed by two sons of Haji Zeyn al-'Abedin by the will of their father. After deduction of the salary of the administrator (ten percent) and expenditure for the maintenance, one-half of the income was to be spent on the mourning ceremony of the Imams and the other one-half was to be used for aid to the poor in the time of the Ghadir Festival. The founders and their descendants were appointed as *vaqf* administrators.

ζ Sara-ye 'Alam-Shekan (built before 1826, forty-eight rooms)

In 1846, Haji 'Abd al-Vahhab Tehrani founded a *vaqf* with a one-fourth share of the *saray* and shares of thirteen shops. After deducting the salary of the administrator (20 percent) and expenditure for the maintenance, one-half of the income was to be used for the aid to the poor and the other one-half was to be spent for the following purposes: poor pilgrims to Najaf and Karbala' (20 percent), the mourning ceremonies outside of Muharram and Safar (15 percent), the mourning ceremony at Takye-e Pahlavan Sharif (10 percent), and the wax of candles for sojourners in Najaf and Karbala', which were used when they visited the shrines.[93] Because Haji 'Abd al-Vahhab controlled a three-fourths share of the *saray* as a *vaqf* in 1853, he probably added one-fourth of the *saray* to the *vaqf*.[94]

So far, out of the thirty-two *sarays* found in the map of 1858, twenty-four *sarays* (75 percent) contained a *vaqf* portion. In this regard, the *vaqf* had a significant role in the *sarays*, the most important commercial facilities in the Grand Bazaar. However, one point cannot be ignored: it was quite rare that a *saray* was built as *vaqf* property. Rather, a portion of an existing *saray* tended to be endowed as a *vaqf* long after its construction. Further, the fact that only five *sarays* became *vaqf* property as a whole supports the observation that *sarays* were generally not built as *vaqf* properties. Therefore, it is difficult to argue that the *vaqfs* contributed to the expansion of the Grand Bazaar. The project of constructing new *sarays* such as Sara-ye Amir and Timche-e Hajeb al-Dowle did not relate to the *vaqf*. Instead, the *vaqf* penetrated into the *sarays* little by little over the course of decades. Therefore, it might be said that while the *vaqf* did not contribute to the expansion of the Grand Bazaar, it contributed to the maintenance of the *sarays*.

Vaqf as an option

It is difficult to say that the *vaqf* was exclusively dominant in the property management of individuals as well as in the management of commercial property in the Grand Bazaar. Out of the four individuals whose records I analyzed, only Haji Mohammad Hasan Kolahduz made more than half of his property a *vaqf*. Even in this case, he used his last will and testament along with the *vaqf* to manage his property. In other cases, only a small part of their property was endowed as a *vaqf.* In sum, the *vaqf* was only one option for the management of their property. Other legal devices such as a last will and testament and a deed for dividing the legacy were also employed. Only around 10 percent of the shops in the Grand Bazaar were a *vaqf.* Seventy percent of the *saray*s in the Grand Bazaar contained the *vaqf* portions, but they rarely became *vaqf* property as a whole all at one time. Instead, they were fragmentally divided into small portions and the portions were endowed one by one over a longer period of time. In this regard, the *vaqf* system did not contribute to the expansion of the Grand Bazaar. Instead, the *vaqf* penetrated gradually into the Grand Bazaar after it expanded. Also, legal devices such as conditional sale were employed for these commercial properties.

Therefore, one can say that a *vaqf* was one of the legal devices utilized by individuals to deal with their properties. While individuals sometimes opted to establish *vaqfs* for the purposes of managing their property, it was only one option. However, the *vaqf* had two distinct features in comparison to other legal devices. Primarily they had a spiritual meaning in the sense that the *vaqf* brought the founder to a higher stage of heaven. They also had a permanency that made the *vaqf* unchangeable. The secondary aspect will be examined in the next chapter.

Notes

1 This does not mean that people always used *vaqf* system to deal with inheritance. See Naofumi Abe, "Preserving a Qajar Estate: Analysis of Fath-'Ali Khan Donboli's 'Property Retention Tactics'," *Studia Iranica* 43 (2014): 129–150.
2 Khavari, *Tarikh-e Zu al-Qarneyn*, 150–151.
3 *Vaqf* deed of Madrase-e Sadr, dated Rabi' I 1227AH, Owqaf no.36.
4 Mohammad 'Ali Hedayati, ed. *Astane-e Rey: Majmu'e-e Asnad va Faramin* (Tehran, 1344Kh), 46–47; 'Abd -allah 'Aqili, ed. *Tarikh-e Astane-e Rey* (Qom, 1380Kh), 396–397.
5 *Ketabche-e Sabt-e Qavalejat*, 133–135.
6 Ibid., 144–145, 150. The last transaction of Alale village in Farahan was mistakenly listed among the transactions related to Mazandaran.
7 *Ketabche-e Sabt-e Qavalejat*, 147–150. The total price of the rural properties was only 343 *tomans* and 5,500 *dinars*, which might not have been the market price.
8 *Ketabche-e Sabt-e Qavalejat*, 137.
9 Ibid., 135–143, 146.
10 *Surat-e Khalesejat va Mowqufat va Raqabat* I, 153, 157, 159, 160, 162–163, 165.
11 Khavari, *Tarikh-e Zu al-Qarneyn*, 988, 1113.
12 For his life, see Nobuaki Kondo, "The Vaqf and the Religious Patronage of Manuchihr Khan Mu'tamad al-Dawlah," in *Religion and Society in Qajar Iran*, ed. Robert Gleave (London, 2005), 228–231.
13 Ibid. 232–235. The *vaqf* deed is preserved in the Vaqf Organization as Owqaf no. 676. The text was published recently. See Haji 'Abbasi and Reza'i, eds. *Asnad-e Mowqufat-e Boluk-e Ghar va Fashapuye*, 98–112.
14 *Surat-e 'Adad-e Khaneha*, 77a, 78a, 82b, 83b.
15 *Ketabche-e Sabt-e Qavalejat*, 159–163.
16 Ibid., 155–159, 170.
17 Ibid., 163–164, 171.
18 Ibid., 165–166.

19 Ibid., 167–170.
20 *Vaqf* deed of Mahmud Khan Kalantar, dated 1250AH, Owqaf, no.52.
21 Khormuji, *Hadayeq al-Akbbar*, 265; Heinrich Brugsch, *Reise der K. Preussischen Gesandtschaft nach Persien 1860 und 1861* (Leizpig, 1862–63), 2:332–333.
22 Bahman Bayani, ed. "Taqsim-name-e Ma-tarak-e Mirza Mahmud Khan Kalantar," *Payam-e Baharestan* no.10 (1389Kh): 963–991. The edited text is helpful but needs to be compared with the facsimile.
23 A *taqsim-name* from the Qajar period has already been analyzed. Abe, "Preserving a Qajar Estate," 141–142.
24 The number of shops is twenty-eight and one-half in the facsimile of the documents instead of twenty-seven and one-half in the edited text. Meydan-e Bolurforushan is not found in any other sources, but it is certain that seventeen out of all twenty-two crystal sellers in Tehran were located around Sabze Meydan. *Surat-e 'Adad-e Khaneha*, 170a.
25 The *vasiyat-name* of Haji Mohammad Hasan Kolahduz, dated 10 Jomada II 1263AH, Owqaf, no.523. This document has been published. Haji 'Abbasi and Reza'i, eds. *Asnad-e Mowqufat-e Boluk-e Ghar va Fashapuye*, 130–133.
26 Werner, "Pious Merchants."
27 *Surat-e 'Adad-e Khaneha*, 172a–b.
28 The *saray* is referred to in a *vaqf* deed. The *vaqf* deed of Aqa Abu al-Qasem Tehrani, dated 28 Jomada I 1255AH, Owqaf no.2199.
29 *Daftar-e Shar'i-e Sangelaji*, 406b.
30 Ibid., 289b.
31 *Surat-e 'Adad-e Khaneha*, 172a–173b, 174b, 178b.
32 Ibid., 81a, 166a–b. For the *vaqf* deed of the *madrase*, see Reza'i, "Tabibi Mosannef," 283–305.
33 *Ketabche-e Dehat-e Khalese va Mowqufat*, II 259; *Surat-e Khalesejat va Mowqufat*, II 318.
34 *Ketabche-e Dehat-e Khalese va Mowqufat*, I 356; II 259; *Ketabche-e Amlak-e Jenab-e Aqa'i az Babat-e Azarbayijan va 'Eraq*, MS 5556, Central Library, University of Tehran, 38.
35 Hedayat, *Malhaqat-e Rowzat al-Safa*, 10:814; E'temad al-Saltane, *al-Ma'aser va al-Asar*, 93–94.
36 *Vaqaye' al-Ettefaqiye* no.4:2, 26 Jomada II 1267AH; no.215:1, 26 Jomada II 1271AH. "Varaqi as Tarikh-e Tehran: Sabze Meydan va Majma'-e Dar al-Sanaye'," *Yadgar* no.39/40 (1327Kh): 64.
37 Sayyed Mohammad Hoseyn Manzur al-Ajdad, ed. "Do Sanad az Monsuban-e Amir-e Kabir," *Ganjine-e Asnad* no.10/11 (1372Kh): 108–109; Edward B. Eastwick, "Persia: Report by Mr. Eastwick, Her Majesty's Secretary of Legation, Camp near Tehran, July 5, 1861," *British Parliamentary Papers, Accounts and Papers* 58 (1862), 74. Fatema Soudavar Farmanfarmaian noted that sale deeds of the Bazar-e Amir were preserved in the Private Archives of Mrs. Sima Malek, but I could not refer to them. Fatema Soudavar Farmanfarmaian, "Politics and Patronage: The Evolution of the Sara-ye Amir in the Bazaar of Tehran," in *the Bazaar in the Islamic City*, ed. Mohammad Gharipour (Cairo, 2012), 208.
38 *Surat-e 'Adad-e Khaneha*, 166b, 173a–178b, 179b. For the bibliography of Mirza Mahdi Navvab, see Al-e Da'ud's introduction to his work. Mirza Mahdi Navvab Tehrani, *Dastur al-A'qab*, ed. Sayyed 'Ali Al-e Da'ud (Tehran, 1376Kh), 2–5.
39 E'temad al-Saltane, *al-Ma'aser va al-Asar*, 177.
40 Akhzar 'Ali Shah, *Ta'in va Sabt-e Mahat-e Khandaq*, Bazar, 80.
41 Ibid., 81–82. For his life, see Heidi A. Walcher, *In the Shadow of the King: Zill al-Sultan and Isfahan under the Qajars* (London, 2008).
42 Akhzar 'Ali Shah, *Ta'in va Sabt-e Mahat-e Khandaq*, Bazar, 79.
43 Ibid., 80–81.

44 Ibid., 17.
45 The article "caravansaray," in *Encyclopaedia Iranica* deals only with the inns by the highways. See Mohammad-Yusuf Kiani and Wolfram Kleiss, s.v. "Caravansaray," *Encyclopaedia Iranica* 4 (1990): 798–802. Yusofifar and Habibi follow this explanation for *karvansara*, but they also define *sara* as "*karavansara* inside the city." Yusofifar and Habibie d. *Sargozasht-e Bazar-e Tehran*, 36–41.
46 Here I omitted eleven *karvansarays* outside the city wall, which could have a different function from those inside the city. Also, I counted Sara-ye Amir as one although the survey counted as five. Eastwick counted them as twenty-seven *karvansarays* besides Sara-ye Amir. Eastwick, "Persia," 74.
47 γ. Sara-ye Hajji Hadi was not mentioned in the building survey of 1853, but was indicated in the map of 1858.
48 Concerning the architecture of Sara-ye Amir, see Soudavar Farmanfarmanian, "Politics and Patronage," 213–218. The plan of the *saray* is found in Ibid. 211; Kanbiz Haji Qasemi, ed. *Ganjname vol. 9: Benaha-ye Bazar Part 1* (Tehran, 1383Kh), 186–188. Yusofifar and Habibi do not explain much about the *saray*. Yusofifar and Habibi, *Sargozasht-e Bazar-e Tehran*. The number of the rooms was written as 336 in the Official Gazette. Eastwick reported ninety-six rooms, which appears too small. See, *Vaqaye' al-Ettefaqiye* no.4:2, 26 Jomada II 1267AH; Eastwick, "Persia," 74.
49 Mahdavi, *For God, Mammon and Country*, 44.
50 E. Orsolle, *Le Caucase et La Perse* (Paris, 1885), 237.
51 *Surat-e 'Adad-e Khaneha*, 168a–b.
52 Eastwick, "Persia," 74.
53 Five documents were recorded in the Sangelaji's second register. *Daftar-e Shar'i-e Sangelaji*, 370b, 372a, 375b, 406b, 407b. See also Soudavar Farmanfarmanian, "Politics and Patronage," 220, 225 n.49.
54 The list of documents relating to *sarays* is also found in Yusofifar and Habibi, *Sargozasht-e Bazar-e Tehran*, 302–306.
55 The *vaqf* deed has been published. 'Ali Farhani, "Barrasi va Bazkhani-e Vaqf-name-e Sara-ye Hajji Molla 'Ali dar Bazar-e Tehran," *Pazhuhesh-name* 4 (1381Kh): 135–139.
56 *Surat-e 'Adad-e Khaneha*, 171b.
57 "Kholase-e Mozakerat raje' be-Sara-ye Haji Sayyed Mohsen," dated 24 Hut 1328AH, Owqaf no.759.
58 *Ketabche-e Sabt-e Qavalejat*, 51; *Surat-e Khalesejat va Mowqufat*, I 150.
59 *Surat-e Khalesejat va Mowqufat* I 150; *Surat-e 'Adad-e Khaneha*, 172b; *Dastur al-'Amal*, 27a.
60 *Vaqf* deed of Hajiye Shah Soltan Khanom, dated 4 Jomada II 1251AH, Owqaf no.964.
61 *Vaqf* deed of Haji Mohammad 'Ali Nuri, dated Safar 1264AH, Owqaf no.526.
62 *Taqsim-name* of Sara-ye Khoda'i, dated 13 Rabi' II 1292AH, Owqaf no.526.
63 Omid Reza'i, "Mowqufe-e Mosha' va Taqsimha-ye Bi-saranjam-e An dar Bazar-e Tehran-e Dowre-e Qajar," *Name-e Anjoman* no.35/36 (1388Kh): 161–162.
64 *Surat-e 'Adad-e Khaneha*, 174a; Akhzar 'Ali Shah, *Ta'in va Sabt-e Mahat*, Bazar, 85.
65 Ibid.
66 *Vaqf* deed of Haji Abu Taleb Tajer Tehrani, dated Shavval 1202AH, Owqaf no.151.
67 *Vaqf* deed of Haji Abu Taleb Bonakdar Tehrani, dated Safar 1214AH, Owqaf no.808.
68 *Surat-e 'Adad-e Khaneha*, 175b.
69 Ettehadiye and Ruhi, eds. *Dar Mahzar*, 526.
70 Akhzar 'Ali Shah, *Ta'in va Sabt-e Mahat*, Bazar, 82. The survey mentions the *saray* as Sara-ye Zarrabkhane.
71 *Vaqf-name-e Sara-ye Shah*, the inscription at Sara-ye Jomuhuri, Bazar-e Tehran.
72 Akhzar 'Ali Shah, *Ta'in va Sabt-e Mahat*, Bazar, 82.
73 *Vaqf* deed of Haji Mohammad 'Ali Tehrani, dated Ziqa'de 1271AH, Owqaf no.2206.
74 Akhzar 'Ali Shah, *Ta'in va Sabt-e Mahat*, Bazar, 85. The survey refers to the *saray* as Sara-ye Qazviniha.

75 *Surat-e 'Adad-e Khaneha*, 176a; Akhzar 'Ali Shah, *Ta'in va Sabt-e Mahat*, Bazar, 85.
76 Ettehadiye and Ruhi, eds. *Dar Mahzar*, 294.
77 Ibid., 364–365.
78 Akhzar 'Ali Shah, *Ta'in va Sabt-e Mahat*, Bazar, 85.
79 *Vaqf* deed of Haji Sayyed Mohammad, dated 1 Rabi' II 1242AH. Owqaf no.840; Haji 'Abbasi and Reza'i, eds. *Asnad-e Mowqufat-e Boluk-e Ghar va Fashapuye*, 54–60.
80 *Vaqf* deed of Hoseyn 'Ali Khan Mo'ayyer-bashi, dated Ramazan 1246AH, Owqaf no.642.
81 *Vaqf* deed of Haji Sayyed Mohammad; Haji 'Abbasi and Reza'i, eds. *Asnad-e Mowqufat-e Boluk-e Ghar va Fashapuye*, 54–60.
82 Hoseyni Balaghi, *Tarikh-e Tehran: Qesmat-e Markazi va Mazafat*, 75.
83 *Surat-e 'Adad-e Khaneha*, 178b.
84 *Vaqf* deed of Jan Jahan Khanom, dated 20 Ziqa'de 1309AH, Owqaf no.3046.
85 *Surat-e 'Adad-e Khaneha*, 178b.
86 *Vaqf* deed of 'Abbas Tajer Farshforush, dated Jomada II 1277AH, Owqaf no.1507.
87 Ibid.
88 *Surat-e 'Adad-e Khaneha*, 179a.
89 Akhzar 'Ali Shah, *Ta'in va Sabt-e Mahat*, Bazar, 85.
90 *Surat-e 'Adad-e Khaneha*, 180a; Akhzar 'Ali Shah, *Ta'in va Sabt-e Mahat*, Bazar, 85.
91 The *vaqf* deed of Sheykh Mohammad Emam-e Jama'at, dated 3 Rabi II, 1264AH, Owqaf no.334.
92 *Surat-e 'Adad-e Khaneha*, 181a.
93 *Vaqf* deed of 'Abd al-Vahhab Tehrani, dated 27 Rajab 1262AH, Owqaf no.562.
94 *Surat-e 'Adad-e Khaneha*, 181b.

8 Transformation of *vaqfs*

As has already been mentioned, one of the most important features of the *vaqf* is its perpetuity, which is also stipulated by Islamic law. In theory, it must be maintained forever. Therefore, by examining a history of *vaqfs*, it is possible to see the extent to which these stipulations of Islamic law were observed.

Akio Iwatake has described how a Timurid *vaqf* in Yazd was maintained for at least 400 years in almost exactly its original form.[1] However, in some cases, the *vaqf* properties were lost or underwent drastic changes. For example, the Zahiriye *vaqf*, whose history was investigated by Christoph Werner, was originally created on behalf of the *madrase* complex in Tabriz during the Safavid period, but it was converted into a family estate during the Qajar period.[2]

The question is: what conditions were necessary to ensure the long-term survival of a *vaqf*? The answer reflects how the law of *vaqfs* was observed or violated in society. Here, I take two cases: the *vaqf* of the Old Friday Mosque and the Chahardah Ma'sum *vaqf*. Both were established during the Safavid period and were still active during the Qajar period. The Vaqf Organization has preserved important documents concerning both cases, which have never previously been referred to by researchers.

Old Friday Mosque

The Old Friday Mosque (Masjed-e Jame') in Tehran is located in the middle of the Grand Bazaar. At first glance, although the building appears quite modern, it was built during or before the Safavid period. Neither books on the general history of Persian architecture nor Iranian travel guidebooks refer to it.[3]

Unfortunately, there is no inscription in the mosque showing the date of its construction. Some researchers believe that it was built in 1661–1662 by a certain Razi al-Din, as indicated by the nineteenth-century historian, E'temad al-Saltane.[4] However, it is not clear what evidence E'temad al-Saltane was using. As mentioned in Chapter 1, Shah Tahmasp Safavi constructed the city wall of Tehran around 1557: this was the point at which it came to be considered as a city (*shahr*). It seems unlikely that the city existed without the Friday Mosque for 100 years. At the very least, our documents call into question the date 1661–1662.

The first document (1651)

All of the documents relating to the Old Friday Mosque are preserved in the same file in the Vaqf Organization, and they are all later transcripts.[5] The oldest one is a *vaqf* deed dated 1651, for which two different transcripts are preserved.

After praising God, the endower is named as Mowlana Mohammad Moqima Razi. Then the document explains the situation of the mosque: it and another small mosque next to it were in ruins at that time, and Mohammad Moqima made efforts to repair them. After completing the repairs, he found that the mosque had no *vaqf* property except one shop that had been destroyed, and no funds to pay for candles and mats, or for the maintenance of the building and the salary of a *mo'azzen*.

As a result of this, he decided to build shops around the mosque. Rich and pious people agreed with his proposal and provided money for the building. With their help, he succeeded in building six shops on the unutilized ownerless land around the mosque. With these shops, and another shop previously belonging to the mosque that he repaired, he established a *vaqf* on behalf of the mosque. The income from the six new shops was to be used for candles and maintenance, while that from the repaired shop was to provide for a *mo'azzen*.

The document states that the first *vaqf* administrator was the endower himself, and he was to be succeeded by Mowlana Molla Mohammad 'Ashura Kermanshahi after his death. After this, the successors were to be male descendants of Molla Mohammad 'Ashura, generation by generation. No one but the administrator could interfere with the *vaqf*, and the administrator was not permitted to use the *vaqf* income for any other purposes. The *vaqf* deed had six endorsements by the 'ulama and twenty-eight confirmations by witnesses.[6]

First, from the content of this document, it is clear that the mosque already existed in 1651, and that it had fallen into ruin, which means that it was built some years before. The document also gives some information about the local area around the mosque. A small mosque was attached to the Friday Mosque, and still unutilized land was available nearby at that time. The area around the mosque had not become a part of the Grand Bazaar.

On the other hand, most of the people mentioned in the document are difficult to identify. The endower might be the same person as Moqim al-Razi, who is found in Shi'i biographical literature as the author of the book entitled *al-Tawhid*, dated 1671.[7] One feature of the document is that the *vaqf* had little relationship with the Safavid state or provincial officials. No one mentioned in the document had an official title, not even a military one such as *khan* or *beg*. Concerning the witnesses, there are few mentions of their professions, but we can at least find a cloth dealer (*bazzaz*) and a perfume dealer (*'attar*). Only twelve witnesses are described with their geographical origins; eight were from Rey and four from Tehran. Clearly, the *vaqf* was not concerned as much with the Safavid state as with the local population. It is probable that, for a local medium-sized city like Tehran, which was neither a state nor a provincial capital, the Safavid state did not contribute much to public buildings such as the Friday Mosque.

The more important point here is that the endower created the *vaqf* by receiving funds from anonymous "wealthy people." This seems strange because these people could have established *vaqfs* on behalf of the mosque by themselves, and thus would have gained the associated spiritual or worldly rewards. This information also reveals a feature of the mosque: it was not a monumental mosque built and funded by a king or political figure, nor was it considered a masterpiece of the age. It was a practical mosque, needed and funded by local people for their daily religious lives.

The mosque in the nineteenth century

After Tehran became a capital under the Qajars, the situation of the Old Friday Mosque changed significantly. First, Fath 'Ali Shah built a magnificent mosque, the Shah Mosque (Masjed-e Shah), in 1809–1810, which was larger than the Old Friday Mosque. Secondly, as the population of Tehran grew, the Old Friday Mosque was expanded with new buildings.

The original part of the mosque was the prayer room (*shabestan*) located on the west side close to the main entrance (right side at the entrance). According

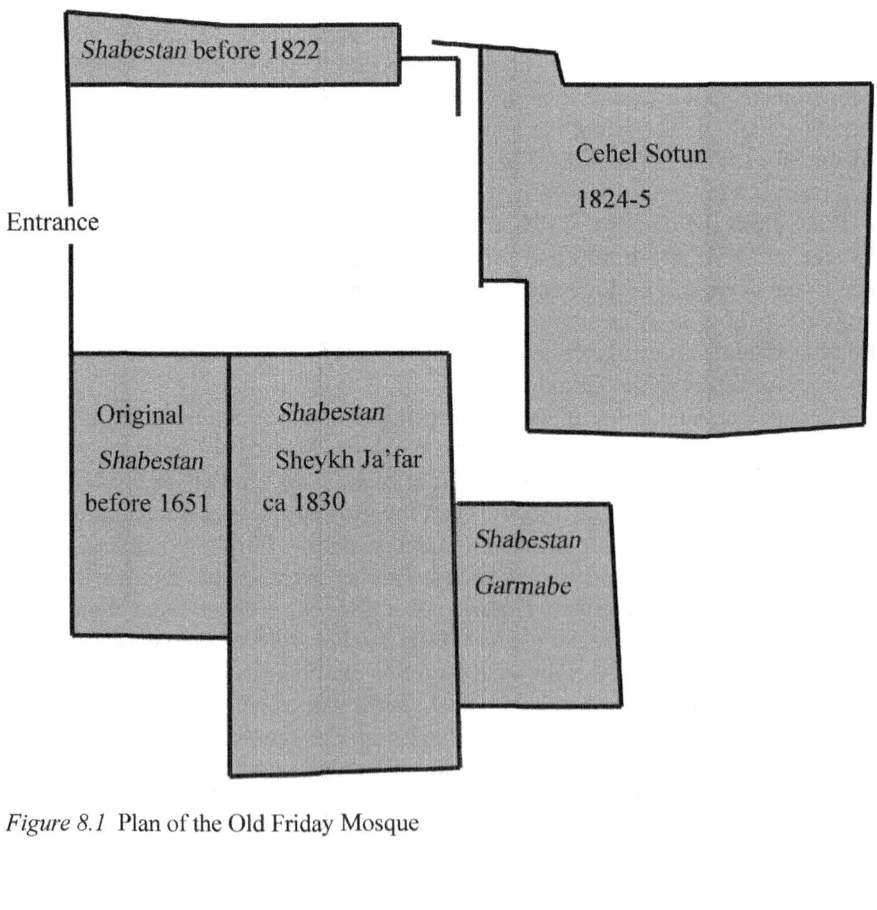

Figure 8.1 Plan of the Old Friday Mosque

to E'temad al-Saltane, another prayer room was added to the original section by Sheykh Ja'far I b. Haji Molla Mohammad probably early in the nineteenth century.[8] The third prayer room, attached to the older two prayer rooms, and known as the prayer room of the hothouse (Shabestan-e Garmkhane), was built by a certain Haji Soltan.[9] The original prayer room was repaired by Sheykh Reza, brother of Sheykh Ja'far I, in 1836–1837.[10] Mirza Masih Astarabadi built a larger independent prayer room named Chehel Sotun (Forty Pillars) on the east side opposite to the main entrance in 1824–1825.[11] In addition, Dust 'Ali Khan Mo'ayyer al-Mamalek constructed another independent prayer room on the north side close to the main entrance (to the left of the entrance) before 1822.[12] Therefore, by the first half of the nineteenth century, the Old Friday Mosque had five prayer rooms.

The mosque was controlled by the family of Emam-e Jama'at, who appear to have been descendants of the second administrator of the Safavid *vaqf*, Molla Mohammad 'Ashura. The first person to be described in the documents from the Qajar Period is Haji Molla Mohammad Kermanshahi, who was active between 1799 and 1802. He was succeeded by his son, Sheykh Ja'far I, whose documents were drawn up from 1826 to 1831. He held the title Emam-e Jama'at-e Dar al-Khelafe (the leader of congressional prayers in the capital). This was distinguished from Emam-e Jom'e-e Dar al-Khelafe (the leader of Friday prayers in the capital), who controlled Shah Mosque. Sheykh Ja'far was succeeded by his brother, Sheykh Reza (d.1861), and then by Sheykh Mohammad (d.1877), son of Sheykh Ja'far I, who was succeeded by Sheykh Ja'far II Soltan al-'Olama (d. 1917–8), his own son.

Struggles over the vaqf property

The *vaqf* property continued to exist during the nineteenth century. The first appendix of the original *vaqf* deed (no date, probably from the early nineteenth century), shows that the imam of the mosque, Haji Molla Mohammad Kermanshahi, collected funds and purchased eleven shops next to the six existing *vaqf* shops, making them too a *vaqf* on behalf of the mosque. In this case, the salary of the *vaqf*-administrator (i.e., the imam), which is not mentioned in the old *vaqf* deed, was fixed as one-fifth of the *vaqf* income. Now the mosque had eighteen *vaqf* shops.[13] In addition, the land next to the mosque was also purchased and included as part of the *vaqf* property.[14] Here we can see that not only the Safavid-period *vaqf*, but also the local support for the mosque, had continued.

However, Qajar state officials (*divaniyan*) illegally occupied most of the *vaqf* property, including the eighteen *vaqf* shops and the land. They built bazaars on part of the *vaqf* land, while another part became a garbage dump. The imams of the mosque struggled to retrieve the property.

The second document, a deed of settlement (*mosalehe-namae*) dated 1815, was written at this time. The imam, Hajji Molla Mohammad, who wanted to protect the remaining *vaqf* land from illegal occupation, consulted with a merchant in Tehran,

Hajji Mohammad Mohsen, and the merchant agreed to build a public bath on the *vaqf* land at his own expense; after completion, a half share of the bath would be a *vaqf* for the mosque. He completed the bath, but he did not originally prepare a well and a water reservoir because he thought that they would be included in the land. Through this document, the two men exchanged ownership of a half share of the land and a half share of the bath, and the merchant arranged to dig a well and make a water reservoir at his own expense.[15] The merchant also built a *saray* next to the public bath and made it a *vaqf* on behalf of the mosque.[16] In sum, the imam tried to keep and improve the *vaqf* property by cooperating with the merchant. Here, we can see a similar example of local cooperation to that of the Safavid period. On the other hand, the state officials did not support the *vaqf*, but instead usurped the *vaqf* property.

The next imam, Sheykh Ja'far, also struggled to recover the *vaqf* property. An edict of the governor of Tehran, 'Ali Mirza Zell al-Soltan, dated 1826, shows the imam's final effort. The edict ordered state officials to give back all the usurped *vaqf* property to the imam. The property that was recovered included the shops in front of the mosque, a bazaar of tailors, a bakery, and some vacant land.[17]

The imam also purchased seven more shops in the alley in front of the mosque: he repaired them and made them a *vaqf*. Now the mosque had twenty-five *vaqf* shops, which had the value of fifty shops from an earlier period, because rents had doubled as the neighborhood prospered.[18]

In spite of the illegal occupation of *vaqf* property by Qajar state officials, the imams succeeded in recovering and expanding it. A main factor, of course, was the imams' efforts, but we cannot ignore the support of the local people. Even without state protection, such as that enjoyed by Shah Mosque the mosque was able to survive with this local support.

Changes in the *vaqf* structure

The financial structure of the mosque, and the status of the imams, changed drastically in the nineteenth century. This was due to the mosque expansion projects. When Mirza Masih built the largest prayer room, named Chehel Sotun, in 1824–1825, he became an independent leader of prayers there. He endowed the Chehel Sotun (although not the mosque as a whole) with some property as a *vaqf*.[19] According to the building survey of 1853, Abu al-Hasan, the son of Mirza Masih, administered at least three shops that were among the *vaqf* properties of the mosque in the Grand Bazaar.[20] Moreover, according to the survey, the *saray* of Sheykh Ja'far, which was also a *vaqf* property of the mosque, was operated by a certain Mirza Abu Taleb rather than by the imam, Sheykh Reza.[21] The *takye* of the mosque had nine *vaqf* shops, which were separated from the other *vaqf* property of the mosque. It is clear that these nine shops were not under the control of Sheykh Reza, as the third appendix to the original *vaqf* deed, which lists the *vaqf* properties, does not refer to them.[22] During this stage, the mosque became a complex of prayer rooms and *takye*, and the imam's family did not control all of the *vaqf* property.

The list also shows that the Sheykh Reza controlled many other *vaqf* properties in addition to those directly connected to the mosque. It includes five other *vaqfs* alongside the mosque's *vaqfs*, as follows:

- A Takye and Hammam of Nowruz Khan, located in front of the house of the imam, along with three pieces of land for shops, to fund the mourning ceremonies of the Shi'i Imams at the *takye*. Sheykh Reza received one-tenth of the income from these properties as a salary.
- B Half of the Hammam of Abu Taleb, on behalf of the Fourteen Infallibles.
- C The land of Vaziri, to fund the mourning ceremonies and pilgrims.
- D Qasem-abad hamlet, to fund an *emamzade*, *sayyeds*, pilgrims, and the poor.
- E Half of Esma'il-abad, for the mourning ceremonies.[23]

The Vaqf Organization has preserved the *vaqf* deeds of B and C. *Vaqf* B was established by Zeynab Khanom and Shahr Banu Khanom in 1802, while *vaqf* C was founded by Mirza Mohammad 'Ali Khan, *vazir* of 'Ali Mirza Zell al-Soltan, in 1831, and was revised in 1862.[24]

Furthermore, there are three other extant *vaqf* deeds that appointed the imam's family as administrators.

- F The *vaqf* of 'Abedin Beg Sanduqdar-e Sarkar-e Khase-e Sharife, dated 1799. Haji Molla Mohammad and his descendants administered a one-twentieth share of Mehrjerd Qanat.[25]
- G The *vaqf* of Haji Abu Taleb Bonakdar, dated 1799 on behalf of the Fourteen Infallibles. Haji Molla Mohammad and his descendants administered five shops and a one-third share of a *saray* in the Grand Bazaar.[26]
- H The *vaqf* of Aqa Mohammad Baqer Tehrani, dated 1850, on behalf of the mourning ceremonies. Sheykh Mohammad and his descendants administered a one-eighth share of one shop and a one-fourth share of another shop in the Grand Bazaar.[27]

All of these *vaqfs* were established by people other than the imam of the mosque and were not related to the Old Friday Mosque. However, the endowers appointed the imam's family as the *vaqf* administrators. The imams no longer belonged only to the mosque, and not all *vaqf* properties were controlled by the imams.

The Old Friday Mosque of Tehran encountered two crises during and after the Safavid period. During the first crisis in the middle of the seventeenth century, the mosque and its *vaqf* shop fell into ruins: a local jurist in collaboration with local people rebuilt them and established a new *vaqf* on behalf of the mosque. During the second crisis early in the nineteenth century, Qajar officials occupied most of the *vaqf* property illegally: the imams struggled to get it back and to expand the amount of *vaqf* property in collaboration with a local merchant. By the middle of the century, the imams had succeeded in recovering and expanding the property. Moreover, the imams came to control other *vaqfs* than that of the Old Friday Mosque, while newly-established *vaqfs* for the mosque were managed by other 'ulama than the imams.

The Chahardah Ma'sum *vaqf*

The Chahardah Ma'sum, or the Fourteen Infallibles, refers to the Prophet Muhammad, his daughter Fatima, and the twelve Imams of Twelver Shi'ism. The *vaqf* on behalf of the Chahardah Ma'sum, known by was established under the Safavids and has been partially studied by modern researchers.[28] However, until now no one has examined what happened to this *vaqf* after the fall of the Safavids. Here, I describe the history of the Chahardah Ma'sum *vaqf* in Tehran, showing how and why the *vaqf* changed during its first 300 years.

Only Hoseyni Balaghi, in his book on the history of Tehran, has attempted to explain the later history of Chahardah Ma'sum *vaqf* in Tehran. According to him, this *vaqf* was established by Shah 'Abbas in 1608–1609 and it encompassed a vast area, from the center to the southern part of the city of Tehran. After the fall of the Safavids, there was some confusion surrounding the *vaqf* and part of it was converted to a cemetery. In the twentieth century, Mohammad Reza Pahlavi converted this cemetery into a residential area that contained approximately 100 houses. However, there were still remaining legal issues concerning the land; in 1957, the *vaqf* administrator initiated legal proceedings to confirm his right over the *vaqf* property. As a result, seven areas in southern Tehran, measuring more than 150,000 square meters, were confirmed as *vaqf* property.[29]

Hoseyni Balaghi's story is quite interesting, but lacks references and accuracy. Here I refer to unpublished documents preserved at the Vaqf Organization in Tehran, which were kept in a thick file.[30] Although the file includes a great number of documents pertaining to the twentieth century, I refer only to the documents from the eighteenth and nineteenth centuries.

Origins

The oldest document in the file relating to the Chahardah Ma'sum *vaqf* is a royal edict (*farman*), dated 1723. Unfortunately, the transcript lacks the seal of the issuer, but it was probably issued by Shah Tahmasp II. The edict authorized the payment of a pension of sixteen *tomans* in cash and sixteen *kharvar* (= 4,800 kilograms) of grain, from the income of the Chahardah Ma'sum *vaqf* in the Rey province, located to the south of Tehran, to five brothers, who were the heirs of Mir Qanbar 'Ali. The *vaqf* properties consisted of four *qanat*s, a water share of the Kan River, and some land outside the city of Tehran. This edict does not mention who established the *vaqf*. Therefore, the first question to be explored is who established the *vaqf*.[31]

Our first candidate is Shah 'Abbas. Hoseyni Balaghi mentions that Shah 'Abbas established a *vaqf* on behalf of the Chahardah Ma'sum. A few transcripts of the *vaqf* deed of 1604–1605 are available and one of them has been analyzed by Robert McChesney.[32] According to this deed, the ruler of the time was the appointed *vaqf* administrator, and the *vaqf* income was to be spent on pensions and grants for the *sayyed*s (i.e., the descendants of the Prophet Muhammad).

The problem is that these transcripts do not mention the *vaqf* property. Another source, a chronicle entitled *Tarikh-e 'Abbasi*, describes some of the *vaqf* properties, but these are not related to the ones in Tehran or Rey.[33] No proof has been found supporting Hoseyni Balaghi's claim.

Another possibility is that the *vaqf* might have been established by Shahzade Soltanam (also known as Moheymin Khanom), a sister of Shah Tahmasp I. Her *vaqf*, which was established before her death in 1562, consisted of lands located in various provinces, from Shirvan to Isfahan.[34] Since this *vaqf* property included land in Rey and Shahriyar near Tehran, it is possible that the origin of the Chahardah Ma'sum *vaqf* in Tehran could also be traced back to Shahzade Soltanam's *vaqf*. The *vaqf* administrator was the ruler at that time, and the beneficiaries were male Shi'i *sayyed*s who had not been granted *soyurghal*s and female Shi'i *sayyed*s who did not have husbands.

A special feature of the Chahardah Ma'sum *vaqf* during the Safavid period is that the Safavid government was fully involved in its administration with its nominal administrator, the Shah. The Safavid administrative manuals mention a special department called the *sarkar-e feyz-asar* (God's favored department), which has not been clearly defined by previous studies.[35] However, the title *vazir-e mowqufat-e sarkar-e feyz-asar-e chahardah ma'sum* ("Minister of the Vaqf Properties of God's Favored Fourteen Infallibles") indicates that the department looked after the administration of the Chahardah Ma'sum *vaqf*.[36] According to the administration manuals, a *vazir* (minister) and a *mostawfi* (financial officer) controlled this department.[37]

Regarding the department's procedures, one can assume that the government sent its officers to collect the *vaqf* income and that this revenue was then spent on pensions and grants to the *sayyed*s. However, the royal edict of 1723 ordered the officers of the *sarkar-e feyz-asar* to make the five *sayyed* brothers responsible for cultivation of the *vaqf* land and the collection of their own pensions. The edict appears to have reflected the political situation in Iran at the time. After the fall of Isfahan, the Safavid government stopped controlling the *vaqf* property, and it was left in the hands of the beneficiaries.

The second document – the royal edict of Nader Shah, dated 1731 – followed the content of the edict of 1723 and also mentioned the financial officers of *sarkar-e feyz-asar*.[38] However, a third document – the royal edict of Fath 'Ali Shah, dated 1798–1799 – contained a significant change. This edict ordered the governor of Tehran to grant the tenure of the *vaqf* lands to the *sayyed*s in lieu of their pensions. The edict did not mention any other officer related to the Chahardah Ma'sum *vaqf*. In fact, by this time, the Qajar government had stopped controlling the *vaqf* land directly, and the *sayyed* family changed from being simply the beneficiaries of the *vaqf* to being its administrators.[39]

In addition, another document shows that the government completely lost control of the property. The inventory of state property compiled in 1842 mentioned the Chahardah Ma'sum *vaqf* and stated that "the property was mentioned in Nader Shah's inventory but now it is unknown where it is."[40] Moreover, another state inventory, which was compiled around 1853, did not mention this property at all.[41]

The reason why the file preserved in the Vaqf Organization does not include the original *vaqf* deed or the name of the founder is obvious. There was no *vaqf* deed to prove that the *sayyed* family had a legitimate right to be the *vaqf* administrators, because they were originally only one of many beneficiaries of the huge state *vaqf*. As there was no deed and no stipulation, after they assumed control, the *sayyed* family was able to use the *vaqf* income as they wished. However, it was not easy for them to control the vast *vaqf* land by themselves, as we will see below.

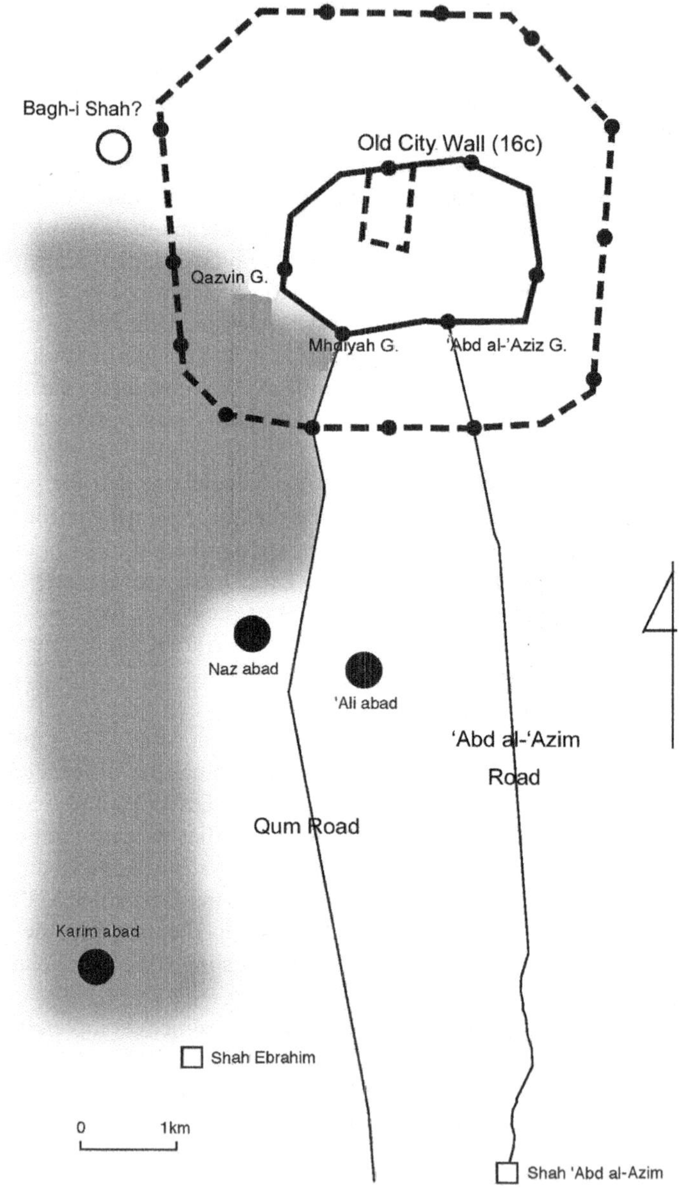

Figure 8.2 Chahardah Ma'sum *vaqf* during the eighteenth century

Changes to the boundaries

When we observe the descriptions of the *vaqf* land carefully, we can see that changes were made to the boundaries of the *vaqf* land over the course of time. The royal edict of 1723 defined the *vaqf* boundaries as follows:

> West: Takhte-e Sang (?);
> East: Kenar-e Gerd Road (Qom Road);
> North: Bagh-e Shah (?) and the lands near the Qazvin Gate;
> (South): Shah Ebrahim.

It is clear that the *vaqf* land was located outside Tehran to the south-west. Some of these place-names are not identified, but Shah Ebrahim must be the shrine that is named Emamzade Ebrahim today.[42]

However, in 1798–1799, the *sayyeds* defined the boundaries in their petition to Fath 'Ali Shah as follows:

> (West): Takhte-e Sang;
> (East): Shah 'Abd al-'Azim Road;
> North: Bagh-e Shah and the lands near the Qazvin Gate;
> (South): Shah Ebrahim and Naz-abad.

In this description, the eastern boundary was shifted further east by more than a kilometer from Qom Road to Shah 'Abd al-'Azim Road. The *sayyed* family probably intended to expand the area of their *vaqf* property.

Nevertheless, on many occasions, the *sayyed* family had to struggle with usurpers. According to a legal edict dated 1835, a Qajar officer named Mohammad Karim Khan Farrash-bashi illegally occupied some land on the southern edge of the *vaqf* property, and constructed a hamlet called Karim-abad. A *mojtahed*, Molla Abu al-Hasan Tehrani, attempted to reclaim the land and make it a *vaqf*; however, he only succeeded in reclaiming part of the land. Here, the southern boundary of the *vaqf* had shifted contrary to the *sayyeds*' interests. Moreover, this legal edict described the western boundary as "Takhte-e Sang and Naz-abad Road (Shar'-e Naz-abad)." Naz-abad Road probably referred to Qom Road, and if so, the western boundary of the property might also have been shifted.[43]

In fact, this shift was confirmed in 1844, after the legal disputes between the *sayyed* family and the head (*khadkhoda*) of the Sangelaj district, one of the five city districts of Tehran. The *rishsefids* (elders) testified in this dispute, and the court examined related documents belonging to both sides. Finally, it was agreed that the *vaqf* property was located between Shah 'Abd al-'Azim and Naz-abad (Qom) roads.[44] No further documents after 1844 mentioned the Qazvin Gate as the northern boundary of the *vaqf*. Instead, in a lease of deed of *vaqf* property dated 1860, for example, the northern boundary of the property was described as being situated between the Mohammadiye and the 'Abd al-'Azim Gates.[45]

On the other hand, the loss of the southern parts of the *vaqf* property was also gradually confirmed. A lease deed of *vaqf* property dated 1841, mentioned the southern boundary as "'Ali-abad and Naz-abad, where the shrine Shah Ebrahim was located."[46] In fact, Shah Ebrahim was located at about five kilometers south of 'Ali-abad and Naz-abad. Finally, another lease deed of *vaqf* property, dated 1862, referred only to 'Ali-abad as the southern boundary and omitted Shah Ebrahim and Naz-abad.[47] These revised boundaries were confirmed by the royal edict of Nasir al-Din Shah, dated 1891.[48]

In fact, within a hundred years or so, the whole of the *vaqf* land shifted approximately two kilometers from west to east. The southern boundary also shifted, contrary to the *vaqf* administrators' interests, approximately five kilometers to the north. When measured on a map, the property in the late nineteenth century was trapezoid: the two bases measured 2.0 and 2.2 kilometers, and it was 7.5 kilometers in height. It covered 1,575 hectares but included some barren land.

Vaqf land in central Tehran

According to the 1731 edict of Nadir Shah and the 1798–1799 petition of the *sayyed* family, the *vaqf* property included some farmland (*mazra'e*), which was located partly inside and partly outside the city wall. From this description, it appears that the farmland was located on the periphery of the city.

However, in later documents, the *vaqf* property relating to the Chahardah Ma'sum is described as in Central Tehran. In a legal edict dated 1865, the four boundaries of the *vaqf* property were defined as follows:

> (North): Khodabandlu Allay;
> (South): Small bazaar belonging to the *vaqf* of Marvi Madrase;
> (East): The house of Mirza Mohammad Khan Sepahsalar;
> (West): Street known as 'the moat' (now known as Naser Khosrow Street).

This was located in the 'Udlajan district and adjoined to the Arg. Its area was 27,500 square meters when measured on a map.

The earliest record found describing the land of the Chahardah Ma'sum *vaqf* within the city was in the *vaqf* deed for Marvi Madrase, which adjoined the *vaqf* land, dated 1816.[49] A small *madrase* that was built separately from the main *madrase*, a well that supplied water to the students, and the *vaqf* public bath, were all situated on the land of the Chahardah Ma'sum *vaqf*. The founder of the *madrase*, Mohammad Hoseyn Khan Marvi, made a contract to lease this land for the term of one hundred years and paid for it from the *vaqf* income of the *madrase*.[50]

The question is: who was the legitimate representative of the Chahardah Ma'sum *vaqf* in the city? The *vaqf* deed of the *madrase* did not refer to the administrator's name, but just mentioned "the jurist who is fully conditioned as the deputy of the Imam." This procedure was used in cases where someone leased a land the owners of which were unknown. Therefore, this deed indicates that the Chahardah Ma'sum *vaqf* did not have an administrator at that time.

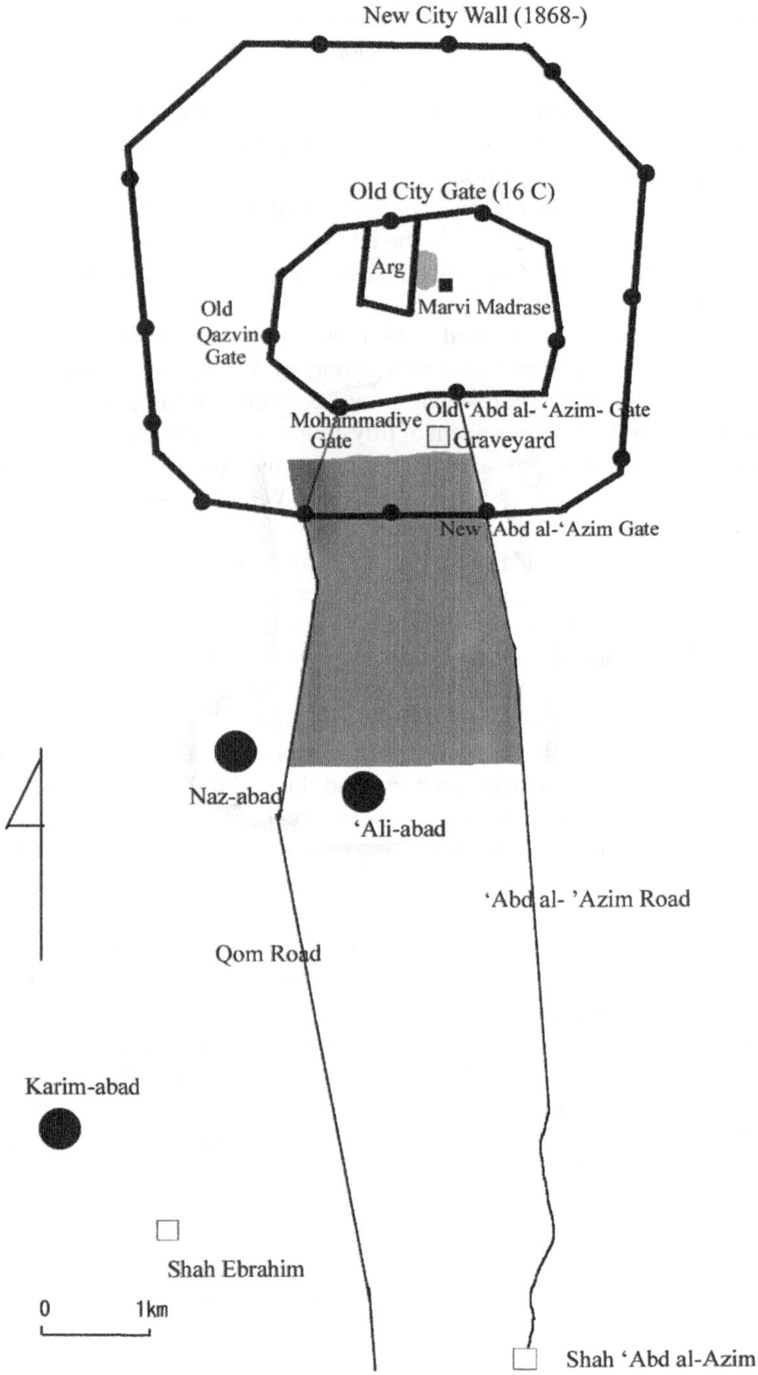

Figure 8.3 Chahardah Ma'sum *vaqf* after 1856

Another document, a lease deed dated 1842, is also notable. Aqa Naqi Qazvini leased about 100 square meters of land belonging to the Chahardah Ma'sum *vaqf* in the city for the term of three years with a rent of six *tomans*. The lender, who legally must have been the representative of the *vaqf*, was a person named Sayyed Yusof Musavi.[51] Apparently, he did not have any connection with the Mir Qanbar 'Ali family, who were Hoseyni *sayyeds*.

From these two documents, one can conclude that the Mir Qanbar 'Ali family did not control the *vaqf* property in the city during the early nineteenth century. In 1816, there was no *vaqf* administrator, and in 1842, it was being managed by other *sayyeds*.

However, this situation changed in 1856, when Mirza Mohammad Andarmani, a famous jurist, issued a legal edict. The deputy of Aqa Sayyed Aqa from the Mir Qanbar 'Ali family sued six residents, who, according to the plaintiff, had been leasing the land of his house at a rent of fifty-four *tomans*. The claim of the accused was as follows: "both the houses and the sites in which we live are our own private properties. We know we have a legitimate right. We do not know about the lease deeds that the plaintiff showed in court."[52]

Many witnesses testified in court. Most of them supported the plaintiff and clarified the four boundaries of the *vaqf* land. Other residents who lived on this land also stated that they had leased the land and that the plaintiff's lease deeds were authentic. Three jurists, including famous *mojtaheds* Molla Mohammad Ja'far Chalmeydani and Sheykh Mohammad from the Old Friday Mosque, and Sayyed Yahya from the Akhavi family (a notable *sayyed* family in Tehran), also confirmed the statement of the plaintiff. As a result, Mirza Mohammad Andarmani confirmed the four boundaries of the *vaqf* property and the plaintiff's position as the *vaqf* administrator. He ordered the accused to pay a rent to the plaintiff.[53]

At first glance, the case appears to have been simple: the residents on the *vaqf* land had simply tried to avoid paying their rent, but they lost the case. However, when we pay attention to the number of witnesses, including the famous jurists and the Akhavi *sayyed*, the case appears to be quite extraordinary. Why did the plaintiff need so many and such respectable witnesses? One reason could have been the lack of a *vaqf* deed. As pointed out above, the property did not have its own *vaqf* deed and there was no documentary evidence to help fix the boundaries of the *vaqf* land. For example, the leaseholders who supported the plaintiff had a vague idea about the boundaries and said that "all of the lands around here are the *vaqf* of Chahardah Ma'sum." As Andarmani's edict was the first document that legally fixed the boundaries of the *vaqf* property in the city, he needed many respectable witnesses.

On the other hand, it is not clear why the Mir Qanbar 'Ali family were given control of the *vaqf* land in the city. The main issue of the dispute was the boundaries of the *vaqf* property, not the *vaqf* administration itself. Apparently, the Mir Qanbar 'Ali family was recognized as administering the Chahardah Ma'sum *vaqf*. Though the document alleged that the *vaqf* had been controlled by the family's ancestors, as pointed out above, the *vaqf* property in the city was not administered by the family, at least during the early nineteenth century. Based on the eighteenth-century documents, it is doubtful that they had any legitimate grounds to claim control over the *vaqf* property in the city. However, it might be natural that, after being recognized as the administrators of Chahardah Ma'sum *vaqf* in the suburbs, they could also claim a right to the administration of the *vaqf* property in the city. In addition, the fact that the residence of the *sayyed* family was located near the *vaqf* land probably helped them to claim control over the *vaqf* property.[54]

Even after Andarmani's edict, it seems that some residents on the *vaqf* land did not pay the rents to the Mir Qanbar family. In 1865, a jurist issued an edict to confirm the *sayyed* family's control of the *vaqf* property in the city and the boundaries of the *vaqf* land, and ordered the leaseholders to pay their rents.[55] Furthermore, in 1871, Haji Molla 'Ali Kani, a leading jurist, issued an edict for the same purpose. According to this edict, some people had objections to the *vaqf* and the position of the *vaqf* administrator. Kani's edict was endorsed by six leading *mojtaheds*, including Abu al-Qasem Kalantari and Mirza Mohammad Hasan Ashtiyani.[56] The royal edict of Naser al-Din Shah, dated 1885, also mentioned Kani's edict and confirmed it.[57] Moreover, in 1894, three question/answer legal edicts were issued by three different jurists. All of them confirmed the boundaries of the *vaqf* property in the city and the collection of the rents by the *sayyed* family.[58] Another *vaqf* deed of a house on the land of the Chahardah Ma'sum *vaqf*, dated 1874, does not mention the rent for the *vaqf*.[59] In other words, in the late nineteenth century, the *sayyed* family was still encountering difficulties in collecting rent.

Interestingly, Kani's edict of 1871 shows his interpretation of the purpose of Chahardah Ma'sum *vaqf*: he suggested that the *vaqf* income should be spent on mourning ceremonies (*ta'ziye-dari*) for the imams or for other necessary purposes. As described above, the Chahardah Ma'sum *vaqf* was originally established for the purpose of providing pensions to the *sayyeds*, descendants of Chahardah Ma'sum. However, Kani interpreted the purpose of the Chahardah Ma'sum *vaqf* as similar to that of the other *vaqfs* during the Qajar period, the mains aims of which were to promote the mourning ceremonies of the Imams. He did not have any specific information on the *vaqf* during the Safavid period, and his interpretation reflects the views of his time.

Leaseholders

The next question to be explored is how the Chahardah Ma'sum *vaqf* was actually managed. The *vaqf* land in the city was mainly occupied by houses, and the residents leased the land and paid their rent. The file of unpublished documents preserved at the Vaqf Organization includes three lease deeds of *vaqf* lands in the city. The leaseholders were not notable persons, and the rents were comparatively inexpensive at less than one *toman* per year. The lease contracts were signed for a five-year term.

Table 8.1 Leaseholders of the Chahardah Ma'sum *vaqf* property in the city

Leaseholder	*Property*	*Period*	*Rent*	*Date*
Karbala'i Mohammad Kangavari	Site of his house	5 years	1.25t	1 Moharram 1272AH
Aqa Mohammad Hoseyn Khan Gholam-e Pishkhidmat	Site of his house	5 years	5t	1 Ramazan 1286AH
Mirza Mohammad Hoseyn Tehrani	Site of his house	5 years	5t	17 Ramazan 1286AH

t: *toman*

Table 8.2 Leaseholders of the Chahardah Ma'sum *vaqf* property outside the city

Leaseholder	*Property*	*Period*	*Rent*	*Date*
Haji Mirza Aqasi	All outside the old city wall	3 lunar years	150t	10 Rajab 1257AH
Mirza 'Isa	All outside the old city wall	10 years	700t 35kh wheat	10 Safar 1277 AH
Mirza Mohammad Hoseyn Dabir al-Molk[60]	All outside the old city wall	5 years	60kh wheat	1 Safar 1279AH
Mirza 'Ali Asghar Khan Amin al-Soltan[61]	All outside the old city wall	12 years	120t 80kh wheat 40kh barley	Ziqa'de 1301AH
Mirza 'Isa Vazir	Between two city walls	3 years	420t	Rajab 1306AH
Majd al-Dowle Khansalar[62]	Outside new city wall	10years	2000t 100kh wheat 100kh straws	16 Jomada II 1313AH

t: *toman*, kh: *kharvar*

On the other hand, the leaseholders of the *vaqf* properties outside the old city were high officials of the central or provincial government, including two Grand Vazirs. The rents varied greatly but most of them ranged from 50 to 200 *toman*s per year in cash. It seems that some contracts were cancelled before the end of the term.

Why were high officials the only ones to lease this *vaqf* land? This is probably because the *vaqf* land was so vast that only rich and politically powerful persons were able to control it. For the *vaqf* administrators, it was easier to lease the property to those who were powerful enough to control the entire *vaqf* land. In addition, the *vaqf* administrators expected these high officials to protect the *vaqf* property from usurpation.

However, a leaseholder could also become a usurper. As shown in Table 8.2, Mirza 'Isa, the *vazir* of the Tehran province, rented the *vaqf* property between the old and the new city walls in 1889.[63] The *vaqf* administrator sent three petitions to Naser al-Din Shah concerning his lease. According to the first petition,

Mirza 'Isa had rented the *vaqf* land outside the (old) 'Abd al- 'Azim Gate for three years but had not paid the rent. The *vaqf* administrator begged the Shah to issue a royal edict ordering the return of the *vaqf* land to the *vaqf* administrator.[64]

In a second petition, dated 1890, the *vaqf* administrator claimed that Mirza 'Isa had stopped paying rent again after a few years. Moreover, he had sold a part of the *vaqf* property for 5,000 *tomans*, and also built and sold an ice house (*yakhchal*). The *vaqf* administrator implored the Shah to issue an edict protecting the *vaqf* property.[65] Although a royal edict was issued after eight months, it only confirmed in general terms, the rights of the *vaqf* administrator and the boundaries of the *vaqf* property.[66] According to an undated third petition, Mirza 'Isa had occupied the *vaqf* property without paying rent for some years. He farmed the *vaqf* land outside the new city wall, and sold part of the *vaqf* property between the old and new city walls for 10,000 *tomans*.[67]

Mirza 'Isa was deeply involved in the expansion project of the city of Tehran, which began in 1868. It is not clear whether he abused his authority. However, as mentioned in Chapter 5, he sold or donated vacant land between the old and the new city walls – areas that were newly developed as part of the expansion project. The shari'a court registers of Sangelaji contained 323 records of such sales and 53 records of such donations in the years 1876–1879. Among them, 119 records concerned property outside the Mohammadiye Gate or the old 'Abd al-'Azim Gate: some of this property may have been the lands of the Chahardah Ma'sum *vaqf*. Therefore, if Mirza 'Isa did actually sell the *vaqf* land, the sale was made possible because he was involved in the city expansion project and because Sangelaji endorsed it.

It is not clear whether the *vaqf* administrator reclaimed all of the *vaqf* land. It is apparent that he at least reclaimed the land outside the new city wall because he lent it to Majd al-Dowle Khansalar in 1895.[68] The old map of 1891 still refers to the lands of the Chahardah Ma'sum *vaqf* as containing kilns for bricks, steel, and plaster inside the new city wall, but its boundaries were not clear. Probably, some parts of the *vaqf* land between the old and new city walls were usurped and "owned" by individuals.

The *vaqf* administrator needed rich and powerful leaseholders for the control of the vast *vaqf* lands outside the city, as only these people could afford to lease and maintain such vast lands. However, there was also a risk of these powerful leaseholders usurping the land.

The Chahardah Ma'sum *vaqf* in Tehran underwent drastic changes during these 300 years. It was originally a state-administered *vaqf* and the *sayyed* family was only one of its beneficiaries. However, after the fall of the Safavids, the *sayyed* family began to control the *vaqf* property directly, and tried to acquire as much of the land as they could. They succeeded in expanding the *vaqf* property outside the city to the east and in acquiring the *vaqf* property within the city. However, it was difficult to control the vast *vaqf* lands, and they always faced the risk of usurpation. Therefore, the *vaqf* was heavily affected by the *sayyed* family's efforts to expand their land and the constant threat of usurpation.

Strengths and weaknesses of the law of *vaqfs*

The cases of the Old Friday Mosque and the Chahardah Ma'sum *vaqf* indicate both strengths and weaknesses of the law of *vaqfs*. The former shows what was necessary for the survival of the *vaqfs*. A *vaqf* must be perpetual in Islamic Law, but it needed to be supported and maintained by the people of the time. In this case, the main factors were local supporters as well as the endeavors of the imam (i.e., the administrator). Though most of the names of local supporters are not mentioned in the documents, they provided the funding for the *vaqf*. This is because the local population required the mosque for their own practical use for public worship. On the other hand, the role of state or provincial officials was very small with regards to the maintenance of the mosque and the *vaqf*. The Safavid officials rarely participated in the management of the *vaqf*, and the Qajar officials were usurpers of *vaqf* property. The Safavids are famous for their patronage of religious institutions, especially in Isfahan, but their hands never reached the Friday Mosque of Tehran, which was not a state or provincial capital. This is partly because the mosque was not a splendid memorial built by a king to show his power and dignity, but a practical place used by local people for their worship.

In the case of the Friday Mosque, the local support for the *vaqf* was related to the nature of the mosque. I believe that this is also true for other Friday mosques in various cities in Iran. Most of them are very old in origin, and their buildings have usually been repaired multiple times and have lost their original form. From an architectural point of view, these mosques are of little consequence. But they were supported and maintained by local people, and repaired again and again in order to meet the daily religious needs of the local communities.

On the other hand, the Chahardah Ma'sum *vaqf* did not have much local support: one can note the struggles of the *sayyed* family to keep and maintain the *vaqf* property. The Zahiriye *vaqf* faced a similar situation, but the changes in the Chahardah Ma'sum *vaqf* were much more drastic: in the Zahiriye *vaqf* case, although the purpose of the *vaqf* – the *madrase* complex – had vanished, and the conditions and stipulations had changed, the land remained *vaqf* property, at least in name. In the case of Chahardah Ma'sum, the *vaqf* land was also shifted and extended. When we consider its form during the late nineteenth century, it is difficult to conceive of its original form. Here we can see the binding power of *vaqf* law. Even though the *vaqf* had undergone drastic changes, the fact still remains that someone established a *vaqf* in this area more than 300 years ago. This fact continued to affect property rights even after several hundred years.

Naturally, the binding power of *vaqf* law makes property rights fragile. One can imagine the many conflicts and litigations that occurred when the location of the Chahardah Ma'sum *vaqf* land had shifted to the east. I have not examined the litigations concerning the *vaqf* property in the twentieth century; however, it is apparent from the huge volume of related documents that these litigations were complicated and hard-fought. The *vaqf* system not only contributes to the welfare and maintenance of Muslim societies, but also sometimes leads to long-lasting property conflicts.

Notes

1 Akio Iwatake, "The Continuity of Waqf in Iran: A Case of Amir Chaqmaq's Waqf in Yazd," *Isramu-Sekai* 42 (1993): 1–19. For the original *vaqf*, see Akio Iwatake, "The Waqf of a Timurid Amir: The Example of Chaqmaq Shami in Yazd," in *Persian Documents: Social History of Iran and Turan in the Fifteenth-Nineteenth Centuries*, ed. Nobuaki Kondo (London, 2003), 87–105.
2 Werner, *An Iranian Town*, 99–122; idem. "A Safavid Vaqf in Qajar Times: The Zahiriya in Tabriz," in *Matériaux pour l'histoire économique du monde iranien*, eds. Rika Gyselen and Maria Szuppe (Paris, 1999), 233–248.
3 For previous research on the Old Friday Mosque, see Mahdi Rajabi and Sayyed Sa'id Mir Mohammad Sadeq, "Masjed-e Jame'-e Tehran ya Jame'-e 'Atiq," *Masjed* 24 (1374Kh): 70–79; Haji Qasemi, ed. *Ganj-name: Benaha-ye Mazhabi-e Tehran*, 22–31; Habibi, ed. *Masajed-e Dirinesal-e Tehran*, 135–150. None of them refers to the related documents preserved in the Vaqf Organization.
4 E'temad al-Saltane, *Mer'at al-Boldan*, 2004.
5 Owqaf no.836.
6 *Vaqf* deed of Masjed-e Jame'-e dated Zihejje 1061AH.
7 Agha Buzurg al-Tihrani, *Tabaqat al-A'lam al-Shi'a: al-Qarn al Hadi 'Ashar*, ed. 'Ali Naqi Monzavi (Qom, n.d.), 582. The book was a commentary on the Shi'i hadith.
8 E'temad al-Saltane, *Mer'at al-Boldan*, 2004.
9 Haji Qasemi, ed. *Ganj-name: Benaha-ye Mazhabi-e Tehran*, 22; Habibi, ed. *Masajed-e Dirinesal-e Tehran*, 135.
10 E'temad al-Saltane, *Mer'at al-Boldan*, 2004–2005.
11 The date is based on the inscription in the Chehel Sotun. E'temad al-Saltane referred to the year 1202/1787–1788, which is not probable because Mirza Masih was less than ten years old at that time.
12 Dust 'Ali Khan died in 1822. Khavari, *Tarikh-e Zu al-Qarneyn*, 567.
13 First appendix to the *vaqf* deed of Masjed-e Jame', no date.
14 Second appendix to the *vaqf* deed of Masjed-e Jame', no date. The land was the legacy of Aqa Mohammad Taqi Arbab Tehrani.
15 Deed of Settlement between Haji Molla Mohammad and Haji Mohammad Mohsen, dated Rajab 1230AH.
16 Second appendix to the *vaqf* deed of Masjed-e Jame'.
17 Edict of 'Ali Mirza Zell al-Soltan, the governor, dated Moharram 1242AH.
18 Second appendix to the *vaqf* deed of Masjed-e Jame'.
19 Hoseyni Balaghi, *Tarikh-e Tehran: Tarikh-e Markazi-e Tehran*, 34.
20 *Surat-e 'Adad-e Khaneha*, 167b, 172a.
21 Ibid., 174b.
22 Third appendix to the *vaqf* deed of Masjed-e Jame', no date.
23 Ibid.
24 *Vaqf* deed of Zinat Khanom and Shahr Banu Khanom, dated 22 Sha'ban 1217AH, Owqaf no.123; *vaqf* deed of Mirza Mohammad 'Ali Khan dated Zihejje 1246AH and the revised version dated 12 Ziqa'de 1278AH, Owqaf no.588.
25 *Vaqf* deed of 'Abedin Beg Sanduqdar, dated 8 Safar 1214AH, Owqaf no.484.
26 *Vaqf* deed of Haji 'Abu Taleb Tehrani, dated Safar 1214AH, Owqaf no.808.
27 *Vaqf* deed of Aqa Mohammad Baqer Tehrani, dated Zihejje 1266AH, Owqaf no.890.
28 Bert Fragner, "Social and Economic Affairs," in *The Cambridge History of Iran, vol. 6: The Timirid and Safavid Period*, eds. Peter Jackson and Laurenc Lockhart (Cambridge, 1986), 521; Robert D. McChesney, "Waqf and Public Policy: The Waqfs of Shah 'Abbas, 1011–1023/ 1602–1614," *Asian and African Studies* 15 (1981): 170–178.
29 Hoseyni Balaghi, *Tarikh-e Tehran: Qesmat-e Jonubi va Mozafat*, 15–19.
30 Owqaf no.73.
31 Royal edict of Shah Tahmasp II dated Moharram 1136AH.

32 'Abd al-Hoseyn Sepanta, *Tarikhche-e Owqaf-e Esfahan* (Esfahan, 1346Kh), 65–72; Vali Qoli Shamlu, *Qesas al-Khaqani*, ed. Hasan Sadat-e Naseri (Tehran, 1371–1374Kh), 186–197; Manuchehr Sotude, "Vaqf-name-e Shah 'Abbas," *Vaqf, Miras-e Javidan* no.47/48 (1383Kh): 10–14; McChesney, "Waqf and Public Policy," 170–178.

33 The chronicle only mentions Isfahan, Qazvin, Kashan, Natanz, Jushqan, Khurasan, Monajjem, *Tarikh-e 'Abbasi*, 340–341.

34 Her *vaqf* properties were located in Shirvan, Arasbaran, Tabriz, Qazvin, Savojbolagh, Shahriyar, Rey, Isfahan, and Garmrud-e Astrabad. Qommi, *Kholasat al-Tavarikh*, 430–431.

35 Vladimir Minorsky, *Tadhkirat al-Muluk: A Manual of Safavid Administration* (London, 1943), 146; Floor, *A Fiscal History of Iran*, 91; idem. "The Sadr or Head of the Safavid Religious Administration, Judiciary and Endowments and other Members of the Religious Institution," *ZDMG* 150 (2000): 471; Muhammad Ismail Marcinkowski, *Mirza Rafi'a's Dastur al-Muluk: A Manual of Later Safavid Administration* (Kuala Lumpur, 2002), 258–268; Mansur Sefatgol, *Sakhtar-e Nehad va Andishe-e Dini dar Iran-e 'Asr-e Safavi* (Tehran, 1381Kh), 355–357.

36 Mohammad Ebrahim Nasiri, *Dastur-e Shahriyaran*, ed. Mohammad Nader Nasiri Moqaddam (Tehran, 1373Kh), 273.

37 The *vazir* named Vazir-e Sarkar-e Feyz-asar as well as Vazir-e Mowqufat-e Chahardah Ma'sum. Mirza Sami'a Ansari, *Tazkerat al-Moluk*, ed. Sayyed Mohammad Dabir-e Siyaqi (Tehran, 1368Kh), 44. Ansari, "Dastur al-Moluk," 553; Yusof Rahimlu, ed. *Aqab va Mavajeb-e Dowre-e Salatin-e Safaviye* (Mashhad, 1371Kh), 48.

38 Royal edict of Nader Shah, dated Sha'ban 1143AH.

39 Royal edict of Fath 'Ali Shah with the petition of Mir Qanbar 'Ali family, dated 1212AH.

40 *Surat-e Khalesejat va Mowqufat*, I 151; II 166.

41 *Ketabche-e Dehat-e Khalese va Mowqufat.*

42 Sarvqadi, *Beqa'-e Motatarakke*, 96.

43 Legal edict of Akhond Molla Abu al-Hasan Tehrani, dated 2 Jomada II 1251AH.

44 Legal statement, dated 15 Rajab 1260AH.

45 Lease deed of Mirza 'Isa, dated 10 Ṣafar 1277AH.

46 Lease deed of Haji Mirza Aqasi, dated 14 Rajab 1257AH.

47 Lease deed of Mirza Mohammad Hoseyn Dabir al-Molk, dated 1 Safar 1279AH.

48 Royal edict of Naser al-Din Shah, dated Zihejje 1308AH.

49 For this *vaqf* deed, see Chapter 6.

50 *Savad-e Vaqf-name-e Madrase-e Khan-e Marvi*, 15a–b, 17a; Ostadi, ed. "Vaqf-name-e Madrase-e Marvi," 61–62.

51 Lease deed between Aqa Sayyed Yusof Tehrani and Aqa Naqi Qazvini, dated 12 Ṣafar 1258/25 March 1842.

52 Legal edict of Mirza Mohammad Andarmani, dated Shavval 1272AH.

53 Ibid.

54 *Surat-e 'Adad-e Khaneha*, 17b; *Ketabche-e Te'dad-e Nofus*, 90. Their house was located in the Khodabanelu Alley. The family consisted of five males, four females, and eight children.

55 Legal edict, dated 9 Zihejje 1281AH.

56 Legal edict of Haji Molla 'Ali Kani, dated Safar 1288AH.

57 Royal edict of Nasir al-Din Shah, dated Rajab 1302AH.

58 Legal edict of Mohammad 'Ali, dated Zihejje 1311AH; Legal edict of Mohammad Hadi b. Mahmud, dated 11 Zihejje 1311AH; Legal edict, dated 12 Zihejje 1311AH.

59 Owqaf no.593. *Vaqf* deed of Mashhadi Hasan Zargar Kashani, dated 5 Rabi' II 1291AH.

60 He held the office of the Chief of the Secretary Department of the Shah (*riyasat-e daftar-e rasa'el-e khasse*) in 1858 and became a member of the governmental council (*majles-e showra-e dowlati*) in 1859. He was appointed as the *vazir* of Tehran in 1866. *Vaqaye' al-Ettefaqiye* no.399:2. 14 Safar 1275AH; no.450:2, 29 Rabi' I 1276AH; *Ruz-name-e Dowlat-e Aliye* no.589:5, 21 Safar 1283AH. See also Guity Nashat, s.v, "Dabir al-Molk," *Encyclopaedia Iranica* 6 (1993): 539–540.

61 He was *de facto* Grand Vazir from September 1883. He was a minister of the Imperial Court after the death of his father. See, Jean Calmard s.v. "Atabak-e A'zam, Amin al-Soltan," *Encyclopaedia Iranica* 2 (1987): 878–890.
62 Mahdi Qoli Khan Qajar Qoyunlu, a cousin of Naser al-Din Shah. After 1885, he became the head steward (*khansalar*) and remained in this position until the assassination of Naser al-Din Shah in 1896. Bamdad, *Sharh-e Hal*, 4:180–181.
63 Lease deed of Mirza 'Isa Vazir, dated Rajab 1306AH.
64 Petition of the *vaqf* administrator to Naser al-Din Shah, no date.
65 Petition of the *vaqf* administrator to Naser al-Din Shah, dated Rabi' I 1308AH.
66 Royal edict of Naser al-Din Shah, dated Zihejje 1308AH.
67 Petition of the *vaqf* administrator to Naserr al-Din Shah, no date.
68 Lease deed of Majd al-Dawle Khansalar, dated 16 Jomada II 1313AH.

Conclusion

This book has discussed the relationship between Islamic law and society in Qajar Iran, focusing on the court system and *vaqf.* Through an analysis of court registers and unpublished documents, it has arrived at the following conclusions.

First, the *'orf* court was not found as a single institution based on customary law. Instead, one finds the *divankhane* and criminal punishments separately administrated by the Shah and the provincial governors. The *divankhane,* following the tradition of the *mazalem* accepted the petitions and complaints of the people, who were thus protected from injustice. Still one could consider the *divankhane* as a court of law; however, the petitions and complaints heard there were not restricted to legal matters, but also included complaints concerning administration or economic matters. For this reason, it is difficult to consider a *divankhane* as a genuine court of law. As part of local administrative duties, provincial governors were primarily responsible for criminal cases. The Shah and the governors respected shari'a as the absolute law, and their decisions did not violate it. If a case was too legally complicated, the *divankhane* and police officers referred it to the legal experts, *mojtahed*s. Naturally, the shahs and the governors had executive power, which the *mojtahed*s lacked. In fact, the shahs and governors executed shari'a and *mojtahed*s*' hokm*s; the shari'a and its experts, the *mojtahed*s, possessed higher authority in legal interpretation rather than did the shahs and the governors. Therefore, it is difficult to affirm that the *'orf* court was dominant over the *shari'a* court. However, in the course of the modern reform inspired by the West, the *divankhane* gradually became court of laws, as explicitly stipulated in the Supplementary Fundamental Law of 1907.

Qajar shari'a courts had some distinctive features. Each court belonged to an individual *mojtahed,* not to the state or district. The 'ulama, who had learned mainly *'usul* and *fiqh* in the 'Atabat and who had reached the status of *ejtehad*, opened the court. For this reason, the Qajar state could not control the shari'a courts. The question is whether the shari'a courts were courts of justice where trials took place. Though we speak of the shari'a courts, only a few records in the court registers directly concern trials. The *mojtahed*s issued legal edicts called *hokm*s, but most of these were not the final decisions of trials; rather, they were opinions in substantial legal cases. They were more authoritative than Sunni fatwas, since the Shi'i theory of *taqlid* requests people to follow the *mojtahed*s' opinions. However, when one of the litigants did not obey them, the edicts were not decisive, unlike the decisions of modern trials. Moreover, the shari'a courts preferred to arrange settlement. It is not clear if attendants actually negotiated at court or somewhere else, but, at the very least, a deed of settlement was drawn up at court and endorsed by the *mojtaheds*. In summary, shari'a courts were places where legal documents, such as *hokms* and deeds of settlement, were issued, rather than places of trials.

If the shari'a court did not judge cases, how were disputes solved in Qajar Tehran? The "Double Vaqf" case gives us an insight. The litigants of the case appealed to both shari'a courts and a *divankhane*. Mohammad Shah issued the royal edict, but its content was denied by a *hokm* of a certain *mojtahed*, which was confirmed by Mohammad Hasan Najafi, one of the most distinguished jurists of the 'Atabat. Here, one institution did not settle the case: both parties appealed to various institutions to secure their interests. Many *mojtaheds* were involved in the case, but the shari'a courts did not make the final judgment. Instead, the courts issued separate *hokms*, each supporting a litigant. The disputes continued for more than sixty years, until finally the *vaqf* village appeared to have been divided by the litigants. The shari'a courts were thus quite independent and were not influenced by royal edicts: only high-ranking jurists in the 'Atabat held sway over the courts since most of the *mojtaheds* in Tehran studied under them.

Another important function of the shari'a courts was the attestation and endorsement of private deeds. The records of sales, leases, or donations of real estate comprised a major portion of the court registers. Moreover, conditional sales, secured loans with interest, were common transactions. Even loans with interest without security, which were clearly forbidden by jurists, were sometimes arranged; in these transactions, interest was termed "fees of agreement." Although *riba* (high rates of interest) are prohibited by Islamic law, a rate of 24 percent was most common in these transactions. In this regard, the shari'a courts, which were quite pragmatic, responded well to the needs of society. Other functions, such as the confirmation of the deeds issued by other courts, the issuance of the deed copies, the review of court registers were also conducted at the shari'a courts.

Socially and economically, the *vaqf* deeds were most influential deeds arranged at the shari'a courts, since, once established, a *vaqf* cannot, in principle, be altered until the end of the world. The analysis of 260 *vaqf* deeds permits a description of the features of Qajar *vaqfs* in Tehran. The Qajar state partially controlled the *vaqfs* because *vaqf* deeds were drawn up at the shari'a courts and never fully registered in the state archives. Large *vaqfs*, such as those of the Shah Mosque and the Naseri Madrase (Mottahari Madrase) were established by shahs and high-ranking officials. However, many *vaqfs* that were not directly related to religious facilities were also founded: most of these *vaqfs* were small and supported the mourning ceremonies of Shi'i Imams. Two groups of people, bureaucrats/military officers and merchants/artisans were significant *vaqf* founders. Thus, various sorts of people established *vaqfs*, which supported not only the religious institutions and ceremonies, but also provided urban necessities, such as water.

How much did people use the *vaqf* system at that time? An analysis of the properties of four individuals clearly indicates that, in most cases, they founded *vaqfs* with comparatively small parts of their property. They did not convert all their property into *vaqfs*. In other words, they did not rely on the *vaqf* system as the sole means to protect it. Instead, they also used other tools, such as the legal division of inheritance and the last wills and testaments for the transference of property to next generation. If we take a look at the Grand Bazaar, only one-tenth of the total shops were *vaqf* properties. On the contrary, most *sarays* had a *vaqf* portion; however, they were not originally built as *vaqf* endowments. Instead, they were created as private property, divided into small portions over the course of time, and then gradually converted into *vaqf* properties, portion by portion. In other words, the *vaqf* system did not contribute much to the development of the Grand Bazaar, although the system might have assisted in its maintenance, as the *vaqfs* gradually penetrated commercial facilities. From this perspective, we cannot say that the *vaqf* system exercised a dominant role in the property management of individuals or commercial activity of the Grand Bazaar. However, it is also true that all property transactions were conducted through the use of the legal devices of Islamic law, of which the *vaqf* was one.

The study of *vaqf* documents also permits the examination of longer term effects. The first case, concerning the Old Friday Mosque, indicates the factors in survival of a *vaqf*. The *vaqf* endured more than 300 years because the imams of the mosque tried to recover the *vaqf* property, and the local inhabitants supported them. The state did not provide much protection to the *vaqf*; on the contrary, state officials tried to usurp its property. In other words, the law of *vaqf* was not well enforced by the state, but it was observed and defended by local society. The second case, that of the Chahardah Ma'sum Vaqf, shows the dynamic change of a Safavid state *vaqf* into a private *vaqf*, controlled by its beneficiaries. A *vaqf* deed, which proved the rights of the beneficiaries, did not exist, and the conditions of the *vaqf* were not well understood in the nineteenth century. The border of the *vaqf* lands had also significantly altered. Even so, once the *vaqf* had been founded, it still affected society for 300 years. Here, we can see the strengths and weaknesses of the law of *vaqf*: the *vaqf* did not survive in its original form but had a continuing influence.

Thus, we can recognize the existence of a highly developed system of law in Qajar Tehran, and the main part of this law was derived from the shari'a. People used various legal devices, such as *vaqfs*, loans, conditional sales, and wills. Their private rights were confirmed by the endorsements of the *mojtaheds*. To prove their right over land, even the Qajar shahs preserved legal deeds endorsed by the *mojtaheds*. Most criminal cases were dealt with by the governors or their officials, but if a case was legally too complicated for them, they referred it to the *mojtaheds*, the higher legal authority. At least, the texts of the sources did not refer to the term *'orf* explicitly; what they mentioned as law was the shari'a. Contrary to the modernist discourse that emphasizes the absence of law in Qajar Iran, we argue that the rule of law existed there.

This body of law was quite pragmatic and accorded well with social practices. It was not very strict and allowed for some adaptations, as is evident in the transactions of the shari'a courts, where even loans with interest were frequently permitted. Of course, the authority of the law depended on Islam, and the *mojtaheds* presided over legal matters. However, the law was not excessively dogmatic. In fact, one may hesitate to call it "religious" law.

The legal order was maintained not by the state but by society. The *mojtaheds* were not appointed by the state; they achieved this status through social recognition. This is the largest difference between Qajar Iran and the Ottoman Empire, where the qadis were incorporated into the state organization. In Iran, the state did not intervene in the shari'a courts. Naturally, the modernizing reforms of the state affected the shari'a courts very slowly. However, we can see the case in which the supreme jurist in the 'Atabat had some influence over the shari'a courts.

Naturally, the system of shari'a courts was based on the Shi'i-Usuli doctrine: only *mojtaheds*, those capable of exercising *ejtehad*, the deduction of legal rules from legal sources, could take part in them. Here, we can see a significant aspect of Qajar 'ulama: the 'ulama as legal experts. Most leading *mojtaheds* in Tehran engaged in legal matters and presided over shari'a courts. Their daily duties included the endorsement of legal documents and issuance of legal edicts. In other words, people needed them when they bought properties or borrowed money. Though the 'ulama mainly been considered as fulfilling the role of clerics in previous studies, we must take into account their function as legal experts, which undoubtedly affected their social position.

Even if the Qajar legal system was highly developed, it was not free from problems. As a judicial institution, the shari'a courts sometimes did not function well. If two parties came to terms with each other at court or if both accepted a *hokm* issued by a *mojtahed*, a dispute terminated. However, if one party did not accept the *hokm*, the shari'a court could not end the dispute. The political authority was then expected to execute the *hokm*, but sometimes it did not do so. The other party could respond by acquiring another *hokm* that supported its position; as a result, both parties would have been justified by *hokms*, resulting in long disagreements and negotiations.[1] Each shari'a court carried on its work, but the general court system was not well organized. Moreover, no archives, beyond the individual shari'a courts which functioned as notary offices, provided information to the public. These might be reasons why some 'ulama took part in the reformist movements such as the Constitutional Revolution.

Given their practical and pragmatic nature, it is difficult to consider all Qajar legal practices old-fashioned or outdated. The Qajar and modern legal systems differ in their transparency and efficiency. The Qajar system always allowed for and required flexibility. This tractability permitted the *mojtaheds* to monopolize the legal reasoning that was not obvious to the public. Further, the flexibility of the system sometimes left cases unsolved, which increased inefficiency, in comparison to the modern system. Further, new elites challenged the legal monopoly of the 'ulama. It was natural, therefore, that the modernized state sought to abolish the shari'a courts and to introduced the modern court system. The civil code of 1928–1936 and the establishment of Daftar-e Asnad-e Rasmi in 1920s were the final blows to the shari'a courts.[2] Though the judicial system of Iran was Islamized after 1979, it does not resemble the Qajar shari'a courts; it is based on the modern court system.[3]

Even so, the serviceable operation of Islamic Law in nineteenth-century Iran is evident from the study of legal documents. In Muslim creeds, the shari'a, seen as God's law, has never changed since the emergence of Islam. However, Islamic law has been interpreted differently by each society, and its legal practices have always been modified, in time and by place. The practical and pragmatic aspect of Qajar legal practices indicated that there were many ways to implement Islamic law, which may have originated with God, but was then interpreted and executed by human beings.

Notes

1 Negotiation and bargaining are keywords describing Qajar society. See, Martin, *The Qajar Pact* (London, 2005).
2 Enayati, *Law, State, and Society*, 113–143; Ahmad Mahdawi Damgani, s.v. "Daftar-e Asnad-e Rasimi," *Encyclopaedia Iranica* 6 (1993): 564–565.
3 Majid Mohammadi, *Judicial Reform and Reorganization in 20th Century Iran: State-Building, Modernization and Islamization* (New York, 2008), 109–215.

Appendix

List of *vaqf* deeds referred to in Chapter 6

1 Haji Abu Taleb Tajer Tehrani. Shavval 1202AH. Owqaf no.151.
2 Mohammad Karim Mostowfi-e Tehran. Safar 1212AH. Owqaf no.856.[1]
3 Mirza 'Ali Qoli Khan. Rabi' I 1213AH.[2]
4 Haji Abu Taleb Bonakdar Tehrani. Safar 1214AH. Owqaf no.808.
5 'Abdin Beg Sanduqdar-e Sarkar-e Khasse-e Sharife. 8 Safar 1214AH. Owqaf no.484.
6 Akhond Molla Mohammad Kermanshahi 18 Rabi' I 1214AH.[3]
7 Aqa Sayyed 'Aliya. Ziqa'de 1216AH. Owqaf no.798.
8 Zinat Khanom and Shahr Banu Khanom. 22 Sha'ban 1217AH. Owqaf no.123.
9 Haji Mirza Hoseyn. Rajab 1223AH. Owqaf no.879.
10 Haji Zeyn al-'Abedin Tehrani. End of Zihejje 1227AH. Owqaf no.717.
11 Mirza Mohammad Shafi' Sadr-e A'zam. Rabi' I 1227AH. Owqaf no.36.
12 Haji Esma'il Tehrani Mehrjerdi. 22 Rabi' I. Owqaf no. 242.
13 Mirza Yusof Ashrafi Mostowfi-e Divan. Rabi' II 1228AH.[4]
14 Nabat Khanom. Zihejje 1228AH. Owqaf no.36.
15 Fath 'Ali Shah Qajar. 1230AH. Owqaf no. 816; Gate inscription of Masjed-e Emam, Tehran.
16 Aqa Mohammad Ja'far Tehrani. 8 Safar 1230AH. Owqaf no.1031.
17 Haji Mohammad Hoseyn Khan Marvi. Zihejje 1231AH.[5]
18 Mirza Mohammad Shafi' Sadr-e A'zam. Shavval 1233AH. Owqaf no.36.
19 Mohammad Reza Khan Savadkuhi. Rajab 1235AH. Owqaf no.975.
20 Mirza Abu al-Hasan Ilchi. 1 Rabi' II 1237AH. Owqaf no.502.
21 Esma'il Khan Qajar Shambayati. 23 Jomada II 1238AH. Owqaf no.130.
22 Mina Khanom. Ziqa'de 1239AH. Owqaf no.483.
23 Haji Sayyed Mohammad. 1 Rabi' II 1242AH. Owqaf no.840.[6]
24 Bibi Kuchek Khanom. 1 Rabi' II 1242AH. Owqaf no.840.[7]
25 Mirza Mohammad Saleh Mostowfi Tehrani. 2 Rajab 1242AH. Owqaf no.298.
26 Mohtaram Khanom. Zihejje1242AH. Owqaf no.578.
27 Haji Mirza Mohamamd 'Ali. 9 Sha'ban 1244AH. Owqaf no.590.
28 Karbala'i Qorbani Tehrani. Rabi' I 1244AH. Owqaf no. 742.
29 Hoseyn Khan Khazanedar. Zihejje 1245AH. Owqaf no.1180.
30 Hoseyn 'Ali Khan Mo'ayyer-bashi. Ramazan 1246AH. Owqaf no.642.
31 Mirza Mohammad 'Ali Khan Vazir-e Zell al-Soltan. Zihejje 1246AH. Owqaf no.588.

32 Haji Sayyed 'Ali Tehrani. Jomada II 1247AH. Owqaf no.191.
33 Haji Sayyed 'Ali Tehrani and Haji Mohammad Hoseyn Shirazi. Zihejje 1247AH. Owqaf no. 26.
34 Karbala'i Mohammad. 18 Zihejje 1247AH.[8]
35 Aqa Khan, Molla Hoseyn and Molla Esma'il. Moharram 1248AH. Owqaf no.1149.
36 Haji Molla Mohammad 'Ali. 1 Jomada II 1249AH. Owqaf no.590.
37 Mahmud Khan Kalantar-e Dar al-Khelafe-e Tehran 1250AH. Owqaf no.52.
38 Golnadam Khanom. 23 Jomada I 1250AH.[9]
39 Haji Qasem 'Ali Tehrani. 15 Sha'ban 1250AH. Owqaf no.946.[10]
40 Haji Molla Hoseyn Semnani. 30 Sha'ban 1250AH. Owqaf no.883.
41 Hajiye Badr Nesa' Khanom. 1 Ramazan 1250AH. Owqaf no.530.
42 Hajiye Shah Soltan Khanom. 4 Jomada II 1251AH. Owqaf no. 964.
43 Haji Mir 'Ali Hoseyn. Rajab 1251AH.Owqaf no.764.
44 Zell al-Soltan. 21 Rajab 1251AH. Inscription at Sara-ye Shah, the Grand Bazaar of Tehran.
45 Mirza Zaki Nuri . 26 Rabi' 1253AH. Owqaf no.71.
46 Aqa Mohammad Mahdi Tajer Shirazi. Rajab 1253AH. Owqaf no.842.
47 Haji Mir 'Abedin. 14 Moharram. 1254AH. Owqaf no.833.
48 Fateme Khanom, Morvarid Khanom and Shirin Khanom. 17 Rajab 1254AH.[11]
49 Aqa Abu al-Qasem. 28 Jomada 1255AH. Owqaf no.2199.
50 Haji Mohammad Ebrahim and Khanom Khan Khanom. 16 Rajab 1255AH. Owqaf no.69.
51 Haji Mohammad Zaman Tajer. 14 Rabi' II 1256AH.[12]
52 Haji Sayyed Hasan Tajer Tehrani, Jomada II 1256AH. Owqaf no.1093.
53 Mirza Ahmad Hakimbashi. Moharram 1257AH.[13]
54 Haji 'Ali Asghar Tajer Tehrani. 26 Safar 1257AH. Owqaf no.1486.
55 Karbala'i Mohammad Baqer Tehrani. Jomada I 1257AH.[14]
56 Ostad Hoseyn Hammami Kashani. 1 Shavval 1257AH. Owqaf no.208.
57 Haji Mir Mohammad 'Ali Tajer Shirazi. 11 Ziqa'de 1257AH. Owqaf no.1497.
58 Mohammad Qoli Khan 'Arab Lalu'i. 27 Ziqa'de 1257AH. Owqaf no.624.
59 Haji Abu Taleb Tajer Tehrani Kolahduz, I. 16 Ramazan 1258AH. Owqaf no.511.
60 Haji Abu Taleb Tajer Tehrani Kolahduz, II. 16 Ramazan 1258AH. Owqaf no.511.
61 Haji Mohammad Hasan 'Arab. 6 Moharram 1259AH. Owqaf no.194.
62 'Isa Khan Beglarbegi-e Dar al-Khelafe. Safar 1259AH. Owqaf no.135.
63 'Isa Khan Beglarbegi-e Dar al-Khelafe. 5 Safar 1259AH. Owqaf no.135.
64 Haji Mirza 'Ali Reza. 25 Jomada I 1259AH. Owqaf no.673.
65 Haji 'Ali Mohammad Tehrani. Rajab 1259AH. Owqaf no.491.[15]
66 Haji Molla Mohammad 'Ali. 1 Zihejje 1259AH. Owqaf no.590.
67 Sheykh Mohammad 'Ali Tehrani. 15 Zihejje 1259AH. Owqaf no.321.
68 Manuchehr Khan Mo'tamad al-Dowle. Rabi' 1260AH. Owqaf no.676.[16]
69 'Isa Khan Beglarbegi-e Dar al-Khelafe. 29 Zihejje 1260AH. Owqaf no.135.
70 Haji Gorgin Beg Gorji. 2 Rabi' 1261AH. Owqaf no.1831.

71 Sayyed Sadeq Bazzaz Tehrani. Jomada II 1261AH. Owqaf no.344.
72 'Isa Khan Beglarbegi-e Dar al-Khelafe.13 Shavval 1261AH. Owqaf no.135.
73 Haji 'Ali Qoli and Haji Mohammad Baqer. Rajab 1262AH. Owqaf no.529.
74 Hajiye Bibi Khanom. 10 Rajab 1262AH. Owqaf no.571.
75 'Abd al-Vahhab Tehrani. 27 Rajab 1262AH. Owqaf no.562.
76 Haji Mirza Mohammad Tehrani. 28 Ramazan 1262AH. Owqaf no.605.
77 Haji Rajab 'Ali Tehrani. 17 Sha'ban 1262AH. Owqaf no.25.[17]
78 Khadije Khanom. 1 Jomada 1263AH. Owqaf no.976.
79 Haji Mohammad Hasan Tajer Kolahduz. 16 Jomada 1263AH. Owqaf no.523.
80 Haji Mohammad 'Ali Nuri. 11 Safar 1264AH. Owqaf no.526.
81 Sohrab Khan Gorji. Rabi' II 1264AH. Owqaf no.550.
82 Sheykh Mohammad Emam-e Jama'at-e Tehran. 3 Rabi' II 1264AH. Owqaf no.334.
83 Hajiye Hajer Khatun Khanom. 7 Sha'ban 1264AH. Owqaf no.981.[18]
84 Haji Qasem Tabarestani, 25 Sha'ban 1264AH. Owqaf no.1308.
85 Molla Gholam Hoseyn. 29 Rabi' I 1265AH. Owqaf no. 322.
86 Mirza Zaki Nuri. Rabi' II 1265AH. Owqaf no.71.
87 Karbala'i Rajab 'Ali 'Attar. Rabi ' II 1265AH. Owqaf no.1820.
88 Hajiye Nane Khanom. 1 Rajab 1266AH. Owqaf no.782.
89 Haji Mohammad Ebrahim Tajer Tanbakuforush Esfahani. 17 Ziqa'de 1266AH. Owqaf no.69.[19]
90 Aqa Mohammad Baqer Tehrani. Zihejje 1266AH. Owqaf no.890.
91 Karbala'i Mohamamd Hasan Kuzegar Dulabi. Rabi' I 1267AH. Owqaf no.839.
92 Haji 'Ali Asghar Tajer Tehrani. 1 Rajab 1267AH. Owqaf no.1486.
93 Bibi Khanom. Rajab 1267AH. Owqaf no.973.
94 Homayun Soltan Khanom. Moharram 1268AH. Owqaf no.165.
95 Mohammad Kazem's father. 11 Rajab 1268AH.[20]
96 Haji Faridun Beg Gorji. 19 Sha'ban 1268AH. Owqaf no.348.
97 Haji Mohammad Esma'il Tehrani. 1269AH. Owqaf no.216.[21]
98 Khadije Khanom. 24 Rabi' I 1269AH. Owqaf no.976.
99 Rajab 'Ali Baqqal. 30 Rajab 1269AH. Owqaf no.1492.
100 Haji 'Ali Akbar Tehrani. Sha'ban 1269AH. Owqaf no.1934.
101 Haji Mohammad Taqi Hajjar. 9 Sha'ban 1269AH. Owqaf no.199.
102 Haji 'Ali Akbar Tajer Tehrani. 22 Ramazan 1269AH. Owqaf no.2201.
103 Mohammad Esma'il Khan Kashani. 15 Ziqa'de 1269AH. Owqaf no.2536.
104 Shokr-allah Khan Kojuri Gholam-e Pishkhedmat, I. 24 Moharram 1270AH. Owqaf no.471.
105 Shokr-allah Khan Kojuri Gholam-e Pishkhedmat, II. 24 Moharram 1270AH. Owqaf no.471.
106 Molla Gholam Hoseyn. 6 Rabi' I 1270AH. Owqaf no.322.
107 Mahmud Khan Kalantar Dar al-Khelafe. Jomada II 1270AH. Owqaf no.52.
108 Haji Mohammad Hoseyn 'Attar Qazvini. 8 Ramazan 1270AH. Owqaf no.798.
109 Aqa Mirza Mo'in Nuri. Moharram 1271AH. Owqaf no.719.
110 Haji Safar 'Ali Me'mar. 12 Safar 1271AH. Owqaf no.352.
111 Karbala'i Mohammad Baqer Tehrani. 20 Safar 1271AH. Owqaf no.576.

112 Haji Mohammad Esma'il Beg Damghani. Jomada II 1271AH. Owqaf no.761.
113 Haji Mohammad 'Ali Tehrani. Ziqa'de 1271AH. Owqaf no.2206.
114 Aqa Mohammad Mahdi Malek al-Tojjar. 13 Ziqa'de 1271AH.[22]
115 Aqa Mirza Mo'in Nuri. Moharram 1272AH. Owqaf no.719.
116 Hajiye Fateme Khanom Tehrani. 17 Moharram 1272AH. Owqaf no.1294.
117 Haji Sayyed Asad-allah and Haji Sayyed Nasr-allah Tehrani. Rabi' I 1272AH. wqaf no.699.
118 Mahd-e 'Olya. 15 Rabi' I 1272AH.[23]
119 Mirza Aqa Khan Nuri E'temad al-Dowle. 15 Shavval 1272AH. Owqaf no.666.
120 Naser al-Din Shah Qajar. Rabi' I 1273AH.[24]
121 Aqa Sayyed Sadeq Akhavi Tehrani. 2 Sha'ban 1273AH. Owqaf no.874.
122 Musa Khan Nuri. 10 Sha'ban 1273AH.[25]
123 'Aziz-allah b. Mirza Esma'il. Shavval 1273AH. Owqaf no.1295.
124 Mahmud Khan Pishkhedmat-e Khasse. 11 Ziqa'de 1273AH. Owqaf no.1489.
125 Mirza Aqa Khan Nuri E'temad al-Dowle. 4 Rabi' I 1274AH. Owqaf no.666.[26]
126 Haji Hasan 'Ali Tehrani 'Alaqeband. 10 Shavval 1274AH. Owqaf no.196.
127 Mirza 'Ali Akbar Monshi and Haji 'Ali Aghar Sarraf Yazdi. 15 Shavval 1274AH. Owqaf no.478.
128 Haji Aqa Mohammad Qazvini. 26 Sha'ban 1275AH. Owqaf no.522.
129 Haji Sayyed Reza. 5 Ramazan 1275AH. Owqaf no.2406.
130 Mirza Aqa Khan Nuri E'temad al-Dowle. 25 Jomada II 1275AH. Owqaf no.666.[27]
131 Mir Qanbar 'Ali Tehrani. Jomada II 1275AH. Owqaf no.2552.
132 Sheykh 'Abd al-Hoseyn Tehrani. 18 Shavval 1276AH. Owqaf no.664.[28]
133 'Abbas Tajer Farshforush. Jomada II 1277AH. Owqaf no.1507.
134 Karbala'i 'Abd al-Hamid Tuprizi Tabrizi. 17 Jomada 1277AH. Owqaf no.275.
135 Mirza Mohammad Mahdi Mostowfi Nuri. 27 Sha'ban 1277AH. Owqaf no.231.
136 Mohammad Rahim Khan Qajar Shambayati and Shahr Banu Khanom. Ramazan 1277AH. Owqaf no.130.
137 Aqa Musa Tajer Tehrani. 21 Shavval 1277AH. Owqaf no.320.
138 Karbala'iye Balus? 1 Moharram 1278AH. Owqaf no.1325.
139 Haji 'Abd al-Razzaq Tajer Kashani. Rabi' I 1278AH. Owqaf no.118.
140 Varase-e Mahmud Khan Kalantar-e Dar al-Khelafe. Rabi' II 1278AH. Owqaf no.52.
141 Haji Mohammad Ja'far Tajer. Rajab 1279AH. Owqaf no.2207.
142 Khadije Soltan Khanom. 24 Sha'ban 1279AH. Owqaf no.1352.
143 Aqa Mirza Mo'in Nuri. Zihejje 1279AH. Owqaf no.719.
144 Haji Kayumars Mirza. 29 Jomada 1280AH. Owqaf no.2485.
145 Mohammad Taqi Tajer Tehrani and Sheykh 'Ali Akbar. 29 Sha'ban 1280AH. Owqaf no.590.
146 Mirza Mohammad 'Ali-abadi Vazir-e Kerman. 24 Zihejje 1280AH. Owqaf no.540.
147 Karbala'i Gholam Reza Esfahani. 1 Safar 1281AH. Owqaf no.219.
148 Aqa Mirza Mo'in Nuri. Jomada I 1281AH. Owqaf no.719.

149 Haji 'Abd al-Mohammad Chaychi Lavasani Tehrani. 3 Jomada II 1281AH. Owqaf no.34.
150 Mirza Aqasi Tehrani. 26 Jomada II 1281AH. Owqaf no.681.
151 'Isa Khan Beglarbegi. 29 Rajab 1281AH. Owqaf no.135.
152 Aqa Mirza Mo'in Nuri. 17 Jomada I 1282AH. Owqaf no.719.
153 Mirza Mohammad Khan Qajar Sepahsalar. I Rabi' 1283AH. Owqaf no.31.[29]
154 Esma'il Musavi Behbahani. 15 Rabi' I 1283AH. Owqaf no.244.
155 Haji Ramazan Halimpaz Qazvini. 2 Jomada II 1283AH. Owqaf no.1556.
156 Mohammad Naser Khan Zahir al-Dowle. 1 Ramazan 1283AH.[30]
157 Haji Mohammad Hoseyn Khan Shehab al-Molk. 19 Zihejje 1283AH. Owqaf no.742.[31]
158 'Aziz-allah b. Mirza Esma'il. 1284AH. Owqaf no.1295.
159 'Aziz-allah b. Mirza Esma'il. Rabi' II 1284AH. Owqaf no.1295.
160 Sakine Khatun. Rabi' II 1284. Owqaf no.803.
161 Sayyed Zeyn al-'Abedin Akhavi Tehrani. 2 Zihejje 1284AH. Owqaf no.312.
162 Haji Aqa Tajer Tehrani. 10 Moharram 1285AH.[32]
163 Haji Aqa Tajer Tehrani. 25 Moharram 1285AH.[33]
164 Shir Khan Khaje-bashi-e Mahd-e 'Olya. 10 Safar 1285AH.[34]
165 Fath 'Ali Khan Qajar. 15 Jomada II 1285AH. Owqaf no.816.
166 Naser al-Din Shah. 24 Rajab 1285AH. Owqaf no.276.
167 Sakine Khatun Khanom. 2 Ramazan 1285AH. Owqaf no.116.
168 Haji Sayyed Kazem Tehrani. 19 Ramazan 1285AH. Owqaf no.2511.
169 Hajiye Nuri Jahan Khanom. 2 Ziqa'de 1285AH. Owqaf no.805.
170 Shahzade Fakhr al-Dowle. Sha'ban 1286AH. Owqaf no.519.
171 Mohammad Taqi Khan Qajar Shambayati. 1287AH. Owqaf no.130.
172 Aqa Mohammad Ebrahim Abdarbashi-e Amin al-Soltan. 26 Moharram 1287AH. Owqaf no.218.
173 Haji Molla 'Ali. 11 Rabi' II 1287AH. Owqaf no.887.
174 Shahzade Fakhr al-Dowle. 18 Jomada I 1287AH. Owqaf no.519.
175 Shahzade Fakhr al-Dowle. 15 Jomada II 1287AH. Owqaf no.519.
176 Kowkab Soltan Khanom. 15 Rajab 1287AH. Owqaf no.254.
177 Karbala'i Mohammad Hoseyn Kardsaz Tehrani. Sha'ban 1287AH. Owqaf no.701.
178 Haji Abu al-Qasem Tajer and Mohammad 'Ali Tajer. 27 Shavval 1287AH. Owqaf no.238.
179 Haji Mahdi Qoli Beg Farrashbashi. Zihejje 1287AH. Owqaf no.720.
180 Aqa Sayyed Esma'il Hammami. 20 Rabi' I 1288AH. Owqaf no.774.
181 Mashhadi Rahim Yuzbashi-e Farrashkhane. 12 Jomada 1288AH. Owqaf no.602.
182 Mostafa Qoli Beg. Late Ramazan 1288AH.[35]
183 Aqa Mirza 'Ali Mostowfi. 14 Shavval 1288AH. Owqaf no.223.
184 Aqa Mashhadi Mohammad Hoseyn Khorasani. 4 Ziqa'de 1288AH. Owqaf no.516.
185 Haji Sayyed Hoseyn Larijani and Haji Molla Hadi Mojtahed. 28 Zihejje 1288AH. Owqaf no.119.

186 Haji Mehr 'Ali Kolahduz. 6 Rabi' II 1289AH. Owqaf no.1890.
187 Aqa Sheykh Mahmud Tehrani and Haji Mohammad Ebrahim 'Attar. 1 Jomada 1289AH. Owqaf no.591.
188 Aqa Mirza Ebrahim Emam-e Jama'at. 10 Jomada I 1289AH. Owqaf no.226.
189 Haji 'Abd al-Razzaq Me'mar Kashani. Jomada II 1289AH. Owqaf no.957.
190 Mashhadi Aqa Qannad. 2 Jomada II 1289AH. Owqaf no.763.
191 Mah Banu Khanom Zartoshti. Sha'ban 1289AH. Owqaf no.50.
192 Aqa Mohammad Khan; Aqa 'Ali Khan Pishkhedmat-e Khasse. 25 Sha'ban 1289AH. Owqaf no.310.
193 Haji Qanbar 'Ali Khan Sa'd al-Dowle. 1 Moharram 1290AH. Owqaf no.865.
194 Ehtesab al-Molk Kashani. 1 Safar 1290AH. Owqaf no.669.
195 Akhond Molla Zeyn al-'Abedin 'Eraqi. 1 Safar 1290AH. Owqaf no.665.
196 Aqa Nasr-allah Tajer Shirazi. 1 Sha'ban 1290AH. Owqaf no.466.
197 Hajiye Nuri Jahan Khanom. 29 Sha'ban 1290AH. Owqaf no.805.
198 Sheykh Fazl-allah Nuri. Rabi' I 1291AH.[36]
199 Mashhadi Hasan Zargar Kashani. 5 Rabi' II 1291AH. Owqaf no.593.
200 Begom Jan Khanom. 14 Rajab 1291AH. Owqaf no.368.
201 Aqa Sayyed 'Ali Naqi Tafreshi. 18 Zihejje 1291AH. Owqaf no.2643.
202 Jan Jahan Khanom. End of 1291AH. Owqaf no.13.[37]
203 Aqa Mirza Mostafa Vakil-e Lashkar. 18 Safar 1292AH. Owqaf no.1200.
204 Haji Sha'ban 'Ali Tanbakuforush. 3 Rabi' 1292AH.[38]
205 'Abd-allah Beg Musavi. Jomada II 1292AH. Owqaf no.1090.
206 Homayun Soltan Khanom. Sha'ban 1292AH. Owqaf no.165.
207 Mohammad Rahim Khan Khazen al-Molk. Sha'ban 1292AH. Owqaf no.363.
208 Haji Rajab 'Ali Bazzaz. 23 Safar 1293AH. Owqaf no.758.
209 Maryam Beygom Khanom and Qamar Nesa' Khanom. Jomada I 1293AH. Owqaf no.2486.
210 Sheykh 'Abbas and Aqa Najaf Qoli, I. 22 Jomada I 1293AH. Owqaf no.527.
211 Sheykh 'Abbas and Aqa Najaf Qoli, II 22 Jomada 1293AH. Owqaf no.527.
212 Haji Molla Hadi Mojtahed and Aqa Sayyed Taqi Larijani, 1 Rajab 1293AH. Owqaf no.32.
213 Mashhadi Hoseyn Jahromi. 2 Ramazan 1293AH. Owqaf no.174.
214 Fath-allah Khan. 7 Ramazan 1293AH.[39]
215 Mirza Reza Vakil al-Ro'aya'. Ziqa'de 1293AH. Owqaf no.278.
216 Haji 'Abd al-Rahman Golmari. 1 Zihejje 1293AH. Owqaf no.283.
217 Qoli Khan Tork-e Mafi. 14 Moharram 1294AH.[40]
218 Haji Rajab 'Ali Bazzaz. 17 Safar 1294AH. Owqaf no.758.
219 Habib-allah Khan Pishkhedmat. Jomada I 1294AH. Owqaf no.1495.
220 Khatan Jan Khanom. 10 Ramazan 1294AH. Owqaf no.780.
221 Sadeq Khan Sartip. 18 Ziqa'de 1294AH. Owqaf no.824.
222 Zobeyde Khanom Amin-e Aqdas. 4 Zihejje 1294AH.Zihejje.[41]
223 Molla Nazar 'Ali Taleqani. 29 Moharram 1295AH. Owqaf no.127.
224 Haji Mohammad Esma'il Arbab Tehrani. 5 Safar 1295AH. Owqaf no.568.

225 Mashhadi Haji Aqa Arbab Tehrani. 5 Safar 1295AH. Owqaf no.78.
226 Khatun Jan Khanom. 7 Jomada II 1295AH.[42]
227 Mohammad Ebrahim Emam-e Jama'at. Sha'ban 1295AH. Owqaf no.1104.
228 Sheykh Mohammad Hasan. 13 Shavval 1295AH.[43]
229 Haji Mohammad Rahim Khan Khazen al-Molk. Ziqa'de1295AH. Owqaf no.363.
230 'Olya-ye Mokhaddere bt. Haji Gorgin Beg Gorji. Moharram 1296AH. Owqaf no.1831.
231 Sayyed Yahya Akhavi Musavi Tehrani. 14 Jomada II 1296AH. Owqaf no.656.
232 Hajiye Sharaf Nesa' Khanom. 6 Rajab 1296AH. Owqaf no.895.
233 Haji Mohammad Hoseyn Javaheri Shirazi. 15 Sha'ban 1296AH. Owqaf no.353.
234 Anis al-Dowle. 9 Zihejje 1296AH. Owqaf no.837.
235 Khatun Jan Khanom (Haji Bibi). 3 Safar 1297AH. Owqaf no.185.
236 Haji Abu al-Fath Tajer Tehrani. 25 Jomada 1297AH. Owqaf no.635.
237 Mortaza Khan Yavar-e Fowj-e Tehran. Rajab 1297AH. Owqaf no.687.
238 Mortaza Khan Nazer Kashani. 22 Sha'ban 1297AH. Owqaf no.851.
239 Mirza Hoseyn Khan Sepahsalar-e A'zam. 7 Shavval 1297AH.[44]
240 Hajiye Hajer Khatun and Hajiyye Sare Soltan Khanom. Rabi' I 1298AH. Owqaf no.5.
241 Haji Mohammad Taqi Me'mar. Rabi' II 1298AH. Owqaf no.351.
242 Mirza Sayyed Kazem Mostowfi-e Divan. 22 Rabi' II 1298AH. Owqaf no.236.
243 Haji Mohammad Reza Nuri, I. Jomada I 1298AH. Owqaf no.719.
244 Haji Mohammad Reza Nuri, II. Jomada I 1298AH. Owqaf no.719.
245 Haji Mohammad Reza Nuri, III. Jomada I 1298AH. Owqaf no.719.
246 Hajiye Shahzade Khanom. Jomada II 1298AH. Owqaf no.165.
247 Anis al-Dowle. 5 Rajab 1298AH. Owqaf no.837.
248 'Abd al-Rahim Khan Khodabandelu Kermanshahani. Moharram 1299AH.[45]
249 Hajiye Bibi Khanom. Moharram 1299AH. Owqaf no.359.
250 Haji Aqa 'Ali Me'mar Kashani. 1 Rabi' II 1299AH. Owqaf no.572.
251 Morvarid Khanom. Jomada II 1299AH. Owqaf no.978.
252 Haji Sayyed Yahya Akhavi. 9 Rajab 1299AH. Owqaf no.233.
253 Haji Aqa Mohammad Esfahani. 1 Ramazan 1299AH. Owqaf no.1177.
254 Haji Mohammad Qasem 'Attar Tehrani. 13 Sha'ban 1299AH. Owqaf no.281.
255 Sha'ban 'Ali Tajer and Abu al-Qasem Bazzaz. 16 Sha'ban 1299AH. Owqaf no.765.
256 Haji Abu al-Hasan Yavar-e Qurkhane. 11 Shavval 1299AH. Owqaf no.4.
257 Mashhadi Rahim Tehrani. 25 Ziqa'de 1299AH. Owqaf no.1837.
258 Mirza Zeyn al-'Abedin Lashkar-nevis. Zihejje 1299AH. Owqaf no.159.
259 Mohammad Taqi Khan Qajar Shambayati. 11 Rabi' I 1300AH. Owqaf no.130.
260 Yahya Khan Moshir al-Dowle. 26 Jomada 1300AH.[46]

Notes

1 Haji 'Abbasi and Reza'i, eds. *Asnad-e Mowqufat-e Boluk-e Ghar va Fashapuye*, 29–44.
2 Habibi, ed. *Masajed-e Dirinesal-e Tehran*, 519.
3 Ibid.
4 Sotude, ed. "Vaqf-name-e Mirza Mohammad Yusof Ashrafi," 38–45.
5 *Savad-e Vaqf-name-e Madrase-e Khan-e Marvi*; Ostadi, ed. "Vaqf-name-e Madrase-e Marvi."
6 Haji 'Abbasi and Reza'i, eds. *Asnad-e Mowqufat-e Boluk-e Ghar va Fashapuye*, 54–60.
7 Ibid., 60–62.
8 Ettehadiye and Ruhi, eds. *Dar Mahzar*, 450.
9 'Abd -allah 'Aqili, ed. *Tarikh-e Astane-e Rey*, 326–328.
10 Haji 'Abbasi and Reza'i, eds. *Asnad-e Mowqufat-e Boluk-e Ghar va Fashapuye*, 81–84.
11 Ettehadiye and Ruhi, eds. *Dar Mahzar*, 451.
12 *Daftar-e Shar'i-e Sangelaji*, 104a.
13 Hoseyni Balaghi, *Tarikh-e Tehran: Qesmat-e Markazi va Mazafat*, 75.
14 Habibi, ed. *Masajed-e Dirinesal-e Tehran*, 519.
15 *Daftar-e Shar'i-e Sangelaji*, 359b.
16 Haji 'Abbasi and Reza'i, eds. *Asnad-e Mowqufat-e Boluk-e Ghar va Fashapuye*, 98–112.
17 Ibid., 120–125.
18 Werner, "Zanan-e Vaqef," 119.
19 Mir Mohammad Sadeq, ed. "Vaqf-name-e Haj Mohammad Ebrahim Tajer Esfahani," 105–108.
20 Reza'i, ed. *Asnad-e Mahkame*, 20.
21 Ibid., 78.
22 Marziye Mortazavi, ed. "Vaqf-name'i az Aqa Mohammad Mahdi Malek al-Tojjar," *Vaqf, Miras-e Javidan* no.79/80 (1391Kh): 210–215.
23 *Vaqf-name-e Mahd-e 'Olya*, MS 8079, Institute for Iranian Contemporary Historcial Studies, Tehran; 'Abd al-Hoseyn Nava'i, ed. *Mahd-e 'Olya be-Revayat-e Asnad* (Tehran, 1383Kh), 17–30.
24 *Savad-e Vaqf-name va Taqsim-name-e Ab-e Shah*, 1–11; Karimiyan, "Vaqf-name-e Qanat-e Naseriye," 102.
25 Reza'i, ed. *Asnad-e Mahkame*, 43.
26 Dabir-e Siyaqi, "Vaqf-name-e Do Qanat," 32–33.
27 Ibid., 34–35.
28 Manzur al-Ajdad, "Do Sanad," 108–109.
29 'Emad al-Din Kazeruni, ed. "Vaqf-name-e Masjed-Madrase-e Sepahsalar-e Qadim (Tehran)," *Vaqf, Miras-e Javidan* no.33/34 (1380Kh): 122–132.
30 Mahmud Ahmadi, "Yek Toghra Vaqf-name az Marhum-e Zahir al-Dowle," *Barrasiha-ye Tarikhi* 12 (2536Sh): 118–136.
31 Mortazavi, ed. "Vaqf-name-e Qanat-e Hoseyniye," 127–136.
32 Reza'i, ed. *Asnad-e Mahkame*, 223.
33 Ibid., 222.
34 Ibid., 149.
35 *Daftar-e Shar'i-e Sangelaji*, 298a.
36 Ettehadiye and Ruhi, eds. *Dar Mahzar*, 165.
37 Haji 'Abbasi and Reza'i, eds. *Asnad-e Mowqufat-e Boluk-e Ghar va Fashapuye*, 227–234.
38 *Daftar-e Shar'i-e Sangelaji*, 432b.
39 Ibid., 116a.
40 Ibid., 420b.
41 Ibid., 154b.
42 Ibid., 386a.

43 Marziye Mortazavi, ed. "Vaqf-name'i marbut be Mahalle-e Sangelaj-e Tehran." *Vaqf, Miras-e Javidan* no.82 (1392Kh): 151–157.
44 *Vaqf-name-e Madrase-e Naseri*; Sahab, *Tarikh-e Madrase-e 'Ali-e Sepahsalar*, 51–102; Sheykh al-Hokama'i, *Asnad-e Me'mari-e Iran*, 1:93–138.
45 Ettehadiye and Ruhi, eds. *Dar Mahzar*, 663.
46 Sahab, *Tarikh-e Madrase-e 'Ali-e Sepahsalar*, 104–107.

Bibliography

Archival and unpublished sources

Akhzar 'Ali Shah, Hasan. *Ta'yin va Sabt-e Mahat-e Khandaq-e Shahr-e Dar al-Khelafe-e Bahere*. MS 20-ba. Central Library, University of Tehran, Tehran.

Arshiv-e Melli: Arshiv-e Melli, National Library and Archives of Iran, Tehran.

Chulavi, Mirza 'Ali Qoli Eqbal. *Tarikh-e Molk-ara*. MS 4161. Malek Library, Tehran.

Daftar-e Shar'i-e Sangelaji. Arshiv-e Melli, Tehran.

Dastur al-'Amal-e Hazih al-Sane-e Yunat-'il-e Kheyriyat-Tahvil-e Dar al-Khelafe-e Tehran. MS Hoquq J-373. Central Library, University of Tehran, Tehran.

Golestan: Golestan Museum, Tehran.

Ketabche-e Amlak-e Jenab-e Aqa'i az Babat-e Azarbayijan va 'Eraq. MS 5556. Central Library, University of Tehran, Tehran.

Ketabche-e Dehat-e Khalese va Mowqufat va Amlak-e Enteqali-e Divan-e A'la. I. MS 8891. Central Library, University of Tehran, Tehran; II. MS 7868. Mar'ashi Library, Qom.

Ketabche-e Jam' va Kharj-e hazih al-Sane-e Takhaqoy-' il-e Dar al-Khelafe-e Tehran Abvab-jam'i-e 'Alijenab Moqarrab al-Khaqan 'Isa Khan Beglarbegi. MS Hoquq J-371. Central Library, University of Tehran, Tehran.

Ketabche-e Jam' va Kharj-e Koll-e hazih al-Sanat-e It-'il-e Mamlekat-e Mahruse motabeq-e Sanne-e 1304 Hejri. MS 776. Majles Library, Tehran.

Ketabche-e Sabt-e Qavalejat va Neveshtejat-e mowjudi dar Khazane-e Mobarake-e Andaruni va Sanduqkhane-e Mobarake. Mr. Bahman Bayani Private Library, Tehran.

Ketabche-e Te'dad-e Nofus-e Mahallat-e Dar al-Khelafe-e Tehran. MS. Melli Library, Tehran.

Owqaf: Daftar-e Asnad va Shenasayi-e Mowqufat, *Vaqf* and Charity Organization, Tehran. Files of Tehran.

Picot, H. *Bibliographical Notices of Members of the Royal Family, Notable, Merchants, and Clergy*. FO881/7028. December 1897. National Archives, United Kingdom.

Savad-e Vaqf-name-e Madrase-e Khan-e Marvi. MS 2850. Madrase-e 'Ali-e Mottahari Library, Tehran.

Surat-e 'Adad-e Khaneha va Sayer-e Benaha-ye Dar al-Khelafe-e Bahere-e Tehran. Or Ms. K9(9). E.G. Browne Collection, Cambridge University, Cambridge.

Surat-e Khalesejat va Mowqufat va Raqabat. I. MS 7619. Majles Library, Tehran; II. MS Mar'ashi Library. Microfilm 4819. Central Library, University of Tehran, Tehran

Vaqf-name-e Madrase-e Naseri. MS 463. Madrase-e 'Ali-e Mottahari Library, Tehran.

Vaqf-name-e Mahd-e 'Olya. MS 8079. Institute for Iranian Contemporary Historical Studies, Tehran.

Vaqf-name-e Sara-ye Shah. The Inscription at Sara-ye Jomuhuri, Grand Bazaar, Tehran.

Published primary sources

'Abd al-Ghaffar. *Naqshe-e Dar al-Khelafe-e Naseri-e Tehran*. 1891 Reprint, Tehran: Sahab, 1984.

Afshar, Iraj. "Ruzname-e Mahallat-e Dar al-Khelafe 1292." In *Daftar-e Tarikh*, vol. 4, edited by Iraj Afshar, 267–277. Tehran: Bonyad-e Mowqufat-e Doktor Mahmud Afshar, 1389Kh.

Ahmadi, Mahmud. "Yek Toghra Vaqf-name az Marhum-e Zahir al-Dowle." *Barrasiha-ye Tarikhi* 12 (2536Sh): 117–136.

Al-e Davud, Sayyed 'Ali, ed. *Asnad va Nameha-ye Amir-e Kabir*. Tehran: Sazman-e Asnad-e Melli-e Iran, 1379Kh.

Almanach de Gotha, annuaire généalogique, diplomatique et statistique: cent-vingt-huitième année. Gotha: Justus Perthes, 1891.

al-Amili, Muhammad b. al-Hasan al-Hurr. *Amal al-Amil*. Edited by Ahmad al-Husayni. 2 vols. Baghdad: al-Andalus, 1385AH.

al-Amili, Shaykh Hasan b. Zayn al-Din. *Ma'alim al-Din wa Maladh al-Mujtahidin*. Qom: al-Islamiya, 1417AH.

Ansari, Mirza Rafi'a. "Dastur al-Moluk." In *Daftar-e Tarikh*, vol. 1, edited by Iraj Afshar, 479–621. Tehran: Bonyad-e Mowqufat-e Mahmud Afshar, 1380Kh.

[Ansari, Mirza Sami'a]. *Tazkerat al-Moluk*. Edited by Sayyed Mohammad Dabir-e Siyaqi. Tehran: Amir-e Kabir, 1368Kh.

'Aqili, 'Abd-allah, ed. *Tarikh-e Astane-e Rey*. Qom: Dar al-Hadis, 1380Kh.

Astarabadi, Sayyed Hasan Hoseyni. *Az Sheykh Safi ta Shah Safi az Tarikh-e Soltani*. Edited by Ehsan Eshraqi. Tehran: 'Elmi, 1364Kh.

'Azod al-Dowle, Soltan Ahmad Mirza. *Tarikh-e 'Azodi*. Edited by 'Abd al-Hoseyn Nava'i. Tehran: Babak, 2535Sh.

Bafqi, Mohammad Mofid Mostowfi. *Mokhtasar-e Mofid*. Edited by Iraj Afshar. Tehran: Mowqufat-e Doktor Afshar, 1390Kh.

Bayani, Bahman, ed. "Taqsim-name-e Ma-tarak-e Mirza Mahmud Khan Kalantar." *Payam-e Baharestan*, no. 10 (1389Kh): 963–991.

———, ed. *Ketabche-e Jam' va Kharj-e Koll-e hazih al-Sanat-e It-'il-e Mamlekat-e Mahruse motabeq-e Sanne-e 1304 Hejri*. Tehran: Ketabkhane, Muze va Markaz-e Asnad-e Majles-e Showra-ye Eslami, 1391Kh.

——— and Mansure Ettehadiye, eds. *Ketabche-e Qabalejat-e Khazane-e Mobarake, Amlak-e Haji Mirza Aqasi, Khalasejat va Mowqufat-e Divan-e A'la*. Tehran: Nashr-e Tarikh-e Iran, 1387Kh.

Binning, Robert B. M. *A Journal of Two Years' Travel in Persia, Ceylon etc*. 2 vols. London: W.H. Allen and Co., 1857.

Brugsch, Heinrich. *Reise der K. Preussischen Gesandtschaft nach Persien 1860 und 1861*. 2 vols. Leizpig: J.C. Hinrichs'sche Buchhandlung, 1862–1863.

Conte di Monteforte. *Ketabche-e Avval-e Qanun*. Tehran, 1296AH. Reprint, in Mortaza Seyfi Fami Tafreshi, *Nazm va Nazmiye dar Dowre-e Qajariye*, 294–319. Tehran: Yasavoli, 1362Kh.

Curzon, George N. *Persia and the Persian Question*. 2 vols. 1892. Reprint, London: Frank Cass, 1966.

Dabir-e Siyaqi, Sayyed Mohammad, ed. "Vaqf-name-e Do Qanat-e Sadr-abad va Kazem-abad va Dokkanha-ye Piramun-e Bagh-e Nezamiye-e Tehran." *Vaqf, Miras-e Javidan*, no. 28 (1378Kh): 29–36.

Della Valle, Pietro. *I Viaggi di Pietro Della Valle: lettere dalla Persia*. Edited by F. Gaeta and L. Lockhart. Roma: Instituto Pligrafico Dello Stato, 1972.

Divan-begi, Mirza Hoseyn Khan. *Khaterat-e Divan-begi*. Edited by Iraj Afshar and Mohammad Rasul Daryagasht. Tehran: Asatir, 1383Kh.

Donboli, ‘Abd al-Razzaq. *Ma’aser-e Soltaniye: az ru-ye Noskhe-e Muze-e Boretaniya*. Edited by Firuz Mansuri. Tehran: Keyhan, 1383Kh.

———. *Ma’aser-e Soltaniye*. Edited by Gholam Hoseyn Zargarinezhad. Tehran: Ruzname-e Iran, 1383Kh.

Dupré, A. *Voyage en Perse fait dans les annes 1807, 1808, et 1809*. 2 vols. Paris: J.G. Dentu, 1819.

Eastwick, Edward B. “Persia: Report by Mr. Eastwick, Her Majesty’s Secretary of Legation, Camp near Tehran, July 5, 1861.” *British Parliamentary Papers, Accounts and Papers* 58 (1862): 68–75.

———. *Journal of a Diplomat’s Three Years’ Residence in Persia*. 2 vols. London: Smith, Elder and Co., 1864.

Esfahani, Mohammad b. Sabz ‘Ali. *Vajizat al-Tahrir: dar Chegunegi-e Tanzim-e Asnad Shar‘i, Melli va Hoquqi dar Dowre-’e Safavi va Qajar*. Edited by Rasul Ja‘fariyan. Qom: Mo’arrekh, 1393Kh.

E‘temad al-Saltane, Mohammad Hasan Khan. *Ruzname-e Khaterat*. Tehran: Amir-e Kabir, 2536Sh.

———. *al-Ma’aser va al-Asar*. Edited by Iraj Afshar. Tehran: Asatir, 1363Kh.

———. *Tarikh-e Montazam-e Naseri*. Edited by Mohammad Esma‘il Rezvani. Tehran: Donya-ye Ketab, 1363–1367Kh.

———. *Mer’at al-Boldan*. Edited by ‘Abd al-Hoseyn Nava’i and Mir Hashem Mohaddes. Tehran: Daneshgah-e Tehran, 1367Kh.

E‘tezad al-Saltane, ‘Ali Qoli Mirza. *Eksir al-Tavarikh*. Edited by Jamshid Kiyanfar. Tehran: Visman, 1370Kh.

Ettehadiye, Mansure and Sa‘id Ruhi, eds. *Dar Mahzar-e Sheykh Fazl-allah Nuri: Asnad-e Hoquqi-e ‘Ahd-e Naseri*. Tehran: Nashr-e Tarikh-e Iran, 1385Kh.

Farhad Mirza Mo‘tamad al-Dowle. *Zanbil*. Tehran: Padide, 1367Kh.

Farhani, ‘Ali. “Barrasi va Bazkhani-e Vaqf-name-e Sara-ye Hajji Molla ‘Ali dar Bazar-e Tehran.” *Pazhuhesh-name* 4 (1381Kh): 130–140.

Fasa’i, Haj Mirza Hasan Hoseyni. *Farsname-e Naseri*. Edited by Mansur Rastegar Fasa’i. Tehran: Amir-e Kabir, 1367Kh.

Forugh, Mirza Mohammad Monshi Na’ini. *Safinat al-Faramin: Safinat al-Ensha’*. Edited by Mohammad Golbon. Khorram-abad: Peygham, 1377Kh.

Ghaffari Kashani, Abu al-Hasan. *Golshan-e Morad*. Edited by Gholam Hoseyn Tabatabayi Majd. Tehran: Zarrin, 1369Kh.

Haji ‘Abbasi, Sa‘id and Omid Reza’i, eds. *Asnad-e Mowqufat-e Boluk-e Ghar va Fashapuye*. Tehran: Osve, 1387Kh.

Hakim, Mohammad Taqi. *Ganj-e Danesh: Joghrafiya-ye Tarikhi-e Shahrha-ye Iran*. Edited by Mohammad ‘Ali Suti and Jamshid Kiyanfar. Tehran: Zarrin, 1366Kh.

Hamadani, Haji Mirza Esma‘il Khan Mostowfi. *Asar al-Razaviye men Motabakhat al-Sadiqiye*. Tehran: Sheykh Mohammad Tehrani, 1317AH.

Harz al-Din, Muhammad Husayn. *Ma‘arif al-Rijal fi Tarajum al-‘Ulama’ wa al-’Udaba’*. 2 vols. Qom: Mar‘ashi, 1405AH.

Hedayat, Reza Qoli Khan. *Malhaqat-e Rowzat al-Safa-ye Naseri*. vols. 8–10. Tehran: Khayyam, 1339Kh.

Hedayati, Mohammad ‘Ali. *Astane-e Rey: Majmu‘e-e Asnad va Faramin*. Tehran, 1344Kh.

Herbert, Thomas. *Travels in Persia, 1627–1629*. Edited by William Foster. London: Routledge, 1928.

al-Hilli, al-Muhaqqiq. *Shara'i' al-Islam fi masa'il al-Halal wa al-Haram*. Edited by 'Abd al-Husayn Muhammad 'Ali Baqqal. Qom: Dar al-Tafsir, 1377Kh.

———. *Tarjome-e Farsi-e Sharaye' al-Eslam*. Translated by Abu al-Qasem b. Ahmad Yazdi. Edited by Mohammad Taqi Daneshpazhuh. 4 vols. Tehran: Entesharat-e Daneshgah-e Tehran, 1373Kh.

Hoseyni, Majd al-Din Mohammad. *Zinat al-Majales*. Edited by Ahmad Ahmadi. Tehran: Sana'i, 1362Kh.

Karimiyan, 'Ali. "Vaqf-name-e Qanat-e Naseriye-e Dowlatkhane (Bagh-e Shah)." *Ganjine-e Asnad*, no. 45/46 (1381Kh): 95–104.

Kazeruni, 'Emad al-Din, ed. "Vaqf-name-e Masjed-Madrase-e Sepahsalar-e Qadim (Tehran)." *Vaqf, Miras-e Javidan*, no. 33/34 (1380Kh): 121–132.

Khavari, Mirza Fazl-allah Shirazi. *Tarikh-e Zu al-Qarneyn*. Edited by Naser Afshar far. Tehran: Vezarat-e Farhang va Ershad-e Eslami, 1380Kh.

Khormuji, Mohammad Ja'far. *Haqayeq al-Akhbar-e Naseri*. Edited by Hoseyn Khadivjam. Tehran: Ney, 1363Kh.

Kojuri, Mohammad Baqer Va'ez. *Ruh va Reyhan ya Jannat al-Na'im va al-'Eysh al-Salim*. Edited by Sayyed Sadeq Hoseyni Eshkevari. 4 vols. Qom: Dar al-Hadis, 1382Kh.

Krziz, A. *Naqshe-e Dar al-Khelafe-e Tehran*. 1275AH. Reprint, Tehran: Sazman-e Joghrafiya'i-e Niruha-ye Mosallah, 1370Kh.

Mahdavi, Asghar and Iraj Afshar, eds. *Asnad-e Tejarat-e Iran dar Sal-e 1287 Qamari*. Tehran: 'Elmi va Farhangi, 1380Kh.

Mahmud Mirza Qajar. *Tarikh-e Sahebqerani*. Edited by Nadere Jalali. Tehran: Ketabkhane, Muze va Markaz-e Asnad Majles-e Showra-ye Eslami, 1389Kh.

Malcolm, John. *The History of Persia from the Most Early Period to the Present Time*. New edition. 2 vols. London: John Murray, 1829.

Manzur al-Ajdad, Sayyed Mohammad Hoseyn, ed. "Do Sanad az Monsuban-e Amir-e Kabir." *Ganjine-e Asnad*, no. 10/11 (1372Kh): 107–111.

Mir Mohammad Sadeq, Sayyed Sa'id, ed. "Vaqf-name-e Haj Mohammad Ebrahim Tajer Esfahani (Masjed-e Jazayeri)." *Vaqf, Miras-e Javidan*, no. 28 (1378Kh): 103–114.

Monajjem, Molla Jalal al-Din. *Tarikh-e 'Abbasi ya Ruzname-e Molla Jalal*. Edited by Seyf-allah Vahid-niya. Tehran: Vahid, 1366Kh.

Mortazavi, Marziye, ed. "Vaqf-name'i az Aqa Mohammad Mahdi Malek al-Tojjar." *Vaqf, Miras-e Javidan*, no. 79/80 (1391Kh): 207–216.

———, ed. "Vaqf-name'i marbut be Mahalle-e Sangelaj-e Tehran." *Vaqf, Miras-e Javidan*, no. 82 (1392Kh): 149–160.

———, ed. "Vaqf-name-e Qanat-e Hoseyniye-e Tehran." *Vaqf, Miras-e Javidan*, no. 84 (1392Kh): 127–136.

Mostowfi, 'Abd-allah. *Sharh-e Zendegani-e Man ya Tarikh-e Ejtema'i va Edari-e Qajar*. 3 vols. Tehran: Zavvar, 1365Kh.

Mostowfi Qazvini, Hamd-allah. *Nozhat al-Qolub: al-Maqalat al-Salesat*. Edited by G. Le Strange. 1915. Reprint, Tehran: Donya-ye Ketab, 1362Kh.

Najm al-Dowle, Mirza 'Abd al-Ghaffar. "Tashkhis-e Nofus-e Dar al-Khelafe." Edited by Naser Pakdaman. *Farhang-i Iran-zamin* 20 (1353Kh): 348–385.

Name-e Daneshvaran-e Naseri: dar Sharh-e Hal-e Sheshsad Tan az Daneshmandan-e Nami. 9 vols. Qom: Dar al-Fekr and Dar al-'Elm, 1338Kh.

Naser al-Din Shah Qajar. *Yaddashtha-ye Ruzane-e Naser al-Din Shah: 1300–1303AH*. Edited by Parviz Badi'i. Tehran: Sazman-e Asnad-e Melli-e Iran, 1378Kh.

Nasiri, Mohammad Ebrahim. *Dastur-e Shahriyaran*. Edited by Mohammad Nader Nasiri Moqaddam. Tehran: Bonyad-e Mowqufat-e Iraj Afshar, 1373Kh.

Nasr-abadi, Mohammad Taher. *Tazkere-e Nasr-abadi*. Edited by Mohsen Naji Nasr-abadi. 2 vols. Tehran: Asatir, 1378Kh.

Nava'i, 'Abd al-Hoseyn, ed. *Mahd-e 'Olya be-Revayat-e Asnad*. Tehran: Asatir, 1383Kh.

Olivier, G. A. *Voyage dans l'Empire ottoman, l'Égypte et la Perse*. 6 vols. Paris: Chez H. Agasse, 1801–1807.

Orsolle, E. *Le Caucase et la Perse*. Paris: Libraire Plon, 1885.

Ostadi, Reza, ed. "Vaqf-name-e Madrase-e Marvi." *Vaqf, Miras-e Javidan*, no. 13 (1375Kh): 56–71.

Qa'em-maqami, Jahangir, ed. "Asnad-e Khanedan-e Amir Divan-e Nuri." *Barrasiha-ye Tarikhi* 8, no. 1 (1352Kh): 279–354.

Qommi, Mirza Abu al-Qasem. *Jame' al-Shatat*. Edited by Mortaza Razavi. 4 vols. Tehran: Keyhan, 1371–1375Kh.

Qommi, Qazi Ahmad. *Kholasat al-Tavarikh*. Edited by Ehsan Eshraqi. 2 vols. Tehran: Daneshgah-e Tehran, 1363Kh.

Rahimlu, Yusof, ed. *Alqab va Mavajeb-e Dowre-e Salatin-e Safaviye*. Mashhad: Daneshgah-e Ferdowsi, 1371Kh.

Razi, Amin Ahmad. *Haft Eqlim*. Edited by Javad Fazeli. 3 vols. Tehran: Elmi, n.d.

Reza'i, Omid, ed. *Panjah va Yek 'Arize va Hokm-e Shar'i az 'Olama-ye Dowre-e Qajar dar bare-e Omur-e Jari-e Mowqufat*. Tehran: Mo'avenat-e Farhangi-e Sazman-e Owqaf va Omur-e Kheyriye, 1383Kh.

———, ed. *Asnad-e Mahkame-e Sayyed Sadeq Tabataba'i (Sangelaji) Mojtahed-e 'Asr-e Naseri*. Tehran: Nashr-e Abi, 1387Kh.

Ruzname-e Dowlat-e 'Aliye-e Iran. no. 472–650. Tehran. 1277–1287AH. Reprint, Tehran: Ketabkhane-e Melli-e Jomhuri-e Eslami-e Iran, 1370–1372Kh.

Ruzname-e Iran. no. 1–1032. Tehran. 1288–1320AH. Reprint, Tehran: Ketabkhane-e Melli-e Jomhuri-e Eslami-e Iran, 1374–1378Kh.

Ruzname-e Vaqaye' al-Ettefaqiye. no. 1–471. Tehran. 1267–1277AH. Reprint, Tehran: Ketabkhane-e Melli-e Jomhuri-e Eslami-e Iran, 1373–1374Kh.

Sa'dvandiyan, Sirus and Mansure Ettehadiye, eds. *Amar-e Dar al-Khelafe-e Tehran: Asnadi az Tarikh-e Ejtema'i-e Tehran dar 'Asr-e Qajar*. Tehran: Nashr-e Tarikh-e Iran, 1368Kh.

Sahab, Abu al-Qasem. *Tarikh-e Madrase-e 'Ali-e Sepahsalar*. Tehran, 1329Kh.

Salname-e Iran. Tehran, 1290–1312AH.

Saravi, Mohammad Fath-allah b. Mohammad Taqi. *Tarikh-e Mohammadi: Ahsan al-Tavarikh*. Edited by Gholam Hoseyn Tabatabayi Majd. Tehran: Amir-e Kabir, 1371Kh.

Savad-e Taqsim-name va Taqsim-name-e Ab-e Shah. Tehran, 1306Kh. Reprint, in *Farhang-e Iranzamin* 24 (1358Kh).

Shamlu, Vali Qoli. *Qesas al-Khaqani*. Edited by Hasan Sadat-e Naseri. Tehran: Vezarat-e Farhang va Ershad-e Eslami, 1371–1374 Kh.

Sheil, Marry. *Glimpses of Life and Manners in Persia*. London: John Murray, 1856.

Sheykh al-Hokama'i, 'Emad al-Din, ed. "Masjed-Madrase-e Me'mar-bashi-e Tehran." *Vaqf, Miras-e Javidan*, no. 37 (1381Kh): 25–32.

———, ed. *Asnad-e Me'mari-e Iran*. vol. 1. Tehran: Matn, 1388Kh.

Sheykh Reza'i, Anise and Shahla Azari, eds. *Gozareshha-ye Nazmiye az Mahallat-e Tehran*. Tehran: Sazman-e Asnad-e Melli, 1377Kh.

Sotude, Manuchehr, ed. "Vaqf-name-e Mirza Mohammad Yusof Ashrafi." *Vaqf, Miras-e Javidan*, no. 18 (1376Kh): 38–45.

———, ed. "Vaqf-name-e Shah 'Abbas.'" *Vaqf, Miras-e Javidan*, no. 47/48 (1383Kh): 10–14.

Stahl, A. F. "Teheran und Umgegend." *Dr. A. Petermanns Mitteilungen aus Justus Perthes' geographischer Anstalt* 46 (1900): 49–54.

Tarab, Mohammad Ja'far Na'ini. *Jame'-e Ja'fari*. Edited by Iraj Afshar. Tehran: Anjoman-e Asar-e Melli, 1353Kh.

Taraz, 'Abd al-Vahhab. "Ketabche-e Mowqufat-e Yazd." Edited by Iraj Afshar. *Farhang-e Iranzamin* 10 (1341Kh): 5–123.

Tasdiqi, Mohammad Reza, ed. *Yadgar-e Mandegar: Majmu'e-e Mowqufat-e Yazd*. vol. 1. Tehran: Setayesh, 1380Kh.

Tehrani, Mirza Mahdi Navvab. *Dastur al-A'qab*. Edited by Sayyed 'Ali Al-e Da'ud. Tehran: Nashr-e Tarikh-e Iran, 1376Kh.

Tonekaboni, Mohammad b. Soleyman. *Qesas al-'Olama*. Edited by Mohammad Reza Barzgar Khaleqi and 'Effat Karbasi. Tehran: Ney, 1383Kh.

Vahid Qazvini, Mirza Mohammad Taher. *Tarikh-e Jahan-ara-ye 'Abbasi*. Edited by Sayyed Sa'id Mir Mohammad Sadeq. Tehran: Pazhuheshgah-e 'Olum-e Ensani va Motale'at-e Farhangi, 1383Kh.

Vaqaye'-e 'Adliye. no. 1–3. Tehran. 1287–1288AH.

Wills, C. J. *Perisa as It Is: Being Sketches of Modern Persian Life and Character*. London: Sampson Low, Marston, Searle & Bivingston, 1886.

Zabihi, Masih and Manuchehr Sotude, eds. *As Astara ta Estarbad*. 10 vols. Tehran: Anjoman-e Asar-e Melli and Anjoman-e Asar va Mafakher-e Farhangi, 1349–1380Kh.

Zare'i Mehrvarz, 'Abbas. "Asnad-e Divan-e 'Adalat-e 'Ozma." In *Khaterat va Asnad-e Mohammad 'Ali Ghaffari*, edited by 'Abbas Zare'i Mehrvarz, 271–319. Tehran: Nashr-e Tarikh-e Iran, 1380Kh.

Secondary sources

Abe, Naofumi. "Preserving a Qajar Estate: Analysis of Fath-'Ali Khan Donboli's 'Property Retention Tactics.'" *Studia Iranica* 43 (2014): 129–150.

———. "The Ambivalent Position of the Landlord: A Dispute over Ownership of an Iranian Village in the 19th Century." *Islamic Law and Society* 23 (2016): 52–88.

Adamiyat, Faridun. *Amir-e Kabir va Iran*. Tehran: Kharezmi, 1354Kh.

Adle, Chahryar. "Le jardin habité, ou Téhéran de jadis des orignes aux Safavides." In *Téhéran: capitale bicentenaire*, edited by C. Adle and B. Hourcade, 15–37. Paris and Tehran: Institute Français de Recherche en Iran, 1992.

Adle, Chahryar and Bernard Hourcade, eds. *Téhéran: Capitale bincentenaire*. Paris and Tehran: Institute Français de Recherche en Iran, 1992.

Afshar, Iraj, ed. *Khaterat va Asnad-e Zahir al-Dowle*. Tehran: Zarrin, 1367Kh.

Ahmadi, Nozhat. *Dar bab-e Owqaf-e Safavi*. Tehran: Ketabkhane, Muze va Markaz-e Asnad-e Majles-e Showra-ye Eslami, 1390Kh.

Algar, Hamid. *Religion and State in Iran 1785–1906: Role of the Ulama in Qajar Period*. Berkley and Los Angeles: University of California Press, 1969.

———. *Mirza Malkum Khan: A Biographical Study in Iranian Modernism*. Berkley and Los Angeles: University of California Press, 1973.

Amanat, Abbas. *Pivot of the Universe: Nasir al-Din Shah Qajar and the Iranian Monarchy 1851–1896*. London: I.B. Tauris, 1997.

———. s.v. "E'tezad-al-Saltana, 'Aliqoli Mirza." *Encyclopaedia Iranica*. Vol. 8. 669–672. 1998.

al-Amin, Sayyid Muhsin. *A'yan al-Shi'a*. Edited by Sayyid Hasan al-Amin. Beirut: al-Ta'aruf, 1998.

Arjomand, Sayyed Amir. *The Shadow of God and the Hidden Imam: Religion, Political Order, and Societal Change in Shi'ite Iran from the Begininng to 1890*. Chicago: The University of Chicago Press, 1984.

Bakhash, Shaul. *Iran: Monarchy, Beureacracy and Reform under the Qajars: 1858–1896*. London: Ithaca Press, 1978.

Baladiye-e Tehran, *Sarshomari-e Nofus-e Shahr-e Tehran*. 1312Kh. Reprint, in Ja'far Shahri, *Tarikh-e Tehran dar Qarn-e Sizdahom*, vol. 1, 7–40. Tehran: Mo'assese-e Khadamat-e Farhang-e Rasa, 1367Kh.

Bamdad, Mahdi. *Sharh-e Hal-e Rejal-e Iran dar Qarn-e 12 va 13 va 14 Hejri*. 3rd edition. 6 vols. Tehran: Zavvar, 1363Kh.

Bayındır, Abdülaziz. s.v. "Bey' bi'l-Vefâ." *Türkiye Diyanet Vakfı İslâm Ansiklopedisi*. Vol. 6. 20–22. 1992.

Bémont, Frédy. *Les Villes de l'Iran: des cités d'autrefois à l'urbanisme contemporain*. 2 vols. Paris, 1969–1973.

Bhalloo, Zahir. "Judging the Judge: Judicial Competence in 19th Century Iran." *Bulletin D'études Orientales* 63 (2014): 276–293.

Bonine, Michael. "Islam and Commerce: Waqf and the Bazaar of Yazd, Iran." *Erdkunde* 41 (1987): 182–196.

Calder, Norman. "The Structure of Authority in Imami Shi'i Jurisprudence." Ph.D Dissertation, University of London, 1980.

Calmard, Jean. s.v. "Atabak-e A'zam, Amin al-Soltan." *Encyclopaedia Iranica*. Vol. 2. 878–890. 1987.

———. s.v. "Tihran (b) Urbanisation, Monuments Cultural and Socio-Economic Life until the Time of Pahlavis." *The Encyclopaedia of Islam*, new edition. Vol. 10. 487–493. 2000.

Dabir-e Siyaqi, Mohammad. "Ketabche-e Amlak va Khalese va Arbabi-e Iran." *Vaqf, Miras-e Javidan*, no. 56 (1385Kh): 25–32.

Damghani, Mohammad Taqi. *Avvalin Qavanin-e Iran qabl az Mashrutiyat*. Tehran: Behzad, 1357Kh.

Deguilhem, Randi. "The Waqf in the City." In *The City in the Islamic World*, vol. 2, edited by Renata Holod, Attilio Petruccioli, and Andre Raymond, 923–950. Leiden: Brill, 2008.

Enayati, Hadi. *Law, State, and Society in Modern Iran: Constitutionalism, Autocracy, and Legal Reform, 1906–1941*. New York: Palgrave Macmillan, 2013.

Ettehadieh Nezam-Mafi, Mansoureh (Ettehadiye, Mansure). "Patterns in Urban Development; the Growth of Tehran (1852–1903)." In *Qajar Iran: Political, Social and Cultural Exchange*, edited by Edmond Bosworth and Carole Hillenbrand, 199–212. Edinburgh: Edinburgh University Press, 1983.

———. "The Emergence of Tehran as the Cultural Centre of Iran." In *Téhéran: capitale bicentenaire*, edited by C. Adle and B. Hourcade, 127–139. Paris and Tehran: Institute Français de Rechershe en Iran, 1992.

———. *Inja Tehran Ast: Majmu'e-e Maqalati dar bare-e Tehran 1269–1344 H.Q.* Tehran: Nashr-e Tarikh-e Iran, 1377Kh.

———. "Mowqufat-e Tehran va Tahavvol-e Shahr, 1269–1320 H.Q." *Vaqf, Miras-e Javidan*, no. 28 (1378Kh): 7–16.

Farhang-e Jogharafiya'i-e Iran. 10 vols. Tehran: Sazman-e Joghrafiya'i-e Keshvar, 2535Sh.

Floor, Willem. "The Office of *Kalantar* in Qajar Persia." *Journal of the Economic and Social History of the Orient* 14 (1971): 253–268.

———. "The Police in Qajar Persia." *ZDMG* 123 (1973): 293–315.

———. "Bankruptcy in Qajar Iran." *ZDMG* 127 (1977): 61–76.

———. "Bankers (*Sarrafs*) in Qajar Iran." *ZDMG* 129 (1979): 263–281.

———. "Change and Development in the Judicial System of Qajar Iran (1800–1925)." In *Qajar Iran: Political, Social and Cultural Exchange*, edited by Edmond Bosworth and Carole Hillenbrand, 113–147. Edinburgh: Edinburgh University Press, 1983.

———. *A Fiscal History of Iran in the Safavid and Qajar Periods, 1500–1925*. New York: Bibliotheca Persica Press, 1998.

———. "The Sadr or Head of the Safavid Religious Administration, Judiciary and Endowments and Other Members of the Religious Institution." *ZDMG* 150 (2000): 461–500.

———. "The Secular Justice System in Safavid Persia." *Studia Iranica* 29 (2000): 9–60.

———. *Guilds, Merchants & Ulama in Nineteenth Century Iran*. Washington, DC: Mage Publisher, 2009.

———. s.v. "Judicial and Legal Systems: IV. Judicial System from the Advent of Islam through the 19th Century." *Encyclopaedia Iranica*. Vol. 15. 199–204. 2009.

Fragner, Bert. "Social and Economic Affairs." In *The Cambridge History of Iran, vol. 6: The Timirid and Safavid Period*, edited by Peter Jackson and Laurenc Lockhart. 491–567. Cambridge: Cambridge University Press, 1986.

Gilbar, Gad. G. "Demographic Developments in Late Qajar Persia, 1870–1906." *Asian and African Studies* 11 (1976): 125–156.

Gleave, Robert. *Inevitable Doubt: Two Theories of Shi'i Jurisprudence*. Leiden: Brill, 2000.

Gurney, John. "The Transformation of Tehran in the Later Nineteenth Century." In *Téhéran: capitale bicentenaire*, edited by C. Adle and B. Hourcade, 51–71. Paris and Tehran: Institute Français de Recherche en Iran, 1992.

Habibi, Hasan, ed. *Emamzadeha va Torbat-e Barkhi az Pakan va Niyakan-e Tehran, Shemiranat va Shahr-e Rey*. vol. 1. Tehran: Bonyad-e Iranshenasi, 1388Kh.

———, ed. *Masajed-e Dirinesal-e Tehran*. Tehran: Bonyad-e Iranshenasi, 1388Kh.

———, ed. *Shomari az Boq'eha, Marqadha va Mazarha-ye Ostanha-ye Tehran va Alborz*. 2 vols. Tehran: Bonyad-e Iranshenasi, 1389Kh.

Habibi Mozaheri, Mas'ud. "Bargozide-e Aznad-e Tanzimi dar Mahzar-e Sayyed Mohammad Mojtahed Tabataba'i." *Payam-e Baharestan, Vizhename-e Qanun va Hoquq*, no. 3 (1391Kh): 354–406.

———. "Gozide-e Asnad-e Tanzimi dar Mahazer-e Shar'." *Payam-e Baharestan, Vizhename-e Maliye va Eqtesad*, no. 1 (1392Kh): 381–404.

Hairi, A. s.v. "Akund Korasani: i. Life and Political Role." *Encyclopaedia Iranica*. Vol. 1. 732–734. 1984.

Haj Sayyed Javadi, Kamal and 'Abd al-Hoseyn Nava'i, eds. *Asar-e Afarinan: Zendeginame-e Nam-avaran-e Farhangi-e Irani*. 6 vols. Tehran: Ajoman-e Asar va Mafakher-e Farhangi, 1377–1380Kh.

Haji Qasemi, Kambiz, ed. *Ganj-name, Farhang-e Asar-e Me'mari-e Eslami-e Iran, vol. 3: Benaha-ye Mazhabi-e Tehran*. Tehran: Sazman-e Miras-e Farhangi-e Keshvar, 1377Kh.

———, ed. *Ganj-name, Farhang-e Asar-e Me'mari-e Eslami-e Iran, vol. 9: Benaha-ye Bazar, part 1*. Tehran: Sazman-e Miras-e Farhangi-e Keshvar, 1383Kh.

Hallaq, Wael B. *Shari'a: Theory, Practice, Transformations*. Cambridge: Cambridge University Press, 2009.

Hambly, Gavin R. G. "An Introduction to the Economic Organization of Early Qajar Iran." *Iran* 2 (1964): 69–81.

———. "Agha Muhammad Khan and the Establishment of the Qajar Dynasty." In *The Cambridge History of Iran*, vol. 7, edited by Peter Avery, Gavin Hambly, and Charles Melville, 104–143. Cambridge: Cambridge University Press, 1991.

———. "The Traditional Iranian City in the Qajar Period." In *The Cambridge History of Iran*, vol. 7, edited by Peter Avery, Gavin Hambly, and Charles Melville, 542–589. Cambridge: Cambridge University Press, 1991.

Haneda, Masashi and Miura Toru, eds. *Islamic Urban Studies: Historical Review and Perspectives*. London: Kegan Paul International, 1994.

Hayashi, Kayoko. "The Vakıf Institution in 16th-Century Istanbul: An Analysis of the Vakıf Survey Register of 1546." *The Memoires of the Research Department of the Toyo Bunko* 50 (1992): 93–113.

Heyd, Uriel. "Some Aspects of the Ottoman Fetva." *Bulletin of the School of Oriental and African Studies* 32 (1969): 35–56.

———. *Studies in Old Ottoman Criminal Law*. Edited by V. L. Ménage. Oxford: Oxford University Press, 1973.

Hoexter, Miriam. "Waqf Studies in the Twentieth Century: The State of the Art." *Journal of the Economic and Social History of the Orient* 41 (1998): 474–495.

Hoseyni Balaghi, Sayyed 'Abd al-Hojjat. *Tarikh-e Tehran*. 2 vols. Qom, 1350Kh.

Hoseyni Eshkevari, Sayyed Sadeq. *Asnad-e Shar'i dar Ketabkhane-e Mirza Mohammad Kazemeyni*. Qom: Zakha'er-e Eslami, 1387Kh.

Isogai, Ken'ichi. "Research of Formal Aspects of Central Asian Documents: Deeds of Bay'-i Ja'iz." [in Japanese]. In *Historical Research on Common Identity and Islam in Central Asia*, edited by Yashushi Shinmen, 51–66. Hachioji: Chuo University, 2002.

Iwatake, Akio. "The Continuity of Waqf in Iran: A Case of Amir Chaqmaq's Waqf in Yazd." [in Japanese]. *Isramu-Sekai* 42 (1993): 1–19.

———. "The Waqf of a Timurid Amir: The Example of Chaqmaq Shami in Yazd." In *Persian Documents: Social History of Iran and Turan in the Fifteenth-Nineteenth Centuries*, edited by Nobuaki Kondo, 87–105. London: RoutlegeCurzon, 2003.

Jennings, Ronald C. "Kadi, Court and Legal Procedure in 17th C. Ottoman Kayseri." *Studia Islamica* 48 (1978): 133–172.

Kazemi Musavi, Ahmad. *Religious Authority in Shi'ite Islam: From the Office of Muft to the Insititution of Marja'*. Kuala Lumpur: ISTAC, 1996.

Kiani, Mohammad-Yusuf and Wolfram Kleiss. s.v. "Caravansaray." *Encyclopaedia Iranica*. Vol. 4. 798–802. 1990.

Kondo, Nobuaki. "Private Property and *Vaqf* of Manuchehr Khan Mo'tamad al-Dowle." [in Japanese]. *Toyoshi-kenkyu* 60/61 (2001): 5–7.

———. "The Waqf of Ustad 'Abbas: Rewrites of Deeds in Qajar Tehran." In *Persian Documents: Social History of Iran and Turan in the Fifteenth-Nineteenth Centuries*, edited by Nobuaki Kondo, 106–128. London: RoutlegeCurzon, 2003.

———. "The *Vaqf* and Religious Patronage of Manuchihr Khan Mu'tamad al-Dawlah." In *Religion and Society in Qajar Iran*, edited by Robert Gleave, 227–244. London: RoutlegeCurzon, 2005.

———. "Shi'i 'Ulama and *Ijaza* during the Nineteenth Century." *Orient* 44 (2009): 55–76.

———."Between Tehran and Sultaniyya: Early Qajar Rulers and Their Itineraries." In *Turko-Mongol Rulers, Cities and City Life*, edited by David Durand-Guédy, 385–416. Leiden: Brill, 2013.

———."The Lives of *Qabalah*s: Annotation, Transcription and Registration of Documents in Early Modern Iran." In *Lecteurs et copistes dans les traditions manuscrites iraniennes, indiennes et centrasiatiques*, edited by Nalini Balbir and Maria Szuppe, *Eurasian Studies* 12 (2014): 561–575.

———. "Migration and Multi-Ethnic Coexixtance in Qajar Tehran." In *Human Mobility and Mutliethinic Coexistence in Middle Eastern Urban Societies 1: Tehran, Allepo,*

Istanbul, and Beirut, edited by Hidemitsu Kuroki, 5–25. Fuchu, Tokyo: Research Institute for Languages and Cultures of Asia and Africa, 2015.

Lambton, Ann K. S. "The Case of Hajji Nur Al-Din, 1823–47: A Study in Land Tenure." *Bulletin of the School of Oriental and African Studies* 30 (1967): 54–72.

———. s.v. "Kadjar." *The Encyclopaedia of Islam*, new edition. Vol. 4. 387–399. 1978.

———. *Qajar Persia: Eleven Studies*. Austin: University of Texas Press, 1987.

———. s.v. "Mahkama 3. Iran." *The Encyclopaedia of Islam*, new edition. Vol. 6. 11–22. 1991.

———. s.v. "Wakf III in Persia." *The Encyclopaedia of Islam*, new edition. Vol. 11. 81–87. 2002.

Libson, G. and F. H. Stewart. s.v. " 'Urf." *The Encyclopaedia of Islam*, new edition. Vol. 10. 887–892. 2000.

Litvak, Meir. *Shi'i Scholars of Nineteenth-Century Iraq: The 'Ulama' of Najaf and Karbala'*. Cambridge: Cambridge University Press, 1998.

Mahdavi, Asghar. "The Significance of Private Archives for the Study of the Economic and Social History of Iran in the Late Qajar Period." *Iranian Studies* 16 (1983): 243–278.

Mahdavi, Shireen. *For God, Mammon and Country: A Nineteenth-Century Persian Merchant*. Boulder: Westview Press, 1999.

Mahdawi Damgani, Ahmad. s.v. "Daftar-e Asnad-e Rasmi." *Encyclopaedia Iranica*. Vol. 6. 564–565. 1993.

——— (Mahdavi Damghani, Ahmad). "Mahakem-e Qaza'i dar Zaman-e Qajariye." *Hafez*, no. 3 (1383Kh): 30–35.

———. "Tarikhche-e Mahzar va Daftar-e Asnad-e Rasmi." *Hafez*, no. 7 (1383Kh): 7–18.

Marcinkowski, Muhammad Ismail. *Mirza Rafi'a's Dastur al-Muluk: A Manual of Later Safavid Administration*. Kuala Lumpur: International Institute of Islamic Thought and Civilization, 2002.

Martin, Vannesa. *Islam and Modernism: The Iranian Revolution of 1906*. New York: Syracuse University Press, 1989.

———. *The Qajar Pact: Bargaining, Protest and the State in Nineteenth-Century Persia*. London: I.B. Tauris, 2005.

———. "Murder in Bushehr in 1844: The Case of Bibi Asilu." *Iran*, no. 46 (2008): 285–292.

McChesney, Robert D. "Waqf and Public Policy: The Waqfs of Shah 'Abbas, 1011–1023/1602–1614." *Asian and African Studies* 15 (1981): 165–190.

Minorsky, Vladimir. s.v. "Teheran." *The Encyclopaedia of Islam*, 1st edition. Vol. 4. 713–720. 1927.

———. *Tadhkirat al-Muluk: A Manual of Safavid Administration*. 1943. Reprint, London: Luzac, 1980.

Mir Mohammad Sadeq, Sayyed Sa'id. "Masjed va Madrase-e Marvi." *Masjed* 29 (1375Kh): 70–83, 122.

Mo'allem Habib-abadi, Mirza Mohammad 'Ali. *Makarem al-Asar dar Akhval-e Do Qarn-e 13 va 14 Hejri*. 8 vols. Isfahan: Nashr-e Nafa'es-e Makhtutat-e Esfahan and Anjoman-e Ketabkhaneha-ye 'Omumi-e Esfahan, 1337–1381Kh.

Modarresi Tabataba'i, Hoseyn. "Ketabche-e Sabt-e Mowqufat va Khalesejat-e Keshvar dar Dowre-e Naseri." *Rahnama-ye Ketab* 18/4–6 (1354Kh): 435–442.

——— (Modarressi Tabataba'i, Hossein). *Introduction to Shi'i Law: A Bibliographical Survey*. London: Ithaca Press, 1984.

Mohammadi, Majid. *Judicial Reform and Reorganization in 20th Century Iran: State-Building, Modernization and Islamization*. New York: Routledge, 2008.

Mohit-e Tabatabayi, Mohammad. "Dadgostari dar Iran az Sadr-e Eslam ta Aghaz-e Mashrutiyat." *Kanun-e Vokala'* 119 (1351Kh): 75–115.

Mo'tamadi, Mohsen. *Joghrafiya-ye Tarikhi-e Tehran*. Tehran: Markaz-e Nashr-e Daneshgahi, 1381Kh.

Nashat, Guity. *The Origins of Modern Reform in Iran, 1870–1880*. Urbana: University of Illinois Press, 1982.

———. s.v. "Dabir al-Molk Farahani." *Encyclopaedia Iranica*. Vol. 6. 539–540. 1993.

Nasr, Seyyed Hossein. *Islamic Philosophy from Its Origin to the Present: Philosophy in the Land of Prophecy*. Albany: State University of New York Press, 2006.

Nurbakhsh, Mas'ud. *Tehran be-Revayat-e Tarikh*. 4 vols. Tehran: 'Elm, 1381Kh.

Perry, John R. *Karim Khan Zand: A History of Iran, 1747–1779*. Chicago: The University of Chicago Press, 1979.

———. s.v. "Aga Mohammad Khan Qajar." *Encyclopaedia Iranica*. Vol. 1. 602–605. 1984.

Rajabi, Mahdi and Sayyed Sa'id Mir Mohammad Sadeq. "Masjed-e Jame'-e Tehran ya Jame'-e 'Atiq." *Masjed* 24 (1374Kh): 70–79.

Ravandi, Mortaza. *Tarikh-e Ejtema'i-e Iran*. vol. 4. Tehran: Amir-e Kabir, 1341Kh.

———. *Seyr-e Qanun va Dadgostari dar Iran*. Tehran and Babol: Nashr-e Chashme and Ketabsara-ye Babol, 1368kh.

Reza'i, Omid. "Ravande Shekrgiri-e Edare-e Ma'aref va Owqaf-e Kerman va Qom." *Vaqf, Miras-e Javidan*, no. 31/32 (1379Kh): 47–57.

———. "Barrasi-e Runeveshtha-ye Vezarat-e Ma'aref va Owqaf as Asl-e Vaqf-nameha." *Vaqf, Miras-e Javidan*, no. 38 (1381Kh): 87–94.

———. "Dastur al-'Amalha-ye Edari-e Owqaf be Edarat-e Nowbonyad dar khosus-e 'Estensakh-e Vaqf-name' va 'Estekhlas-e Mowqufe'." *Vaqf, Miras-e Javidan*, no. 39/40 (1381Kh): 36–41.

———. "Khatt va Mohr-e Omana-ye Shar'-e Tehran dar Dowre-e Qajar." *Vaqf, Miras-e Javidan*, no. 43/44 (1382Kh): 60–91.

———. "Ashnayi ba Daftar-e Asnad va Shenasayi Mowqufat-e Sazman-e Owqaf." *Ganjine-e Asnad*, no. 51/52 (1382Kh): 10–13.

———. "Selsele-e Sheykh al-Eslamiye-e Tamami-e Shiraz Pishgam-e dar Sabt-e Neveshtejat-e Shar'iye-e Dowre-e Qajar." *Vaqf, Miras-e Javidan*, no. 54 (1385Kh): 77–94.

———. "Aqa Sayyed Sadeq Mojtahed Sangelaji va Neveshtejat-e Shar'iye." *Vaqf, Miras-e Javidan*, no. 56 (1385Kh): 57–68.

———. *Jostarhayi dar Sanad-shenasi-e Farsi*. Tehran: Bonyad-e Pazhuhesh va Towse'-e Farhang-e *Vaqf*, 1385Kh.

———. *Fehrest-e Asnad-e Mowqufat-e Iran, vol. 4: Ostan-e Tehran va Tababe'*. 2 vols. Tehran: Bonyad-e Pazhuhesh va Towse'e-e Farhang-e *Vaqf*, 1386Kh.

———. "Jaygah-e Khanedan-e Behbahani dar Towlid va Sabt-e Neveshtejat-e Dowre-e Qajariye." *Vaqf, Miras-e Javidan*, no. 57 (1386Kh): 44–55.

———. "Barrasi va Tahlil-e Mohrha-ye bi-Yaddasht dar Qabaleha-ye Dar al-'Elm-e Shiraz." *Vaqf, Miras-e Javidan*, no. 60 (1386Kh): 26–38.

———. *Dar-amadi bar Asnad-e Shar'i-e Dowre-e Qajar*. Tokyo: Research Institute for Languages and Cultures of Asia and Africa, 2008.

———. "Mowqufe-e Mosha' va Taqsimha-ye Bi-saranjam-e An dar Bazar-e Tehran-e Dowre-e Qajar." *Name-e Anjoman*, no. 35/36 (1388Kh): 153–170.

———. *Qabaleha-ye Farsi: Pardazesh-e Suri va Mohtavayi*. Tehran: Osve, 1388Kh.

———. "Tabibi Mosannef ba Masjed, Madrase va Ketabkhane-e *Vaqfi*-ash dar Tehran-e Dowre-e Shah Soleyman Safavi." *Owraq-e 'Atiq* 2 (1389Kh): 267–305.

———. "Pishine va Nahve-e Sabt-e Asnad-e Shar'i dar Bandar-e Bushehr (1308HQ–1350HQ)." *Asnad-e Baharestan*, no. 1 (1390Kh): 79–94.

Ritter, Markus. *Moscheen und Madrasabauten in Iran 1785–1848: Architectur zwichen Rückgriff und Neuerung*. Leiden: Brill, 2006.

Rodinson, Maxime. *Islam and Capitalism*. Translated by Brian Pearce. London: Allen Lane, 1974.

Sa'dvandiyan, Sirus. *Dar-amadi bar Jam'iyat-shenasi-e Tarikhi-e Iran dar 'Asr-e Qajar*. Tehran: Vezarat-e Farhang va Ershad-e Eslami, 1379Kh.

———. *'Adad-e Abniye, Shomar-e Nofus az Dar al-Khelafe ta Tehran 1231–1311 Khorshīdī*. Tehran: Vezarat-e Farhang va Ershad-e Eslami, 1380Kh.

Sa'edlu, Hushang. "Ketabche-e Raqabat-e Mohammad Shahi va Naser al-Din Shahi." In *Haftad Maqale*, edited by Yahya Mahdavi and Iraj Afshar, vol. 1, 189–197. Tehran: Asatir, 1369Kh.

Sakamoto, Tsutomu, "The Demoghraphic Census of Teheran in 1868." [in Japanese]. *Oriento* 27 (1984): 92–108.

Sarvqadi, Mohammad Ja'far. *Beqa'-e Motabarrake-e Ostan-e Tehran*. Tehran: Edare-e Koll-e Owqaf va Omur-e Kheyriye-e Ostan-e Tehran, 1383Kh.

Schacht, Joseph. *An Introduction to Islamic Law*. Oxford: Clarendon Press, 1982.

Schneider, Irene. "Muhammad Baqir Šafti (1180–1260/1766–1844) und Die Isfahaner Gerichtsbarkeit." *Der Islam* 79 (2002): 240–273.

———. "Religious and State Jurisdiction during Naser al-Din Shah's Reign." In *Religion and Society in Qajar Iran*, edited by Robert Gleave, 84–110. London: RoutlegeCurzon, 2005.

———. *The Petition System in Iran: State, Society and Power Relations in the Late 19th Century*. Wiesbaden: Harrassowitz, 2006.

Sefatgol, Mansur. *Sakhtar-e Nehad va Andishe-e Dini dar Iran-e 'Asr-e Safavi*. Tehran: Rasa, 1381Kh.

Sepanta, 'Abd al-Hoseyn. *Tarikhche-e Owqaf-e Esfahan*. Esfahan: Edare-e Koll-e Owqaf, 1346Kh.

Seyed-Gohrab, A. A. and S. McGlinn. *The Essence of Modernity: Mirza Yusof Khan Mustashar ad-Dowla Tabrizi's Codified Law (Yak Kalima)*. Amsteldam and West Lafayette: Rozenberg Publishers and Purdue University Press, 2008.

Seyfi Fami Tafreshi, Mortaza. *Nazm va Nazmiye dar Dowre-e Qajariye*. Tehran: Yasavoli, 1362Kh.

Shabana, Ayman. *Custom in Islamic Law and Legal Theory: The Development of the Concepts of 'Urf and 'Adah in the Islamic Legal Tradition*. New York: Palgrave Macmillan, 2010.

Shah Hoseyni, Parvane. "*Vaqf* shenasi-e Joghrafiyayi-e Shahr-e Tehran: Dowre-e Qajar va Pahlavi." *Tahqiqat-e Joghrafiya'i* 42 (1375Kh): 117–133.

Shahri, Ja'far. *Tarikh-e Tehran dar Qarn-e Sizdahom: Zendegi, Kasb va Kar*. 6 vols. Tehran: Mo'assese-e Khadamat-e Farhang-e Rasa, 1367Kh.

———. *Tehran-e Qadim*. 5 vols. Tehran: Mo'in, 1371Kh.

Sharif Razi, Mohammad. *Akhtaran-e Foruzan-e Rey va Tehran ya Tazkerat al-Maqaber fi Ahval al-Mafaher*. Qom: al-Zahra, n.d.

Sheikholeslami, A. Reza. *The Structure of Central Authority in Qajar Iran 1871–1896*. Atlanta: Scholars Press, 1997.

Sheykh al-Hokama'i, 'Emad al-Din. "Asnad-e *Vaqf*-e Ostan-e Tehran dar Baygani-e Markazi-e Sazman-e Owqaf va Omur-e Kheyriye." *Vaqf, Miras-e Javidan*, no. 28 (1378Kh): 141–167.

Shimizu, Naomi and Koji Kamioka. *Sacred Places in Tehran Province*. [in Japanese]. Fuchu: Research Institute for Languages and Cultures of Asia and Africa, 2009.

Soleymani, Mohammad Hoseyn. "Dar al-Shar'-e Mashhad dar Dowre-e Qajar va Barrasi-e Chand Saj'-e Mohr." *Payam-e Baharestan*, no. 21 (1392Kh): 211–223.

———. "Sakhtar-e Dar al-Shar' va Sazokar-e Tahrir-e Ashnad-e Shar'i." *Ketab-e Mah, Tarikh va Joghrafiya*, no. 192 (1393Kh): 45–48.

Soudavar Farmanfarmaian, Fatema. "Politics and Patronage: The Evolution of the Sara-ye Amir in the Bazaar of Tehran." In *The Bazaar in the Islamic City*, edited by Mohammad Gharipour, 203–227. Cairo: The American University in Cairo Press, 2012.

Stewart, Devin J. *Islamic Legal Orthodoxy: Twelver Shiite Responses to the Sunni Legal System*. Salt Lake City: University of Utha Press, 1998.

Tamdoğan, Işık. "*Sulh* and the 18th Century Ottoman Courts of Üsküdar and Adana." *Islamic Law and Society* 15 (2008): 55–83.

al-Tihrani, Agha Buzurg. *Nuqba' al-Bashar al-Qarn al-Rabi' 'Ashar*. Mashhad: Dar al-Murdada, 1404AH.

———. *Tabaqat al-A'lam al-Shi'a: al-Qarn al Hadi 'Ashar*. Edited by 'Ali Naqi Monzavi. Qom: Esma'iliyan, n.d.

"Varaqi as Tarikh-e Tehran: Sabze Meydan va Majma'-e Dar al-Sanaye'." *Yadgar*, no. 39/40 (1327Kh): 59–70.

Walcher, Heidi A. *In the Shadow of the King: Zill al-Sultan and Isfahan under the Qajars*. London: I.B. Tauris, 2008.

Werner, Christoph. "A Safavid *Vaqf* in Qajar Times: The Zahiriya in Tabriz." In *Matériaux pour l'histoire économique du monde iranien*, edited by Rika Gyselen and Maria Szuppe, 233–248. Paris: Association pour l'Avancement des études iraniennes, 1999.

———. *An Iranian Town in Transition: A Social and Economic History of the Elites of Tabriz*. Wiesbaden: Harassowitz, 2000.

———. "Zanan-e Vaqef dar Tehran-e 'Ahd-e Qajar." Translated by Nasim Majidi Qahrudi. *Vaqf, Miras-e Javidan*, no. 28 (1378Kh): 115–122.

———. "Stiftungen von Frauen im Teheran der Qagarenzeit." In *Akten des 27. Deutschen Orientalistentages (Bonn-28, September bis 2. Oktober 1998)*, edited by Stefan Wild and Hartmut Schild, 797–807. Würzburg: Ergon, 2001.

———. "Formal Aspects of Qajar Deeds of Sale." In *Persian Documents: Social History of Iran and Turan in the Fifteenth-Nineteenth Centuries*, edited by Nobuaki Kondo, 13–49. London: RoutlegeCurzon, 2003.

———. "Pious Merchants: Religious Sentiments in Wills and Testaments." In *Religion and Society in Qajar Iran*, edited by Robert Gleave, 211–226. London: RoutlegeCurzon, 2005.

———. " 'Urf oder Gewohnheitsrecht in Iran: Quellen, Praxis Und Begrifflichkeit." In *Rechtspluralismus in Der Islamischen Welt: Gewohnheitsrecht Zwischen Staat Und Gesellschaft*, edited by Michael Kemper and Maurus Reinkowski, 153–175. Berlin: Walter de Gruyter, 2005.

———. *Vaqf en Iran: aspects culturels, religieux et sociaux*. Paris: Association l'avancement des études iraniennes, 2015.

Yeganeh, Naser. s.v. "Civil Code." *Encyclopaedia Iranica*. Vol. 5. 648–650. 1992.

Yusofifar, Shahram and Hasan Habibi. *Sargozasht-e Bazar-e Bozorg-e Tehran: Bazarha, Bazarcheha-ye Piramun-e An dar Devist Sale-e Akhir*. Tehran: Bonyad-e Iranshenasi, 1389Kh.

Ze'evi, Dror. "The Use of Ottoman Shari'a Court Records as a Source for Middle Eastern Social History: A Reappraisal." *Islamic Law and Society* 5 (1998): 35–56.

Index